THE LAW, POLITICS AND THEORY OF TREATY WITHDRAWAL

This book explores how the law of treaty withdrawal operates. Many commentators have observed a wider sense of crisis in international law as governments of different ideological stripes withdraw or threaten to withdraw from international organisations and treaties. There are different political forces behind all of these cases, but they all use the same basic device in international law – a treaty withdrawal clause. This book focuses on withdrawal clauses within multilateral treaties, providing a detailed overview of their operation, drawing on a range of case studies including Brexit, nuclear weapons treaties and investment arbitration agreements. The obligations a withdrawal clause places on a withdrawing state help regulate the withdrawal process, providing a notional form of stability. Using insights from international relations theory and legal theory, this book unpacks how and why the law of withdrawal operates and what its limitations are.

The Law, Politics and Theory of Treaty Withdrawal

Frederick Cowell

• HART •
OXFORD • LONDON • NEW YORK • NEW DELHI • SYDNEY

HART PUBLISHING

Bloomsbury Publishing Plc

Kemp House, Chawley Park, Cumnor Hill, Oxford, OX2 9PH, UK

1385 Broadway, New York, NY 10018, USA

29 Earlsfort Terrace, Dublin 2, Ireland

HART PUBLISHING, the Hart/Stag logo, BLOOMSBURY and the Diana logo are trademarks of Bloomsbury Publishing Plc

First published in Great Britain 2023

A catalogue record for this book is available from the British Library.

A catalogue record for this book is available from the Library of Congress.

Library of Congress Control Number: 2023940198

ISBN: HB: 978-1-50993-856-8
ePDF: 978-1-50993-858-2
ePub: 978-1-50993-857-5

Typeset by Compuscript Ltd, Shannon

This book is dedicated to my daughter, Eleanor Ruth Anna Cowell.

It is also in memory of her Great Grandfather, Thomas Percy Cowell, who like many men of his generation had to fight in a war (Royal Artillery and Royal Army Medical Core Western Front 1914–1915, Salonika 1916–1918) caused by the failure of international treaties.

May treaties work a bit better for your generation Eleanor.

Acknowledgements

The work on the ideas for this book began as part of a paper for a special meeting of the European Society of International Law Interest Group on International Organisations on 'Exiting Organisations' in Naples in September 2017. Out of that came a special edition of the *International Organizations Law Review*, and some of the articles are cited in this book. I am deeply indebted to Richard Collins of University College Dublin and Sufyan Droubi of the University of Manchester for their helpful feedback on my paper, which helped shape my thinking on this area.

There are three people who need a specific and detailed thank you, as without them this book probably would not have come into being. First, my former masters' student Dia Kolarski now a researcher at the Humboldt University, Berlin. Supervising her thesis on ICC withdrawal, many chats in 2019 and discussions on her PhD proposal, all helped shaped this book, and her suggestions on the drafts of the manuscript were invaluable. Second, my research assistant Nishana Shukul, whose painstaking work double-checking all of the references, building the treaty sample in the appendix and crunching all of the numbers was invaluable. Without her this book would have taken another year, and she remains an invaluable colleague. Finally, Professor Larry Helfer, of Duke Univeristy who basically invented study into treaty withdrawal, was a reviewer of my original proposal and draft chapter. He also read through what became the conclusion, which was my paper at the Paths in International Law Conference at the Geneva Graduate Institute in October 2022, which he was chairing. I am so grateful to everyone who came and asked questions at that point as, with the pandemic, I had really had only a couple of opportunities to showcase the work in this book and get feedback.

There are a number of other thanks that need to be made. Some of my students at Birkbeck and NYU London need thanking – in particular Tayla Bland, who helped with the early stages of research, and Stephanie Anais and Viran Solanki, who acted as guinea pigs in reading through chapters and finding sources. Many thanks also to my friend Jonathan Leader-Maynard of Kings College, London, who helped me on some of the international relations theory. My colleagues at Birkbeck Department of Law, Michelle Everson and Giulia Leonori, helped me plug the gaps in my understanding of some areas of law, or helped in a couple of other ways – which were small for them but ultimately so helpful to me. Other thank yous must also be extended to Susan Quarell the research officer at Birkbeck School of Law, who helped me secure the extra funding and time needed to complete the research on this book. Finally, so many thanks to the team at Hart Publishing, who had to endure my lateness in completing the manuscript, for being so patient every step of the way. A very special thanks also to Catherine Minahan who helped with the extensive copyediting of the final manuscript.

This book was a good four years in the making, during which time the subject matter of the book crashed and evolved around my ears. Some examples and cases will be talked about more than others, and I have tried to give as detached a sense as one can when narrating as history events that are happening and being reported on the news. There has also had to be a lot of re-writing, as events changed the moment final drafts were written. My wife Rosie endured a lot of me explaining in micro detail the ups and downs of all of these developments. Also, thanks to my in-laws Sue and Tony as I wrote most of chapters two – four on your dining room table in Somerset. The law and events described within these pages are correct as at 20 December 2022, at which point, for the sake of clarity and closure, I have drawn the line. Even if things change subsequently, I hope the theoretical templates will stand the test of time. Any errors are mine.

Contents

Introduction

I. TOWARDS A LAW OF WITHDRAWAL

On 14 October 1933, there was an address on German radio explaining one of the first international acts of the country's new Government. Chancellor Hitler explained, in a broadcast heard by millions, due to the new habit of listening collectively in town squares, beer halls and other public locations, that the ongoing disarmament negotiations between Germany and other great powers, namely Britain and France, had broken down. Germany, Hitler argued, had been humiliated by the peace settlement created by the Treaty of Versailles 14 years earlier, and withdrawal from the League of Nations was necessary to rectify these failures and humiliations.[1] Ever the democrat, Hitler announced that the League of Nations withdrawal policy would be put to a referendum for the German people to decide. This referendum was ultimately successful, although reliant on a significant level of voter intimidation and street violence. Even then this was probably unnecessary; anti-League sentiment had been a central feature of German politics for many years, and when the then Foreign Minister Gustav Stresemann took Germany into the League of Nations in 1925, it was in the face of strong opposition from nationalist politicians.[2] When the peace process and disarmament were linked to the worsening economic conditions in Germany, which Hitler expressly did, national decline was intertwined with the actions of the international community, and particularly those of the League of Nations. Reporting on this a day later, one British newspaper described withdrawal from the League of Nations as completing 'the moral isolation which the triumph of Nazism has gradually brought on Germany'.[3] Under the League of Nations withdrawal clause, however, it took two years from the date of notifying an intention of withdrawal to it becoming effective, and for the withdrawing state to be legally outside the League.

Yet months before the withdrawal became effective, on 16 March 1935 Hitler went even further, reintroducing conscription. This was in direct defiance of the provisions of the 1919 Treaty of Versailles, which forbade the use of conscription as a means to constrain overall German military power, and Germany was still technically bound by Article 8 of the League Covenant requiring it to reduce

[1] R Evans, *The Third Reich in Power* (Penguin Books, 2006) 618–19.
[2] JW W-B, 'Germany and the League' (1931) 7 *Bulletin of International News* 3, 7.
[3] 'The German Decision' *The Manchester Guardian* (16 October 1933) 8.

its armaments.[4] An April 1935 resolution from the Council of the League of Nations condemned the action as a 'unilateral repudiation of international obligations', but the Nazi Government did not care.[5] As the Government saw it, international disarmament negotiations, which had begun in 1932, had been marred by the refusal of Britain and France to accept Germany's status as a great power, and as a consequence Germany was being discriminated against. Legally speaking, it was a unilateral denunciation of the Treaty of Versailles following an allegation of non-performance, and this was the case put forward by the German Government.[6] But this was deeply cynical, as German rearmament was proceeding apace, regardless of any international negotiations. Despite this, though, the Nazi Government tried to frame its actions in legal terms, and even made the notional concession of signing up to the Anglo-German Naval Agreement a few months later, effectively committing itself to limiting the *Kriegsmarine* fleet in proportion to the British Royal Navy.

These were perhaps the most infamous treaty denunciations in human history, as they were crucial steps on the road to the breakdown of the international order and, eventually, to World War Two. But, as with Italy's withdrawal from the League of Nations in 1937 following its invasion of Abyssinia, states withdrawing from the League of Nations did not bring it to a close. Britain remained a member of the organisation until 1946, even though the League had long ceased to have any useful function. Article 1 of the League of Nations Covenant expressly envisaged states' being able to leave the League and for its business to carry on regardless. As odd as it seemed, given that the Nazi regime ended with the commission of heinous international crimes, in the 1930s it was concerned about the legalities of its actions, trying to denounce treaties within the law and using legal arguments to justify their actions.

A. What is Withdrawal?

Treaty denunciation has a long history. The law of treaties evolved in the late eighteenth century as the principle became established that an individual treaty could outlive the monarch who signed it. By the nineteenth century, the principle of when a legal obligation came to an end began to assume greater significance, as international commerce conquered the globe and governments relied increasingly on the expectations created by multilateral treaties. Early studies of the question attempted to distinguish treaties terminated as a result of changing circumstances, such as a war, from treaties that expired over time and treaties

[4] K Magliveras, 'The Withdrawal from the League of Nations Revisited' (1991) 10 *Penn State International Law Review* 25, 37–38.

[5] CG Fenwick, 'The Denunciation of the Disarmament Clauses of the Treaty of Versailles' (1935) 29 *American Journal of International Law* 675, 676.

[6] ibid.

that a state might leave in order to protect its interests.[7] As one legal scholar put it in 1929, the doctrine of *pacta sunt servanda* or, as he put it, that 'one civilized state should be able to rely upon the pledged word of another civilized state' required some acknowledgement that changed circumstances or a state's determination of its own interests might require the state to leave a treaty.[8] The 1871 London Declaration confirmed the principle that no state could 'liberate itself from the engagements of a Treaty, nor modify the stipulations thereof, unless with the consent of the Contracting Parties by means of an amicable arrangement', essentially linking the idea of state consent to the termination of treaties, although the precise legal legacy of the London conference was somewhat contested.[9] Prior to 1945, what was perhaps underdeveloped in international legal scholarship was the idea that a state might wish to leave a multilateral treaty, leaving behind a permanent multilateral legal structure. In 1933, Harold Tobin noted in his book on the termination of treaties that around one-third of all treaties concluded since the 1880s had a provision allowing for the unilateral denunciation of treaties by one state party.[10] Various attempts to codify international law surrounding the operation of treaties in the 1930s recognised the existence of a right to withdraw from a treaty.[11] In the 1969 Vienna Convention on the Law of Treaties (VCLT),[12] the right of a state to withdraw from a treaty was recognised in a number of provisions in Part V, although during the drafting process these were, as accounts at the time noted, some of the most contested parts of the entire Convention.

The terms 'denunciation' and 'withdrawal' are sometimes used interchangeably in the case of treaty withdrawal, and some have suggested that 'denunciation' refers to a state's exiting from a bilateral treaty whereas 'withdrawal' describes a state's leaving a multilateral treaty.[13] There is an important distinction with respect to withdrawal, however, as in the case of bilateral treaties a denunciation that takes the number of parties down to one does not leave any international structures or functioning international legal regime behind, whereas withdrawal from a multiparty agreement can leave behind functioning institutions. For example, in 2018, the Government of President Rodrigo

[7] T Ion, 'Sanctity of Treaties' (1911) 20 *The Yale Law Journal* 268.

[8] GW Keeton, 'The Revision Clause in Certain Chinese Treaties' (1929) 10 *British Yearbook of International Law* 111, 111.

[9] D Bederman, 'The 1871 London Declaration, Rebus Sic Stantibus and a Primitivist View of the Law of Nations' (1988) 82 *American Journal of International Law* 1, 6.

[10] H Tobin, *The Termination of Multipartite Treaties* (Columbia University Press, 1933) 194–99.

[11] For this see A McNair, 'The Functions and Differing Legal Character of Treaties' (1930) 11 *British Yearbook of International Law* 100; Harvard Draft on the Law of Treaties, 'Article 34. Denunciation' (1935) 29 *American Journal of International Law* 1173.

[12] Vienna Convention on the Law of Treaties 1969 (opened for signature 23 May 1969, entered into force 27 January 1980) 1115 UNTS 331.

[13] L Helfer, 'Terminating Treaties' in DB Hollis (ed), *The Oxford Guide to Treaties* (Oxford University Press, 2012) 624–642, 635.

Duterte in the Philippines was incensed at the prospect of the International Criminal Court's (ICC's) investigation of his Government's 'war on drugs' policy for crimes against humanity, and announced the Philippines' withdrawal from the Rome Statute of the ICC.[14] This did not have any impact on the ICC's ability to function as a court, nor did it automatically end the obligations of the Philippines to comply with the ICC whilst the investigation was ongoing. Article 127 of the Rome Statute, the treaty's withdrawal clause, stipulated that after the issuing of a notice of denunciation, it did not come into effect until one year later; until then the Philippines was still bound by the Rome Statute like any other state.[15] After the United Kingdom's (UK's) formally notified the European Council that it was withdrawing from the European Union (EU) in March 2017, this kickstarted the legal process of withdrawing from the EU, which was only formally completed in December 2020. During that time there were various legal arguments about the status of the UK's contribution to the EU budget as a withdrawing state, the revocability of the UK's notification of withdrawal and many other subjects, all concerned with the process of formally leaving the EU and ceasing the UK's obligations to EU institutions.

It makes sense to conceive of denunciation as the legal lever that states have to pull as part of the process of initiating withdrawal from a multilateral legal regime. The 'how' of denouncing a treaty is often straightforward; it involves a state issuing a very simple written communiqué to the treaty depository, usually the United Nations, saying that it denounces the treaty. Laurence Helfer's influential study of treaty withdrawal notes that withdrawal clauses are very common in most post-1945 treaties, with publication by the United Nations Office of Legal Affairs and the Council of Europe of templates of final clauses, including denunciation clauses, to assist government officials with the drafting of treaties.[16] This commences the process of withdrawal in line with that treaty's withdrawal clause or, in those cases where there is no withdrawal clause, initiates the beginning of the process of withdrawal if the treaty permits it or other parties agree to allow it.[17] Withdrawal describes the entire process from beginning to end of leaving a multilateral treaty or international organisation

[14] T Regencia, 'Duterte announces Philippines' "immediate" withdrawal from ICC' *Al-Jazeera* (14 March 2018) at www.aljazeera.com/news/2018/3/14/duterte-announces-philippines-immediate-withdrawal-from-icc; H Ellis-Petersen, 'Rodrigo Duterte to pull Philippines out of international criminal court' *The Guardian* (14 March 2018) at www.theguardian.com/world/2018/mar/14/rodrigo-duterte-to-pull-philippines-out-of-international-criminal-court-icc (accessed 10 March 2022, as are all subsequent URLs unless stated otherwise); The relevant withdrawal clause is found in Rome Statute of the International Criminal Court (concluded 17 July 1998, entered into force 1 July 2002) 2187 UNTS 3, Article 127(b).

[15] The Philippines officially left the ICC on 17 March 2019. International Criminal Court, 'President of the Assembly of States Parties regrets withdrawal from the Rome Statute by the Philippines' ICC Press Release (18 March 2019) at www.icc-cpi.int/Pages/item.aspx?name=pr1443.

[16] L Helfer, 'Exiting Treaties' (2005) 91 *Virginia Law Review* 1579, 1596.

[17] This complicated position is analysed in full in ch 4.

or, for the sake of shorthand, an international legal regime to which a state is a party. It describes the process of moving from a state of affairs where a state has legal obligations under a regime, to a state of affairs where it no longer has legal obligations to that regime. In their book *Treaties in Motion*, Malogosia Fitzmaurice and Panos Merkouris describe treaties as being in motion through time, advancing from their *Genesis* (formation as a treaty) to *Phthora* (the termination or end of a treaty for a party, potentially through withdrawal).[18] Some treaties can have an obvious end point; for example, when states agree an older treaty can terminate automatically, and this is often the case in trade law, where countries may create fresh treaties that supersede an earlier trading agreement. A lot of treaties do not have an obvious terminal point in time: when in 1995 the Treaty on the Non-Proliferation of Nuclear Weapons (NPT) was due to expire, states opted to renew the treaty in perpetuity, essentially saying that the legal state of affairs it created, where the division between states that possessed nuclear weapons and non-nuclear states was enshrined into law, should remain a fixed part of the international legal order.[19] Yet Article X of the NPT allowed for states to withdraw in the event that they decided 'that extraordinary events' had 'jeopardized the supreme interests' of their country.[20] Whilst the treaty envisioned an ongoing legal relationship, an individual state could exit from that relationship, effectively terminating the legal obligations placed upon it by the NPT, whilst leaving the rest of the regime unaffected. It is this part of the *Phthora*, or ending of treaties, that this book is about.

Treaties have become increasingly complex over time, and often underpin international organisations, associations of states and ongoing processes of conferences and summits, which can issue declarations, recommendations and resolutions. These networks of what are often termed 'hard law obligations' (those coming from treaties) and 'soft law' (such as the resolutions of an organisation) are best described as regimes. As Duncan French and Karen Scott note, the term 'regime' was originally developed by scholars of international relations, in the context of the dynamic nature of the international legal systems created to tackle climate change or pollution.[21] From the perspective of the withdrawing state, it is seeking to remove itself from a broader constellation of obligations, both current and prospective, that operate under the broad umbrella of a regime, by using the withdrawal clause in that regime's founding

[18] M Fitzmaurice and P Merkouris, *Treaties in Motion: The Evolution of Treaties from Formation to Termination* (Cambridge University Press, 2020) 16.

[19] See J Pilat and CW Nakhleh, 'A Treaty Reborn? The NPT After Extension' in RGC Thomas (ed), *The Nuclear Non-Proliferation Regime: Prospects for the 21st Century* (Routledge, 1998) 41–55.

[20] Treaty on the Non-Proliferation of Nuclear Weapons (adopted 1 July 1969, entered into force 5 March 1970) 729 UNTS 161, Art X.

[21] D French and KN Scott, 'International Environmental Law' in M Bowman and D Kritsiotis (eds), *Conceptual and Contextual Perspectives on the Modern Law of Treaties* (Cambridge University Press, 2018) 677–709, 685.

treaty. It therefore makes sense to delineate regimes – the structures from which a state wishes to withdraw – and a treaty with a withdrawal clause – the instrument a state uses to execute its withdrawal. Thinking of regimes also helps in understanding a further issue common in contemporary cases of withdrawal: a state that is withdrawing from a treaty leaves a permanent legal structure in place with which it may still need to have relations. Article 50 of the Treaty on European Union (TEU), the clause covering withdrawal from the EU, was in part designed to facilitate a negotiation between the withdrawing state and the EU about their post-withdrawal relationship.[22] Withdrawal is therefore different from termination of a treaty, and it is also different from the legal arguments surrounding the validity of a treaty or the arguments surrounding the circumstances that the treaty was based on changing. Withdrawal, as this book goes on to show, is a way of recognising the autonomous decision of a state to discontinue its international legal obligations whilst leaving intact the legal regime from which it is departing.

B. What is the Law of Withdrawal?

Helfer's data shows that over a nearly 60-year period from 1945–2005, only 3.5 per cent of all multilateral treaties were denounced at least once.[23] Yet whilst it may be something that is not that common, it is something that is sufficiently high-profile and controversial that there is now what can be described as a law of withdrawal. It is first worth a brief legal note on the sources of the law of withdrawal. The VCLT, which, as scholars have been at pains to note, is not the final word on treaty law, is often the starting point for disputes over the interpretation of treaties.[24] This is especially important when it comes to withdrawal, as the political climate is often heated, and the withdrawing state is actively trying to remove its legal obligations. The VCLT therefore plays an important role in confining arguments to the terms of a treaty's withdrawal clause and in providing a framework within which disputes about withdrawal can take place.[25] Even in cases where there is a distinct regional legal order or specialised legal regime – known as a *lex specialis* by international lawyers – the VCLT is often used as a reference point about how the law on withdrawal ought to function. There are also grounds for thinking that the law of withdrawal exists beyond

[22] For an analysis of this, see M Dougan, *The UK's Withdrawal from the EU: A Legal Analysis* (Oxford University Press, 2021) 24–30.

[23] Helfer (n 16) 1606.

[24] For the definitive overview of scholarship in this area, see E Cannizzaro (ed), *The Law of Treaties Beyond the Vienna Convention* (Oxford University Press, 2011).

[25] The impact of VCLT, Klabbers argues, is to confine disputes to a treaty's specific provisions; see J Klabbers 'Reluctant Grundnormen: Articles 31(3)(C) and 42 of the Vienna Convention on the Law of Treaties and the Fragmentation of International Law' in M Fitzmaurice, M Vogiatzi and M Craven (eds), *Time, History and International Law* (Brill Nijhoff, 2007) 141–162, 142.

the VCLT, either as a principle of customary international law or as a general principle of law. The law of withdrawal could arguably pass the two-element test for recognition as a norm of customary international law, as recognised by the International Law Commission (ILC), in that it is a general international practice and there is widespread acceptance of that practice as law.[26] The codification of large parts of the law of withdrawal into the VCLT does not preclude its customary status, and there are some areas where in practice the law of withdrawal goes beyond the provisions of the VCLT.[27] Importantly there is, as demonstrated throughout this book, a strong consensus among states that the core principles of the law of withdrawal, as set out below, ought to be followed by the withdrawing state.[28]

Beyond the discussion about the source of the law of withdrawal, there is the question of what the substance of the law is, and there have been some important attempts at a synthesis of the law in this area, looking at the VCLT, contemporary state practice and case law on the subject. Campbell McLachlan, an arbitration panel member of the International Centre for Settlement of Investment Disputes (ICSID), has set out a fairly comprehensive synthesis of the law of withdrawal as it relates to withdrawal from international adjudication regimes, arguing that whilst international law sets out a framework of checks and balances, domestic courts have a role to play to in the process of withdrawal.[29] Helfer's 2012 contribution to the *Oxford Guide to Treaties* gives perhaps the most comprehensive and easy to understand synthesis on the law of withdrawal, and is certainly the starting point for any newcomer to international law.[30] Even though not a synthesis of the law of withdrawal, Barbra Koremenos and Alison Nau's study of withdrawal clauses is vital for understanding the subject matter of the law of withdrawal, the treaty terms regulating how states exit their legal obligations.[31] More recent works by Joseph Crampin and Antonio Morelli have, with reference to recent highly publicised cases such as Brexit, attempted to deliver a comprehensive synthesis of the law on withdrawal that addresses its changing nature.[32] Based on these and other works, it is possible to identify four core principles that collectively constitute the law of withdrawal, as shown below.

[26] 'Draft conclusions on identification of customary international law, with commentaries' in *Yearbook of the International Law Commission*, 2018, vol II, pt two.

[27] *Military and Paramilitary Activities in and against Niceragua (Niceragua v United States of America)* (Merits) (Judgment of 27 June 1986) [1986] ICJ Rep 14, paras 174–79.

[28] Reus-Smit argues that interactions can create obligations but need the 'valuing' of the substantive underlying idea involved in the obligation; see C Reus-Smit, 'Obligation through Practice' (2011) 3 *International Theory* 339, 346.

[29] C McLachlan, 'The Assault on International Law and the Limits of Withdrawal' (2019) 68 *ICLQ* 499.

[30] Helfer (n 13).

[31] B Koremenos and A Nau, 'Exit, No Exit' (2010) 81 *Duke Journal of Comparative & International Law* 81.

[32] J Crampin, 'Treaty withdrawal and recalcitrant States' (2020) 9 *Cambridge International Law Journal* 225; A Morelli, *Withdrawal from Multilateral Treaties* (Brill, 2021).

i. Withdrawal is a Legal Action that Can Only be Done through the Legal Provisions for Exiting a Regime

Article 54 VCLT outlines that states have a right to withdraw in accordance with a treaty's withdrawal clause or 'at any time by consent of all the parties after consultation with the other contracting States'. This is complemented by other clauses in Part III of the Convention, most notably Article 56, which clarifies what to do in the event that there is no withdrawal clause. In general, where there is no withdrawal clause, withdrawal is not possible unless one of two conditions can be established: first, it can be shown that the parties intended to allow for withdrawal; or, second, that 'a right of denunciation may be implied by the nature of the treaty'.[33] This formulation has come in for some criticism for the lack of clarity over what the 'nature' of a treaty is, yet, as is shown in chapter 1, the basic position entailed by both of these provisions is that there is no unfettered right to withdrawal.[34] Any discussions about this point have usually concluded that any such right to withdraw would be inherently destabilising to the entire framework of international law. Concerns about the international rule of law are reflected in the structure of Article 42 VCLT, which effectively extinguishes any unilateral right to withdraw by clarifying that withdrawal 'may take place only as a result of the application of the provisions of the treaty or of the present Convention'.[35] It almost certainly restricts the autonomy of state decision making, confining the termination of legal obligations to something done primarily through the terms of a withdrawal clause. But this provides effective stability in the international legal system, allowing states to have certainty when entering into legal regimes about how they can terminate the obligations they are acquiring.

ii. The Obligations Contained in a Withdrawal Clause are Like Any Other Clause Binding on States

The implication of Article 44 VCLT, which maintains that treaty provisions are not separable from one another in the event of withdrawal, is that withdrawal clauses are the same as other provisions in a treaty.[36] This principle was key to the reasoning of the Court of Justice of the European Union (CJEU) in *Wightman*, which looked at whether the UK could withdraw its notice to leave the EU.[37] Under Article 50 TEU, upon giving notice, a Member State had

[33] Art 56(2) VCLT.

[34] T Giegerich 'Article 56' in O Dörr and K Schmalenbach (eds), *Vienna Convention on the Law of Treaties: A Commentary* (Springer, 2018) 1039–1060.

[35] Art 42(2) VCLT.

[36] Art 44(1) VCLT.

[37] Case C-621/18 *Wightman v Secretary of State for Exiting the European Union* (CFI, 10 December 2018) para 59. In the decision emphasis was placed on Art. 65-68 of the VCLT.

two years before the notice of withdrawal became effective and it was formally outside the EU. But during this period the UK was still a Member State, shared all the rights of a Member State and was entitled to take actions like any other Member State, including withdrawing its declaration of withdrawal. There was no special status that arose from withdrawal clauses.

As will be shown in chapters 2 and 3, as well as guiding how states exit from a legal regime, withdrawal clauses often place obligations on the state following withdrawal. At a simple level these can relate to paying outstanding organisational funds, and at a more complex level can involve the continuation of certain rights and obligations. These are binding on a withdrawing state, a principle that can be politically controversial, as a state, by withdrawing, is trying to alter the nature of its legal obligations, but at the same time is obliged to maintain certain legal obligations as the result of a withdrawal clause. Because withdrawal clauses are the same as any other treaty clauses, and in some cases clearly do envisage obligations on a state following withdrawal, the principles of good faith and state consent in international law, which apply to every other obligation of the state, as chapters 2 and 3 set out, continue to apply to these obligations.

iii. Withdrawal and All Actions During the Withdrawal Process are Subject to the Good Faith Principle

When the ILC was codifying the principles of international treaty law, one basic common area of agreement noted by Paul Gormley was 'the fundamental nature of *pacta sunt servanda* to the entire corpus of international law'.[38] As will be outlined in chapter 1, the principle that obligations once accepted bind states to fulfil them – the doctrine of *pacta sunt servanda* – is fundamental to international law and the idea that international law can provide stability in the wider international order. Good faith is central to the codification of the doctrine in Article 26 VCLT. Sir Gerald Fitzmaurice, a former judge at both the International Court of Justice (ICJ) and the European Court of Human Rights (ECtHR), described good faith as 'a principle, of general principle, as opposed to a rule'; instead it 'underlies a rule and explains or provides a reason for it'.[39] It requires the withdrawing state to comply both with the particulars surrounding withdrawal and the specific provisions of a withdrawal clause, but also not to

[38] WP Gormley, 'The Codification of Pacta Sunt Servanda by the International Law Commission: The Preservation of Classical Norms of Moral Force and Good Faith' (1970) 14 *St Louis University Law Journal* 367, 373.

[39] G Fitzmaurice, 'The General Principles of International Law considered from the Standpoint of the Rule of Law' (1957) 92 *Recueil des Cours de l'Academie de Droit International* 7 Op cit S Reinhold, 'Good faith in international law.' (2013) 2 *UCL Journal of Law and Jurisprudence* 40.

act in bad faith whilst attempting or engaging in an act of withdrawal. A state cannot simply terminate its obligations under a treaty by claiming, for example, that there was a breach of obligations by another party.[40] When a state has issued a declaration submitting to the jurisdiction of a tribunal, the good faith principle still applies when that state withdraws the declaration or uses another legal mechanism to remove itself from the jurisdiction of that tribunal.[41] States will sometimes try to withdraw from the jurisdiction of a tribunal when a case is about to be brought against them, or where they are at risk of losing a case before an international tribunal. Even though this might not be classified as a withdrawal, as technically they are suspending a declaration under a treaty protocol, and in many instances a state can often remain a member of a legal regime but not submit to its tribunal's jurisdiction, this still ought to be considered an act of withdrawal. In such instances the withdrawing state is seeking to alter its legal obligations by withdrawing a declaration, which can have a real impact on the rights of individuals, denying them access to an international body that can hear their case and protect their rights.

iv. Withdrawal Cannot be Used to Extinguish Certain Categories of Rights

The International Covenant on Civil and Political Rights (ICCPR), one of the founding international human rights instruments, does not contain a withdrawal clause. When North Korea attempted to withdraw from the ICCPR in 1997, the ICCPR's treaty body, the Human Rights Committee (HRC), and the Secretary General of the United Nations both noted that the absence of a withdrawal clause in the ICCPR meant that withdrawal from the treaty was not possible.[42] The HRC clarified that this was in part because of the universal nature of human rights, stating that 'the rights enshrined in the Covenant belong to the people living in the territory of the State party'.[43] As shown in more detail in chapter 4, the principle that there are certain rights that a state is bound to protect regardless of treaty obligations – the doctrine of peremptory norms – is an often contested but widely acknowledged concept in international law, and this aspect of the law of withdrawal is consistent with this doctrine. Sunset provisions in withdrawal clauses, discussed in chapter 3, which in some treaties prevent the withdrawing state from using its withdrawal to terminate the

[40] *Gabčíkovo-Nagymaros Project (Hungary v Slovakia)* (Merits) [1997] ICJ Rep 7, paras 108–118.

[41] *Military and Paramilitary Activities in and against Nicaragua (Nicaragua v United States of America)* (Jurisdiction and Admissibility) (Judgment) [1984] ICJ Rep 392; International Covenant on Civil and Political Rights (adopted 16 December 1966, entered into force 23 March 1976) 999 UNTS 171 (ICCPR).

[42] Y Tyagi, The denunciation of human rights treaties' (2009) 79 *British Yearbook of International Law* 86.

[43] Human Rights Committee, 'General comment on issues relating to the continuity of obligations to the International Covenant on Civil and Political Rights' CCPR/C/21/Rev.1/Add.8/Rev.1 (8 December 1997) para 7.

hearing of a case pending before a tribunal or dispute resolution body, or using withdrawal to carry out human rights abuses underway while the state was still party to the treaty, also notionally protect certain rights during the withdrawal process. This form of argument is best described as 'rights transcendency' – the idea that the protection of certain rights transcends the legal moment of termination. There are also other provisions in the VCLT protecting rights acquired under a treaty from being extinguished. Collectively, this network of different doctrines and principles adds up to one overarching principle in the law of withdrawal – there are certain rights that cannot be extinguished by the act of withdrawal. Nevertheless, as chapter 4 demonstrates, this is patchy and inconsistent in application, and in practical terms it is unclear if this provides any substantive rights protection.

II. WHY DOES IT ALL WORK? THE PURPOSE OF THIS BOOK

Like all good ideas, this book began its life in the pub. More specifically, at the tables outside the 'Holborn Whippet' in glorious sunshine on 24 June 2016. The UK had the day before voted to leave the EU, and on that Friday I was at the pub mulling over (with beers) what was happening with Jamie and Gareth, old friends from undergraduate days. Neither of them was a lawyer or worked in international relations (having the good sense to be, respectively, a web developer and an archaeologist), but as I was foolish enough to have that as my line of work, they were keen to know what I thought was going to happen now. I sketched out the structure of Article 50 TEU and the good faith principle, but crucially became stuck on one simple question: Why did all of this work? Why, having decided to leave, would a country obey the law?

In a way this question is a variant on a much larger question that scholars from a number of different disciplines have posed: Why does international law work? Realist theorists, such as Eric Posner and Jack Goldstone, maintain that international law 'works' because it emerges from 'states acting rationally to maximize their interests given their perceptions of the interests of other states and state power'.[44] Related to this are rationalist theories of international law, which argue that the way international law shapes a state's behaviour, and ultimately compliance with its obligations, is by creating a predictable framework for dispute settlement.[45] From a slightly different direction, Andrew Guzman argued that states were rationally concerned about their reputation and other forms of consequences, sometimes referred to as 'collateral consequences', and

[44] J Goldsmith and E Posner, *The Limits of International Law* (Oxford University Press, 2005) 3.
[45] J Trachtman, 'International Law and Domestic Political Coalitions: The Grand Theory of Compliance with International Law' (2010) 11 *Chicago Journal of International Law* 127.

would therefore be motivated to comply with international law.[46] Others have more specifically examined the way in which reputation works in order to create a set of structured incentives to comply with human rights law and trade law.[47] Various constructivist theorists have analysed the way that states interact with one another, reasoning that compliance with international law emerges out of the shaping of states' identities by interactions.[48] Constructivism has also been criticised from a variety of different directions, but it helps explain the more complicated nature of how states operate within international regimes and build up a sense of fidelity to those institutions.[49] However, the question that has been under-examined in the increasingly voluminous literature on this subject is why, when a state has taken the decision to terminate its legal obligations through the process of withdrawal, does it comply with the laws governing and regulating how it leaves?

The obligations contained in withdrawal clauses are often highly controversial, requiring the withdrawing state to pay sums of money to the regime it is leaving, preserve and respect property rights of large corporations who are politically unpopular, or even stay the execution of convicted criminals. They are often intimately connected to the political case for withdrawing from a regime. As a consequence, it is unsurprising that in some instances, the obligations constructed by withdrawal clauses are ignored by the withdrawing state. Withdrawal from the ICC enabled the Philippines to stall progress into investigations into crimes against humanity, slowing cooperation and denying that the ICC has jurisdiction over the country, despite an obligation in the withdrawal clause in the Rome Statute of the ICC that states were obliged to continue cooperation with ongoing investigations after withdrawal.[50] At a basic level, states

[46] A Guzman, 'Reputation and international law' (2005) 34 *Georgia Journal of International & Comparative Law* 379; R Bewster, 'Reputation in International Relations and International Law Theory' in J Dunoff and M Pollack (eds), *Interdisciplinary Perspectives on International Law and International Relations: The State of the Art* (Cambridge University Press, 2013) 524–543.

[47] H Hongju Koh, 'How is international human rights law enforced' (1998) 74 *Indiana Law Journal* 1397; JA Conti, 'Learning to dispute: repeat participation, expertise, and reputation at the World Trade Organization' (2010) 35 *Law & Social Inquiry* 625.

[48] J Brunnée and S Toope, *Legitimacy and Legality in International Law: An Interactional Account* (Cambridge University Press, 2010): For a summary of the literature, see E Stubbins Bates, 'Sophisticated Constructivism in Human Rights Compliance Theory' (2015) 25 *European Journal of International Law* 1169.

[49] For critiques of constructivism, see M Zehfuss, *Constructivism in International Relations: The Politics of Reality* (Cambridge University Press, 2002) 250–51; B Bowring, 'What is Realism in International Law and Human Rights?' in J Joseph and C Wight, *Scientific Realism and International Relations* (Springer, 2010) 101–114.

[50] AJ Yogaswara, 'Impact of Philippines' Withdrawal from International Criminal Court on Crime Against Humanity Investigation in Philippines' (2020) 4 *Padjadjaran Journal of International Law* 226, 237–38; H Woolaver, 'Withdrawal from the International Criminal Court: International and Domestic Implications' in G Werle and A Zimmermann (eds), *The International Criminal Court in Turbulent Times* (Springer, 2019) 23–42, 26–29; G Engelbrecht, 'Philippines: The International Criminal Court Goes After Duterte's Drug War' International Crisis Group (17 September 2021) at www.crisisgroup.org/asia/south-east-asia/philippines/philippines-international-criminal-court-goes-after-dutertes-drug-war.

are still obliged to comply with the terms of a withdrawal clause in a procedural sense, with their withdrawal only becoming legally effective at a particular time, the correct notification being sent to the depository of the treaty and other administrative steps met. Even this can be extraordinarily controversial; for nearly a year after voting to leave the EU, the UK was involved in a domestic constitutional and legal battle about how to actually issue a notification of denunciation.[51] The pressure to simply walk away from legal obligations is all the more tempting because withdrawal is a means of terminating obligations or ceasing to be bound by obligations, and politically speaking the distinction between denunciation and ceasing to perform obligations can at first glance appear trivial.

Writing in 1940, a rather sceptical Hans Morgenthau noted that 'laymen were much quicker to recognize the gap between the rules of international law as represented by science, and the rules of international law as they exist in actual experience'.[52] At the time Morgenthau was writing, western Europe had been overrun by the Nazis, Japan was threatening a wider war in South East Asia and Britain was being bombed. Morgenthau was sceptical about legal positivists, who he thought had unmoored international law from its social reality. Writing about 20 years later at the height of the Cold War, Morton Kaplan and Nicholas deB Katzenbach, seeking to explain the effectiveness of international law, noted that compliance came from the habits of the bureaucratic operations of individual states, as they navigated shared interests on the international plane.[53] Both of these theories are united in their explanation of how international law's operation is dependent on the social reality in which the law operates – mere structures of international law were not enough. In the late 1980s, there was the growth of a theory often termed 'rationalist institutionalism', which drew on realist thought and maintained that international law could facilitate different types of cooperation that might not otherwise occur, by reducing transaction costs and increasing certainty.[54] This theoretical work offered a sketch of how international law could, to a degree, order and shape the social reality in which it operated, and goes someway to understanding the aims of a withdrawal clause. Helfer's 2005 analysis of treaty withdrawal examined how exit clauses create different incentives for states and can help solve problems like the 'prisoners' dilemma', where uncertainty is created by not knowing how another party to a treaty would act in a given situation.[55] Koremenos and Nau's analysis of

[51] The case was *Miller v Secretary of State for Exiting the European Union* [2017] UKSC 5.

[52] H Morgenthau, 'Functionalism, and International Law' (1940) 34 *American Journal of International Law* 260.

[53] MA Kaplan and N de B Katzenbach, *The Political Foundations of International Law* (John Wiley & Sons, 1961).

[54] R Steinberg, 'Wanted – Dead or Alive: Realism in International Law' in Dunoff and Pollack (eds) (n 46) 156–57.

[55] Helfer (n 16).

withdrawal clauses shows how their design encourages states to act rationally, pursuing predictable courses of action.[56]

There is, however, more to the law of withdrawal than just the design of withdrawal clauses; their design works, to the extent that it does, only because of the wider social reality of the international legal system. International law and the increasing legalism of international relations create an important signalling effect, and a significant function of withdrawal clauses, this book argues, is to create a framework for distinguishing between the lawful and unlawful actions of states in what can be moments of crisis for international law.[57] The analysis of international law used by the English school of international relations maintains that the most significant feature of international law's impact on state behaviour is the way that relatively broad principles can, in the long run, have an effect on states.[58] By itself a withdrawal clause in an individual treaty cannot shape state behaviour; multilateral treaty regimes are not standalone islands in the broader international order. But the norms of the law of withdrawal set out a set of expectations on states and their operation in international society.[59] Hedley Bull, CAW Manning and other theorists of the English school of international relations saw international law as performing an 'institutional' function in an otherwise anarchical international society, providing mechanisms that allowed states to interact with one another predictably.[60] The examples of institutions given in this literature are the law of diplomatic relations and the laws of war, but the law of withdrawal also plays a crucial role as one of these institutions.

A lot of different states at some point have wanted to terminate legal obligations under a treaty or exit a legal regime. As one former judge of the European Court of Human Rights (ECtHR) observed, in almost all signatory states of the European Convention on Human Rights (ECHR), the receipt of a ruling against them by the Court leads some political figures to argue that defying the Court or leaving the ECHR is an appropriate response.[61] Yet the Convention's withdrawal clause in a couple of different ways envisages that a state will be bound by legal

[56] Koremenos and Nau (n 31).

[57] This will be discussed more in ch 5, but the key concepts of international law creating an insider/outsider signalling effect can be seen in HH Koh, 'Why do nations obey international law' (1996) 106 *Yale Law Journal* 2599; F Johns, *Non-Legality in International Law: Unruly Law* (Cambridge University Press, 2013) Introduction.

[58] For a simple overview, see D Armstrong, T Farrell and H Lambert *International law and International Relations* (Cambridge University Press, 2012) 116–18; B Buzan, *An Introduction to the English School of International Relations: The Societal Approach* (Polity, 2014) ch 2.

[59] Even though often referred to, as will be shown, the 'international community' is a complex concept that is difficult to define; see C Tams, 'The International Community as a Legal Concept' in J d'Aspremont and S Singh (eds), *Concepts for International Law Contributions to Disciplinary Thought* (Edward Elgar, 2019) 505–523.

[60] A Linklater and H Suganami, *The English School of International Relations: A Contemporary reassessment* (Cambridge University Press, 2006) 46–48.

[61] E Myjer, 'Why much of the criticism of the European Court of Human Rights is unfounded' in S Flogaitis, T Zwart and J Fraser (eds), *The European Court of Human Rights and Its Discontents: Turning Criticism into Strength* (Edward Elgar Publishing Ltd, 2013) 37–53.

obligations beyond the moment it has left. There are also obligations and treaties that states cannot ignore or leave; even though the Charter of the United Nations contained no withdrawal clause, states nevertheless attempted to withdraw from it. In these cases, the social identities of states, and their socialisation, both in institutions and in broader international society, can be more important than the presence of rational incentive structures. As the state in question is either seeking to withdraw from a legal regime or has withdrawn from that legal regime, and the regime is either seeking to continue its authority over a state or protect rights, there is a limited set of shared interests and goals between the regime and the withdrawing state. Constructivist theory focuses on the ideational factors behind commitment and compliance with international law, and the way that a state's identities and interactions are a basis for commitment.[62] However, the complex and often patchwork way in which obligations continue and rights are protected during the process of withdrawal is in many ways an illustration of the limits of constructivist theory concerning compliance with a state's legal obligations.

III. THE STRUCTURE OF THE BOOK AND SOME PRELIMINARY CAVEATS

Although withdrawal is relatively rare, there is no room to explore all instances of withdrawal, even superficially, and invariably the reader will find some omissions in the following pages. The main methodological selection criteria for the examples and case studies in this book has been to look at instances where there has been doctrinal development, or where there is illumination of an underlying principle. That said, a range of various withdrawals, from human rights to investment treaties, are examined throughout the book. Some case studies loom larger than others: Brexit and the NPT feature in this book chiefly because they generated so many legal and political flashpoints, which help clarify doctrinal matters about the law and played out some of the theoretical tensions both in the formation and application of the law of withdrawal. Chapter 1 looks at the basic question of what the law of withdrawal is for – what purpose it serves for those states that utilise it. Withdrawal conceptually speaking is not the inverse of consenting to be bound by international obligations; instead it is better to conceive of it as an independent doctrine designed to recognise the political autonomy of a state. But even on these terms, the law of withdrawal facilitates the recognition of autonomy more in theory than in practice, as it operates in a context of sovereign inequality and prescribes the actions a state can take in determining its legal obligations, effectively limiting autonomy.

[62] J Checkel, 'Why Comply? Social Learning and European Identity Change' (2001) 55 *International Organization* 553; A Sinclair *International Relations Theory and International Law: A Critical Approach* (Cambridge University Press, 2010); C Reus-Smit, 'Politics and international legal obligation' (2003) 9 *European Journal of International Relations* 591.

In chapter 2, the structure and operation of withdrawal clauses is analysed, looking at both the theoretical assumptions behind their structure and how they shape state behaviour in practice. The text of over 200 withdrawal clauses is examined, to see how they impose different restrictions on withdrawing states, such as controlling the time a state has to be a party to a treaty before it can withdraw. There is no one theoretical model that explains the rationale behind the different features of withdrawal clauses and why they work. In fact, a common theme of this book is that withdrawal clauses challenge existing theories of international obligation, testing the idea that committing to international law is part of a rational calculation by states, or that international obligations exist as a means of solving common problems, and the concept that international obligation are an ideational expression of political values.[63] At a number of points this book will look at the position that someone from a particular theoretical school of thought might take in explaining an aspect of the law of withdrawal, in order to analyse competing arguments about why the law of withdrawal does or does not have a particular effect. Where possible, some of the different nuances of the various schools of thought will be set out, although the main purpose of this exercise is to map different theoretical templates onto the law of withdrawal and instances where it has been applied.

Chapter 3 examines the different ways in which obligations on the withdrawing state continue after withdrawal – either through the creation, by elements of withdrawal clauses, of obligations designed to continue after withdrawal, or by the withdrawing state's retaining responsibility for breaches from when it was a member of a legal regime. Continuing obligations or the continuing authority of legal regimes are conceptually different, and the legal obligations involved are justified in different ways, from obligations and legal regimes from which a state cannot withdraw, which are the subject matter of chapter 4. Underpinning the discussion in both chapters 3 and 4 is the importance of human rights as a justification for maintaining a set of obligations on a state, even when that state, by commencing withdrawal, is clearly expressing a preference that it no longer wishes to be bound by those obligations. Whilst this is broadly consistent with other principles in public international law, the continued protection of rights, whether a right to access a tribunal or a right to property, can conflict with the political preference of a state's population to commence a treaty withdrawal, even if that removes or restricts individual rights. If part of the law of withdrawal's function is to acknowledge the autonomy of states, then a state that withdraws from a human rights treaty in order to facilitate the execution of convicted criminals is exercising its autonomy. An obligation on the withdrawing

[63] For an overview and a discussion of these different theoretical approaches, see C Reus-Smit, *The Politics of International Law* (Cambridge University Press, 2004); B Koremenos, 'Institutionalism and International Law' in Dunoff and Pollack (eds) (n 47) 59–82; K Raustiala and A-M Slaughter, 'International Law, International Relations and Compliance' in W Carlsnaes, T Risse and B Simmons (eds), *Handbook of International Relations* (Sage Publications, 2002) 538–558.

state to recognise decisions from a human rights court about the death penalty effectively stymies the desired effect a state hopes to have by withdrawing from that regime, hence constricting its autonomy. If (as the author does) you believe the death penalty to be abhorrent and a violation of human rights, then recognising the political desire to execute someone is not a pressing concern.

But this is the wrong way to understand the politics of withdrawal. The existence of a withdrawal clause can act as a legal device to incentivise participation in a regime and ratification of a treaty because it offers a state the possibility of flexibility in the future – an argument often made in relation to other legal devices such as treaty reservations.[64] If, as is the case with withdrawal clauses requiring compliance with decisions of a tribunal after withdrawal, that flexibility is restricted, this in turn means that something that a domestic population may want is denied to them. The law of withdrawal can help mediate the messier end of domestic politics and allow its interaction with international law. When in March 2019 the UK, due to its own internal political tensions, could not ratify a post-withdrawal agreement by the two-year deadline imposed by Article 50 TEU (the EU's withdrawal clause), the clause also provided a framework for mediating a political solution, leading to an extension of the deadline. Adapting Michael Dougan's personal comment from the introduction to his book on the law of leaving the EU,[65] it is possible to conclude that leaving the EU was a bad idea, and, like Dougan, this is the view taken by this author. But from the scholarly perspective of this book, the UK's withdrawal from the EU is an example of a successful withdrawal; it took place within the law and the UK left the EU according to the law at 11pm on 31 January 2020. Although this book tries to cover a lot of theoretical ground, the seemingly grubby and mundane aspects of the domestic politics of states feature heavily; this is because they are often the forces that drive withdrawal. The underlying political ideas behind a withdrawal may be the subject of fierce ideological and moral debate, the political and economic consequences of a withdrawal may be on any objective assessment highly negative, yet the act of withdrawal itself can be legal on the international plane supporting and reinforcing the international legal order.

Chapter 5 looks at the way that the law of withdrawal underpins the rule of law at an international level, creating a form of stability in the international system by making the process of withdrawal, which might otherwise be chaotic and destabilise legal regimes, a predictable and bounded process. Although there is a lot of emphasis in the academic literature, and from legal experts involved in drafting and the interpretation of legal instruments, about the need to promote stability as a core purpose of the law of withdrawal, there is surprisingly little

[64] See E Neymayer, 'Qualified Ratification: Explaining Reservations to International Human Rights Treaties' (2007) 36 *Journal of Legal Studies* 397, 403.

[65] Dougan (n 22) 19–20.

agreement on what substantively stability is and what it is for. Stability is presented as one of the metaphorical goods of the rule of international law, and regulating withdrawal is a means of preserving that stability. But, in so doing, the law of withdrawal limits certain political choices and cannot in practice treat states as equal parties, due to their asymmetrical bargaining power, even though the legal fiction of sovereign equality can be maintained. Stability also does not necessarily mean the protection of other basic goods of the international system, such as the protection of human rights; and even though it supports the position that such rights are in effect transcendent, the law of withdrawal is limited as to what it can and cannot achieve. Instead, the stability the law of withdrawal creates is one where states that withdraw, but do not comply with the law of withdrawal, are categorised as law breakers, outside of the norms of international society. This is a stability of form, and boundary setting, not of substance. International society and the states within in it are considered stable because of their adherence to the procedural norms of the law withdrawal, even if the nature of a given withdrawal detrimentally affects the substantive interests of other states, groups or individuals.

1

What is the Law of Withdrawal For? A Sketch of the Objectives

INTRODUCTION

THOMAS BATY WAS a traditional member of the British intellectual establishment, a founder of the Hugo Grotius Society, renowned writer on international law and the defender of some particularly heinous international crimes. As legal advisor to the Imperial Japanese Government, he put forward arguments rooted in natural law to suggest that 1920s China was not really sovereign, and therefore the Japanese annexation of Manchuria in 1932 and the subsequent attempt to conquer China in 1937 were legal due to the Chinese absence of statehood.[1] After the 1931 Mukden incident, when a railway line and a Japanese Army base were attacked, the League of Nations had appointed an international commission of inquiry to look into the incident. Baty, framed the League's actions as interference by the great powers of Europe with Japan's sovereign interests.[2] Baty's thinking on both sovereignty and the legal status of China was utilised by Japan to advance its case against the League of Nations. The Japanese government claimed the League was undermining its attempts to create peace in the region and was disputing the legitimacy of Japan's recognition of the puppet state of Manchukuo.[3] The League, however, did not believe the Imperial Japanese Government and continued its investigation. Outraged, the Japanese ambassador served notice on the League that under the terms of Article 1 of the League Covenant, Japan intended to

[1] For an overview of Baty's thoughts, see P Olbas, 'Naturalist Law and Japan's Legitimization of Empire in Manchuria: Thomas Baty and Japan's Ministry of Foreign Affairs' (2008) 15 *Diplomacy and Statecraft* 35. For an example of Baty's thinking, see T Baty, 'Can an Anarchy be a State?' (1934) 28 *American Journal of International Law* 444.

[2] S Murase, 'Thomas Baty in Japan: Seeing Through the Twilight' (2003) 73 *British Yearbook of International Law* 315, 329. As Olbas (n 1) notes, there is some evidence that Baty was not strongly connected to the workings of the Japanese Foreign Ministry and formed his opinions in 1931–32 based on partial evidence from the Japanese Foreign Ministry. See A Carty, 'Thomas Baty: An International Lawyer as Public Intellectual between Imperial Japan and the Republic of China' (2013) 56 *Japanese Yearbook of International Law* 70, 76.

[3] T Burkman, *Japan and the League of Nations: Empire and World Order, 1914–1938* (University of Hawaii Press, 2008) 172.

withdraw from the League. For the Japanese delegation, the law surrounding withdrawal (as it existed at the time) served a relatively clear purpose; as its members ceremonially exited the League of Nations Assembly in a scene later immortalised by Hergé in the Tintin book *The Blue Lotus*, they symbolically ended their cooperation with the League over Manchuria.[4]

The politics of each act of withdrawal may look very different, and certainly for each individual country involved the political decision to withdraw from a given regime, will be individually important and significant to the political elites and population of that country. Yet the law of withdrawal, as a system of law, exists to facilitate the alteration of the legal relationships that the withdrawing state currently has. This is a summary of what the law of withdrawal is designed to do, but it gives little actual sense of what the justification is for the existence of these legal principles nor an insight into what that legal system recognises as a legitimate reason for its exercise. Justifications for the law of withdrawal, this chapter explains, revolve, directly or indirectly, around two assertions of state sovereignty. First, the procedural assertion. By the sovereign act of denunciation and the acknowledgement of that act as the legitimate act of a sovereign power by other international actors, a state is deemed to have asserted its sovereignty. The acknowledgement by the international community of the act of withdrawal as legal, and hence legitimate, is what the law of withdrawal provides to the withdrawing state. This is important, as acts of withdrawal are often politically destabilising and contested; and even if they are not, withdrawal can pose a wider danger to the stability of international law. Oliver Lissitzyn noted, at an American Society of International Law conference in 1967, that the existence of a unilateral right of withdrawal from treaties was a fiercely debated topic, but that because of the destabilising impact withdrawal would have on international stability, the conclusion was that such a right should be defined in a limited manner.[5] Second, the substantive assertion of sovereignty. By altering the obligations a state has, withdrawal allows that state to lawfully take or refrain from taking a particular course of action, which it would otherwise not be able to do because of its international obligations. This asserts a state's sovereignty in that it allows the state to enact a decision it has taken as a political entity about its international obligations. In this respect the law of withdrawal, as Antonio Morelli argues, is a form of risk management, balancing the turbulent nature of domestic politics, and the often asserted sovereign right of a state to decide its international relations, with the need for predictability and stability

[4] JJ Burnes, 'Conditions of Withdrawal from the League of Nations' (1935) 29 *American Journal of International Law* 40, 45–46. Note Japan's ceremonial exit was in February, but its formal notice of denunciation was dated 27 March 1933.

[5] OJ Lissitzyn, 'Stability and Change: Unilateral Denunciation or Suspension of Treaties by Reasons of Changed Circumstances' (1967) 61 *Proceedings of the American Society of International Law at Its Annual Meeting (1921–1969)* 186, 187.

in international law.[6] Many of the arguments a state makes about sovereignty in the process of withdrawal revolve around the second form of assertion of sovereignty. But the first type of remains important from the perspective of the withdrawing state, in order to ensure that its actions are recognised as legal by other actors.

Concluding that the law of withdrawal is necessary to prevent anarchy, as the American Society of International Law did in the 1960s, replicates a standard pattern of legal argument that Martti Koskenniemi has dubbed the 'tension between the demands of international law's normativity and its concreteness'.[7] On the one hand, international law imposes a requirement for reality by prescribing how a state may withdraw and what the stipulations are for such an act, but absent an understanding of the 'concreteness' of withdrawal – in this case the tangible justifications a state uses to justify an actual or a contemplated act of withdrawal – any analysis of the law of withdrawal runs the risk of becoming a set of 'abstractions'.[8] The presumed practical outcome of the operation of withdrawal clauses, as the next chapter demonstrates in more detail, is to regulate the operation of the withdrawal process, attempting to impose some sort of order over a potentially anarchic situation.[9] But this chapter's project is to delve slightly deeper into the presumptions behind the underlying principles of the law, first by looking at how obligations are created and then by synthesising the core justifications for the law of withdrawal's existence.

I. STATE CONSENT, SOVEREIGNTY AND WITHDRAWAL

In August 1926, a French mail ship collided with a Turkish coal ship, with 10 sailors tragically losing their lives. The resulting arrest of the French ship's captain in Turkey triggered a legal dispute over jurisdiction at the Permanent Court of International Justice (PCIJ). Although the issue of jurisdiction is what the famous case bearing the French ship's name, *The Lotus*, focused on, there also was an exploration of the nature of international legal obligations. The PCIJ concluded that the 'rules of law binding upon states … emanate from their own free will', conflating international obligation with the idea of state consent.[10] Starting from

[6] A Morelli, *Withdrawal from Multilateral Treaties* (Brill Publishing, 2021) 31–33.

[7] M Koskenniemi 'International law in the world of ideas' in J Crawford and M Koskenniemi (eds), *The Cambridge Companion to International Law* (Cambridge University Press, 2012) 47–63.

[8] ibid.

[9] Anarchy in international society is a core tenet of the realist theory of international relations, maintaining that in the absence of centralised government each state has no alternative but look after its own security and interests; A Hurrell, *On Global Order: Power, Values and the Constitution of International Society* (Oxford University Press, 2007) 29–30. The relationship between the international law and the anarchy of the international system is explored in F Mégret, 'International Law as Law' in Crawford and Koskenniemi (eds) (n 7) 64–92, 67.

[10] '*The Lotus' (France v Turkey)* (Judgment) Judgment No 9, PCIJ Rep Series A No 10, ICGJ 248 (PCIJ 1927).

the principle that a state's legal constraints are an expression of sovereign will reflects an absolutist understanding of the sovereign as law maker. The sixteenth-century philosopher Jean Bodin, widely considered one of the founding fathers of the modern doctrine of sovereignty, expressed a version of this principle when he argued that the 'absolute and perpetual power' exercised by a sovereign is 'not subject to the law', which would in Bodin's definition include laws passed by other sovereigns or the sovereign's predecessors.[11] This form of sovereignty can be termed the 'classic' definition of sovereignty, which, as Robert Jackson notes, treats international law as a series of legal arrangements constructed by states in the course of their mutual relations.[12] The overall meta principle of *The Lotus*, Martti Koskenniemi notes, is that in the 'absence of clear prohibitions, the state must be assumed free', even if the nature of freedom in this case was a somewhat circular proposition that glossed over some of the choices and contradictions involved in that freedom.[13]

The idea stemming from *The Lotus* and its definition of the source of legal obligations was highly significant in shaping the law of withdrawal. If states entered into obligations freely then an extension of that freedom was presumed to be the freedom to undo obligations. A few years after *The Lotus*, the legal scholar and former reader of International Law at the University of Hong Kong, George Keeton, noted, in an article on the treaties used to control colonial concessions in China, that the 'whole law relating to treaties' was reliant on one 'civilized state' being able to rely on the word of another 'civilized state'.[14] If that was no longer possible then Keeton argued that international law recognised the principle that such treaties should not 'continue … to be regarded by civilized states as a whole as binding'.[15] The idea of withdrawal as a right of states is discussed in more detail in section II of this chapter, but the assumption coming from *The Lotus* about state consent is what concerns us here. The interpretation of *The Lotus* principle as being that, in the absence of prohibition, international law permits a state's choice of action has been often criticised for its highly laissez-faire approach to international obligations, and some scholars have doubted that the judges of the PCIJ were actually making such a decisive statement about the nature of international legal obligations.[16] That said,

[11] J Bodin, 'Bodin on Sovereignty' in J Franklin (ed), *Cambridge Texts in the History of Political Thought* (Cambridge University Press, 1992) 1, 11–12.

[12] R Jackson, *Sovereignty: Evolution of an Idea* (Polity, 2007) 55.

[13] M Koskenniemi, 'The Politics of International Law' (1990) 1 *European Journal of International Law* 4, 18.

[14] G Keeton, 'The Revision Clause in Certain Chinese Treaties' (1929) 10 *British Yearbook of International Law* 111, 111.

[15] ibid.

[16] For a summary see A Hertogen, 'Letting *Lotus* Bloom' (2016) 26 *European Journal of International Law* 901; see also O Spiermann, '*Lotus* and the Double Structure of International Legal Argument' in P Sands and L Boisson de Chazournes (eds), *International Law, the International Court of Justice and Nuclear Weapons* (Cambridge University Press, 1999).

the idea of state consent as a sovereign act and of withdrawal functioning as the undoing of that sovereign act is relatively pervasive in early thinking on the law of withdrawal. To understand this, it is first important to critically unpack the references to sovereignty and state consent in arguments about the law of withdrawal.

A. Defining Sovereignty

Even though some of the early literature on withdrawal makes implicit or explicit reference to sovereignty, it is a misapprehension to proceed on the assumption that there is a clear idea or definition of sovereignty on which the law of withdrawal relies. Stephen Krasner argues there are at least four different meanings of the word 'sovereignty': (i) domestic (authority over law within a state); (ii) interdependent (the authority to control transborder movements); (iii) international legal sovereignty (recognition by other states); and (iv) Westphalian sovereignty (the ability to exclude external forces).[17] Others have outlined the existence of other overlapping definitions and refinements of the meaning of the term 'sovereignty' in international law.[18] The different definitions of the term are also, to an extent, historical moments; in his seminal article 'The S Word', Louis Henkin notes how understandings of what sovereignty meant changed at various points in the twentieth century, resulting in an understanding that required states to acknowledge (albeit in a minimal fashion) the impact of international forces, such as human rights law, by the end of the twentieth century.[19] Although the late 1990s and early 2000s encouraged a lot of speculation about the end of the state or the waning of sovereignty, in reality this was simply another historical episode shaping an alternative definition of what sovereignty could mean and how the concept of sovereignty could be invoked.[20]

Definitions of sovereignty also mask deep inequalities between entities considered sovereign. From the sixteenth century onwards colonialism produced a reimagining of the world, which led to the generation of legal principles concerning the possession of territories and the creation of separate categories

[17] SD Krasner, *Sovereignty: Organized Hypocrisy* (Princeton University Press, 1999) 12.

[18] See, for an outline of the different uses, S Beaulac, *The Power of Language in the Making of International Law: The Word Sovereignty in Bodin and Vattel and the Myth of Westphalia* (Brill Publishing, 2004) 2.

[19] L Henkin, 'That S Word: Sovereignty, and Globalization, and Human Rights, Et Cetera' (1999) 68 *Fordham Law Review* 1.

[20] For an illustrative text charting this, see JE Alvarez, 'The Return of the State' (2011) 20 *Minnesota Journal of International Law* 268. There was an earlier tendency in the 1990s to assume that there was a decline of the state sovereignty in international law: see O Schachter, 'The Decline of the Nation-State and its Implications for International Law' (1998) 36 *Columbia Journal of Transnational Law* 7; K Jayasuriya, 'Globalization, Law, and the Transformation of Sovereignty: The Emergence of Global Regulatory Governance' (1999) 6 *Indiana Journal of Global Legal Studies* 425.

of sovereignty; broadly speaking, the world was divided up into the territories created by international law and those who created international law.[21] When nations became independent, they not only did so on terms shaped by international law, but also had to be bound by international norms and laws which they often had had little say over.[22] This was to have a variety of consequences, such as entrenching systemic material inequalities, but it also meant that the doctrine of sovereign equality was more of a juridical construction than a description of political reality.[23] International law emerged as a means of both defining sovereignty's status quo and determining its future possibilities. There is then the deeper question of whether sovereignty is a creature of interantaional law, or whether it describes a pre-legal phenomenon on which the international legal order is itself based. In Medieval Europe and Asia, sovereignty described a form of superiority; it was in the formation of the modern nation state, when sovereignty and the sovereign became associated with a right to command, that the concept of sovereignty begin to emerge as an abstract concept not directly linked with an individual person.[24] What happened after that was a series of revolutions, beginning with the Peace of Westphalia in 1648, that redefined what sovereignty could be, recognising both political and physical senses of sovereignty.[25] As these revolutions reshaped the meaning of what could be sovereign, so too did international law reimagine what legal obligations were, but it was not clear that one automatically preceded the other.[26] In fact international law often defended sovereignty; as Stewart Motha notes in a wide-ranging study of colonial and post-colonial sovereignty in the Indian Ocean, 'weakened' sovereign power often relied on law to shore up 'the artifice that is its edifice', arguing that law acted as a means of preserving the trappings of sovereignty, particularly the power to give acts of violence legitimacy.[27]

The issue that then arises is how to approach a working definition of sovereignty in order to appreciate what states are referring to in the process of

[21] A Anghie, *Imperialism, Sovereignty and the Making of International Law* (Cambridge University Press, 2004) 110–14; Mégret (n 9).

[22] A Anghie, 'The Evolution of International Law: Colonial and Postcolonial Realities' (2006) 27 *Third World Quarterly* 739.

[23] S Pahuja, *Decolonising International Law: Development, Economic Growth and the Politics of Universality* (Cambridge University Press, 2011) 26. For a critique of the doctrine of sovereign equality, see M Cosnard, 'Sovereign Equality – "The Wimbledon sails on"' in M Byers and G Nolte (eds), *United States Hegemony and the Foundations of International Law* (Cambridge University Press, 2003) 117–134.

[24] M Loughlin, 'The Ten Tenets of Sovereignty' in N Walker (ed), *Sovereignty in Transition* (Oxford University Press, 2003).

[25] D Philpott, *Revolutions in Sovereignty: How Ideas Shaped Modern International Relations* (Princeton University Press 2001) ch 1.

[26] A Cassese, 'States: Rise and Decline of the Primary Subjects of the International Community' in B Fassbender and A Peters (eds), *The Oxford Handbook of the History of International Law* (Oxford University Press, 2012) 49–70.

[27] S Motha, *Archiving Sovereignty: Law, History, Violence* (University of Michigan Press, 2018) 4, 18.

withdrawal, which is more difficult than it initially seems. 'It is impossible to define "sovereignty"', Koskenniemi argues, because any definition that attempts to encompass a state's 'full subjective freedom' ends up being forced into a conclusion that 'no state is free' or that the 'international order is not really binding'.[28] The point of this is that references to '"sovereignty"' or 'statehood' cannot lead to 'determinate consequences' or an ascertainment as to whether a state is free or not.[29] If this seems circular it is because essentially the argumentative structure at work here starts with the existence of a legal obligation and works backwards to determine whether or not that is an interference with a state's sovereignty; and if it is, whether a state consented to that obligation. As a set of intuitions in legal argument, this is given coherence by a particularly Eurocentric conception of sovereignty, relying on standardised conceptions of space and time that emerged during the seventeenth and eighteenth centuries. These allowed maps defining a state's jurisdiction to be drawn, and administrative authorities and institutions exercising legal control over the population to be created – all part of what Teemu Ruskola calls the 'homogenous conceptions of individual subjectivity and state-based sovereignty'.[30] The protection of sovereignty in international law is, and remains, a series of claims that refer to the changing of its subject, and in international law are both interdependent and co-dependent on one another. As Gerry Simpson notes, paraphrasing Baty's words, 'it is universally agreed that … [international law] has something to with States'.[31] Simpson's contention, building on Baty's rather pithy observation, is that international law has structurally been positioned around two sets of arguments: one about the material and immaterial qualities of statehood, and the other about the stability of the state itself.[32] Withdrawal is an argument about the latter concept – what a state can or cannot do, and how those actions relate to the stability both of the state and of the wider international society within which the state exists.

In the context of understanding what the law of withdrawal is for, it makes sense to focus on the types of arguments states make about their sovereignty and capacity to engage in sovereign decision making. Wouter Werner and Jaap de Wilde, in a 2001 article, argued that rather than being preoccupied with the substantive meaning of the term 'sovereignty', it instead made sense to think of sovereignty as series of claims and examine who was making those claims and to whom those claims were addressed, rather than simply constructing and

[28] M Koskenniemi, *From Apology to Utopia: The Structure of International Legal* Argument, 2nd edn (Cambridge University Press, 2005) 245.

[29] ibid.

[30] T Ruskola, 'China in the Age of the World Picture' in A Orford and F Hoffmann (eds), *The Oxford Handbook of the Theory of International Law* (Oxford University Press, 2016) 138–155, 145.

[31] G Simpson, 'Something to do with States' in Orford and Hoffmann (eds) (n 30) 564, 564–65.

[32] ibid.

reconstructing concepts and searching for their corresponding realities.[33] In its essence, the law of withdrawal is about providing a legal framework for a state to alter its legal obligations, exercising its sovereign decision-making capacity to undo its previous commitment to an international legal regime, which itself was a sovereign act. This can lead to the use of the concept of sovereignty in a series of different and often contradictory ways. In 2017, President Donald Trump issued a statement saying that the United States (US) was withdrawing from Paris Climate Change Treaty because the commitments to reduce CO_2 emissions had led to a situation where '[f]oreign leaders in Europe, Asia … [had] more to say with respect to the US economy than our own citizens and their elected representatives'. Withdrawal from the Treaty therefore represented 'a reassertion of America's sovereignty'.[34] James Crawford, commenting on this, noted that the US had in fact exercised its sovereignty 'in negotiating, signing and ratifying the Paris Agreement', with the Administration of President Obama, who had ratified the Paris Agreement, agreeing that 'all countries should have general obligations to reduce emissions'.[35] That Presidents Obama and Trump might disagree on what it meant to exercise the nation's sovereignty is relatively unsurprising – they disagree on most things. Obligations bind states regardless of changes in domestic political office, but, as shown in section II of this chapter one of the functions of the law of withdrawal is that it allows for a state's preferences to change, so that following a change of individuals in a political office, a state can exercise its sovereign decision-making capacity and take another legal act to initiate withdrawal from a treaty. Yet withdrawal does not make the act of legal commitment to a treaty any less of a sovereign act. Understanding sovereignty as a set of claims allows for interrogation of the claims made by states in the process of withdrawal, and can be situated within a wider trend in international relations and international legal theory to recognise the changing nature of sovereignty as a concept.[36]

B. Critically Appraising State Consent

As a term, 'state consent' is used to refer both to the 'free will' of states and to their 'acceptance' of obligations in international law, but these two ideas are often

[33] W Werner and J de Wilde, 'The Endurance of Sovereignty' (2001) 7 *European Journal of International Relations* 283.

[34] White House Press Secretary, 'Statement by President Trump on the Paris Climate Accord' (1 June 2017) at www.whitehouse.gov/the-press-office/2017/06/01/statement-president-trump-paris-climate-accord (accessed 23 March 2022 unless stated otherwise).

[35] J Crawford, 'The Current Political Discourse Concerning International Law' (2018) 81 *MLR* 1, 16.

[36] WG Werner, 'State Sovereignty and International Legal Discourse' in IF Dekker and Werner (eds), *Governance and International Legal Theory* (Utrecht University Press, 2004); J Cohen, 'Whose Sovereignty? Empire Versus International Law' (2004) 18 *Ethics & International Affairs* 1; this review essay also analyses some of the developments in the scholarship on sovereignty, J Bartelson, 'The Concept of Sovereignty Revisited' (2006) 17 *European Journal of International Law* 463.

described in ways that overlap and interlink.[37] It is the basis of legal principles, such as *pacta sunt servanda*, and the rules found in Articles 11–18 of the Vienna Convention on the Law of Treaties (VCLT). Early theorists of international law, such as Emer de Vattel and Johann Jacob Mose, drew a direct line from the importance of honouring contracts in the civil sphere to the importance of rulers' honouring their agreements with other rulers.[38] Histories of the doctrine trace its origins within such writings as a move away from a personalised approach to treaties, which bound individuals for their lifetime and was underpinned by religious oath taking, towards a doctrine of good faith, underpinned by reciprocal understandings made in the wider context of an international order.[39] Others, such as Anthony Carty and Anna Irene Baka, have argued that the historical provenance of positivistic reasoning about the nature of international obligations was rooted in the expansion of liberal capitalism and colonialism from the sixteenth century onwards, which was the context of de Vattel's work, who saw consent in terms of the 'virtual liberty of nations'.[40] Similar thinking can be found in the nineteenth-century writings of Henry Wheaton, who argued that states 'are moral beings capable of contracting by direct positive consent … the rules for the regulation of their mutual intercourse'.[41]

The nineteenth-century German jurist Heinrich Triepel explained the role of state will in creating binding international law in neo-Hegelian terms, arguing that it was the meeting of collective will that gave rise to international law as law; and absent such an expression of will, legal relations could not arise.[42] In the early twentieth century, writers attempting to explain the source of international obligations focused on consent as the most significant feature of what gave international law its binding quality.[43] Writing in 1925, Percy Corbert noted that the consent of states is the 'formal' but not necessarily the 'material' source of international law.[44] These arguments came to underpin positivist approaches to

[37] S Besson, 'State Consent and Disagreement in International Law-Making. Dissolving the Paradox' (2016) 29 *Leiden Journal of International Law* 289, 295.

[38] H Wehberg, 'Pacta Sunt Servanda' (1959) 53 *American Journal of International Law* 775.

[39] R Lesaffer, 'The Grotian Tradition Revisited: Change and Continuity in the History of International Law' (2002) 73 *British Yearbook of International Law* 103.

[40] A Carty and AI Baka, 'Sources in the Metas-History of International Law: From Liberal Nihilsm and the Anti-Metaphyiscs of Modernity to an Aristotelian Ethical Order' in S Besson and J d'Aspremont (eds), *The Oxford Handbook of International Law* (Oxford University Press, 2017) 253.

[41] H Wheaton, *Elements of International Law with a Sketch of the History of the Science* (Carey, Lee and Blanchard, 1836) 43.

[42] J Shen, 'The Basis of International Law: Why Nations Observe' (1999) 17 *Penn State International Law Review* 287, 312–313 gives a description of Triepel's work.

[43] See, eg, R Foulke, 'Definition and Nature of International Law' (1919) 19 *Columbia Law Review* 429; Q Wright, 'The Understanding of International Law' (1920) 14 *American Journal of International Law* 565, 575; G Wickersham 'The Codification of International Law' (1926) 4 *Foreign Affairs* 237. It is noteworthy that some were sceptical of an adherence to the doctrine of consent, eg C Eagleton, 'The Current Status of International Law' (1930) 69 *Proceedings of the American Philosophical Society* 203, 205.

[44] PE Corbett, 'The Consent of States and the Sources of the Law of Nations' (1925) 6 *British Yearbook of International Law* 20, 25.

international law, as for positivists state consent was a known source from which obligations could emerge.[45] Although more recent scholars have attempted to distinguish positivism from state-centricism, the voluntarist paradigm – the idea that, apart from some commonly acknowledged and limited exceptions, a state's obligations in international law are characterised by the voluntary sovereign act of consent – was at the forefront of understanding legal obligations by the early twentieth century.[46] The PCIJ, in the *SS Wimbledon* case explicitly endorsed the voluntarist paradigm when it observed that any treaty creating an obligation 'places a restriction upon the exercise of the sovereign rights of the State' but that the 'right of entering into international engagements is an attribute of state sovereignty'.[47] As Mónica García-Salmones Rovira notes, there is something quasi-theological about the idea of voluntarism in classic legal positivism; for example a fourteenth-century theologian would argue that 'no rationality can bind the will of God'; and even if this statement conflicted with their observations of the reality around them, they would instead focus on their 'epistemological view on the normative character of God's command'.[48] Voluntarism, and voluntarist thinking about international law, promoted sovereign will as the central epistemological tenet for understanding where international obligations came from, even though from the nineteenth century onwards, writers on international law were clear that there were different sources of international obligation that stemmed from the wider interests of the international community.[49]

Voluntarism has a lot of critics, and branches of international law that exist to protect basic rights or regulate the social interactions of states sit uneasily with the idea that international legal obligation exists solely out of states' volunteering to enter into such commitments.[50] It does provide a justificatory logic to the doctrine of *pact sunt servanda*, as the basic principle of expecting a state to fulfil its obligations can be justified by the fact that a state consented to

[45] Hans Morgenthau critically explores the growth of this thought in H Morgenthau, 'Positivism, Functionalism, and International Law' (1942) 34 *American Journal of International Law* 260, 271.

[46] For a critical description of classic legal positivism and voluntarism, see R Collins, 'Classical Legal Positivism in International Law Revisited' in J d'Aspremont and J Kammerhofer, *International Legal Positivism in a Post-Modern World* (Cambridge University Press, 2014) 35. For an example of those trying to separate it voluntarism from J d'Aspremont, 'Reductionist Legal Positivism in International Law' (2012) 106 *American Society of International Law Proceedings* 368.

[47] *SS Wimbledon*, 1923 PCIJ Rep Series A No 1, 25 (28 June).

[48] M García-Salmones Rovira, 'Faith, Ritual and Rebellion in 21st Century (Positivist) International Law' (2015) 26 *European Journal of International Law* 537, 540.

[49] There is considerable scepticism of the narrative that situates the history of international law in the 19th century as a clash between naturalism and positivism (see Collins (n 46)); see also M Koskenniemi, 'The Legacy of the Nineteenth Century' in D Armstrong (ed), in *Routledge Handbook on International Law* (Routledge, 2009) 141–153.

[50] These ideas are discussed from a human rights perspective by Theodore Christakis, who is not unsympathetic to the idea that voluntarism should underpin the creation of human rights law. See T Christakis, 'Human Rights from a Neo-Voluntarist Perspective' in J Kammerhofer and J d'Aspremont (eds) in *International Legal Positivism in a Post-Modern World* (Cambridge University Press, 2014).

those obligations.[51] As codified in the VCLT, *pact sunt servanda* requires parties to perform obligations in good faith, and Article 11 situates the entire act of becoming a party to a treaty as an exercise of consent on the part of the state.[52] The existence of a legal obligation therefore can be surmised from the act of consent. Even though this has been criticised as narrowing assumptions about what constitutes legal obligation, the mere existence of consent is, as subsequent chapters of this book set out, politically useful both to explain legal obligations and to appeal to a state to comply with those obligations.[53] Some have been careful to stress the distinction between the treatment of *pacta sunt servanda* simply as a trite statement to the effect that 'one should obey the law' and its actual status as a quasi-constitutional doctrine that governs the formation of legal obligations.[54] As a doctrine, *pacta sunt servanda* is based on the idea that a state's expression of consent has meaning and it is rooted within a positivist justification of international legal obligations. Even outside the confines of a positivistic understanding of the sources of international law, state consent can provide an important justificatory function for the existence of international legal obligations and provides a neat shorthand explanation as to the legitimacy of any such obligations.[55]

First, the doctrine of state consent, and legal doctrines based on state consent such as *pacta sunt servanda*, provides some connection between the domestic population of a state, and their general political will, and the international obligations imposed on that state, meaning that state consent can provide an evaluative function for assessing whether a political unit wishes to restrict itself in a particular manner.[56] Whilst this is somewhat idealistic, as states are not necessarily all built on democratic consent and the content of international legal obligations can be difficult to assess through political processes, this is a description of the ideal.[57] This argument for consent has also been cited with approval

[51] Guzman points out that this can create a 'compliance pull' for treaty obligations: A Guzman 'Against Consent.' (2012) 52 *Virginia Journal of International Law* 747, 752–753.

[52] Art 11 VCLT provides that 'The consent of a State to be bound by a treaty may be expressed by signature, exchange of instruments constituting a treaty, ratification, acceptance approval or accession or by any other means if so agreed.' Art 26 VCLT, codifying *pacta sunt servanda*, provides 'Every treaty in force is binding upon the parties to it and must be performed by them in good faith.' 1969 Vienna Convention on the Law of Treaties (opened for signature 23 May 1969, entered into force 27 January 1980) 1155 UNTS 331.

[53] A Pellet, 'The Normative Dilemma: Will and Consent in International Law-making' (1988) 12 *Australian Yearbook of International Law* 22.

[54] JL Kunz, 'The Meaning and the Range of the Norm Pacta Sunt Servanda' (1945) 39 *American Journal of International Law* 180.

[55] M Lister, 'The Legitimating Role of Consent in International Law' (2011) 11 *Chicago Journal of International Law* 633; Guzman (n 51).

[56] M Craven, 'The Ends of Consent' in D Kritsiotis and MJ Bowman (eds), *Conceptual and Contextual Perspectives on the Modern Law of Treaties* (Cambridge University Press, 2014).

[57] As Jens Steffek suggests, the 'traditional idea' of what makes international law legitimate, contractual consent, can operate independently of the type of government actually making that argument. See J Steffek, 'Legitimacy in International Relations: From State Compliance to Citizen Consent' in A Hurrelmann et al (eds), *Legitimacy in an Age of Global Politics* (Springer, 2007) 178.

by those who argue that the doctrine can prevent coercion into legal obligations and thus serve as some form of redress to sovereign inequality.[58]

Second, the idea of *pacta sunt servanda* plays an important moral function in underpinning the stability of the international order and international law, and hence the material and political goods that accrue to individuals from a stable international order.[59] There is also a wider normative benefit to the state as a whole in terms of rationalising and limiting inter-state conflict and stopping coercion into obligations.[60] Rationalist theorising on international law often focuses on the way in which obligations create reputational concerns for states, lest they should end up violating an international obligation, but this rests on understanding state consent as providing a form of international stability that 'good' states aspire to maintain because they are concerned about their reputation.[61]

Third, as Besson notes, because state consent is rarely totalising and more of a structured 'agreement to disagree further', with arguments about interpretation, reservations and implementation all forming legitimate parts of international law, the overall loss of sovereign capacity and identity through an act of state consent is often relatively minimal.[62] In this respect, the rules of state consent serve to preserve the procedural autonomy of states in terms of negotiating their obligations, so that the formal process of being bound as a matter of law comes after securing agreement, or at the point of maximal potential agreement between states.[63] Again, this is another description of a normative ideal, not of practical reality; many states do not get to bargain over the content of treaties. Some treaties, such as human rights treaties, contain provisions that are difficult for states to challenge, and represent a particular definition and codification of rights to which many states have not contributed.[64] Some treaties, such as

D'Aspremont describes this argument as a pastiche of authority which creates a reality for international law – see J d'Aspermont 'Consenting to International Law in Five Moves' in S Besson (eds.) *Consenting to International Law* (Cambridge University Press, Forthcoming 2023).

[58] Brad Roth argues that sovereign consent can help preserve formal legal equality between states, when there are clear political inequalities between states. See B Roth, *Sovereign Equality and Moral Disagreement, Premises of a Pluralist International Legal Order* (Oxford University Press, 2011) 7–9.

[59] H Suganami, 'A normative enquiry in international relations: the case of "pacta sunt servanda"' (1983) 9 *Review of International Studies* 35.

[60] O Spiermann, 'Twentieth Century Internationalism in Law' (2007) 18 *European Journal of International Law* 785, 789.

[61] A leading example of this is A Guzman, *How International Law Works: A Rational Choice Theory* (Oxford University Press, 2008). There has also been some criticism of the dependency of this thinking on contractual analysis. See A Kydd, 'Reputation and cooperation: Guzman on international law' (2009) 1 *International Theory* 295.

[62] Besson (n 37) 292.

[63] See A Bolintineanu 'Expression of Consent to be Bound by a Treaty in the Light of the 1969 Vienna Convention' (1974) 68 *American Journal of International Law* 672, 674.

[64] The presence of reservations to human rights treaties has been argued as being necessary to ensure state consent from prospective parties. This is discussed in R Goodman, 'Human Rights Treaties, Invalid Reservations, and State Consent' (2002) 96 *American Journal of International Law* 531.

investment treaties, require states that are in a relatively weaker economic position to accept their provisions with minimal scope for disagreement, in order for them to benefit from increased inward investment into their economy.[65]

To what extent a state's intention regarding legal relations can be divined from an act of consent has been called into question. As Koskenniemi argues, a state's intention 'can only be known in its manifestations' and arguments over 'which manifestations (text, behaviour, teleology etc) count' for the purposes of determining intention 'depend on whether they express intent', leading him to conclude that the doctrine is 'hopelessly circular'.[66] Doctrines of treaty interpretation, especially evolutive interpretations of individual provisions, create arguments about the intention of states on entry into a legal regime and the scope of what they consented to, which are difficult to dismiss with a simplistic reading of state consent as proof of intent.[67] In fact a rigid assessment of notions of legality in determining state consent can end up diluting the idea that state consent can be a useful mechanism for determining the intention of state parties.[68] However, whilst it might be reasonable to conclude that the doctrine of state consent is an unreliable proxy for divining state intent, the doctrine remains the dominant heuristic for explaining why international legal obligations exist and ought to bind states.[69] Many of the arguments about consent are in fact structured arguments about the changing nature and meaning of sovereignty, being fought out under the overall guise of the formalist doctrine of state consent.[70] The arguments surrounding state consent have become, as Werner describes it, part of a 'foundational myth' about international law, designed to present it as 'more coherent, unitary and encompassing than it actually is'.[71] Legal and political arguments over withdrawal often involve contestations over the precise meaning of this foundational myth. What a state consented to in agreeing to an arbitration clause in a bilateral investment treaty, and whether that consent involves consent to arbitration under the International Convention

[65] See G Van Harten, 'Five Justifications for Investment Treaties: A Critical Discussion' (2010) 2 *Trade, Law and Development* 19.

[66] M Koskenniemi, *From Apology to Utopia: The Structure of International Legal Argument* (Cambridge University Press, 2005) 337.

[67] For an overview of this general issue, see M Kumm, 'The Legitimacy of International Law: A Constitutionalist Framework of Analysis' (2004) 15 *European Journal of International Law* 907.

[68] OA Elias and CL Lim, *The Paradox of Consensualism in International Law* (Brill, 1998) 241.

[69] For a discussion on this point, see S Besson, 'Theorizing the Sources of International Law' in S Besson and J Tasioulas (eds), *The Philosophy of International Law* (Oxford University Press, 2010) 165–66. Some scholars have emphasised the sources doctrine in state consent whilst arguing that considerations of political authority should be taken into account. See D Hollis, 'Why State Consent Still Matters: Non-State Actors, Treaties, and the Changing Sources of International Law' (2005) 23 *Berkley Journal of International Law* 137.

[70] S Ranganathan, *Strategically Created Treaty Conflicts and the Politics of International Law* (Cambridge University Press, 2014) 131–38.

[71] WG Werner, 'State consent as foundational myth' in C Brölmann and Y Radi (eds), *Research Handbook on the Theory and Practice of International Lawmaking* (Edward Elgar, 2016) 13–31, 15.

on the Settlement of Investment Disputes (ICSID), is often an area of dispute when a state is seeking to withdraw from an investment treaty and presumes it can escape arbitration under ICSID as well.[72]

C. Withdrawal as the Undoing of State Consent?

Withdrawal can be understood as proof of the exercise of consent, in that whilst a state is free to consent to an obligation, it is also free to end its consent. There are of course obligations from which withdrawal is not possible as a matter of law, but this is a subject for later chapters.[73] This chapter is concerned with the stated reasons for withdrawal when withdrawal is legally possible which can, intuitively speaking, be understood as the inverse of consent. Writing in 1625, Hugo Grotius in *On the Law of War and Peace* noted that a king could make treaties that were binding on the king and his successors, but under-explored the unmaking or termination of treaties, with the analysis focusing on the impossibility of performance and unequal terms in treaties.[74] Nevertheless, the first major study of withdrawal, Harold Tobin's *The Termination of Multipartite Treaties*, noted that it had 'always been an accepted rule' that bilateral treaties could not be terminated by denunciation without the consent of the other parties, and this principle did not really change with the growth of multilateral treaties.[75] Arie David, in a 1975 study of treaty termination, argued that *pacta sunt servanda* was a mechanism for claiming authority in bargaining during treaty breakdown, encouraging states to use the legal mechanisms of denunciation to affect treaty termination.[76]

Early literature on withdrawal often conflated withdrawal as a result of a state's decision and withdrawal using the doctrine of changed circumstances rendering performance impossible – *rebus sic stantibus*. Wheaton, writing in 1836, noted that even treaties designed to exist in perpetuity could be terminated when 'the internal constitution of government of either state is so changed as to render the treaty inapplicable under the circumstances different from those with a view to which it was concluded'.[77] Writing in the *American Journal of International Law* in 1927, JW Garner noted how a few months earlier, the

[72] FM Lavopa, LE Barreiro and MV Bruno, 'How to Kill a BIT and Not Die Trying: Legal and Political Challenges of Denouncing or Renegotiating Bilateral Investment Treaties' (2013) 16 *Journal of International Economic Law* 869, 875–77.

[73] See E Schwelb, 'Some Aspects of International Jus Cogens as Formulated by the International Law Commission' (1967) 61 *American Journal of International Law* 946, 955–57.

[74] H Grotius, *On the Law of War and Peace: Student Edition*, ed S Neff (Cambridge University Press, 2012) 232–37.

[75] H Tobin, *The Termination of Multipartite Treaties* (Columbia University Press, 1934) 194.

[76] A David, *The Strategy of Treaty Termination: Lawful Breaches and Retaliations* (Yale University Press, 1975) 83–84.

[77] Wheaton (n 41) 191.

Chinese Republic had terminated its treaty with Belgium citing the 'recognized principle of *rebus sic stantibus*'.[78] In 1930, Arnold McNair noted that *rebus sic stantibus* had 'a double aspect, legal and political', and noted the analogy between it and domestic contract law, which in both the UK and many jurisdictions in the US recognised that states might be unable to meet obligations to which they had consented.[79] In 1941, the US withdrew from the International Load Lines Convention – a treaty regulating the maximum tonnage of cargo ships – without giving notice to other parties to the Convention as required by the treaty, citing the principle of *rebus sic stantibus* due to needs in time of war and the requirements for maintaining convoys of shipping traffic across the Atlantic, requiring increased tonnage to be loaded on ships. The situation was, the US State Department argued, 'wholly different from that obtaining at the time the convention was signed'. As the then US Attorney General argued, 'of the 36 countries who were party, 10 are at war and 16 are under military occupation', allowing the Government to declare the Convention suspended.[80] As Krzysztof Plec noted, the doctrine of *rebus sic stantibus* was understood in this exchange as a qualification to the principle of *pacta sunt servanda*.[81] However, in the mid-twentieth century, a distinction came to be drawn between arguments about the changed circumstances of the treaty that would or could have consequences for its validity and the right of a state to withdraw from the treaty in exercise of its own autonomy.[82] When codifying the law of treaties in the VCLT, a distinction was drawn between circumstances that would allow a state to argue that obligations were no longer binding on the state, and the right to withdraw as an autonomous decision.

When Japan withdrew from the League of Nations, it had for two years been in protracted negotiations both with the League Council and with the wider international community about the status of Manchuria.[83] The dispute was not about a change of circumstances but about Japan's rights as a sovereign nation and the perceived overreach of the League's power. Withdrawal was a conscious sovereign act, to the extent that in the 1933 *Official Journal* of the League it was referred to it as the 'exercise [of Japan's] privilege of withdrawal'.[84]

[78] JW Garner, 'The Doctrine of Rebus Sic Stantibus and the Termination of Treaties' (1927) 21 *American Journal of International Law* 509, 509.

[79] AD McNair, 'The Functions and Differing Legal Character of Treaties' (1930) 11 *British Yearbook of International Law* 100, 106.

[80] Statement by Secretary of State, 'International Load Line Convention' *The Department of State Bulletin*, vol 5 no 106, 9 August 1941, 114.

[81] K Plec, *Making and Bending International Rules: The Design of Exceptions and Escape Clauses in Trade Law*, 2nd edn (Cambridge University Press, 2018) 75–76.

[82] A Vamvoukos, *Termination of Treaties in International Law: The Doctrines of Rebus Sic Stantibus and Desuetude* (Clarendon Press, 1985) 22–27.

[83] For the history of this, see D Wen-wei Chang, 'The Western Powers and Japan's Aggression in China: The League of Nations and "The Lytton Report"' (2003) 10 *American Journal of Chinese Studies* 43.

[84] Burns (n 4) 46.

The exercise of sovereign autonomy in the process of withdrawal, by acting under the terms of a withdrawal clause in a treaty to which it has already consented, is compatible with the principle of 'performing [an] obligation' under the treaty following the principle of *pacta sunt servanda*, as codified in Article 26 VCLT. Vassilis Pergantis argues that *pacta sunt servanda* as a discursive strategy has little value in relation to withdrawal, as it risks prioritising a form of formalist logic – a state has consented to something therefore it must obey it – that could see states locked in what might have become unjust and unfair arrangements.[85] But formalist logic is important from a withdrawing state's perspective, as the state is seeking an absence of formal legal constraints as a result of treaty withdrawal, or at the very least hopes to generate that assumption in the minds of other parties by threatening such an action.[86] Furthermore, the withdrawing state, by using a withdrawal clause, is attempting to have its actions viewed as legal actions. When Japan was leaving the League of Nations, it exercised its powers under the withdrawal clause in the League Charter, and there was little doubt in contemporary legal sources that, regardless of other actions of the Japanese Empire, withdrawal was a legal act.[87]

Scholarly work on the role of consent during the 2010s often focused either on its diminished role, or on the difficulty of situating it alongside concepts such as global public goods, or its role in sociological legitimacy.[88] These accounts are characterised by a growing scepticism of a strictly formalistic view of consent, which has some merit, especially in light of literature challenging the formation of obligations.[89] State consent does, however, have relevance in explaining how states acquiesce to a process of normative development, which then shapes the rules and frameworks governing their behaviour.[90] As such, the discursive power of a formalist approach to consent is useful in demarcating the existence of the rule-compliant states discharging their obligations from those non-rule-compliant states, or those without any obligation to follow the law.[91] Consent and

[85] V Pergantis, *The Paradigm of State Consent in the Law of Treaties: Challenges and Perspectives* (Edward Elgar, 2017) 156–58.

[86] L Helfer, 'Exiting treaties' (2015) 91 *Virginia Law Review* 1579.

[87] Burns (n 4) 46.

[88] See, eg, N Krisch, 'The Decay of Consent: International Law in an Age of Global Public Goods' (2014) 108 *American Journal of International Law* 1; T Christano, 'Climate Change and State Consent' in J Moss (ed), *Climate Change and Justice* (Cambridge University Press, 2015) 17; D Moeckli, 'Interpretation of the ICESCR: Between Morality and State Consent' (22 January 2016) at https://ssrn.com/abstract=2720351.

[89] E Kassoti, 'Beyond State Consent? International Legal Scholarship and the Challenge of Informal International Law-Making' (2016) 63 *Netherlands International Law Review* 99; E Reynolds et al, 'Attitudes toward Consent-Based and Non Consent-Based International Law in a Regional Power Context' (2018) 44 *International Interactions* 661.

[90] E Hay, *Teaching International Law: State-Consent As Consent to a Process of Normative Development and Ensuing Problems* (Martinus Nijhoff Publishers, 2003) 1.

[91] Pellet (n 53) 22. Alain Pellet described the question over the division between law and non-law 'as a bad question'.

the identification of consent have an important function regarding how a state conceives of how international law should operate. As Pergantis goes on to argue, what the capacity to withdraw says about the underlying principle of state consent can be summarised in two equally plausible schools of thought: first, that consent is conditional, which therefore makes the certainty of international agreements less stable; or, second, that the possibility of withdrawal is necessary to obtain state consent to entry into legal obligations in the first place.[92] Both of these schools of thought are very much in evidence in some of the justifications for the use and existence of the law of withdrawal presented in Section II.

But before considering that, it is important to take a step back and ask a final question: To what extent does state consent imply the existence of a right to withdraw from a legal obligation? This school of thought would, taking a positivist voluntarist position, maintain that because obligations arise from state consent, withdrawal is a presumption of free consent. Thomas Franck and Peter Prows describe a presumption as the position that if 'one fact (or the commission, or omission, of an act) can be demonstrated, then another may (or must) be inferred from it' or, put more succinctly, 'if A then B'.[93] In the context of withdrawal, the presumption, as Emile Giraud summarises, is that if 'states are not obliged to enter into them [international agreements], they must not be prevented from leaving them.'[94] This, however, takes a very narrow view of both the nature of obligations and the context of withdrawal. The obligations a state has operate in a broader framework of international law and, even if not reciprocal, can have a direct effect on other states or the individuals living within states. Examples of these concerns, relating to treaties controlling nuclear weapons and greenhouse gas emissions, are discussed in subsequent chapters. Broader concerns about the stability of international law were paramount during the drafting of the VCLT provisions in this area.[95] President Richard Nixon, in a 1972 letter to the US Congress recommending ratification of the VCLT, made reference to the US 'fighting for the stability' of the treaty system in the drafting process, in particular reference to arbitration over the misuse of invalidity and termination clauses.[96] Indeed, there are few, if any, real

[92] Pergantis (n 85) 157. Both positions are outlined by Pergantis; the latter view is explored by L Helfer, 'Terminating Treaties' in DB Hollis (ed), *The Oxford Guide to Treaties* (Oxford University Press, 2012) 648.

[93] TM Franck and P Prows, 'The Role of Presumptions in International Tribunals' (2005) 4 *Law and Practice of International Courts & Tribunals* 197, 200.

[94] E Giraud, 'Modification et Terminaison des Traités Collectifs' (1961) 49 *Annuaire de l'Institut de droit international* 5, 74.

[95] For indicative examples, see EP Deutsch, 'Vienna Convention on the Law of Treaties' (1971) 47 *Notre Dame Law Review* 297, 304; SE Nahlik, 'The Grounds of Invalidity and Termination of Treaties' (1971) 65 *American Journal of International Law* 736, 746–47.

[96] R Nixon and W Rodgers, 'Vienna Convention on the Law of Treaties' (1972) 6 *The International Lawyer* 428, 436–37.

case studies of states claiming an unfettered sovereign right to withdraw; and even when that may be the case, it is usually cloaked in one of the arguments detailed in section II of this chapter. It is useful to understand voluntarism as part of a broader theory about law and its origins, which privileges a particular set of presumptions about sovereignty, namely, that international law itself is, or ought to be, a reflection of sovereign will.[97] But this does not mean that sovereign will ought to give an unfettered licence to act as a state pleases, not least because of the attendant cost to the stability of the overall international system such a position would entail.

II. FOUR JUSTIFICATIONS FOR THE EXISTENCE OF THE LAW OF WITHDRAWAL

If, as argued in section I, it is not correct to simply see withdrawal as the inverse of consent, the question remains as to what the justification is for the law of withdrawal. From the existing case law and literature on withdrawal, it is possible to discern four distinct objectives for states, or justifications that states might use to explain their actions when engaging in a lawful act of withdrawal. Equally, these four objectives/justifications are important for states in developing or advocating for the inclusion of withdrawal clauses in an instrument. All of these objectives/justifications touch on the international legal doctrines of state consent and good faith but are ultimately distinct arguments. So the object of this section, as indicated by the individual subheadings, is to unpack the legal arguments states make about why they can withdraw from a legal obligation. Framing the answer to the question in the title of this chapter another way, from existing scholarship and practice these are the four leading explanations as to why the law of withdrawal ought to exist. Each of these categories fuses together the arguments used by states to justify an individual act of withdrawal and the justification for the law's existence as a normative framework. On the surface there is little clear distinction between the two justifications, as the withdrawing state, by trying to engineer an act of withdrawal rather than non-compliance or termination, wants both to escape the legal obligations and to justify its actions as legal to internal and external audiences, especially to those states who remain in the legal regime they are withdrawing from. These are not strict legal tests

[97] Subsequent interpretations of and literature on *The Lotus* (n 10) support this general view: H Handeyside, 'The Lotus Principle in ICJ Jurisprudence: Was the Ship Ever Afloat?' (2007) 29 *Michigan Journal of International Law* 71, 79–80. This presumption of sovereignty was heavily criticised shortly after the decision was made as being an example of the 'extreme positivist school, that the law emanates from the free will of sovereign independent states: JL Brierly, 'The "Lotus" Case' (1928) 44 *Law Quarterly Review* 154, 155. See more generally on arguments about what sovereignty means, A de Hoogh, 'The Sovereigns are Dead, Long Live the Sovereigns – Reflections on State Sovereignty and International Law' in E Rieter and H de Waele (eds), *Evolving Principles of International Law* (Brill, 2012) 169–195.

about the legality of a state's actions but different justifications for the existence of the law of withdrawal.

A. Withdrawal Safeguards a State in Light of Changing External Circumstances

Although the VCLT specifically lists a set of safeguards pertaining to the practical circumstances in which a treaty operates and when it might become invalid, some states have tried to use the process of withdrawal as a means of protecting themselves in the event of a change in the political circumstances surrounding the treaty. As Georg Nolte argues, the commitment of parties to a treaty depends in part 'on the situation of the treaty more generally and thus its political viability' as an instrument.[98] Therefore one important aspect of the law of treaties is to provide protections for states as the political circumstances surrounding the obligations they have assumed change over time. The International Law Commission's (ILC) Working Group on treaties over time identified in its initial recommendations some grounds for withdrawal relating to the passage of time, such as the supervening possibility of performance or changing circumstances, all of which describe why a state may wish to withdraw because of the changed political viability of obligations under the treaty.[99] Managing the socio-political reality of treaties is in essence the rationale of Article 61 VCLT, which expressly gives the 'impossibility of performing a treaty' as a basis for 'terminating or withdrawing' from the treaty, and Article 62, which acknowledges that circumstances may change the 'essential basis of the consent of the parties to be bound by the treaty'.[100] There is, however, a distinction between consent as discussed in these provisions and consent as evidence of the positivist contention that international law is an expression of the will of states. These provisions exist as means of defending the state from being put in what it might regard as a punitive position as a result of changing external circumstances.

The *Gabčíkovo-Nagymaros* case[101] was significant, in that one of the parties, Hungary, attempted withdrawal from a treaty that lacked a withdrawal or termination clause. A 1977 treaty concluded between Hungary and Czechoslovakia (which by the time of the proceedings at the International Court of Justice (ICJ) was Slovakia, as the project was on its territory) dammed two parts of the river

[98] Georg Nolte, *Treaties and Their Practice: Symptoms of Their Rise or Decline* (Brill Nijhoff, 2011) 21.

[99] See S-I Lekkas and A Tzanakopoulos, 'Pacta Sunt Servanda versus Flexibility in the Suspen-...n of Treaties' in C Tams, A Tzanakopoulos and A Zimmerman (eds), *Research ... reaties* (Edward Elgar, 2014) 312, 318–322; ILC, *Report of the Interna-... the Work of its 60th Session* (5 May–7 June and 7 July–8 August 2008) ...na-

... *Project (Hungary v Slovakia)* (Merits) [1997] ICJ Rep 7.

Danube with a view to providing hydro-electric power. Both countries were at the time one-party communist states, and environmental concerns received relatively little attention in the political sphere. By 1989 however, when Hungary abandoned its part in the project, there was not only a much greater awareness of the environmental damage that controlled flooding would cause, but also internal political pressure about its consequences.[102] At the ICJ, the Hungarian Government argued that it had given its consent to the damming of the Danube, at considerable expense, only on the basis that this would constitute a joint investment with Slovakia and involve the pooling of resources in relation to protection of the environment.[103] In its decision the Court was clear that the general presumption in international law was that the absence of a withdrawal clause entailed that the parties had not envisaged a unilateral right of termination. There was a set of severe practical consequences from Hungary's decision to terminate – a large amount of construction work had been undertaken and commitments made that would be impossible to unpick. As AE Boyle noted, in a fashion similar to 'major construction contracts in domestic law, the impossibility of returning to the status quo' weighed against unilateral termination.[104] Literature on the decision has focused on the interpretation of Article 62 VCLT and the role of changed circumstances, and the bulk of the decision is concerned with arguments over changed circumstances and the impossibility of performance.[105] But what Hungary was trying to do, in practical terms, was assert a general right to withdrawal under the guise of Articles 61 and 62 VCLT, to, in essence, protect itself from bearing the cost of a changed political reality.

The rejection of these arguments by the ICJ does not resolve the broader dilemma about how external political changes and dynamics affect a treaty and the legal provisions involved in connecting a treaty to political reality.[106] Using a rational design analysis of treaties, which analyses the terms of the treaty through the lens of explaining a collaboration problem between states, the presence of an exit clause can be interpreted as a means of reconciling future changes of political circumstance with existing legal obligations.[107] Tobin recognised this basic underlying point when he argued that a withdrawal clause 'facilitates the securing of consent of doubtful states to conventions aimed at universality', as the presence of a withdrawal clause removes the fear that 'changed conditions

[102] S Stec and GE Eckstein, 'Of Solemn Oaths and Obligations: The Environmental Impact of the ICJ's Decision in the Case of the *Gabcikovo-Nagymaros Project*' (1998) 8 *Yearbook of International Environmental Law* 41.

[103] *Gabčíkovo-Nagymaros Project* (n 101) paras 54–55.

[104] AE Boyle, 'The *Gabcikovo-Nagymaros* Case: New Law in Old Bottles' (1997) 8 *Yearbook of International Environmental Law* 13, 15.

[105] D Reichert-Facilides, 'Down the Danube: The Vienna Convention on the Law of Treaties and the *Case concerning the Gabcíkovo-Nagymaros Project*' (1998) 47 *ICLQ* 837.

[106] Lekkas and Tzanakopoulos (n 98) 326.

[107] B Koremenos and A Nau, 'Exit, No-Exit' (2010) 21 *Duke Journal of Comparative and International Law* 81.

will make continued adherence inconvenient or even dangerous'.[108] Exit clauses can thus be situated alongside other flexibility clauses; and as some research has established, flexibility clauses in trade agreements, allowing for the temporary suspension of the terms of a trade treaty to deal with particular economic conditions, can actually encourage states to ratify them.[109] However, flexibility provisions are not particularly useful for certain types of treaty that want to deter signatory states from withdrawal; for example, human rights treaties, which aim to create a normative climate of respect for human rights, want to discourage states from leaving since that would undermine the general principles that treaty is designed to protect.[110] It is important to note, however, that the inclusion of a withdrawal clause is often a matter of simply acknowledging state preferences at the time of drafting.[111] Withdrawal clauses are often presented in this process as necessary guarantors of state bargaining power in the formation of legal relationships in the international sphere.[112] Or at least, that is the way a state seeking such a clause might perceive the situation.

An interesting example of this is the 1963 Test Ban Treaty, which contained a denunciation clause providing that a state party would have the right, in exercise of its 'national sovereignty', to withdraw 'from the Treaty if it decide[d] that extraordinary events' had 'jeopardized the supreme interests of its country'.[113] The Soviet Union initially opposed the inclusion of a withdrawal clause, arguing, from a highly voluntarist standpoint, that the right to denounce a treaty was an inherent sovereign power.[114] Western nations pushed back at this idea, but the Soviet Union was successful at getting the clause framed so as to include a reference to national sovereignty.[115] Article IV of the final treaty stated that each state party 'shall in exercising its national sovereignty have the right to withdraw from the Treaty', but it also contained the notional safeguard of requiring the withdrawing state to inform other parties three months in advance.[116] How these requirements worked in practice will be discussed in subsequent chapters, but when making the case for ratification of the Test Ban treaty states were

[108] Tobin (n 75) 202.

[109] J Kucik and E Reinhardt, 'Does Flexibility Promote Cooperation? An Application to the Global Trade Regime' (2008) 62 *International Organisation* 477, 499.

[110] G Naldi and K Magliveras, 'Human Rights and the Denunciation of Treaties and Withdrawal from International Organisations' (2013) 33 *Polish Yearbook of international Law* 95.

[111] Helfer (n 92) 636.

[112] ibid; see also T Meyer, 'Power, exit costs, and renegotiation in international law' (2010) 51 *Harvard International Law Journal* 379.

[113] Treaty Banning Nuclear Weapons Tests in the Atmosphere, in Outer Space and Under Water (adopted 5 August 1963, entered into force 10 October 1963) 480 UNTS 43.

[114] J Goldblat, *Arms Control: The New Guide to Negotiations and Agreements* (Sage Publications, 2002) 50.

[115] E Schwelb, 'The Nuclear Test Ban Treaty and International Law' (1964) 58 *American Journal of International Law* 642, 661.

[116] Treaty Banning Nuclear Weapon Tests in the Atmosphere, in Outer Space and Under Water (completed 5 August 1963, entered into force 10 October 1963) 480 UNTS 43, Art IV.

keen to emphasise the flexibility the withdrawal clause gave them. When at the Senate Foreign Relations Committee, the then United States Secretary of State Dean Rusk argued that this clause entailed that the 'US would need to answer to no authority other than its own conscience and requirements' in order to withdraw from the treaty.[117] Although Rusk would later modify this view, the starting point he took was to emphasise the flexibility the state had in being able to respond to changing circumstances and how that flexibility favoured US interests.[118] Ultimately, even though withdrawal and changes of circumstances are treated differently in the VCLT, and are distinct legal concepts, the inclusion of a withdrawal clause in a treaty can operate as a mechanism for a state to manage the changing political and material circumstances around that treaty.

B. Withdrawal as Recognition of a Political Decision by a State Party

This justification deals with the idea that international law should recognise the decision of a sovereign state to leave due to the general desire to respect state autonomy, or out of principled respect for national democracy/national governmental authority. Crucially, the arguments described here are not underpinned by voluntarism, or at least do not require the acceptance of any one underlying set of normative principles about what international law is or ought to be. Yet it is hard not to see the language of right or rights as being present in some withdrawal clauses. For example, the Treaty on the Non-Proliferation of Nuclear Weapons (NPT) withdrawal clause, which provides that a party may exercise 'its national sovereignty … [and] have the right to withdraw from the Treaty if it decides that extraordinary events' have occurred, can be read as a recognition of the right of a party to decide how to respond to political events.[119] The concept of there being a set of sovereign state rights is a somewhat inchoate concept in international law, with more attention having been given to the legal definition of state responsibility or to the rights of individuals living within states.[120] There

[117] C Cohn, 'Interpreting the Withdrawal Clause in Arms Control Treaties' (1989) 10 *Michigan Journal of International Law* 849, 851.

[118] ibid 852.

[119] J Nielsen, 'Interpreting the withdrawal clause of the Treaty on the Non-Proliferation of Nuclear Weapons (NPT): options within the 2010 NPT review cycle' (2008) 2 *International Journal of Nuclear Law* 109.

[120] On this point of state responsibilities, see J Perkins, 'The Changing Foundations of International Law: from State Consent to State Responsibility' (1997) 15 *Boston University International Law Journal* 433. On individual rights, see LB Sohn, 'The New International Law: Protection of the Rights of Individuals Rather Than States' (1982) 32 *American University Law Review* 1; MJ Struett, 'The Transformation of State Sovereign Rights and Responsibilities under the Rome Statute for the International Criminal Court' (2005) 8 *Chapman Law Review* 172. On the point of sovereign rights, see Y Bytyak et al, 'The State Sovereignty and Sovereign Rights: The Correlation Problem' (2017) 97 *Man in India* 577.

is a well-developed literature explaining how a state's right to decide or exercise certain powers is being transformed or eroded (depending on your perspective) by international obligations, which is often associated with delegation to international organisations – dealt with in section II.C.[121] At issue here is the capacity of a state's domestic institutions, its legislature and domestic courts, to take a decision on its international legal obligations, and for that decision to be recognised as lawful and legitimate by the international community at large.

Again, at issue are different versions of arguments about state sovereignty, and there are two versions of this justification. Version one is that the act of withdrawal is a reassertion of the withdrawing state's sovereignty. A good example of this argument can be found in the African Union's (AU) Withdrawal Strategy Document on AU withdrawal from the International Criminal Court (ICC). A decision from the 2017 AU Assembly fully supported 'the sovereign decisions taken by Burundi, South Africa and The Gambia as pioneer implementers' of the AU's withdrawal strategy.[122] But in the AU's Draft Withdrawal Strategy Document, it was conceded that Article 127 of the Rome Statute of the ICC treated denunciation as a unilateral sovereign act, so that in effect all the strategy document was doing was framing what the regional context was for ICC withdrawal. The intention of such an exercise was to articulate to an external audience why withdrawal from the ICC was justified, arguing that the ICC's 'selectivity of cases' unfairly targeted African states, which reflected the 'systemic imbalance of international decision making processes'.[123] These arguments were not just a reaction to a particular case, they spoke to a much deeper sense of sovereign inequality felt by many African states in relation to international institutions.[124] While not explicitly referenced in the Withdrawal Strategy, anti-colonialism and decolonisation had shaped regional integration, and implicitly framing the decision in these terms would have instrumentally served as an internal mechanism of persuasion to other states in the AU that they also ought to withdraw.[125] Withdrawals from

[121] For an overview of these arguments, see M Loughlin, 'The Erosion of Sovereignty' (2016) 45 *Netherlands Journal of Legal Philosophy* 57; P Trimble, 'Review: Globalization, International Institutions, and the Erosion of National Sovereignty and Democracy Reviewed Work(s): Fairness in International Law and Institutions by Thomas M Franck' (1997) 95 *Michigan Law Review* 1944; K Raustiala, 'Rethinking the Sovereignty Debate in International Economic Law' (2003) 6 *Journal of International Economic Law* 841.

[122] Assembly of the African Union, 28th Ordinary Session (31 January 2017). Decision on the International Criminal Court 1 Doc. EX.CL/1006(XXX) para 6.

[123] The Draft Withdrawal Strategy was never officially published, as explained in E Keppler, 'AU's "ICC Withdrawal Strategy" Less than Meets the Eye' *Human Rights Watch* (1 February 2017) at www.hrw.org/news/2017/02/01/aus-icc-withdrawal-strategy-less-meets-eye. AU Withdrawal Strategy Document (Draft 2) Version 12 January 2017 – Human Rights Watch at www.hrw.org › icc_withdrawal_strategy_jan._2017.pdf.

[124] See F Cowell, 'Inherent imperialism: understanding the legal roots of anti-imperialist criticism of the International Criminal Court' (2017) 15 *Journal of International Criminal Justice* 667.

[125] Although the AU was distinct from its predecessor the Organisation of African Unity (OAU), in its legal structure and willingness to countenance intervention, many of the same political forces underpinned it. See C Paker and D Rukare, 'The New African Union and Its Constitutive Act'

the ICC were in part a reflection of the low politics of certain states trying escape investigation of political figures, as was the case in Burundi and Kenya, whose respective withdrawal and attempted withdrawal coincided with indictments or investigations of high-profile political figures in those countries.[126] They were also a means of critiquing the activities of the ICC in Africa, as was the case with the stated reasons given by Gambia and South Africa for their attempted withdrawals.[127] What the Withdrawal Strategy attempted to do was to try to impose a sense of unity on such decisions and link it to an explanation of a shared experience of sovereignty among African states.[128] The claim about sovereignty here was one concerning the marginalisation of post-colonial states by an international institution, argumentatively positioning the ICC as another institution, in a long line, that had, since decolonisation, marginalised African states.[129]

The second version of this justification is the contention that withdrawal is necessary so that an international body will respect a state's decisions or actions. This can be adversarial and likely to arise after a prolonged period of disagreement with or backlash towards the legal regime from which the state is withdrawing. The US withdrawal from the Optional Protocol to the Vienna Convention on Diplomatic Relations Concerning the Compulsory Settlement of Disputes in 2005 was an example of this version of the justification at work. In 1993, 18-year-old José Medellín, who had been born in Mexico, raped and murdered two teenage girls during a gang initiation ritual in Houston, Texas. During police interrogation after his arrest, Medellín was not granted access to consular assistance from the Mexican Embassy. He was later convicted in a Texas court and sentenced to death. Since 1942 there had been a bilateral treaty of consular assistance between Mexico and the US that ran alongside the obligations under the 1963 Vienna Convention on Consular Relations surrounding

(2002) 96 *American Journal of International Law* 365. For the history, see G Nzongola-Ntalaja, 'Pan-Africanism since decolonization: from the Organisation of African Unity (OAU) to the African Union (AU)' (2014) 4 *African Journal of Democracy and Governance* 31.

[126] M Ssenyonjo, 'State Withdrawal Notifications from the Rome Statute of the International Criminal Court: South Africa, Burundi and the Gambia' (2018) 29 *Criminal Law Forum* 63; SD Mueller, 'Kenya and the International Criminal Court (ICC): politics, the election and the law' (2014) 8 *Journal of Eastern African Studies* 25. It was later alleged that some of the evidence in the cases was fabricated as a result of political pressure by outside actors, adding another layer of controversy to these prosecutions and the subsequent attempted withdrawal; see W Kabukuru, 'Kenya: Ocampo's bombshell leaves ICC flat on its face' *New African* (6 March 2014) at https://newafricanmagazine.com/4246.

[127] KD Magliveras, 'The Withdrawal of African States from the ICC: Good, Bad or Irrelevant?' (2019) 66 *Netherlands International Law Review* 419; M Du Plessis and G Mettraux, 'South Africa's Failed Withdrawal from the Rome Statute: Politics, Law, and Judicial Accountability' (2017) 15 *Journal of International Criminal Justice* 361.

[128] PI Labuda, 'The African Union's Collective Withdrawal from the ICC: Does Bad Law make for Good Politics?' *EJIL Talk!* (15 February 2017) at www.ejiltalk.org/the-african-unions-collective-withdrawal-from-the-icc-does-bad-law-make-for-good-politics/ (accessed 2 September 2020).

[129] Cowell (n 124).

access to consular assistance.[130] Medellín's case was one of 53 cases in which a Mexican national had been sentenced to death and consular access denied, which formed the basis of a claim – usually referred to as the *Avena* case – brought before the ICJ in 2003 under the Compulsory Settlement of Disputes Protocol.[131] Two years earlier the ICJ had ruled against the US in *LaGrand* in similar circumstances, although at an earlier stage of proceedings and in 1999, the US had ignored a provisional order by the ICJ and allowed the execution of one of the claimants.[132]

In 2003, an interim ruling involving three of the claimants held that the US should not proceed with executions before the ICJ had ruled on the merits of the case, which, given that the execution of one of the individuals was scheduled by the US State of Louisiana to take place before that point, could be portrayed as a form of interference with sovereign decision making.[133] The eventual decision (which in fairness, the US State Department stated it would comply with), required substantive remedies to be offered in the US legal system, such as review of the sentence, when consular access was denied.[134] The US Supreme Court was later to hold that as a matter of US law, the treaty was not directly binding on Texas, which, given the strongly pro-death penalty stance of politicians in Texas, meant that Medellín's execution went ahead in 2008.[135] Writing shortly after the execution, Ted Cruz, the Solicitor General of Texas (who would go onto become a US Senator and to run for President in 2016), said that the ICJ's decision was 'unprecedented' – no international tribunal in more than '200 years of our nation's history … asserted the authority to bind US courts' – and praised the US Supreme Court for making the correct decision, which preserved 'our nation's fundamental sovereignty'.[136] By this time, however, the US Government had withdrawn from the Dispute Settlement Protocol. In March 2005, just a year

[130] WJ Aceves, 'Consular Notification and the Death Penalty: The ICJ's Judgment in *Avena*' (2004) 8 *ASIL Insights* (2 April 2004) at www.asil.org/insights/volume/8/issue/6/consular-notification-and-death-penalty-icjs-judgment-avena (accessed 9 November 2020).

[131] *Avena and Other Mexican Nationals (Mexico v United States of America)* [2004] ICJ Rep 12.

[132] *LaGrand (Germany v United States of America)* (Merits) [2001] ICJ Rep 466. FL Kirgis, 'World Court Rules Against the United States in LaGrand Case Arising from a Violation of the Vienna Convention on Consular Relations' (2001) 6 *ASIL Insights* (4 July 2001) at www.asil.org/insights/volume/6/issue/16/world-court-rules-against-united-states-lagrand-case-arising-violation (accessed 2 September 2020).

[133] *Avena and Other Mexican Nationals (Mexico v United States of Arnerica)* (Provisional Measures) (Order of 5 February 2003) [2003] ICJ Rep 77.

[134] J Quigley, 'The United States' Withdrawal from International Court of Justice Jurisdiction in Consular Cases: Reasons and Consequences' (2008) 19 *Duke Journal of Comparative & International Law* 263.

[135] P Laidler, 'Lack of Arguments or a Common Sense: Reasons of the US Supreme Court's Preferences to International Community in the Process of Constitutional Interpretation' in A Mania and Ł Wordliczek (eds), *The United States and the World: From Imitation to Challenge The United States and the World: From imitation to challenge* (Jagiellonian University Press, 2009) 223–241, 238–40.

[136] T Cruz, 'Medellin v Texas: A case of more than murder' *Houston Chronicle* (Houston, 30 March 2008) at www.chron.com/opinion/outlook/article/Medellin-v-Texas-A-case-of-more-than-murder-1543234.php (accessed 19 January 2023).

after the ICJ's decision in *Avena*, at a press conference, the US State Department spokeswoman Darla Jordan said the Administration had taken this action in order to protect 'against future International Court of Justice' decisions that would interfere in the US justice system.[137] Although criticised by some lawyers as a 'sore loser move', the way it was presented by figures in the Federal and Texan administrations was that the Protocol allowed a forum-shopping exercise by convicted murderers.[138] There are two ways of reading the US backlash to the ICJ and the withdrawal from the Dispute Settlement Protocol: first, as an example of a great power claiming a form of sovereign exceptionalism, and hence falling into a long line of international legal decisions where the US claimed that the superiority of its domestic constitutional system over international institutions necessitated a particular course of action.[139] Second, as suggested by Jeremey Waldron, the incident can be seen as an example of a state with an 'unwieldy decentralized federal system' proving itself to be unable to follow a basic international legal obligation, and this whole incident was a sign that the US was 'not properly formed … into an entity that is capable of keeping its own promises'.[140]

Both of these readings of the reaction to the *Avena* case were in their own ways arguments about how the US was constructed as a sovereign entity.[141] In this respect the act of withdrawing was a means of getting the international community to respect it *as* a sovereign entity. What links the above examples together is the way in which they both depend on using withdrawal to demonstrate or advance a claim about sovereignty that is implicitly or explicitly being weakened by an international body. Substantively, the form of sovereignty enjoyed between the states described in both case studies differed considerably – the difference, as Anghie framed it, between states that created international law and those that were created by international law.[142] Yet in both case studies the relationship between the state and the international regime from which it was withdrawing provoked and instigated a similar set of tensions surrounding sovereignty. Withdrawal is justified in these scenarios as a means of resolving those tensions, and in doing so defending or protecting a state's sovereign decision making.

[137] A Liptak, 'US Says It Has Withdrawn From World Judicial Body' *New York Times* (New York, 10 March 2005) at www.nytimes.com/2005/03/10/politics/us-says-it-has-withdrawn-from-world-judicial-body.html (accessed 19 January 2023).

[138] Cruz (n 136).

[139] For an outline of the US exceptionalist approach to international law, see H Hongju Koh, 'On American Exceptionalism' (2002) 55 *Stanford Law Review* 1479; A Bradford and E Posner, 'Universal Exceptionalism in International Law' (2011) 52 *Harvard International Law Journal* 3, 35–41.

[140] J Waldron, 'Are Sovereigns Entitled to the Benefit of the International Rule of Law?' (2011) 22 *European Journal of International Law* 315.

[141] ibid 322. See, on the exceptionalism point, H Richardson III, 'The Execution of Angel Breard by the United States: Violating an Order of the International Court of Justice' (1998) 12 *Temple International & Comparative Law Journal* 121.

[142] A Anghie, 'The Evolution of International Law: Colonial and Post-Colonial Realities' in B Rajagopal, J Stevens and R Falk (eds), *International Law and the Third World: Reshaping Justice* (Routledge, 2008) 35–50.

C. An Escape Hatch against 'Delegation Creep'

Delegation involves the effective transfer of a set of decision-making powers from the sovereign state to an international body.[143] Delegations can come in a variety of different forms and cover a range of different issues. Curtis Bradley and Judith Kelley identify eight different types of delegation, ranging from adjudication, as is the case with the North American Free Trade Agreement Tribunal, to agenda setting, as is the case with the Montreal Protocol on Substances that Deplete the Ozone Layer.[144] The motivation for delegations can vary, from there being a collective shared set of externalities that need control or regulation, the collective presence of expertise and knowledge in an international organisation, or the need to demonstrate external credibility to other international actors.[145] Although state consent is formally required for a delegation of authority, it is important to note the choice about whether or not to actually engage in delegation, may, as a matter of political reality, be highly restricted. Some have sought to counter this by arguing that delegations are not particularly widespread and do not involve significant conflict with states.[146] Yet is it is not so much the legitimacy of an act of delegation, or the initial commitment to a body, that is at issue as the way in which those political and legal powers evolve after the act of delegation. In their well-known 2000 article 'The Concept of Legalization', Kenneth W Abbot et al captured this tension in their definition of 'delegation', which they describe as being where 'third parties have been granted authority to implement, interpret, and apply the rules; to resolve disputes; and (possibly) to make further rules'.[147] Some states might argue that the word '(possibly)' in that definition is doing a lot of heavy lifting, as in some cases the growth of institutional powers, even if not formally binding on a state, can be significant.[148]

Withdrawal clauses in these circumstances can operate as a kind of escape hatch, allowing a state to potentially restore prerogatives once delegated to

[143] See C Bradley and J Kelley, 'The concept of international delegation' (2008) 71 *Law & Contemporary Problems* 1. For a provisional definition of delegation, see Hawkins et al, who define delegation as 'a conditional grant of authority from a principal to an agent that empowers the latter to act on behalf of the former': D Hawkins et al, 'Delegation Under Anarchy: States, International Organizations, and Principal-Agent Theory' in D Hawkins et al, *Delegation and Agency in International Organizations* (Cambridge University Press, 2006) 3–38.

[144] The eight types of delegation identified by Bradley and Kelly (Ibid.) are: 1. Legislative; 2. Adjudicative; 3. Regulatory; 4. Monitoring and Enforcement; 5. Agenda Setting; 6. Research and Advisory; 7. Policy Implementation; 8. Re-delegation. See the *Montreal Protocol on Substances that Deplete the Ozone Layer* (opened for signature 16 September 1987, entered into force 1 January 1989) 1552 UNTS 3.

[145] D Lake and M McCubbins, 'The Logic of Delegation to International Organisations' in Hawkins et al (eds) (n 143) 341.

[146] A Guzman and J Landsidle, 'The Myth of International Delegation' (2008) 96 *California Law Review* 1693.

[147] KW Abbott et al, 'The Concept of Legalization' (2000) 54 *International Organization* 401, 401.

[148] Guzman and Landsidle (n 146); H Angé, 'The Myth of International Delegation: Limits to and Suggestions for Democratic Theory in the Context of the European Union' (2007) 42 *Government and Opposition* 18, 20–21.

an institution. As Armin von Bogdandy and Ingo Venzke note in relation to the instruments that underpin international courts and other international legal bodies, once an 'international agreement is in place, it is largely withdrawn from the grasp of its individual makers'.[149] As institutional theorists would argue, this is the point of delegation – it is meant to take decisions away from the short-term political whims of a state party and create a structure for pooling decisions and authority.[150] In these circumstances, a withdrawal clause holds out the possibility of there being a future means for exiting legal commitments that are perceived as excessive, acting as a mechanism of reassurance to governments that their successors could theoretically take such an action. In reality, as von Bogdandy and Venzke argue, this is 'hardly … a sufficient escape hatch' and often does not constitute 'a realistic option' for most states 'because the costs of exit are prohibitively high'.[151] What distinguishes this justification for withdrawal from the justification on changed circumstances, described in section II.A, is that the first justification relates to changing of external circumstances, whereas this one relates to the evolution of the regime itself and its internal features. The creation of a withdrawal clause in the putative Constitution of the European Union, which was later repackaged into the Lisbon Treaty to amend the Treaty on European Union (TEU) following the rejection of the Constitution by voters in France and the Netherlands in the mid-2000s, is an example of the escape-hatch dilemma at work. Article 50 TEU gave notional freedom for a state to leave the European Union (EU) by clearly stating that 'any Member State may decide to withdraw'; but it placed uncertain and unknowable costs on the withdrawing state by containing references to negotiations between the European Council and the withdrawing state regarding 'the arrangements for its withdrawal'.[152]

The founding instruments of the European Economic Community (EEC) did not have an express withdrawal clause and were treaties of unlimited duration.[153] Early rulings of the European Court of Justice had held that the EEC had created a community legal system in which 'States have limited their sovereign rights' and that powers that had been conferred by states could not be unilaterally withdrawn from the Community.[154] Despite this, there was a presumption

[149] A von Bogdandy and I Venzke, 'In Whose Name? An Investigation of International Courts' Public Authority and Its Democratic Justification' (2012) 23 *European Journal of International Law* 7, 21.

[150] For an overview of institutionalist thinking, see B Koremenos, 'Institutionalism and International Law' in J Dunoff and M Pollack (eds), *Interdisciplinary Perspectives on International Law and International Relations: The State of the Art* (Cambridge University Press, 2013) 59. See also B Frischmann, 'A dynamic institutional theory of international law' (2003) 51 *Buffalo Law Review* 679.

[151] von Bogdandy and Venzke (n 149).

[152] Consolidated version of the Treaty on European Union [2016] OJ C202/43.

[153] J Hill, 'The EEC the Right of Member State Withdrawal' (1982) 12 *Georgia Journal of International & Comparative Law* 335.

[154] See respectively Case 6/64, *Costa v ENEL*, Slg 1964, 1251 at 1259 and Case 7/71, *Commission v France*, Slg 1971, 1003, 1018.

that withdrawal could be accomplished using the principles in the VCLT, but that this was likely to be difficult or undesirable. For example, in 1983 the British Labour Party had a commitment in their election manifesto to leave the EEC, but when asked about specifics of this commitment were unclear about what the process would involve even though they were keen to stress the process would be 'orderly' and 'in conformity with international law'.[155] Certainly, no real thinking prior to 2001 had gone into how withdrawal could be achieved despite the arrival during the 1990s of political parties in the European Parliament explicitly committed to leaving the EU.[156] Some territories had left – Algeria in 1962 and Greenland in 1985 (the circumstances of which will be analysed more in subsequent chapters) – but created no real working template or precedents. This was in part because the issues involved were so small – as Phedon Nicolaides rather caustically observed, because of Greenland's 'almost exclusive reliance on fish' there was no economic impact whatsoever on the wider Community.[157] Yet Member States repeatedly threatened withdrawal, using it as tactical leverage in Community politics. In 1965, French President Charles de Gaulle threatened to empty chair a Community meeting; and in 1975, the then Labour Government in the UK held a referendum on withdrawal.[158] The Maastricht Treaty of 1992, which turned the Community into the EU had caused fresh concerns about its relationship with its Member States and their sovereignty.[159] The German Constitutional Court, in its ruling on the Maastricht Treaty, stressed the importance of the democratic foundations of the Community, which would come from its Member States.[160] Reflecting on the Maastricht Treaty in 1999, William Wallace noted that the increasing technocratic nature of the European project, as envisaged by the Treaty, was eroding what could traditionally be thought of as national sovereign interests, and argued that 'the principle of constitutional independence [for Member States] could still be reasserted through withdrawal'.[161] He did not clarify how this could take place but did conclude that 'the costs of

[155] Julia Langdon 'Longer Needed to Quit the Market – MP.' *The Guardian* 17 February 1983, p.5.

[156] As set out by Hofmeister while the case was made that the VCLT provisions on withdrawal would apply, there was also a strong case for thinking this was not so; H Hofmeister, 'Should I Stay or Should I Go? – A Critical Analysis of the Right to Withdraw from the EU' (2010) 16 *European Law Journal* 589.

[157] P Nicolaides, 'Withdrawal from the European Union: a typology of effects' (2013) 20 *Maastricht Journal of European and Comparative Law* 209, 212.

[158] S Lechner and R Ohr, 'The right of withdrawal in the treaty of Lisbon: a game theoretic reflection on different decision processes in the EU' (2011) 32 *European Journal of Law and Economics* 357.

[159] For contemporary reflections on what this meant on sovereignty, see N MacCormick, 'Beyond the sovereign state' (1993) 56 *MLR* 1; D Kugelmann, 'The Maastricht treaty and the design of a European federal state' (1994) 8 *Temple International & Comparative Law Journal* 335.

[160] Decision of the German Federal Constitutional Court of 12 October 1993 in Re Maastricht Treaty Cases 2 BvR 2134/92, 2 BvR 2159/92. For an account of the contemporary issues, see U Everling, 'The Maastricht Judgment of the German Federal Constitutional Court and its Significance for the Development of the European Union' (1994) 14 *Yearbook of European Law* 1.

[161] W Wallace, 'The Sharing of Sovereignty: the European Paradox' (1999) 47 *Political Studies* 503, 505.

withdrawal, in terms of lost status and influence within the European order as well as lost economic advantages, would be very high'.[162]

The 2001 Laeken Declaration, designed to address the challenges faced by the EU as it came into the twenty-first century, called on 'European institutions to be less unwieldy and rigid and, above all, more efficient and open'.[163] It set up the Convention on the Future of Europe, which was made up of 105 delegates from existing and future EU Member States, beginning work in 2002 with the purpose of writing a European Constitution. The proposal for a withdrawal clause came from a number of different sources, including the British delegation, Members of the European Parliament (MEPs) and the steering committee of the Convention, although many were quite sceptical of its inclusion, fearing it would be used by states to 'blackmail' the organs of the EU and each other.[164] David Heathcoat-Amory, a British Member of Parliament and a known Eurosceptic Conservative, argued that the attempt to codify a Constitution for Europe was a technocratic enterprise that did not have the buy-in from the public, and on democratic grounds a new treaty should contain 'the right to secede'.[165] Andrew Duff, a British Liberal Democrat MEP who was distinctly pro-European, later claimed that the insertion of a withdrawal clause was supported by those who were pro-EU federalism and those who were anti-EU federalism alike.[166] The right to withdraw was listed as one of the 10 key principles of the Community in a paper by Alain Lamassoure, a French MEP, as part of what he described as the 'community model' that would in turn ensure that 'Constituent authority resides with the Member States'.[167] Other supporters of the inclusion of a withdrawal clause argued it was necessary for a constitutional model of the EU. But some, such as the German MEP Joschka Fischer, opposed the introduction of such a clause, and the Portuguese national delegation went so far as to claim that 'the nature of the Union is not compatible with such an exit clause'.[168]

The eventual version that made its way unchanged from the Constitution into the Lisbon Treaty positioned withdrawal from the EU as an individual

[162] ibid.

[163] Laeken Declaration on the future of the European Union (15 December 2001). Bulletin of the European Union 2001, No 12. Luxembourg: Office for Official Publications of the European Communities, 'Presidency Conclusions of the Laeken European Council (14 and 15 December 2001)' 9–23.

[164] D Spinant, 'Giscard forum set to unveil controversial EU "exit clause"' *Politico* (Brussels, 4 February 2003) at www.politico.eu/article/giscard-forum-set-to-unveil-controversial-eu-exit-clause (accessed 18 June 2020).

[165] Contribution from the Rt Hon David Heathcoat-Amory, member of the Convention, 'A new future for Europe' (Brussels, 24 September 2004) CONV 291/02.

[166] A Duff, 'Everything you need to know about Article 50' *EURACTIV* (Brussels, 5 July 2016) at www.euractiv.com/section/uk-europe/opinion/everything-you-need-to-know-about-article-50/.

[167] Contribution by M Lamassoure, member of the Convention, 'The European Union: four possible models' (Brussels, 3 September 2002) CONV 235/02.

[168] M Gatti 'Article 50 TEU: A Well-Designed Secession Clause' (2017) 2 *European Papers* 159, 165.

right of states.[169] As the German Constitutional Court later held, Article 50 was evidence of the limitations on future delegation, stating that 'if a Member State can withdraw based on a decision made on its own responsibility, the process of European integration is not irreversible'.[170] Yet in the process of drafting, the clause had been shorn of almost any proposed safeguards, such as requiring a post-exit agreement for states to be in place prior to withdrawal becoming effective or for rights of European citizens to be safeguarded in the process of exit.[171] With hindsight – and certainly at the time of writing this chapter in the summer of 2020 in the midst of the political turbulence caused by Brexit – this seems like a terrifying oversight, but in the context of its drafting it made sense as an inadequate-but-potential escape hatch of the sort described by von Bogdandy and Venzke. Having minimal requirements clearly preserved withdrawal as an individual right of states to push back against delegation to the EU, and the need to preserve and protect withdrawal as an individual right was a position that commanded broad agreement.[172] Yet at the same time the minimalist structure of Article 50 created uncertainty about the process of leaving, which served as a deterrent to states contemplating withdrawal. In February 2016, prior to the referendum on leaving the EU, the British Foreign Office – reflecting the Government of the day's overall position that the UK should stay in the EU – warned that it would be 'difficult to complete a successful negotiation' with the EU under the terms of Article 50 and that leaving the Union would cause 'a decade or more of uncertainty'.[173] For a regime such as the EU, which desired to preserve its powerful single market and independent institutions, whilst at the same time acknowledging the fissiparous nature of democratic sentiment towards it in its Member States, the seemingly contradictory aspects in the textual structure of Article 50 superficially made sense.

[169] There is a strong argument for reading Art 50 as functional part of the Constitutional Order of the EU – see P Eeckhout and E Frantziou, 'Brexit and Article 50 TEU: A Constitutionalist Reading' UCL European Institute Working Paper, December 2016 at https://westminsterresearch.westminster.ac.uk/item/9z863/brexit-and-article-50-teu-a-constitutionalist-reading (accessed 18 June 2020).

[170] BVerfG, Judgment of the Second Senate of 30 June 2009, 2 BvE 2/08 at www.bverfg.de/e/es20090630_2bve000208en.html, para 329. For commentary, see J Arato, 'A Preemptive Strike against European Federalism: The Decision of the Bundesverfassungsgericht Concerning the Treaty of Lisbon' *EJIL Talk!* (9 October 2010) at www.ejiltalk.org/a-preemptive-strike-against-european-federalism-the-decision-of-the-bundesverfassungsgericht-concerning-the-treaty-of-lisbon/ (accessed 18 June 2020); D Thym, 'In the Name of Sovereign Statehood: A Critical Introduction to The Lisbon Judgment of the German Constitutional Court' (2009) 46 *Common Market Law Review* 1795.

[171] For commentary on the final text, see H-J Blanke and S Mangiameli, 'Article 50: Voluntary Withdrawal from the Union' in H-J Blanke and S Mangiameli (eds), *The Treaty on European Union (TEU) A Commentary* (Springer, 2013) 1385.

[172] T Lock, 'Why the European Union is Not a State: Some Critical Remarks' (2010) 5 *European Constitutional Law Review* 407, 409.

[173] Department of Foreign and Commonwealth Affairs, *The process for withdrawing from the European Union Presented to Parliament by the Secretary of State for Foreign and Commonwealth Affairs by Command of Her Majesty* (Cm 9216, 2016) para 2.5–2.9.

D. The Law of Withdrawal as a Guarantee of Good Faith

Unlike the other points about the law of withdrawal's purpose outlined so far, this one concerns not so much the defence of state sovereignty but rather the defence of the overall international legal order. 'Like all other rules of international law,' Lukashuk argued, 'the principle of good faith fulfilment of obligations derives from … the general consent of states.'[174] A similar echo of this point can be found in the *Nuclear Tests* case, where the ICJ was asked to interpret a unilateral declaration from France about stopping nuclear testing in the South Pacific. It noted that in certain circumstances where a such a declaration had been made, it was to be interpreted as binding upon the state – hence restricting its sovereignty – because the 'basic principles governing the creation and performance of legal obligations … is good faith'.[175] Some other attempts to define good faith often implicitly end up cross-referencing the voluntarist assumption that because a state has entered into an obligation, it ought to perform that obligation in good faith.[176] This circular form of reasoning is rejected in other explanations of good faith that focus on its instrumental value in the generation of stability and predictability in international relations, and its facilitative role in international legal argument.[177] Robert Kolb calls this the axiological function of an international obligation, allowing the existence of a 'minimum common ground of values, functions and concepts' that prevent the international legal order from '[dissolving] … into concurring and unrelated legal blocks'.[178] When a state is seeking to withdraw from its obligations, the good faith principle is essential for ensuring that the state stays within the parameters of the withdrawal clauses and does not abuse the withdrawal process.

The principle of only withdrawing in line with the terms of a withdrawal clause, although having earlier origins in state practice, was first expressly codified in the 1928 Havana Convention on Treaties, which stated that where a denunciation clause had 'been agreed upon' a treaty could be 'denounced only on the manner provided thereby'.[179] Subsequent commentary on withdrawal

[174] II Lukashuk, 'The Principle Pacta Sunt Servanda and the Nature of Obligation under International Law (1989) 83 *American Journal of International Law* 513, 513.

[175] *Nuclear Tests (Australia v France)* (Merits) [1974] ICJ Rep 253, 268 (*Nuclear Tests* case).

[176] For a critical outline of this argument see M Koskenniemi, 'Introduction: Sources and Legal Pragmatis.' in M Koskenniemi (eds), *Sources of International Law* (Routledge, 2000) xiv.

[177] ibid. For an analysis of good faith as a principle of international law, see N Monebhurrun, '*Gold Reserve Inc v Bolivarian Republic of Venezuela*: Enshrining Legitimate Expectations as a General Principle of International Law?' (2015) 32 *Journal of International Arbitration* 551. Linderfalk argues that good faith performs a communicative function as regards the intention of states and the general functioning of international law: U Linderfalk, 'What are the Functions of the General Principles? Good Faith and International Legal Pragmatics' (20 April 2017) at https://ssrn.com/abstract=2955648 or http://dx.doi.org/10.2139/ssrn.2955648 (accessed 10 November 2020).

[178] R Kolb, *Good Faith in International Law* (Hart Publishing, 2017) 4–5.

[179] Reproduced in 'Appendix 1. Convention on Treaties' (1935) 29 *American Journal of International Law* 1205.

clauses, pre-dating the VCLT, also noted the general principle that where a withdrawal clause was present in an instrument, that should govern the process of withdrawal.[180] In its 1980 *Advisory Opinion on the Interpretation of the Agreement Between the WHO and Egypt*, the ICJ specifically dealt with withdrawal in the context of good faith. In 1951, the Egyptian city of Alexandria had been made the Regional Office for the Eastern Mediterranean Region of the World Health Organization (WHO), and in correspondence the WHO maintained that the establishment of an Office meant that that Office should have the privileges and immunities of an international body.[181] The World Health Assembly had in 1979 decided, for political reasons, to relocate this regional body to Amman in Jordan, which effectively meant withdrawing from the Agreement, which under section 37 required a party to give two years' notice before denouncing the treaty. The *Advisory Opinion* clarified that the section should, as a matter of law, be interpreted in good faith, which was necessary both for efficacy – to ensure the 'practical arrangements needed to effect an orderly and equitable transfer of the Office' – and to protect the general interests of states and their obligations 'under general international law'.[182] Good faith here required the WHO to limit the exercise of a unilateral prerogative, such as decisions over the allocation of organisational resources and functions between members states, and instead conform to the provisions set out in the withdrawal clause in the Agreement.

In principle, a similar situation arises in respect of withdrawal from instruments that subject a state to the jurisdiction of an international court or tribunal. Withdrawal from such an instrument as soon as a state perceives it is in its interests to do so, in order to avoid an adverse decision, promotes what Kolb describes as 'unilateralist' and 'system damaging attitudes'.[183] In *Nicaragua v United States*, a dispute had arisen in connection with Article 36 of the ICJ Statute under which states made declarations accepting the compulsory jurisdiction of the Court in relation to certain disputes.[184] The jurisdictional powers contained in Article 36 had a long a history, dating back to the Statute of the PCIJ, which, when it was being drafted in the 1920s, had sought to build arbitration regimes to enable the pacific settlement of disputes.[185] The modern iteration, whilst requiring states to make a declaration, also contained a provision that six months' notification needed to be given in cases of termination

[180] McNair observed 'this occurs so frequently it hardly requires illustration': AD McNair, *The Law of Treaties* (Clarendon Press, 1961) 500.

[181] *Interpretation of the Agreement of 25 March 1951 between the WHO and Egypt* (Advisory Opinion) [1981] ICJ Rep 73.

[182] ibid paras 48–50.

[183] Kolb (n 178) 232.

[184] *Military and Paramilitary Activities in and against Nicaragua (Nicaragua v United States of America)*, (Jurisdiction and Admissibility) (Judgment) [1984] ICJ Rep 392.

[185] For this history, see J Charney, 'Compromissory Clauses and the Jurisdiction of the International Court of Justice' (1987) 81 *American Journal of International Law* 855.

of jurisdiction.[186] Since the communist-leaning Sandinista Government had come to power in Nicaragua in 1979, the US Government had pursued a policy of non-recognition, which under the Reagan Administration had covertly turned into a programme of armed assistance to the right-wing rebel group known as the Contras. The proceedings initiated by Nicaragua at the ICJ concerned several different claims relating to violations of the UN Charter in terms of armed assistance and direct support to the Contras, the right wing rebel group fighting against the Nicaraguan government. On 6 April 1984, three days prior to the filing of proceedings by the Nicaraguan Government in the ICJ's registry, the US Secretary of State George Schultz notified the UN Secretary General that the US Article 36 declaration was not to apply 'to disputes with any Central American State', clearly anticipating the proceedings.[187] From the perspective of Schultz and the Reagan Administration, such an action would have been relatively consistent with previous policy towards international bodies they felt were too pro-communist, and the US withdrawal from UNESCO six months previously had been justified on grounds not entirely dissimilar, in that it was an international act to prevent pro-communist countries from utilising international institutions against the US.[188] As an official State Department statement clarified in January 1985, the dispute in Nicaragua involved a 'build-up of Soviet arms and Cuban advisers' and therefore was 'inherently political', going on to conclude in a quasi-voluntarist fashion that when the 'United States accepted the Court's compulsory jurisdiction in 1946, it certainly never conceived of such a role for the Court in such controversies'.[189]

At the ICJ, the US contended that the declaration was not a termination of its 1946 declaration but a modification, as it was its 'sovereign right to qualify an acceptance of the Court's compulsory jurisdiction'.[190] The Court held that the creation of obligations underpinning the compulsory jurisdiction under its Optional Clause system was built on the 'principle of good faith', referencing the *Nuclear Tests* case and other case law on the interconnected nature of legal obligations and the role of good faith.[191] This led to the conclusion that modification in this case had a similar effect to termination; it removed a case from consideration by the ICJ, and therefore the six months' notice clause that formed part of the original acceptance by the US of compulsory jurisdiction was still in effect.[192] The case was then able to progress on to the merits stage of proceedings,

[186] R Lawson, 'The Problem of the Compulsory Jurisdiction of the World Court' (1952) 46 *American Journal of International Law* 219, 223–24.

[187] *Nicaragua v United States of America* (n 184) p.398.

[188] For the general background, see C Joyner and S Lawson, 'The United States and UNESCO: Rethinking the Decision to Withdraw' (1985) 41 *International Journal* 37.

[189] 'Text of US Statement on Withdrawal from case before the World Court' *The New York Times* (New York, 19 January 1985) 4.

[190] *Nicaragua v United States of America* (n 184) p.415.

[191] ibid 418; *Nuclear Tests* case (n 175); *Interhandel (Switzerland v United States)* [1959] ICJ Rep 6, para 23.

[192] *Nicaragua v United States of America* (n 184) p.421.

although the US continued to maintain that its declaration was valid. Even after the Court found against the US in 1986 on a number of issues relating to the merits, including finding that it had assisted forces committing crimes against humanity and assisted in acts of aggression, the US Government continued to maintain that the Court lacked authority to issue such a ruling, refusing to cooperate with the judgment.[193] To many in the wider international community this appeared an outrage, attracting a UN General Assembly resolution criticising the behaviour of the US. However, there was a broader legal issue at play, as the 1984 judgment made it clear it was 'far from established' what the requirements for terminating a declaration actually were and the treatment under the law of treaties was an 'analogy'.[194] As Kolb's commentary on the case notes, although the principle of six months was soon settled on, there was contemporary academic commentary in the 1980s and 1990s expressing pessimism about how this could be emblematic of a broader failure of the entire system of optional declarations.[195] Writing from the vantage point of the 2010s, Kolb concluded that 'pessimistic prognostications' as to the collapse of the optional declaration system had proved unfounded and that there was a fairly clear legal presumption that withdrawal from optional declarations was inadmissible.[196]

This view neglects the political environment in which the legitimacy of courts is shaped, giving some states the confidence to defy the norms of good faith, and the capacity of states to withdraw from optional protocols absent any withdrawal mechanism does encourage procedural abuse (of which more in subsequent chapters). Yet Kolb is right in noting that the good faith principle is a core justification for restricting a state's actions when withdrawing from any legal regime. Whilst the principle of good faith is not an argument for a state's withdrawal from a regime, it is a necessary feature of the law of withdrawal in order to maintain the balance between a state's autonomy of decision making and the stability of the international system as whole, where legal obligations are not only clear but also carry a degree of normative authority leading the state party to comply with the content of the obligation.[197] The principle of good faith also builds all state parties' trust in the bargain between stability and flexibility, as described in the first justification – the bargains of which withdrawal clauses are the end product.[198] Finally, if the process of withdrawal

[193] Scott and Carr argue that even though there is an interesting legal argument about the scope of compulsory jurisdiction, the way the US acted clearly undermined the Court and the 'lawfulness' of the international system; G Scott and C Carr 'The ICJ and Compulsory Jurisdiction: The Case for Closing the Clause' (1987) 81 *American Journal of International Law* 57, 69–72.

[194] *Nicaragua v United States of America* (n 184) 420.

[195] Kolb (n 178) 237–38.

[196] ibid.

[197] This point is made by J Crampin, 'Treaty withdrawal and recalcitrant States' (2020) 9 *Cambridge International Law Journal* 22.

[198] EK Penney, 'Is that Legal? The United States' Unilateral Withdrawal from the Anti-Ballistic Missile Treaty' (2002) 51 *Catholic University Law Review* 1287.

is to result in obligations on the withdrawing state, some of which, as in the case of Article 50 TEU, require the withdrawing state to engage in protracted negotiations after withdrawal, the principle of good faith is vital for creating expectations on the conduct of the withdrawing state and the remaining parties in the legal regime.[199] Good faith therefore is both a justification of, and necessary for, the 'law' in the law of withdrawal.

CONCLUSION: THE TWO CONCERNS

Arguments about sovereignty in cases of withdrawal do not proceed from a determinate position as to sovereignty's substance. Instead, sovereignty is a claim or set of claims, advanced in legal arguments by the states withdrawing from an international legal regime. Understanding this is important for appreciating why the justification for the law of withdrawal, as being the inverse of the act of consent, is too narrow a framework for understanding the overall purpose of the law of withdrawal. States have multi-faceted justifications for wishing to withdraw from a legal regime. Asserting or establishing a right to withdraw based on the nature of legal obligation does little to ensure the recognition of a state's actions as legal or even justified. The four justifications in section II can be grouped together in two related concerns – flexibility and stability – which become a theme throughout the rest of this book. These concerns mirror analytic lenses that are relatively common in discussions about withdrawal clauses; Pergantis, exploring the arguments about the inclusion of withdrawal clauses in the 1958 Law of the Sea Convention, noted the way they revolved around the fairly predictable poles of flexibility and stability.[200]

First, the concern for stability is a distinct goal of the law of withdrawal, formalising in seemingly neutral legal language what can be a deeply destabilising political reality. It is also, to adopt a perspective from critical theory for a moment, a way of masking ideological choices both about the existence of the status quo in international affairs and about the role of law in maintaining the dominant ideological trends in that status quo.[201] Yet the maintenance of stability is why the doctrine of *rebus sic stantibus* is codified the way it is in the VCLT, why Article 54 of the VCLT prioritises the operation of withdrawal clauses and why arguments about delegation creep have to be made within the two aforementioned doctrines.[202] Conflict about the role and powers of international

[199] C Moldovan, 'Brexit and the international law on treaty withdrawal' (2018) 5 *EURINT* 257.
[200] Pegantis (n 85) 160–61.
[201] This theoretical argument derives from the works of Theodor Adorno and Max Horkheimer; for its application in international theory, see C Peoples, 'Theodor Adorno' in J Edkins and N Vaughn-Williams (eds), *Critical Theorists and International Relations* (Routledge, 2009) 7–18, 12–14.
[202] On Art 62 VCLT, see J Kulaga, 'A renaissance of the doctrine of Rebus Sic Stantibus?' (2020) 69 *ICLQ* 477, 478–79.

regimes leading to withdrawal are therefore managed through the processes that were designed to encourage stability. As set out in section I, sovereignty is defined through the process of legal argument, but the resolution of such arguments is often guided by the production of stability. Subsequent chapters set out how the law of withdrawal's focus on stability can end up magnifying sovereign inequalities.

Second, the law of withdrawal is designed to recognise the autonomy of decision making, not necessarily a democratic decision but the autonomy of decision making by states. The act of consent is an imperfect but instrumentally useful mechanism for capturing this autonomy. It makes more sense to think of a decision to withdraw as the recognition of an act of state autonomy than the reversal of consent. The fact that a state once consented to become party to a treaty is a fact of a legal regime's past.[203] A withdrawing state is a state that is availing itself of a right under a clause that allows withdrawal, or that is making a legal argument that it should be allowed to withdraw in the present. Under both scenarios the state is making an argument that its autonomy in exercising its rights in international law ought to be respected. There are two important legal reasons why this is significant: First; as outlined in chapters 2 and 3, the withdrawing state is still bound by the withdrawal clause, both during and potentially after the act of withdrawal, because of the obligations contained in withdrawal clauses. The principle of *pacta sunt servanda*, based on the original act of consent, applies in connection with obligations under those clauses. The original act of consent is not therefore reversed; withdrawal must take place according to the withdrawal provisions of a treaty, and the principle of *pacta sunt servanda* applies in relation to those provisions. Second, bounding a state's autonomy within the law is essential to the international rule of law, which, as set out in chapter 5, relies less on a precise form, or set of provisions, and more on the prevailing assumption that a state's interactions and obligations on the international plane 'are to be ruled by law'.[204] Acts of state consent are not reversed in so much as new legal acts are created, in this case withdrawal, and those acts themselves can be differentiated between the lawful and unlawful versions of those acts.

[203] On consent see D Bodansky and J Shand Watson, 'State Consent and the Sources of International Obligation' (1992) 86 *Proceedings of the Annual Meeting (American Society of International Law)* 108, 111. On the question of time, see R Higgins, 'Time and the Law: International Perspectives on an Old Problem' (1997) 46 *ICLQ* 501.

[204] M Kumm, 'International Law in National Courts: The International Rule of Law and the Limits of the Internationalist Model' (2003) 44 *Virginia Journal of International Law* 19, 22–23.

2

The Structure of Withdrawal Clauses: Theory and Form

INTRODUCTION

MUCH POLITICAL FANFARE had attended the Treaty establishing a Constitution for Europe (the European Constitution) in 2004, with European leaders pledging to make it the start of a new era of European integration. Meanwhile, scholarly attention began to focus on the Constitution's new legal and political framework, which for the first time in the European Union's history contained a withdrawal clause. For some this was a little premature; as Jochen Herbst observed, 'in the morning light of the establishment of a European Constitution' discussions about withdrawal were 'like talking about divorce on your wedding day'.[1] But – to further strain the analogy – engaged couples making a pre-nuptial agreement is seen by many as a form of protection, in particular of their personal financial assets, before entering into a legal union. Equally, although often not expressly, denunciation clauses can be seen as a means of safeguarding certain aspects of sovereignty during treaty negotiations. The German Constitutional Court, when ruling on the Lisbon Treaty, which the Constitution would later become, concluded that the existence of a withdrawal clause operated as a means of protecting a state's sovereignty by providing a limit to further integration.[2] The preceding chapter, which also examined the German Constitutional Court's Lisbon decision, looked at the rationale for withdrawal. Yet the precise way in which a state initiates the act of withdrawal, and the rules surrounding it in a withdrawal clause, is itself an important safeguard both for the interests of the withdrawing state and for the integrity of the legal regime a state is withdrawing from.

Many withdrawal clauses are relatively similar in their construction. Treaties on nuclear weapons control, for example, often have withdrawal clauses derived from the basic template created by the withdrawal clause in

[1] J Herbst, 'Observations on the Right to Withdraw from the European Union: Who are the "Masters of the Treaties"?' (2005) 6 *German Law Journal* 1755, 1755.

[2] BVerfG, Judgment of the Second Senate of 30 June 2009 – 2 BvE 2/08 at www.bverfg.de/e/es20090630_2bve000208en.html, para 329.

the 1963 Partial Test Ban Treaty. Pro-forma withdrawal clauses are often used by international bodies, such as the Council of Europe, to aid efficient treaty construction.[3] Despite the relatively identical nature of these clauses, their individual provisions can protect the interests their parent treaty was designed to protect. For example, the 2015 Paris Climate Change Agreement, in common with other environmental treaties, has a minimum membership requirement before states can withdraw, in part to promote the norms contained within the Agreement. Also, imposing a gap between notification of withdrawal and the withdrawal's coming into effect can provide legal certainty, allowing those who might otherwise be caught unawares by a sudden change in a state's international obligations to adapt accordingly. Given that the obligations contained in a withdrawal clause can be the final legal obligations of a treaty to which the withdrawing state is expected to adhere, the provisions of a withdrawal clause, far from being inconsequential, are an important barometer of a state's respect for the legal regime from which they are departing and the international rule of law in general.

Withdrawal clauses aim, directly or indirectly, to have an effect on state behaviour during the process of withdrawal, and this chapter probes into those intended effects and why the procedural aspects of withdrawal clauses are shaped in the way they are. A temporal narrative is used in this chapter to track the different steps in withdrawal, from a state's decision to withdraw to the moment of the cessation of legal obligations to a legal regime. The process of initiating a withdrawal, and the rules that withdrawal clauses place on the withdrawing state, are discussed in section II. In section III, the process of notification under a withdrawal clause is looked at, while section IV examines the temporal issues of withdrawal, that is how long a state has to be party to a treaty prior to withdrawal and how long it takes from a notification of withdrawal to its becoming effective. The later sections of this chapter draw on an analysis of a dataset of over 200 withdrawal clauses in treaties, ranging from investment arbitration treaties to weapons control treaties, to examine the prevalence of certain features of withdrawal clauses. The full methodological detail of how this sample was constructed, and the treaties included in it, is set out in detail in the Appendix to this book. For this chapter, the data gathered is used to examine what some general trends are in withdrawal clauses and their framing.

Because this chapter is looking at the way in which withdrawal clauses shape state behaviour, it is predominantly focused on treaties that contain a withdrawal clause, which, under the terms of Article 54 of the Vienna Convention on the Law of Treaties (VCLT) requires the withdrawing state to utilise it in the process of treaty exit. However, before launching into such an analysis, it is first

[3] C Ahlström, 'Withdrawal from arms control treaties' (2003) *SIPRI Yearbook* 2004 763; L Helfer, 'Terminating treaties' in DB Hollis (ed), *The Oxford Guide to Treaties* (Oxford University Press, 2012) 624–644.

necessary to give an overview of the theoretical templates used to examine the way in which provisions in international law try to shape state behaviour. These theoretical templates will be important for analysing the effect of withdrawal clauses during the process of withdrawal, the subject of this chapter, and the nature of obligations on a state after withdrawal, the subject of chapter 3. The main effect of withdrawal clauses is iterable – they create a repeatable function for bringing into being the termination of legal obligations for a party, giving the withdrawing state a procedural pathway towards its eventual aim of giving up its obligations. Their iterablity helps standardise time and form in the law of withdrawal, which in turn underpins other legal doctrines, such as good faith.

I. THEORETICAL TEMPLATES FOR UNDERSTANDING HOW WITHDRAWAL CLAUSES SHAPE STATE BEHAVIOUR

International law can often follow quite rigidly formalist lines when explaining the effects of international instruments, focusing on the existence and the performance of obligations without any theorising about the conditions that generate international law's effectiveness.[4] An aggressively formalistic focus on the importance of obligation can obscure the underlying political forces behind the law, and how legal instruments try to shape and use those forces. Withdrawal clauses are legal provisions containing obligations for state parties. Even though they are procedural provisions binding a state as a matter of law, the sense of obligation on states is often at its weakest when states are using withdrawal clauses, because they are designed to remove that state from the scope of obligations under the treaty they are withdrawing from. International relations and international law scholars have for over a quarter of a century used interdisciplinary methods to examine how international law generates compliance and a sense of obligation upon states.[5] A variety of empirical and theoretical work has considered different aspects of state behaviour and incentive structures, although some theoretical templates are more useful than other in understanding withdrawal clauses.

Realist theories of international relations generally maintain that states are principally interested in the acquisition and maintenance of power, with the state as the basic unit of power in the international system. Realists in principle

[4] D Kennedy, 'The Disciplines of International Law and Policy' (1999) 12 *Leiden Journal of International Law* 9; O Jütersonke, 'Realist Approaches to International Law' in A Orford and F Hoffmann (eds), *The Oxford Handbook of the Theory of International Law* (Oxford University Press, 2016) 327–343.

[5] A-M Slaughter, AS Tulumello and S Wood, 'International Law and International Relations Theory: A New Generation of Interdisciplinary Scholarship (1998) 92 *American Journal of International Law* 367; M Burgstaller, *Theories of Compliance with International Law* (Brill Nijhoff, 2004); B Simmons, 'Compliance with international agreements' (1998) 1 *Annual Review of Political Science* 75.

believe that state actions are shaped by rational egoism and that the international system tends towards anarchy.[6] Leading realist theorists, such as Hans Morgenthau, are often quite sceptical regarding the independent effect of international obligations on state behaviour – as Morgenthau once famously said, an 'iron law' of international law was that 'legal obligations must yield to the national interest'.[7] Realists can often take a reductive view of legal obligation, taking little account of the institutional and social forces surrounding or underpinning legal regimes.[8] Some of the scepticism about international law from realists was born in the 1930s out of a wider suspicion of international legal regimes, such as the League of Nations, which many leading realists argued tended towards utopianism.[9] John Mearsheimer, in a major restatement of this school of thought in the early 1990s, criticised the desire to see international legal systems and institutions as a form of escape from power politics.[10] Cooperation between states was dictated far more by the presence of rational self-interest than by formal obligation. Arguments about the rational self-interest of states in the process of withdrawal, or threats to use a withdrawal clause, are a feature of the literature on treaty exit.[11] Examples of extra-treaty sanctions, such as when the US restricted fishing rights in its waters to any state that threatened to withdraw from the 1946 International Convention for the Regulation on Whaling, and of states threatening to withdraw as form of bargaining, such as when Japan threatened to withdraw from the 1911 Fur Seal Treaty, prompting other parties to agree to a renegotiation, seemingly confirm realist beliefs about state behaviour and self-interest.[12] One feature of realist thinking is the way in which different schools of realism have positioned it as a theory describing the way states 'naturally' act, and that the rational egoism of state practice is a natural feature of the international order.[13] Yet realist theory, because of its instance on treating the substance of the law and the legal provisions of treaties as being

[6] For this description, see W Wohlforth, 'Realism' in C Reus-Smit and D Sindal (eds), *The Oxford Handbook of International Relations* (Oxford University Press, 2010)131–149. Leading works advancing these basic propositions include J Mearsheimer, *The Tragedy of Great Power Politics* (Norton, 2001); K Waltz, *Theory of International Relations* (Random House, 1979).

[7] H Morgenthau, *In Defence of the National Interest: A Critical Study of American Foreign Policy* (Alfred Knopf Publishers, 1951) 144.

[8] O Yasuaki, 'International law in and with international politics: The functions of international law in international society' (2003) 14 *European Journal of International Law* 105, 112.

[9] KA Lieber, 'The new history of World War I and what it means for international relations theory' (2007) 32 *International Security* 155; L Ashworth, 'Realism and the spirit of 1919: Halford Mackinder, geopolitics and the reality of the League of Nations' (2010) 17 *European Journal of International Relations* 279.

[10] JJ Mearsheimer, 'The False Promise of International Institutions' (1994) 19 *International Security* 5.

[11] L Helfer, 'Exiting Treaties' (2005) 91 *Virginia Law Review* 1579.

[12] ibid. S Barnett, *Environment and Statecraft: The Strategy of Environmental Treaty-Making: The Strategy of Environmental Treaty-Making* (Oxford University Press, 2003) 160–62.

[13] J Der Derian 'A Reinterpretation of Realism: Genealogy, Semiology, Dromology' in J Der Derian (ed), *International Theory: Critical Investigations* (Macmillan, 1995) 363–393, 386–89.

ultimately subsidiary to the way a treaty figures within the broader scheme of power relations, can be less useful for an insight into the structure of individual treaty provisions. It is not, for example, clear, taking Jack Goldsmith and Eric Posner's position in *The Limits of International Law*, why a state would comply with the terms of a withdrawal clause or ongoing obligations after treaty exit if compliance emerges as the result of 'the *ex ante* choices of rational agents who seek functional benefits *ex post*'.[14]

Institutionalism posits that international institutions play an important role in promoting cooperation among states, countering the realist insistence that such institutions are ultimately subordinate to the *realpolitik* interests of their member states.[15] Drawing on insights from economics and game theory, institutionalism attempts to develop an understanding of why institutional structures, such as treaty regimes and international organisations, emerge and why, despite often lacking coercive powers, they end up ensuring compliance by reducing transaction costs, pooling resources and monitoring state behaviour.[16] There are various forms of institutionalist thinking, but underpinning most of them is the idea of attempting to explain why states cooperate within the confines of legal regimes.[17] Rational choice institutionalism, in particular Andrew Guzman's work in this area, often places a strong emphasis on reputations and the way that states' reputational interests are shaped or defined by their adherence to legal obligations to which they are parties.[18] Although rationalism offers some significant insights into how withdrawal clauses anticipate the way state parties will act or react to a withdrawal clause, withdrawal clauses pose two challenges for it as a theory. First, institutionalism does not give a lot of attention to the dynamics of the domestic politics within a withdrawing state, which can be important in relation to the requirements of withdrawal clauses because, as set out Section IV of this chapter if there are tangible concerns on issues surrounding the timing and duration of a withdrawal, the entire process can become live domestic political issue.[19] Second, institutionalism, by its heavy emphasis on the

[14] J Goldsmith and E Posner, *The Limits of International Law*, 2nd edn (Oxford University Press, 2005). For this critical summary of Goldsmith and Posner's position, see K Raustiala, 'Refining the limits of international law' (2005) 34 *Georgia Journal of International & Comparative Law* 423, 424.

[15] W Aceves 'Institutionalist Theory and International Legal Scholarship' (1997) 12 *American University International Law Review* 227.

[16] K Abbott, 'Enriching Rational choice: Institutionalism for the study of international law' (2008) 1 *University of Illinois Law Review* 5, 6; S Oeter, 'Toward A Richer Institutionalism for International Law and Policy: A Comment on Kenneth W Abbot's Recent Work' (2008) 1 *University of Illinois Law Review* 61.

[17] B Koremenos 'Institutionalism and International Law' in JL Dunoff and MA Pollack (eds), *Interdisciplinary Perspectives on International Law and International Relations: The State of the* Art (Cambridge University Press, 2003) 59, 59–61.

[18] A Guzman, *How International Law Works: A Rational Choice Theory* (Oxford University Press, 2008) ch 1.

[19] R Brewster, 'The domestic origins of international agreements' (2003) 43 *Virginia Journal of International Law* 501, 508–11.

factors that underpin cooperation, can neglect the factors that cause cooperation to break down. Under an institutionalist paradigm, an act of withdrawal is by definition proving the assumptions of realist critics that institutions are unable to independently constrict state behaviour.[20]

Constructivism emphasises the social and relational construction of what states are and what they want, and places a strong emphasis on legal relations emerging through socialisation within other states.[21] Various schools of constructivist thought have examined the way that interaction with other states in international forums can build a sense of fidelity to the law and thus encourage compliance with the law.[22] An important theoretical insight from constructivism is the recognition of how informal or procedural norms can change state behaviour, absent any coercive factors.[23] Literature examining the relationship between constructivist theory and withdrawal has highlighted how the features of an instrument can be designed to maintain socialisation among states, even when that is seemingly breaking down as a state is threatening withdrawal.[24] Constructivism has attracted a considerable amount of criticism from those concerned that its emphasis on the social aspects of state behaviour ignores the role of power and hegemonic states in international relations and analyses the actions of states, such as denouncing a treaty, using a psycho-social methodology that downplays formal legal obligation.[25]

There a number of theories that focus on a state's intention, treating states as rational actors in both the construction of institutions and how they then act in institutions, analysing the legal structure of an institution as evidence of how states go about solving a coordination problem. Rational choice theory looks at the way in which individual states respond to incentives, form preferences and make choices in the context of institutional constraints, as well as at how institutions are created and designed as a function of actor preferences and other exogenous restrictions.[26] Rationalist choice theory is a way of analysing how behavioural approaches to international law function and what factors

[20] For realists arguments in this respect see Mearsheimer (n 10); JM Grieco, 'Anarchy and the Limits of Cooperation: A Realist Critique of the Newest Liberal Institutionalism' (1988) 42 *International Organization* 485.

[21] I Hurd, 'Constructivism' in Reus-Smit and Snidal (eds) (n 6).

[22] J Brunnée and SJ Toope, 'International law and constructivism: elements of an interactional theory of international law' (2000) 39 *Columbia Journal of Transnational Law* 19.

[23] PA Karber, '"Constructivism" as a Method in International Law' (2002) 94 *Proceedings of the American Society of International Law Annual Meeting* 189.

[24] Mingtao Shi, 'State withdrawal from international institutions: changing social relations within divergent institutions' (2018) 55 *International Politics* 221; F Cowell, 'Exit clauses in regional human rights systems: the socialisation of human rights law at work?' (2018) 15 *International Organizations Law Review* 388.

[25] B Bowring, 'What is realism in international law and human rights?' in J Joseph and C Wright (eds), *Scientific Realism and International Relations* (Palgrave Macmillan, 2010) 101–114. For an additional critical exploration of constructivism and legal obligation see M Koskenniemi, 'The mystery of legal obligation' (2011) 3 *International Theory* 319.

[26] A Thompson, 'Rational Choice Theory and International Law: Insights and Limitations' (2002) 31 *The Journal of Legal Studies* 285.

alter and drive a state's behaviour.[27] Analysing the factors behind the creation of legal regimes, what was described as a process of legalisation, is a significant part of this theory, which also relates to the various institutionalist schools of thought described above.[28] Rational design theory looks at the underlying cooperation problem that a legal regime has been created to solve, and links explanations of a regime's legal powers to those problems and explains them as devices to achieve resolution of those problems.[29] Rational design theorists, unlike constructivists, do not maintain that a state's social identity within an organisation or treaty regime is particularly significant, but at the same time do not share the realist conclusion that law will always be subordinate to the political interests of states.[30] One of the leading insights from rational design theorists' focus on the underlying cooperation problem presented to states, is to construct an account of why certain legal regimes have dispute resolution mechanisms and why those mechanisms can be effective.[31] It makes sense when considering withdrawal clauses to treat rationalism separately from rational design, as the latter's focus on the cooperation problem as a means of interpreting the design of a particular provision is distinct from thinking about the behavioural concerns of states, which may be influenced and structured by exogenous factors beyond the regime.

In a related vein, functionalism traces organisational powers back to the underlying aims of an organisation's founding, going beyond rational design theory's more precise focus on the existence of a cooperation as a necessary precondition for the construction of institutional frameworks.[32] A central insight from functionalism is to demonstrate how the legal powers of an institution can evolve through the process of cooperation within an institution.[33] Functionalism, unlike rational design, analytically puts more of

[27] A van Aaken, 'Rationalist and Behavioralist Approaches to International Law' in JL Dunoff and MA Pollack (eds), *International Legal Theory: Foundations and Frontiers* (Cambridge University Press, 2022) 261–281.

[28] J Goldstein et al, 'Introduction: Legalization and World Politics' (2000) 54 *International Organization* 385.

[29] Koremenos (n 17) 62–63; B Koremenos, C Lipson and D Snidal, 'The Rational Design of International Institutions' (2001) 55 *International Organization* 761.

[30] J Duffield 'The Limits of "Rational Design"' (2003) 57 *International Organization* 411; E Kantorowicz-Reznichenko, 'The Enforcement of International Law' in MO Hosli and J Selleslaghs (eds), *The Changing Global Order: Challenges and Prospects* (Springer, 2019) 364.

[31] See on this point B Koremenos, 'If Only Half of International Agreements Have Dispute Resolution Provisions, Which Half Needs Explaining?' (2007) 36 *The Journal of Legal Studies* 189.

[32] J Klabbers, 'Colonial Inspirations: The Emergence of Functionalism in International Institutional Law (2014) 25 *European Journal of International Law* 645.

[33] T Gehring, 'Integrating integration theory: neo-functionalism and international regimes' (1996) 10 *Global Society* 225; see further on this point J Klabbers, 'What Role for International Organizations in the Promotion of Community Interests?: Reflections on the Ideology of Functionalism' in

its focus on cooperation as an ongoing process, or as a process that advances towards a particular objective. Prior to the refinement of rational design and functionalist theories in the 2000s, which was able to draw on experience of the growth in institutional membership and treaty ratification during the 1990s, some scholarship looked at the different types of legal regime or organisation as fulfilling a coordination or collaborative purpose.[34] Andreas Hasenclever et al used the term 'structural-situationism', characterising their argument as a form of contingent structuralism, to explain that collaboration regimes were likely to require formal legal structures to counteract the problem of non-collaboration between states, but coordination regimes were likely to be less formal as they did not suffer from these problems to the same level.[35]

II. INITIATING A DECLARATION OF WITHDRAWAL

What differentiates withdrawal from other processes, such as suspension of membership of an international organisation or treaty regime, is that it originates in a decision made by a state's domestic political authorities. Yet for the most part, withdrawal clauses make scant if any reference to the activities of a state prior to making a notification of withdrawal. As Helfer notes in an empirical study of withdrawal clauses and their use, 'the overwhelming majority of the denunciation and withdrawal clauses do not … require a state to provide any justification for its decision'.[36] Helfer's analysis of this point does not distinguish between the pre-notification political activity of a state and the substance of a notification. The latter point will be discussed in Section III, but in terms of the pre-notification political activity of a state, Helfer's basic position seems correct – out of the more than 200 treaties surveyed in the analysis of withdrawal clauses (see section I and the Appendix to this book for details), only a handful – 12 per cent in total – had any reference to factors that could be considered to relate to the process of deciding to withdraw. Courts have in some cases been willing to restrict the scope of state action in relation to the decision to withdraw.

E Benvenisti and G Nolte, *Community Interests Across International Law* (Oxford University Press, 2018) 86–100.

[34] A Hasenclever, P Mayer and V Rittberger, *Theories of International Regimes* (Cambridge University Press, 1997). Earlier realist scholars pioneering this analysis include A Stein, 'Coordination and collaboration: regimes in an anarchic world' (1982) 36 *International Organization* 299. Departing from the realist framework, see D Snidal, 'Coordination versus Prisoners' Dilemma: Implications for International Cooperation and Regimes' (1985) 79 *The American Political Science Review* 923.

[35] A Hasenclever, P Mayer and V Rittberger, 'Interests, power, knowledge: the study of international regimes' (1996) 40 *Mershon International Studies Review* 177.

[36] Helfer (n 11) 1598.

A. The Process of Withdrawal as a Counterpoint to Accession

The creation of legal obligations upon a state, through the process of ratifying or acceding to a treaty, is often subject to a variety of domestic or international procedures and safeguards. Ratification of a treaty in domestic law usually requires clear actions on the part of the ratifying state, reflected in arguments over the difference between a monist system (where a treaty is treated as self-executing) and dualist orientated systems (where the treaty requires legislation to give it legal effect within a state).[37] There is a relatively extensive literature about the way in which domestic and international courts have recognised or not recognised the existence of legal obligations.[38] Article 46 VCLT also recognises the importance of domestic law in terms of treaty ratification when it allows for a violation that is 'manifest' concerning 'a rule of its internal law of fundamental importance' to invalidate a state's consent to a treaty.[39] Yet the termination of international obligations, through the process of withdrawal, is not only underexamined but also has far fewer clear standards than the process of creating obligations.[40]

The United States' Constitution, for example, requires the executive branch of government, in the course of ratifying a treaty, to seek the advice and consent of two-thirds of the US Senate. This requirement is an internal democratic safeguard, necessary to protect against executive overreach, dating back to the eighteenth century; and in more modern times, it had been a substantial barrier to human rights treaties.[41] But there is no democratic safeguard in reverse. As Jean Galbraith notes, the US Constitution 'says nothing specific about what domestic actor or actors have the power to withdraw the United States from treaties'.[42] Scholars of the relationship between the US Constitution and international law have argued that the power for this rests with the President under

[37] There is an ongoing debate whether treaties that create international norms or public order treaties are affected by this distinction, or whether there is some third category of 'international' treaty: see JG Starke, 'Monism and Dualism in the Theory of International Law' (1936) 17 *British Yearbook of International Law* 66; S Kadelbach, 'International Law and the Incorporation of Treaties into Domestic Law' (1999) 42 *German Yearbook of International Law* 66. This will be discussed further in ch 4.

[38] See, eg, MA Waters, 'Creeping Monism: The Judicial Trend toward Interpretive Incorporation of Human Rights Treaties' (2007) 107 *Columbia Law Review* 628.

[39] Art 46(1) VCLT.

[40] H Woolaver, 'Domestic and International Limitations on Treaty Withdrawal: Lessons from South Africa's Attempted Departure from the International Criminal Court' (2017) 111 *AJIL Unbound* 450.

[41] On the human rights treaties point, see N Kaufman Hevener and D Whiteman, 'Opposition to Human Rights Treaties in the United States Senate: The Legacy of the Bricker Amendment' (1988) 10 *Human Rights Quarterly* 309. There is a way around this requirement, by the executive's essentially authorising treaties that do not contain any fresh obligations – see Section IV.

[42] J Galbraith, 'The President's Power to Withdraw the United States from International Agreements at Present and in the Future' (2017) 111 *AJIL Unbound* at www.cambridge.org/core/journals/american-journal-of-international-law/article/presidents-power-to-withdraw-the-united-states-from-international-agreements-at-present-and-in-the-future/0CBA97AFF0673758960A65AC E23EB5C0 (accessed 20 October 2021, as are all subsequent references unless otherwise stated).

the so-called vesting powers thesis, but this could mean that the President is effectively empowered to remove rights from citizens of the US by presidential fiat.[43] Furthermore, under this doctrine, re-joining a treaty could be accomplished without oversight of the US Senate, as a President would theoretically be entitled to undo an executive action of his or her predecessor, again highlighting the relatively minimal democratic oversight in the process of withdrawal.[44] In 1979, when President Jimmy Carter announced the withdrawal from (and effective termination of) a defence treaty with Taiwan, as part of a process of attempting to normalise diplomatic relations with China after a long period of maintaining no formal relations due to the 1949 communist revolution, a group of Senators and Representatives, led by Senator Barry Goldwater, a strident anti-communist, attempted to challenge the President's power to terminate treaties without congressional approval.[45] In the lower courts, there was an argument about whether the question of the President's power to terminate treaties without democratic oversight was itself justiciable; but when the case went to the US Supreme Court, only two Justices voted to actually consider the case, with the majority concluding that the matter was simply not justiciable.[46] As a pragmatic ruling demarcating political from legal questions, this judgment was relatively routine for a constitutional court like the US Supreme Court. However, in the petitioners' case, there were a number of important points about the role of democratic authority in treaty termination that were never addressed by the Court.[47]

The balance of power was at issue in *Democratic Alliance v Minister of International Relations*, where the South African High Court struck down the Government's withdrawal from the Rome Statute of the International Criminal Court (ICC).[48] The South African Government, in October 2016, had issued a declaration saying that it intended to withdraw under the provisions of Article 127 of the Rome Statute, after a ruling by the South African Supreme Court held that the Government should have arrested President Omar Al-Bashir during a state visit to South Africa in 2015, for whom there was an arrest warrant on charges relating to genocide and crimes against humanity in Darfur.[49] In its press release on the decision to withdraw, the Government highlighted this in vague terms, claiming that its freedom of diplomatic relations was being infringed, but elsewhere referenced the 2014 AU decision urging

[43] C Bradley, 'Treaty Termination and Historical Gloss' (2014) 92 *Texas Law Review* 773, 780–81.

[44] See J Galbraith, 'Rejoining Treaties' (2020) 106 *Virginia Law Review* 73.

[45] *Goldwater v Carter*, 444 US 996 (1979).

[46] ibid.

[47] Some of the points that were not addressed in relation to the allocation of powers are outlined in E McGLynn Gaffney Jr, '*Goldwater v Carter*: The Constitutional Allocation of Power in Treaty Termination' (1979) 6 *Yale Studies in World Public Order* 81, 92–94, 99–100.

[48] *Democratic Alliance v Minister of International Relations and Cooperation and Others* (83145/2016) [2017] ZAGPPHC 53.

[49] *The Minister of Justice and Constitutional Development v The Southern African Litigation Centre* (867/15) [2016] ZASCA 17 (15 March 2016).

states to withdraw from the ICC on anti-imperialist grounds.[50] The decision to withdraw was taken without parliamentary authorisation, and in finding against the Government, the High Court concluded that given that the ratification of treaties required parliamentary approval, in the absence of any guidance in the South African Constitution there was no 'cogent reason' why the withdrawal from treaties should be treated differently.[51] The *acte contraire* reasoning here – the idea that the requirements for amending or undoing a legal act must mirror the requirements for creating that act – preserved the idea of a broader democratic mechanism for the way that legal relations are shaped on the international plane. However, as Hannah Woolaver's analysis of the judgment and its decision showed, this is not a well-established principle in different jurisdictions.[52] It is also unclear whether as a matter of international law the failure to comply with a domestic constitutional requirement would be grounds for not recognising an act of withdrawal as valid.[53] Rather, the conception of democracy in the law of withdrawal is often more about the recognition of the actions and the power of the executive in a state than it is about an expression of consent from the population or a recognition of the constitutional legitimacy of the decision to withdraw from a treaty.[54] From a realist perspective, it makes sense that withdrawal clauses would seek to recognise, and show bias towards, the authority of the party in charge of a state's foreign relations when determining whether an act of this nature was lawful.[55] Yet this argument could also be extended, as from a rationalist perspective the ability to ensure that a withdrawing state is incentivised to cooperate both in withdrawal and afterwards with the legal regime from which it is exiting, gravitates towards recognition on the international plane of the regime's declaration of withdrawal in all but the most narrow procedural grounds.[56]

[50] A Borda, 'South Africa's reasons for leaving the ICC don't quite add up' *The Conversation* (25 October 2016) at https://theconversation.com/south-africas-reasons-for-leaving-the-icc-dont-quite-add-up-67481. On the issue of the AU resolution, see ch 1.

[51] *Democratic Alliance v Minister of International Relations* (n 48) para 57.

[52] Woolaver (n 40).

[53] Woolaver has set out a framework for international law's development in this area – H Woolaver, 'From Joining to Leaving: Domestic Law's Role in the International Legal Validity of Treaty Withdrawal' (2019) 30 *European Journal of International Law* 73.

[54] C McLachlan, 'The assault on international adjudication and the limits of withdrawal' KFG Working Paper Series No 28, February 2019, 6.

[55] Classic realist theory places strong emphasis on states as the source and author of international laws and obligations – for an overview, see E Egede, *Politics of International Law and International Justice* (Edinburgh University Press, 2013) 27–29. A realist would conclude that more powerful states would simply assert the legitimacy of their actions in cases like these, regardless of the substantive legal requirement – see, for an overview of realist analysis of power and the law, C Sylvest, 'Realism and international law: the challenge of John H Herz' (2010) 2 *International Theory* 410, 431–35.

[56] A core feature of rationalism is that 'the agent makes choices in anticipation of the likely choices and reactions of others': RO Kohane 'Rational Choice Theory and International Law: Insights and Limitations' (2002) 31 *The Journal of Legal Studies* 307, 308.

B. Demonstrating the Necessity for Withdrawal

Substantive notification provisions refer to requirements in a withdrawal clause for a state party to demonstrate either the necessity for their notification or some pre-withdrawal procedure. In terms of the former concept, provisions requiring the necessity for withdrawal to be shown, these are relatively rare and occur mainly in arms control treaties. Beginning with the 1963 Partial Test Ban Treaty (PTBT), withdrawal clauses of treaties controlling weapons of mass destruction permitted a state to withdraw if 'extraordinary events' would jeopardise their 'supreme interests'.[57] However, the PTBT formula stopped short of requiring the withdrawing state to explain what those events were. The 1968 Nuclear Proliferation Treaty (NPT) does, however, require the withdrawing state to include 'a statement of the extraordinary events it regards as having jeopardized its supreme interests' in its notice of withdrawal to other parties.[58] Five other multilateral treaties on nuclear weapons, as well as the 1992 Chemical Weapons Convention and the 1972 Convention on Biological Weapons, also contain substantive requirements in their notification provisions for the withdrawing states to outline what the circumstances are that require them to leave the treaty.[59] In the sample of over 200 withdrawal clauses analysed for this chapter, it was only weapons and disarmament treaties that were found to contain a provision of this sort in their withdrawal clause.

The requirement to demonstrate a condition of necessity prior to withdrawal was implicit in the structure of the PTBT's withdrawal clause, and can be read from a rationalist perspective as a means of ensuring that state parties take their respective commitments to the treaty seriously. The refinement of the clause in the Nuclear Non-Proliferation Treaty (NPT) formula shows how these clauses were conceived of as a means of balancing flexibility on the part of state parties, encouraging commitment with the promise that exit could occur quickly if the geopolitical situation changed, with the need for a stable arms-control system; requiring a party to demonstrate the existence of a situation of necessity could prevent the provision from abuse. When the NPT was being drafted, the Swedish representative to the Drafting Committee argued that the reference to extraordinary events in the withdrawal clause was 'a provision which many countries will consider of great importance', because it would allow non-nuclear states to withdraw if the 'effectiveness, stability and power' of the NPT to prevent

[57] Treaty banning nuclear weapon tests in the atmosphere, in outer space and under water (5 August 1963, entered into force 10 October 1963) 480 UNTS 43, Art 4.

[58] Treaty on the Non-Proliferation of Nuclear Weapons (1 July 1968, entered into force 25 May 1970) 726 UNTS 161, Art X.

[59] Ahlström, (n 3); Convention on the Prohibition of the Development, Production, Stockpiling and Use of Chemical Weapons and on their Destruction (opened for signature 3 September 1992, entered into force 29 April 1997) 1975 UNTS 45, Art XVI; Convention on the prohibition of the development, production and stockpiling of bacteriological (biological) and toxin weapons and on their destruction (opened for signature 10 April 1972, entered into force 29 March 1975) 1015 UNTS 163, Art XIII.

proliferation was in some way compromised by the proliferation of nuclear weapons by non-nuclear states and the unwillingness of nuclear-weapon states to pursue disarmament.[60] From looking at the Committee meetings from 1965–68, it was clear that the withdrawal clause was seen as providing an escape hatch for states, both nuclear and non-nuclear, in the event that the normative order constructed by the NPT began to fracture – it allowed nuclear states to leave if they felt that other states were not playing by the rules and allowed non-nuclear states to leave if they felt that the disarmament goals contained in the NPT were not being met.[61] The aim of requiring states to declare what these circumstances were was a means of ensuring that there was something approaching 'legitimate grounds' for withdrawal when a state used that provision.[62] The clause safeguarded the NPT's creation of a community of states, socialising states into constraining their security-oriented incentives to acquire nuclear weapons in the interest of a communal order with a limited number of nuclear powers. From a constructivist perspective, the requirement to outline what those 'extraordinary events' were helped shape an understanding of 'extraordinary events' that was stringent and – it was hoped – would deter states from withdrawing from the community of states defined by the NPT.[63]

Yet implicitly, this requirement also suggests some form of scrutiny of a state's reasons for withdrawing. When in 1993 North Korea attempted to withdraw from the NPT, its stated reasons came under examination, in part because they constituted a bad-faith attempt to evade obligations under the NPT. Having become a party to the NPT in 1985, North Korea was subject to inspections by the International Atomic Energy Agency (IAEA) under the terms of the treaty, but these did not materialise, and by 1987 North Korea had started operating a nuclear facility in Yongbyon. By 1992, it was widely known that it was pursuing nuclear weapons.[64] When announcing its withdrawal under Article X of the NPT in March 1993, there had been warnings from the IAEA that North Korea's failure to cooperate with inspections could lead to further measures, including a reference to the UN Security Council.[65] North Korea's notification of withdrawal claimed that US actions and the military alliance with South Korea had

[60] Final verbatim record of the Conference of the Eighteen-Nation Committee on Disarmament [Meeting 335], ENDC/PV.335 (3 October 1967) 10.

[61] For an illustration, see the US delegates' comments ENDC/PV.325 (24 August 1967) 10; and the Canadian delegates' comments ENDC/PV.336 (5 October 1967) 6. G den Dekker and T Coppen, 'Termination and Suspension of, and Withdrawal from, WMD Arms Control Agreements in Light of the General Law of Treaties' (2012) 17 *Journal of Conflict & Security Law* 25, 35.

[62] ENDC/PV.373 (5 March 1968) 10.

[63] For an exploration of this argument, see B Sutter, 'The Nonproliferation Treaty and the "New World Order"' (1993) 26 *Vanderbilt Journal of Transnational Law* 181, 190; C Evans, 'Going, Going, Gone? Assessing Iran's Possible Grounds for Withdrawal from the Treaty on the Non-Proliferation of Nuclear Weapons' (2021) 26 *Journal of Conflict & Security Law* 309, 321–22.

[64] R Lehman, 'A North Korean Nuclear-Weapons Program: International Implications' (1993) 24 *Security Dialogue* 257, 262; M Klare 'The Next Great Arms Race' (1993) 72 *Foreign Affairs* 136.

[65] A Mack, 'The Nuclear Crisis on the Korean Peninsula' (1993) 33 *Asian Survey* 339.

engineered a state of 'semi-war' on the Korean peninsular, calling the inspections of the IAEA a 'conspiracy' and part of the 'imprudent machinations' of the US that would have the effect of violating North Korea's sovereignty.[66] The allegation of a vast conspiracy, with international organisations being manipulated by the US, was fairly standard North Korean propaganda, but it was far from clear that this would constitute an extraordinary event under Article X, which had a specific requirement that the events in question relate to the 'subject matter' of the treaty – nuclear weapons. In a statement issued on 1 April 1993, the three depositary governments of the NPT – Russia, the UK and the US – questioned 'whether the DPRK's stated reasons for withdrawing from the Treaty constitute extraordinary events' because they did not relate to nuclear weapons.[67] Although, to take North Korea's perspective, a response like this would be exactly how those involved in a conspiracy would respond, it was really not clear that its stated reasons were anything more than a reassertion of North Korea's ideological positions.[68] The 1993 episode appeared instead to be a political move by North Korea, and eventually there was a political resolution to the crisis, with a statement emerging from a June summit in New York in which the North Korean Government agreed to suspend its NPT withdrawal.[69]

Even though the requirement to demonstrate the existence of such a situation is ultimately one that is subjectively determined by the withdrawing state, the interpretation of the clause in practice has revolved around a narrow interpretation of it that bolsters the aims of the Treaty and a good-faith interpretation of it, rather than an unlimited right to withdraw as a state sees fit.[70] The presumption of Security Council involvement in assessing the reasons given by the withdrawing state would also heighten the difficulty any would-be withdrawing state would face in lawfully exiting the treaty.[71] There is, however, a way of reading this requirement as a vision of a world where security guarantees, particularly those made by the US to various European nations, are no longer present and there is an external aggressor making nuclear threats.[72] In that

[66] Statement of the Government of the Democratic People's Republic of Korea, Pyongyang, 12 March 1993 – Contained in IAEA 'Report by the Director of the International Atomic Energy Agency on Behalf of the Board of Governors to all Members of the Agency on the Non-Compliance of the Democratic People's Republic of Korea with the agreement of the IAEA and the Democratic Republic of Korea.' IHFCIRC/419 (8 April 1993) Annex 7.

[67] Conference on Disarmament, 'Letter dated 2 April 1993 addressed to the Secretary-General of the Conference on Disarmament by the representatives of the Depositary Governments of the Treaty on the Non-Proliferation of Nuclear Weapons' Doc CD/1195 (2 April 1993).

[68] Ahlström, (n. 3) 771.

[69] ibid.

[70] T Coppen, 'Good faith and withdrawal from the Non-Proliferation Treaty' (2014) 2 *Questions of International Law* 21; Evans (n 63).

[71] On that presumption, see SZ Kutchesfahani, 'A Staple of Global Nuclear Order' (2018) 48 *Arms Control Today* 6; G Bunn and J Rhinelander, 'NPT Withdrawal: Time for the Security Council to Step In' (2005) 35 *Arms Control Today* 17.

[72] C Ford, 'Deterring or Dissuading NPT Withdrawal: Lessons for the Like-Minded' (2022) 46 *The Fletcher Forum for World Affairs* 19, 25–26.

scenario withdrawal may be a way of trying to legally acquire nuclear weapons as a last resort. This reading situates the joint PTBT and the NPT formula for a withdrawal clause as less a guarantor of sovereign interests and more a vision of a world where the balance of nuclear power is substantially different. But this also highlights a core objective of the NPT; its goal was to preserve the arms balance of the status quo and create a set of international norms that would strengthen the political taboo against acquiring nuclear weapons and in favour of disarmament. The requirement to demonstrate the circumstances behind initiating a withdrawal supports these general aims, by requiring the withdrawing state to either defy an international taboo or demonstrate that the stability of existing norms surrounding weapons has changed.

C. Initiating Withdrawal as a Means of Stopping Proceedings

One area where there is a relatively clear standard regarding the initiation of a withdrawal is when a state withdraws from the jurisdiction of an international court in order to effectively block proceedings. As outlined in chapter 1, the ICJ in *Nicaragua v United States* concluded that an attempt by the US to enter a Declaration to Article 36 of the ICJ's Statute precluding the bringing of disputes in Central America to the Court, was contrary to general principles of good faith.[73] In *Ivcher-Bronstein v Peru*, a case before the Inter-American Court of Human Rights (IACtHR), the claimant, Baruch Ivcher-Bronstein, had been born in Israel but was a naturalised Peruvian citizen and the Director of a leading Peruvian television network, Frecuencia Latina-Canal 2.[74] The network had been airing news programmes that detailed torture committed by the Peruvian Army's intelligence services and illegal spying on opposition politicians. In retaliation, the Government of President Alberto Fujimori revoked Ivcher-Bronstein's citizenship and assumed a majority share of his company.[75] After exhausting his remedies in the domestic courts, he took his case to the IACtHR, alleging amongst other things a violation of his right to freedom of expression.[76] In August 1999, after it had twice requested and been granted procedural extensions by the Court, the Peruvian Government's ambassador in Costa Rica (the seat of the Court) wrote to it saying that the Peruvian Congress

[73] *Military and Paramilitary Activities in and against Nicaragua (Nicaragua v United States of America)* (Jurisdiction and Admissibility) [1984] ICJ Rep 392.

[74] *Ivcher Bronstein v Peru* (Competence) Inter-American Court of Human Rights Series C No 5 (24 September 1999).

[75] S Canton, 'Protecting Truth from Power: 15 Years of The Special Rapporteur For Freedom of Expression' *Americas Quarterly* (19 October 2013) at www.americasquarterly.org/fulltextarticle/protecting-truth-from-power-15-years-of-the-special-rapporteur-for-freedom-of-expression/.

[76] Karen Sokol, 'Ivcher Bronstein. Jurisdiction. Resoluciones y Sentencias, Serie C, No 54 and Constitutional Tribunal. Jurisdiction. Resoluciones y Sentencias, Serie C, No 55.' (2001) 95 *American Journal of International Law* 178.

had passed a resolution approving the withdrawal of Peru from the contentious jurisdiction of the Court. Human rights groups had long been protesting in Peru against Fujimori's Government, and at the same time as Ivcher-Bronstein's case, another case involving judges who had been impeached for refusing to comply with Fujimori's attempt to circumvent constitutional term limits was also due to go before the IACtHR.[77] There was little doubt that this was therefore a tactical manoeuvre by the Peruvian Government to make these politically inconvenient cases go away ahead of an election scheduled for 2000. Moreover, the Government had not attempted a withdrawal from the 1969 American Convention on Human Rights, only from the jurisdiction of the Court. The IACtHR ruling on its competence took note of the Inter-American Commission's report on the question of withdrawal, which argued there was 'no provision that would make it possible to [only] withdraw recognition of the Court's contentious jurisdiction'; and even if a withdrawal were possible, for the sake of 'juridical security and continuity' it was necessary to have a one-year period prior to withdrawal's becoming effective.[78] Directly referencing *Nicaragua v United States*, the Court ruled that a good-faith interpretation of the Convention would require that the only means of withdrawing from the jurisdiction of the Court would be to denounce the American Convention altogether. Due to the sunset clause in the Convention's withdrawal clause (see chapter 3 for more detail), this would mean that Ivcher-Bronstein's case would still have to be heard by the Court, even if Peru wished to withdraw from the Convention overall. But the Court went further, drawing on the International Court of Justice's (ICJ) Advisory Opinion in *Reservations to the Genocide Convention*, to hold that because human rights treaties and courts were of a special character, states should expect to have less discretion in relation to initiating a withdrawal from their jurisdiction than they would from another inter-state tribunal.[79]

In relation to the jurisdiction to hear individual complaints against a state party, the situation with the African Court of Human and People's Rights (ACHPR) is somewhat different from that in the IACtHR, as the majority of state parties have not entered a declaration to the Court Protocol allowing for individual cases to be heard by the Court.[80] The Court has been fairly consistent that, where there has been no declaration under the Court Protocol, the Court lacks the jurisdiction to hear the case before it.[81] Victoire Ingabire

[77] *Constitutional Court v Peru* (Competence) Inter-American Court of Human Rights Series C No 5 (24 September 1999).

[78] *Ivcher-Bronstein v Peru* (Competence) para 24. The reasoning in this and in *Constitutional Court* was identical.

[79] *Ivcher-Bronstein v Peru* (Competence) para 48; *Reservations to the Convention on the Prevention and Punishment of the Crime of Genocide* (Advisory Opinion) [1951] ICJ Rep 15.

[80] A Enabulele, 'The problems of jurisdiction by optional declaration: reflections on Articles 5(3) and 34(6) of the Protocol of the African Court on Human and Peoples' Rights' (2018) 24 *Australian Journal of Human Rights* 223.

[81] Data in 2014 showed that around 55% of all cases being ruled on by the Court were Art 36(4) cases; for the data see at www.african-court.org/en/index.php/2012-03-04-06-06-00/all-cases-and-decisions (accessed 14 August 2014).

was a Rwandan politician and activist of Hutu ethnicity who had, at the time of her case before the ACHPR, been in repeated trouble with the Rwandan authorities since 2010 because of her strident political views, which fell foul of Rwandan genocide laws.[82] The strict penalties imposed by those laws, which prohibited a range of offences, such as revising or questioning core facts of the 1994 Genocide, had been criticised by human rights groups but were of vital importance for the governing Rwandan Patriotic Front (RPF), who saw these as essential in cementing the post-conflict political order in Rwanda.[83] Ingabire was convicted in October 2012 of a number of charges, including spreading the ideology of genocide; and after being unsuccessful in her domestic appeals, the Rwandan Supreme Court in fact increased her term of imprisonment from eight to 15 years.[84] At the time, Rwanda was one of just seven nations that had issued a declaration allowing individual petitions to the ACHPR.[85] In February 2016, as Ingabire's case was under consideration by the ACHPR, the Government of Rwanda issued a letter to the Court secretariat formally withdrawing its declaration under the Court Protocol. Unlike the American Convention, the African Charter on Human and Peoples' Rights contains no withdrawal clause and the Court Protocol was designed to make the individual jurisdiction of Court expressly voluntary, due to concerns from state parties at the time of drafting about the growth of court power and vexatious litigation.[86] In considering the withdrawal of Rwanda's declaration, the Court examined *Nicaragua v United States* and the principle of good faith, but concluded that the principle did not apply in the context of an individual declaration whose 'unilateral character stem[s] from the international principle of state sovereignty'.[87] Instead, they rooted their decision in the collateral consequences of what withdrawal would involve for the rights of individuals and how it would deprive them of access to justice.[88] Citing *Ivcher-Bronstein*, the Court concluded that the principle that a withdrawal would become effective only after one year following notification was necessary for legal certainty.[89]

[82] Bloomberg News, 'Rwanda: Opposition Leader Is Arrested' *New York Times* (14 October 2010) at www.nytimes.com/2010/10/15/world/africa/15briefs-Rwanda.html.

[83] See C Dalporto, 'Genocide Ideology Laws: Violation of Rwandan People's Rights' (2011) 20 *Cardozo Journal of International & Comparative Law* 875; Human Rights Watch, 'Law and Reality Progress in Judicial Reform in Rwanda' (25 July 2008) at www.hrw.org/report/2008/07/25/law-and-reality/progress-judicial-reform-rwanda, ch 7.

[84] Ingabire was later to be successful at the substantive hearing at the Court. For details, see International justice Resource Centre, 'African Court Holds Rwanda Violated Victoire Ingabire's Freedom of Expression' (12 December 2017) at https://ijrcenter.org/2017/12/12/african-court-holds-rwanda-violated-victoire-ingabires-freedom-of-expression/.

[85] These seven states are Burkina Faso, Cote d'Ivoire, Ghana, Malawi, Mali, Rwanda and Tanzania.

[86] On the drafting of the Court Protocol, see G Bekker, 'The African Court on Human and Peoples' Rights: Safeguarding the Interests of African States' (2007) 51 *Journal of African Law* 151.

[87] *Victoire Ingabire Umuhoza v The Republic of Rwanda* App no 003/2014 (ACHPR, 3 June 2016).

[88] ibid paras 57–58.

[89] ibid paras 63–66.

In both of the above cases, these regional human rights courts were willing to link the impact of withdrawal to the rights of those people the act of withdrawal would affect. In essence this challenged the domestic government's decision making, as in both cases the governments had decided for political reasons to ignore the rights of the claimants. Although focusing on issues surrounding the time between denunciation and withdrawal's becoming legally effective, both cases considered the pre-notification decision process and attempted to limit or guide a state in its decision-making process regarding withdrawal. In both cases, the Court's process of interpretation can be read, from an institutionalist perspective, as an attempt to preserve the integrity of the legal regime for its original purpose – the protection of the rights of individuals – which would involve restricting the range of actions that states could take in relation to courts.[90] This can be reconciled with the general aversion of the law of withdrawal towards prescribing the process of sovereign decision making prior to a declaration of withdrawal, because in these cases the withdrawing state's impact undermined or compromised the efficacy of the wider international legal system by directly challenging the authority of the courts.

III. NOTIFICATION PROVISIONS

Having decided to withdraw from a legal instrument, the next stage for a withdrawing state is to make an official declaration of the decision to leave and initiate withdrawal. Even if largely a procedural obligation, these rules arguably have a value that goes beyond the process of administering treaty membership. Notification, from a formal legal perspective, is necessary to distinguish the decision to leave from simple non-compliance with a legal obligation.[91] These rules also serve an important social signalling effect to delineate between the groups of states that are remaining in a legal regime and the state withdrawing from that legal regime. From a constructivist perspective, withdrawal provisions have a normative power for a legal regime as a whole because in delineating the community of states within a legal regime from the states outside, social interactions within the community gain a sense of value and definition.[92] This can be vital because, as Nicolas Onuf has argued, international law is often

[90] This form of institutionalist reasoning, sometimes known as historical institutionalism, is described in K Alter, 'The Evolution of International Law and Courts' in O Fioretos, TG Falleti and A Sheingate (eds), *The Oxford Handbook of Historical Institutionalism* (Oxford University Press, 2016).

[91] From these theoretical perspectives, this is the purpose of a withdrawal clause; E Posner and A Sykes, 'Efficient Breach of International Law: Optimal Remedies "Legalized Noncompliance" and Related Issues' (2011) 110 *Michigan Law Review* 243, 285–86. At the other end of the Treaty process, this principle can be seen in the emergence of the demarcation between signature and ratification; see E Swaine, 'Unsinging' (2003) 55 *Stanford Law Review* 2061.

[92] Posner and Sykes (n 91); see also Cowell (n 24).

challenged on positivist grounds for not being a true form of law, therefore the authorising language contained in the rules of accession to an instrument, and by implication the authorising language contained in rules on withdrawal from an agreement, can provide a foundation for a regime's legal authority.[93]

A withdrawal clause therefore contains authorising language in the sense that its terms remove a legal obligation from a state, providing the logical (but not the legal) inverse to the authorising language of the provisions of a legal instrument that create obligations.[94] All forms of law are built on performative utterances. JL Austin described the existence of certain performative statements, such as 'give and bequeath my watch to my brother' or 'I name this ship', which are part of doing an action and which give that statement meaning and force – in the case of the watch, the act of making a will, and in the case of the ship, the act of formally launching it as a vessel onto the seas.[95] The issuing of a statement is the performance of an action.[96] Formally, the act of denunciation removes, or in most cases begins to remove, a legal obligation, but the performance and performative statement made in the process of denunciation can also be read as way of creating a new legal reality. As a practical matter, the formal process of sending a notification to denounce a treaty provides rich political symbolism for the withdrawing state, and is a substantive communication to both internal and external audiences about a state's legal obligations. In 2017, when Theresa May activated Article 50 of the Treaty of the European Union (TEU), and in 2020, when President Donald Trump formally denounced the Paris Climate Change Agreement, both events were carefully publicised. In May's case, an official photograph at 10 Downing Street (the historic home of the UK Prime Minister) showed her formally signing the letter to the President of the Council of Europe activating Article 50. In Trump's case, at a Whitehouse news conference, which was televised, behind a podium bearing the seal of the President of the United States. In the Austinian sense, these actions were pieces of performative communication, as they not only involved the leader of a government reporting the fact of a withdrawal but also the act itself as affecting it or calling it into being.

This is what gives these moments power, but, as Jacques Derrida noted in his critique of Austin's conception of performativity, this analysis requires a context within which the '"coded" iterable utterance' or the statement gains meaning.[97] As Derrida argues, the action of launching a ship or conducting a marriage conforms to an iterable model; it involves citing something that the receivers of the statement can

[93] Language can 'authorise' a community of states – N Onuf, 'International Legal Order as an Idea' (1979) 73 *American Journal of International Law* 244, 248. On the question of positivism, see N Onuf, 'Do Rules Say What They Do? From Ordinary Language to International Law' (1985) 26 *Harvard International Law Journal* 385.

[94] JL Austin, *How to Do Things with Words* (Clarendon Press, 1962).

[95] ibid 6.

[96] ibid 7.

[97] J Derrida, 'Signature Event Context' in *Limited Inc*, tr S Weber (Northwestern University Press, 1988) 1.

recognise.[98] A withdrawal clause and its procedural obligations create that meaning for the statements made in the notification of denunciation – as set out in the introduction, denunciation describes the notification initiating withdrawal, which in turn describes the whole process of a state terminating its legal obligations. The procedural substance of notification is therefore an important part of the legal form of withdrawal, which can be illustrated by looking at three important issues surrounding the notification provisions in withdrawal clauses. All of these issues relate to broader questions of state power and the framework of law in the withdrawal process.

A. Whom to Notify

In bilateral treaties, the question of notification is relatively straightforward, as there exists only one other party to notify. Article 65 VCLT sets out a series of procedural requirements in terms of whom to notify when 'impeaching the validity of a treaty, terminating it, withdrawing from it or suspending its operation'.[99] The general principle is that other parties – there is no specification that it must be all parties and no minimum number – must be notified of an intended withdrawal. Article 65 describes circumstances where withdrawal is being exercised as a discretionary matter by the withdrawing state, which is distinct from withdrawal following a fundamental change of circumstances as described in Article 62 VCLT. In cases involving a fundamental change of circumstances, the ICJ held in the *Fisheries Jurisdiction* case that an exchange of notes could (but did not in this case) constitute a notification of a change of circumstances, a position which had a basis in customary international law.[100] When the European Court of Justice (ECJ) examined Article 65 VCLT in *Racke GmbH & Co*, it concluded that the procedural requirements contained in the provision did not form part of customary international law.[101] The relatively minimal requirements of Article 65 – which place responsibility for dispute resolution on Article 33 of the Charter of the United Nations and preserve the rights of a state to respond with a notice of denunciation in response to another state's alleging a treaty violation – all point towards the primacy of the provisions of individual treaties in determining procedural rules on notification.

Where notifications should be sent is dealt with in Articles 76–77 VCLT, which describe the powers of the depository. The depository can be a state, an international organisation or a designated individual with responsibility or administrative functions concerning the treaty, which would be formally tasked with receiving and 'keeping custody of any instruments, notifications and

[98] ibid 18.

[99] Art 65(1) VCLT.

[100] *Fisheries Jurisdiction (United Kingdom v Iceland) (Jurisdiction of the Court)* (Judgment) [1973] ICJ Rep 3.

[101] Case C-162/96 *Racke GmbH & Co v Hauptzollamt Mainz* [1998] ECR 1, para 59.

communications' relating to the treaty, including notifications of withdrawal.[102] In respect of other parties to the treaty and as a matter of form, a treaty would terminate, or a member state would commence withdrawal, at the moment a depository receives a notification of denunciation.[103] If the date on the notice of withdrawal, regarding when the act of withdrawal becomes effective, is prior to the date of receipt by the depository then that is in effect an application by the withdrawing state for the withdrawal to be considered pre-dated. Such an eventuality may be explicitly envisaged by the withdrawal clause in question, or it may be open to dispute. Yet the starting point for ascertaining when a withdrawal happened would be the receipt of a notification by the depository.[104] The 1994 Energy Charter Treaty (ECT) contains a provision allowing for provisional application of the treaty by a signatory to it, pending full ratification and implementation by that party. This obligation expires if a party to that treaty makes a 'written notification to the Depository of its intention not to become a Contracting Party'.[105] In 2009, Russia informed the Portuguese Government, who acted as the depository party for the ECT, that it did not intend to become a party to the ECT, effectively terminating its provisional application, but it remained a member of the Treaty five years later as it was still participating in aspects of the Treaty's framework.[106] The operation of Article 45 ECT during the period gave rise to a series of investment arbitrations and subsequent litigation (with one case concluding in 2020) in the Netherlands, who under the Treaty's investment clauses was designated as the location for arbitration.[107] In this case the administrative depository functions for a treaty were performed by a designated state, but in many other cases, especially in treaties promoting general order in international law, or human rights instruments, the Office of the Secretary General of the United Nations performs the depository functions, having absorbed this function from the League of Nations in 1946 shortly after the UN's founding.[108] In the 1986 Vienna Convention on the Law of Treaties

[102] Art 77(c) VCLT.

[103] S Rosenne, 'The Depositary of International Treaties' (1967) 61 *American Journal of International Law* 923, 925.

[104] Notifications to the depository allow other parties to be notified (Art 77(e) VCLT), see M Villiger, *Commentary on the 1969 Vienna Convention on the Law of Treaties* (Brill Nijhoff, 2009) 919; for the pre-VCLT evolution, see C Parry, 'Some Recent Development in the Making of Multi-Partite Treaties' (1950) 36 *Grotius Society Transactions for the Year* 149, 160–65.

[105] Energy Charter Treaty (adopted 17 December 1994, entered into force 16 April 1998) 2080 UNTS 95, Art 45(3)a.

[106] I Mironova, 'Russia and the Energy Charter Treaty' *International Energy Charter* (7 August 2014) at www.energycharter.org/what-we-do/knowledge-centre/occasional-papers/russia-and-the-energy-charter-treaty/.

[107] T Voon and AD Mitchell, 'Ending International Investment Agreements: Russia's Withdrawal from Participation in the Energy Charter Treaty' (2017) 111 *AJIL Unbound* 461 at www.cambridge.org/core/journals/american-journal-of-international-law/article/ending-international-investment-agreements-russias-withdrawal-from-participation-in-the-energy-charter-treaty/E44E5A4DAB45B4767CC357EC948B189A (accessed 21 April 2021).

[108] UNGA Res 24 (I) (12 February 1946).

between States and International Organizations or between International Organizations it is stated that depository functions 'may be made by the negotiating States and negotiating organizations', and the rules on notification in Article 65 of that Convention are virtually identical to those in the VCLT.[109] In the sample of treaties looked at in the Appendix to this book, the overwhelming majority of treaties have the UN Secretary General's office as the location of the depository for receiving a notification of denunciation.

The procedure for legal regimes where there is no clear exit clause is more uncertain. When Indonesia attempted to withdraw from the United Nations in 1965, in the absence of a withdrawal clause, the Deputy Prime Minister of Indonesia wrote a letter on 20 January to the then UN Secretary General U Thant, stating Indonesia's intention to withdraw immediately. Although the legal effect of this was subsequently doubted in a legal memo from the UN General Legal Office in September 1965, the letter had the practical consequence of bringing Indonesia's cooperation with the UN to an end, until the Indonesian Government sent a telegram in September 1966 announcing that it would be resuming cooperation with the UN.[110] When Greenland, which was legally part of Denmark on its accession to the European Community in 1973, wanted to withdraw from the EEC following a 1982 referendum held by its newly independent Home Rule Parliament, the Danish Government simply wrote to the European Council about Greenland's desire to withdraw from the EEC.[111] It went out to consultation at the EEC's other bodies, the Commission and the Parliament, and afterwards a set of proposals from the Commission about the future relationship between Greenland and the EEC was produced.[112] In a sense this was a means of resolving a legally anomalous position; Greenland had always had an usual status in EEC law. Its bespoke constitutional arrangement with Denmark and its political community, which largely comprised First Nation peoples or those doing scientific research, meant that withdrawal took place without any wider political controversy.[113] The interesting point was that in both cases, notification of withdrawal took place with the assumption that there was a process of notification, even though there was no express procedural requirement in a withdrawal clause, making these communications fulfil a performative function.

[109] Vienna Convention on the Law of Treaties between States and International Organizations or between International Organizations (opened for signature 21 March 1986 – not yet in force) Art 77.

[110] Y Blum, 'Indonesia's Return to the United Nations' (1967) 16 *ICLQ* 522.

[111] R Friel, 'Providing a Constitutional Framework for Withdrawal from the EU' (2004) 53 *ICLQ* 407; K Mason, 'European Communities Commission-Greenland-EC Commission Draft Approves Withdrawal of Greenland from the European Community and Proposes Terms for Economic Reassociation' (1983) 13 *Georgia Journal of International & Comparative Law* 865.

[112] This was described as an application for a 'political license' to withdraw – J Weiler, 'Alternatives to Withdrawal from an International Organization: The Case of the European Economic Community' (1985) 20 *Israel Law Review* 282.

[113] For the background, see F Harhoff, 'Greenland's withdrawal from the European Communities' (1983) 20 *Common Market Law Review* 13.

Given that a performative statement depends on making reference to a legal document, the search for some kind of legal structure by states (both the ones withdrawing and the ones remaining) is hardly surprising. Yet there also appears to be an assumed hierarchy in the structure of notification requirements; and even in cases where there are no notification requirements, states have behaved as though there is a central authoritative party to whom a declaration needs to be made. References to a depository as a quasi-centralised body, even though its functions are purely administrative, points towards the necessity for a centre or focal point for the legal authorisation of withdrawal, something that critical scholars of international law would identify as being characteristic of a hierarchy in international law.[114] Others would perceive this search for authority as a form of relational authority, where states have produced some form of rudimentary order almost by default, in order to prevent a state of broader anarchy in international relations and the wider international community.[115] Another perspective would be that the procedural formalism of withdrawal is illustrative of international law's wider 'self-conscious functionalism' and the tendency to look for, and venerate, a set procedure as providing a form of stability and legitimacy.[116] The procedural requirements of withdrawal are perhaps best understood as invoking a form of source-based hierarchy – because these requirements stem from the treaty from which withdrawal is sought, this gives them both a form of legitimacy and determinacy, which is instrumentally useful in managing the potentially highly destabilising process of a member state's withdrawal.[117] The implicit reliance on a form of procedure or form of authority, even where none is specified, points towards a hierarchy as a form of language that orders international relations between states and legal regimes. This is a formal-juridical type of hierarchy made by states' presuming that a procedural framework exists, or adopting a rationalist perspective, by their constructing one in order to resolve the collaboration problem posed by a state's withdrawal from a legal regime.[118]

B. Substance of the Notification

The substance of a notification of denunciation is often simply a notification that a state is withdrawing under the terms of a treaty's withdrawal clause. Yet some

[114] M Koskenniemi, 'Hierarchy in International Law: A Sketch' (1997) 8 *European Journal of International Law* 566, 569–71.

[115] For an overview of relational authority, see H Bull, *The Anarchical Society: A study of Order in World Politics* (Columbia University Press, 1977) ch 3.

[116] A Orford, 'Constituting Order' in J Crawford and M Koskenniemi (eds), *The Cambridge Companion to International Law* (Cambridge University Press, 2012) 286–87.

[117] M Prost, 'Hierarchy and the sources of international law: a critique' (2017) 39 *Houston Journal of International Law* 285.

[118] A Barder 'International Hierarchy' in *Oxford Research Encyclopedia of International Studies* (2017) at https://oxfordre.com/internationalstudies/view/10.1093/acrefore/9780190846626.001.0001/acrefore-9780190846626-e-95 (accessed 16 August 2022).

withdrawal clauses refer to prerequisites that directly affect the substance of the notification. As noted in section II.B, these either require a party to demonstrate the necessity for their notification or, that some pre-withdrawal procedure has been performed. These are relatively rare, the first type of substantive requirement is found only in weapons and disarmament treaties. Article 50 TEU is an example of the second type of notification provision, which requires a state party to demonstrate its adherence to pre-withdrawal procedures. Paragraph 1 of Article 50 preserves the right to withdraw as an autonomous right of states ('Any Member State may decide'), but then a provision follows stating that withdrawal should be 'in accordance with its own [the withdrawing Member State's] constitutional requirements'.[119] Article 50 was, as noted in chapter 1, a provision that was simply carried over from aborted Constitutional Treaty of the early 2000s into the 2009 Lisbon Treaty. During the drafting of the Constitutional Treaty, there was considerable opposition from some states to the inclusion of a withdrawal clause in the Treaty, but others were keen to present it as a necessary extension of a state's sovereignty. Proposals for the European Commission to directly supervise withdrawal, for withdrawal to be made conditional on the agreement of other Member States or for withdrawal to be conditional on a referendum did not make their way into the final text of the clause.[120]

This left an open question as to the meaning of the 'constitutional requirements' clause. The *Bundesverfassungsgericht* – Germany's Federal Constitutional Court – in its ruling on the Lisbon Treaty, held that Article 50 TEU entailed that 'the right to withdraw can be exercised without further obligations' because the withdrawing state not need to give reasons for its decision to withdraw.[121] The reference to constitutional requirements was therefore, as some argued, a requirement that it was the responsibility of withdrawing state to self-assess or demonstrate, maintaining the principle that in the EU, Member States 'remained masters of treaties'.[122] But others maintained that it was a trigger mechanism and that Article 50 clearly envisaged a void withdrawal from a Member State.[123] In the event of a dispute about what the meaning of this was, the Court of Justice of the European Union (CJEU) would ultimately be involved, as Richard Friel argued, because Article 50 TEU was a creature of European law, hence 'the question as to whether or not that decision was constitutionally made would fall ultimately to the ECJ'.[124] Technically this was

[119] Consolidated Version of the Treaty on European Union [2008] OJ C115/13, Art 50.

[120] M Dougan, 'The Convention's Draft Constitutional Treaty: A "Tidying-Up Exercise" that needs some tidying-up of its own' Online Paper 27/03 (August 2003) at http://dx.doi.org/10.2139/ssrn.507782 (accessed 15 August 2022).

[121] BVerfG, Judgment of the Second Senate of 30 June 2009 – 2 BvE 2/08, para 330.

[122] Herbst (n 1); S Wieduwilt, 'Article 50 TEU – The Legal Framework of a Withdrawal from the European Union' (2015) 18 *Zeitschrift für Europarechtliche Studien* 169, 177–79.

[123] C Möllers, 'Pouvoir Constituant-Constitution-Constitutionalisation' in A von Bogdandy and J Bast (eds), *Principles of European Constitutional Law* (Hart Publishing, 2005).

[124] Friel (n 111) 425.

correct, but this line of argument (originally mooted in 2004) seemed blind to the political passions and anger towards European institutions that would characterise any use of Article 50 TEU, and others cast doubt on whether the court would even have this power.[125] Another possible reading of this clause was that it was a reflection of the multiple constitutional orders of the Member States of the EU and the way in which EU was in itself a constitutional order of multiple democracies.[126] Certainly, as regards the issue of whether a notification of withdrawal could be withdrawn (see below), the CJEU noted the way that the clause, as part of the EU, underpinned the constitutional order of the Union more broadly.[127] From a constructivist or institutionalist perspective, referring to 'constitutional requirements' was a means of ensuring that the community values of the EU would continue to apply during the potentially fraught process of a Member State's withdrawal.

After the Brexit referendum in June 2016, there was a heated debate about how exactly to trigger Article 50 TEU in the context of the UK's uncodified constitution. Because the political fallout from the referendum had resulted in a leadership election within the then governing Conservative Party, it had not been settled how the process would be initiated. Treaty ratification had not been required to be put to a parliamentary vote until 2010, with the executive usually acting under what was called (part of the royal prerogative) to ratify or withdraw from a treaty.[128] The same was not necessarily true of treaty withdrawal, and in the absence of a firm position, those vying to become leader of the Conservative Party (a political party that had largely supported the campaign to leave the EU) adopted the position that Parliament should not have a role in EU withdrawal so as to make the outcome quicker. In light of the 1972 European Community Act, which had in the UK's dualist system brought Community law into UK law, a group of challengers argued successfully in the UK High Court in October 2016 that following the UK's doctrine of parliamentary sovereignty meant that withdrawal required parliamentary legislation. Therefore, triggering Article 50 TEU could not be accomplished by an executive act.[129] This provoked

[125] Blanke and Mangiameli note that the CJEU had in the past specifically ruled out such a competence to review purely internal law procedures, citing Case 9/65 *Acciaierie San Michele SpA (in liquidation) v High Authority of the ECSC* (ECJ, 22 June 1965) 29 et seq. See H-J Blanke and S Mangiameli, 'Article 50 [Voluntary Withdrawal from the Union]' In H-J Blanke and S Mangiameli, *The Treaty on European Union (TEU)* (Springer, 2013) 1406.

[126] A broad version of this theory is set out in F Cheneval and F Schimmelfennig, 'The case for demoicracy in the European Union' (2013) 51 *Journal of Common Market Studies* 334.

[127] J Vidmar, 'Unilateral Revocability in Wightman: Fixing Article 50 with Constitutional Tools: ECJ 10 December 2018, Case C-621/18, *Andy Wightman and Others v Secretary of State for Exiting the European Union*' (2019) 15 *European Constitutional Law Review* 359, 370–71.

[128] J Barrett, 'The United Kingdom and Parliamentary scrutiny of Treaties: Recent Reformers' (2011) 60 *ICLQ* 225; I Sinclair, SJ Dickson and G Maciver, 'National Treaty Law and Practice: United Kingdom' in DB Hollis, MR Blakeslee and LB Ederington, *National Treaty Law and Practice: Dedicated to the Memory of Monroe Leigh* (Brill, 2005) 727–762.

[129] *R (Miller) v The Secretary of State for Exiting the European Union* [2016] EWHC 2768 (Admin).

a popular backlash towards the courts because this was seen to be stymying the process of withdrawal from the EU, yet in actuality this was an argument about the mechanism for making a notification of withdrawal, not really an argument about the substance of whether to notify at all.[130] In the UK Supreme Court, the Government argued that actions concerning treaties were a matter for the executive – and lost. A majority of the Court concluding that given the scale of changes involved in withdrawal from the EU, it was clear as a matter of domestic constitutional law that ministers could not cause the UK to withdraw from the EU Treaties without prior parliamentary approval.[131] The resolution of the case in the UK domestic courts did not deal with whether the substantive notification requirement of Article 50 TEU needed to be complied with as a matter of international law.[132] However, by setting out a long and detailed analysis of the status of withdrawal in relation to constitutional statutes, and the publication by the UK Government shortly after the ruling in *Miller* of proposals for the domestic triggering of Article 50, there was visible compliance with provisions on constitutional requirements. In March 2017, the then Prime Minister Theresa May wrote to the President of the European Council describing in detail how the notification was being made in line with the UK's constitutional requirements.[133]

Getting the withdrawing state to act in line with an obligation regarding notification can be understood as the withdrawal clause itself facilitating the socialisation of the withdrawing state within the wider international legal order and incentivising it to act lawfully.[134] This would accord with broader constructivist understandings of legal obligation, where international obligations comprise 'continuous self-constitution for a society, embodying the society's possibilities, and transforming behaviour', so that state action evolves in line with the provisions of an instrument, including a withdrawal clause.[135] Equally, from a rationalist perspective, the advantage of a substantive notification obligation provides an

[130] For an overview of the backlash, see R Breeze, '"Enemies of the people": Populist performances in the Daily Mail reporting of the Article 50 case' (2018) 25 *Discourse, Context & Media* 60. This backlash was the start of a wider constitutional tension in the UK over the constitutional doctrine of parliamentary sovereignty in the Brexit process – see C Bickerton, '"Parliamentary", "popular" and "pooled": conflicts of sovereignty in the United Kingdom's exit from the European Union' (2019) 41 *Journal of European Integration* 887.

[131] *R (on the application of Miller and another) (Respondents) v Secretary of State for Exiting the European Union* [2017] UKSC 5 [77]–[78].

[132] ibid [40]–[63].

[133] M Gatti, 'Art 50 TEU: A Well-Designed Secession Clause' (2015) 2 *European Papers* 159. It was telling that the text of the letter framed the decision in language that was relatively similar to her earlier political speeches attacking those who argued Brexit would be difficult, even though the notional audience was simply the Treaty depository – for an analysis, see R Leung, 'Analysis of the UK Prime Ministerial discourse on Brexit: Thematic choices and their implications' (2018) 11 *Discourse and Interaction* 45, 59.

[134] For examples of this argument of this school of thought, see Brunnée and Toope (n 22); R Goodman, 'International law and state socialization: Conceptual, empirical, and normative challenges' (2004) 54 *Duke Law Journal* 983.

[135] B Kingsbury, 'The concept of compliance as a function of competing conceptions of international law' (1997) 19 *Michigan Journal of International Law* 345, 358–59.

exogenous factor to help shape the withdrawing state's actions and its calculations of rationality. The notification provisions in the NPT are an example of this, as even though the determination of exceptional circumstances is something that a state determines, the existence of a requirement to make a substantive notification shapes the way that determination is made by a state party.[136] At the NPT review conferences, it was highlighted how the notification requirement imposed constraints upon the withdrawing state. A 2005 paper from New Zealand on the question of withdrawal noted that the 'capacity for rapid breakout by a state party to nuclear weapons and then withdrawing from the Treaty has existed since [the NPT's inception' and that the provisions of Article X, including the notification provisions, were a means of safeguarding against that.[137] A proposal a year earlier from the United Nations High-level Panel on Threats, Challenge and Change argued that a notification of withdrawal 'should prompt immediate verification of its compliance with the Treaty, if necessary mandated by the Security Council', and seemingly indicated that the notification itself would contain information relevant to that process.[138] Whilst a substantive notification provision is a rare requirement, with almost all notifications to the depository simply containing a reference to compliance with the duration requirements (see below) or a statement of the relevant provision under which the withdrawal was being made, the inclusion of a notification provision clearly relates both to the treaty's compliance provisions and to the underlying aims of the treaty.

C. Withdrawal of a Notification

The question of whether a notification can be withdrawn once issued should logically be *acte contraire* – if a notification to withdraw is an expression of a state's will to withdraw, withdrawal of the notification to withdraw is an indication that a state no longer possesses the will to withdraw. Article 68 VCLT takes this as the starting point when it provides that a 'notification or instrument provided for in article 65 or 67 may be revoked at any time before it takes effect', but this less clear than it seems: Article 65 does not create a freestanding right of withdrawal or have a customary basis to it, and places strong emphasis on the individual requirements of withdrawal clauses.[139] Therefore, the withdrawal of a notification needs to be analysed in light of the procedural requirements in

[136] Evans (n 62) 319–22; see also DH Joyner, 'What if Iran Withdraws from the Nuclear Nonproliferation Treaty? Part 1: Can They Do That?' *ESIL Reflections* (13 December 2012) at https://esil-sedi.eu/wpcontent/uploads/2012/12/ESIL-Reflections-Joyner.pdf.

[137] 2005 Review Conference of the Parties to the Treaty on the Non-Proliferation of Nuclear Weapons, 'Working paper on article X (NPT withdrawal) submitted by Australia and New Zealand' NPT/CONF.2005/WP.16 (28 April 2005).

[138] UN Secretary General, 'A more secure world: our shared responsibility: Report of the High-level Panel on Threats, Challenges and Change' A/59/565 (2 December 2044) para 134.

[139] Krieger notes the ILC 'did not base Article 65 on a customary rule' instead viewing it as a 'progressive development' of international law Heike Krieger 'Article 65' in O Dörr and K Schmalenbach (eds), Vienna Convention on the Law of Treaties (Springer, 2012) 1211–1232, 1213.

that specific withdrawal clause. After the UK had made its notification under Article 50 TEU in March 2017, some doubted whether the notification could be withdrawn, arguing that Article 68 VCLT did not enjoy customary legal status and Article 50 TEU did not envisage a withdrawal of a lawful notification.[140] Others argued, based on an analysis of private international law, that to permit a revocation of a notification would create instability in the overall framework of European law.[141] The position of the UK Government was that withdrawal of its Article 50 notification was not government policy (regardless of whether such a right existed), and at the UK Supreme Court in *Miller*, all parties had adopted the position that notifications under Article 50 TEU could not be withdrawn, albeit as an operational presumption about the international legal effect on which to litigate the specific point of UK constitutional law.[142]

In December 2017, Andy Wightman, a Member of the Scottish Parliament (MSP), along with other Members of Parliament and Members of the European Parliament for the UK, began domestic proceedings in the UK seeking a declaration on whether an Article 50 application could be unilaterally revoked. All of the politicians involved in the litigation were from political parties committed to either a second referendum on the question of Britain's membership of the EU, or some other policy that would require the revocation of the March 2017 notification under Article 50 TEU. Following an election in June 2017, the Government no longer commanded a parliamentary majority and it was theoretically possible to envisage how a new government could exercise the power of revocation in a number of different scenarios.[143] The ECJ's judgment in *Wightman* in December 2018 was in line with the earlier Advocate General's Opinion that an Article 50 withdrawal notice was fully revocable.[144] As the Court noted during the drafting of Treaty, amendments to avoid abuse of the process by the withdrawing state and to make the withdrawal decision more difficult had all been rejected, and instead there was a strong consensus,

[140] For a discussion on these points see Paul Eden, 'The Revocability of Instruments of Withdrawal from Multilateral Treaties with Particular Emphasis on the United Kingdom's Article 50 TEU Notification' (23 August 2018) at https://ssrn.com/abstract=3238431; see also S Enchelmaier, 'Exit from Brexit: would quitter's remorse count under Article 50 TEU' (2018) 33 *Butterworths Journal of International Banking and Financial Law* 278.

[141] P Ostendorf, 'The withdrawal cannot be withdrawn: the irrevocability of a withdrawal notification under art 50(2) TEU' (2017) 42 *European Law Review* 451.

[142] See *Miller* (n 139). V Miller and S de Mars, 'Brexit questions in national and EU courts' HC Library Briefing Paper No 8415, 1 November 2019, 16. See also the discussion by S Weatherill, 'Can an Article 50 notice of withdrawal from the EU be unilaterally revoked?' *EU Law Analysis* (16 January 2018) at http://eulawanalysis.blogspot.com/2018/01/can-article-50-notice-of-withdrawal.html (accessed 20 November 2021).

[143] For a sample of this argument, see E McGaughey, 'Fraud unravels everything: Brexit is voidable and Article 50 can be revoked' *LSE Brexit Blog* (9 April 2018) at https://blogs.lse.ac.uk/politicsandpolicy/fraud-unravels-everything-brexit/. See also J Maugham QC, 'Britain can legally cancel Brexit. That's EU advice – but will parliament agree?' *The Guardian* (4 December 2018) at www.theguardian.com/commentisfree/2018/dec/04/britain-legally-cancel-brexit-eu-parliament-court-remain; O Patel, 'Brexit: is it possible to stop it?' *The Conversation* (6 December 2018) at https://theconversation.com/brexit-is-it-possible-to-stop-it-107750.

[144] Case C-621/18 *Wightman v Secretary of State for Exiting the European Union* [2018] ECR 1.

withdrawal being seen as a 'voluntary and unilateral' decision of the withdrawing state.[145] The structure of Article 50 TEU kept the withdrawing state as an EU member for a two-year period. Therefore, when read alongside Article 68 VCLT, it was clear that there existed a unilateral right to withdraw a notification of withdrawal.[146] Linking this explicitly to the principle of state consent, the ECJ clarified that the right of revocation had to be unilateral, because a state 'cannot be forced to leave the European Union against its will'.[147] This can only really be read as a statement of European law, as there is no real basis for reading Article 68 VCLT as conferring this right in a general sense.[148] Yet the Court was also careful to imply certain conditions regarding revocation, including that any revocation be 'unequivocal and unconditional', so as to avoid a form of bargaining between the Council and the withdrawing state about the terms of departure.[149]

At issue in the *Wightman* decision was how to assess and protect the changing decision of the withdrawing government. This was also at issue in relation to Gambia's withdrawal from the Rome Statute of the ICC. In October 2016, in one of his last official acts, President Yahya Jammeh sent a notification of withdrawal under Article 127 of the Rome Statute, commencing the withdrawal process.[150] Jammeh had been in office for a long time, first as a military leader then as a civilian autocrat, and had two central objections to the ICC: first, as a leading advocate of the AU's withdrawal strategy from the ICC, his Government wanted to set an example, accusing the Court of focusing on Africa at the expense of Western nations' war crimes, with the Government's Information Minister denouncing the Court as 'an International Caucasian Court for the persecution and humiliation of people of colour, especially Africans'.[151] Second, Jammeh had a record of human rights abuses, and with presidential elections approaching, which he was contesting in the face of mounting opposition, he would have likely been aware of how post-election violence in Guinea led to ICC investigations and in Kenya had resulted in indictments against

[145] ibid para 68.
[146] ibid paras 69–71. References to the VCLT were on the whole much more cautious in the ECJ judgment than in the Advocate General's Opinion; J Vidmar, 'Unilateral Revocability in Wightman: Fixing Article 50 with Constitutional Tools' (2019) 15 *European Constitutional Law Review* 359, 368.
[147] ibid para 72.
[148] Vidmar (n 146).
[149] *Wightman* (n 144) para 74.
[150] Gambia: Withdrawal, Rome Statute of the International Criminal Court 1998 Ref: C.N.862.2016.TREATIES-XVIII.10 (11 November 2016).
[151] Reuters Staff, 'Gambia announces withdrawal from International Criminal Court' Reuters, 26 October 2016 at https://uk.reuters.com/article/uk-gambia-icc/gambia-announces-withdrawal-from-international-criminal-court-idUKKCN12P333. This was also in support of a broader anti-institutional policy in the 2010s, which saw Gambia's withdrawal from the Commonwealth of Nations: M Janson 'Enough is enough: Gambians put faith in democracy as Yahya Jammeh ousted at ballot bo.' *The Conversation* (2 December 2016) at https://theconversation.com/enough-is-enough-gambians-put-faith-in-democracy-as-yahya-jammeh-ousted-at-ballot-box-69825.

senior figures in the Government.[152] However, in December 2016 Jammeh lost the election to Adama Barrow, and although there was a short constitutional crisis, when Jammeh changed his mind about accepting the election result, Barrow assumed office in January 2017 and Jammeh left the country.[153]

Shortly after his election, Barrow had committed to re-joining the ICC, seeing it as part of a wider campaign to improve human rights in the country and hold the Jammeh regime's human rights abuses accountable. This stance was clearly popular with supporters, with reporters from *The Guardian* recording one Barrow supporter in Banjul as saying 'he [Jammeh] killed my father – I promise you, he did … we want him to go to the ICC'.[154] In February 2017, the Ambassador of Gambia to the UN issued a notification to the UN Secretary General, in the latter's capacity as depository of the Rome Statute, rescinding Gambia's notification of withdrawal, saying that it 'still considers itself as a state party and will continue to honour its obligations under the Rome Statute', which was correct, as under the terms of Article 127 of the Rome Statute, Gambia would have formally ceased to be a state party on 10 November 2017.[155] A few days later the President of the Assembly of States Parties to the Rome Statute issued a press release welcoming the Gambia's decision.[156] There was little doubt that Gambia's intentions had changed, the result of the presidential election was proof of that. By contrast, the test of state intention set out by the ECJ was never met (before the UK formally left the EU in January 2020, becoming a third-party state, unable to exercise rights open to Member States).

Changing state intention is not a prerequisite of Article 68 VCLT, but in order to maintain the stability of an international legal regime, requiring proof of a change of intention is a means of preventing the withdrawing state from using withdrawal as a form of leverage to exert changes to that

[152] A key motivation for withdrawal was the self-interest of the Government and Jammeh himself; see K Mills and A Bloomfeild, 'African resistance to the International Criminal Court: Halting the advance of the anti-impunity norm' (2018) 44 *Review of International Studies* 101, 119. See also I Sprouse, 'The Gambia's unsurprising renunciation of the ICC, or the so-called "International Caucasian Court"' *LSE Human Rights Blog* (10 November 2016) at https://blogs.lse.ac.uk/africaatlse/2016/11/10/the-gambias-unsurprising-renunciation-of-the-icc-or-the-so-called-international-caucasian-court/.

[153] D Perfect, 'The Gambian 2016 Presidential Election and its Aftermath' (2017) 106 *Round Table: The Commonwealth Journal of International Affairs* 323.

[154] R Maclean and E Graham-Harrison, 'The Gambia's President Jammeh concedes defeat in election' *The Guardian* (2 December 2016) at www.theguardian.com/world/2016/dec/02/the-gambia-president-jammeh-concede-defeat-in-election. A Kriesch 'The Gambia's new president: "We will not leave the ICC"' *Deutsche Welle* (5 December 2016) at www.dw.com/en/the-gambias-new-president-we-will-not-leave-the-icc/a-36639735.

[155] Gambia: Withdrawal of Notification of Withdrawal Ref: C.N.62.2017.TREATIES-XVIII.10, 16 February 2017.

[156] Assembly of State Parties Press Release, 'ASP President welcomes Gambia's decision not to withdraw from the Rome Statute' *ICC News* (17 February 2017) at www.icc-cpi.int/news/asp-president-welcomes-gambias-decision-not-withdraw-rome-statute#:~:text=The%20President%20of%20the%20Assembly,founding%20treaty%20of%20the%20ICC.

legal regime.[157] Also, from a rationalist perspective, difficulties in retracting a notification provide some kind of disincentive to states' making a notification recklessly. How much of a safety mechanism this provides against use by a state of its withdrawal to exact concessions, something Timothy Meyer suggests can be a feature of withdrawal clauses, remains unknown, as there are a limited number of examples where the withdrawal of a notification has occurred.[158] This also points to the existence of a formal juridical form of hierarchy in international treaty law, which, as described previously, means that states seek and use procedural forms in relation to withdrawal, all of which presume a hierarchical system.[159] The existence of a hierarchy in this area does not necessarily mean that the whole of international treaty law is hierarchic, nor there that there exists some kind of clearly defined hierarchic system in international law, merely that this is an area where having some kind of authoritative ordering language allows for mitigation of what could otherwise be a disorderly or anarchic process, and subsequently generates an expectation on states to comply with that process.[160]

IV. THE TEMPORAL ISSUES OF WITHDRAWAL

The most common substantive feature of withdrawal clauses is some form of temporal constraint, with most of the withdrawal clauses sampled containing a reference to time. Article 56 VCLT specifically refers to the requirement that a party shall give 'not less than twelve months' notice of its intention to denounce or withdraw from a treaty' where there is no withdrawal clause in the treaty,[161] and there are other numerous references to time in other provisions of the VCLT surrounding withdrawal and termination. Controlling the time in relation to withdrawal comes in two separate forms. First, as discussed in section IV.A, withdrawal clauses specify the length of time a state needs to be party to a treaty before it can lawfully denounce that treaty. Second, as discussed in section II.B, withdrawal clauses specify the time between a notice of denunciation and withdrawal's becoming effective – 'effectiveness' meaning the cessation of legal obligations under that treaty (beyond continuing obligations (see chapter 3) and rights that cannot be withdraw from (see chapter 2)). Both types of obligations create obligations on states, as would any other provision in a treaty. The regulation of time helps influence and direct the domestic politics of withdrawal

[157] This falls alongside other provisions in withdrawal clauses preventing a 'cut and run from the withdrawing State'; see L Helfer, 'Exiting Custom: Analogies to Treaty Withdrawal' (2010) 21 *Duke Journal of Comparative & International Law* 65, 67.

[158] T Meyer 'Power, Exit Costs, and Renegotiation in International Law' (2010) 51 *Harvard International Law Journal* 381.

[159] Barder (n 118).

[160] D Lake, *Hierarchy in International Relations* (Cornell University Press, 2009) 61–62.

[161] Art 56(1) VCLT.

by setting the expectations of when legal developments will happen, allowing domestic political actors to act accordingly. Article 50 TEU, with its two-year time limit, helped shape expectations and domestic politics in the UK between March 2017 and March 2019.

The regulation of time is a means of controlling and managing the overall level of flexibility offered by withdrawal clauses to create a level of stability in the regimes created by treaties.[162] Both types of time regulation also serve distinct aims and ends, and help underpin existing legal doctrines. Justifications for temporal constraints implicitly refer back to doctrines such as good faith or compliance, both as a justification and as proof of the importance of such doctrines. If international law is understood as a belief system, which is self-referential in that it constantly refers to itself, and grounds fundamental doctrines in repetition of their existence – almost like a religious faith – then the temporal aspects of withdrawal clauses are examples of that process.[163] Adherence to these temporal constraints helps reinforce the interconnected web of belief surrounding international doctrines. The philosopher Émile Durkheim observed, in his study of the sociology of religion, that religions try to regulate time, moving it from a 'partial or total commemoration of our past life' to becoming a 'continuous canvass' which is 'objectively conceived of by everybody.'[164] When applied to the wider international community, the regulation of time can help form a collective communal reality, as the clauses dictating the time at which obligations cease, or when obligations can be departed from, are given universal definition. This affects the practical reality of international relations; at a particular time the withdrawing state's representatives leave an international organisation's headquarters, or on a given date a state is able to make good on its government's political commitment to leave a legal regime. The regulation of time thus becomes part of the 'iterable model' of denunciation as described in section III, making the act of withdrawal itself legal or of law, rather than a non-legal act of non-compliance.

A. The Time from Accession to Notification

Controls on how long a state needs to be party to a treaty before it can lawfully denounce that treaty are relatively common, but of the treaties that have a withdrawal clause in the sample surveyed for this chapter, just around half are silent on the issue. For example, the 1972 Customs Convention on Containers, which

[162] For an overview on the literature on flexibility, see L Helfer, 'Flexibility in International Agreements' in Dunoff and Pollack (eds): (n 17). See also, on the regulation and creation of certainty, B Koremenos, 'Contracting around International Uncertainty' (2005) 99 *American Political Science Review* 549.

[163] This theory is outlined by J d'Aspremont, *International Law as a Belief System* (Oxford University Press, 2017) 7–9.

[164] É Durkheim, *The Elementary Forms of Religious Life*, tr C Cosman (Oxford University Press, 2001) 12.

facilitates states' bringing shipping containers into a state whilst temporarily exempting them from customs payments, has a withdrawal clause the operative part of which simply states 'any Contracting party may denounce the present Convention by effecting the deposit of an instrument with the Secretary-General of the United Nations'.[165] This is distinct from, although superficially similar to, a provision that a state may withdraw at 'any time'. For example, in the Agreement Establishing the International Tea Promotion Association, which establishes the international body coordinating policy on tea, the withdrawal clause reads 'at *any time* after the entry into force of this Agreement, any Member may withdraw from this Agreement'.[166] The inclusion of the words 'any time' may in practice be relatively inconsequential – in the two examples above there is almost no distinction in terms of how it would condition a state's behaviour when committing to the treaty in question or, if having taken the decision to withdraw from it, how any withdrawal would be conducted. The standard mechanism to interpret silence would be to examine the nature of the treaty to see whether silence could imply that a particular practice was excluded, and in the majority of cases 'any time' would likely be synonymous with silence.[167] It is therefore possible to envisage a situation where silence over when a withdrawal can take place is read in the context of the treaty to conclude that this does not mean a withdrawal can take place at a given moment in time. Although likely to be very rare, this exercise in construction does not seem to have influenced the construction of withdrawal clauses and given the prevalence of the two as concepts (see Figure 2.1) it is hard therefore to conclude anything specific from the use of 'any time' and silence in individual treaties. Therefore the most obvious conclusion is that they are treated as synonymous. But as a matter of law, it is possible to conceive of a future treaty, perhaps on environmental protection or climate change, where silence is interpreted differently.

However, when disaggregated by theme, it possible to see some patterns starting to emerge. Significantly, of the disarmament and weapons control treaties included in the sample all containing withdrawal clauses, all are either silent on withdrawal or contain a specific reference to a declaration's being allowed at 'any time'. Part of this is the general issue to do with what Barbra Koremenos and Alison Nau term 'treaties with underlying enforcement problems' – where the subject matter of the agreement incentivises non-compliance because of the uncertainty created about the intentions of other parties.[168] As Koremenos and Nau demonstrate, with an analysis using a rational design methodology to

[165] Customs Convention on Containers (adopted 2 December 1972, entered into force 6 December 1975) 998 UNTS 43, Art 23 (emphasis added).

[166] Agreement establishing the International Tea Promotion Association (adopted 31 March 1977, entered into force 23 February 1979) 1123 UNTS 367, Art 23.

[167] R Gardiner, *Treaty Interpretation*, 2nd edn (Oxford University Press, 2015) 165–67.

[168] B Koremenos and A Nau, 'Exit, no exit' (2010) 21 *Duke Journal of Comparative & International Law* 81. See also B Koremenos, *The Continent of International Law: Explaining Agreement Design* (Cambridge University Press, 2016) 151–155.

analyse a sample of treaties with withdrawal clauses, treaties with withdrawal clauses allowing a quick withdrawal are those with these underlying commitment problems.[169] Anxieties that the NPT would not offer sufficient flexibility, especially from non-nuclear powers (who would likely be the most affected by a requirement to wait after accession before they could withdraw), were a core feature of the negotiations during the 1960s.[170] At subsequent NPT review conferences there was some consideration of strengthening Article X, mainly to address the issue of withdrawals allowing a state to facilitate its ongoing non-compliance, but there was no real consideration of altering the time a state had to be a party.[171] Even the 2017 Treaty on the Prohibition of Nuclear Weapons, which according to its Preamble is intended to achieve 'effective progress towards general and complete disarmament', contains a similar withdrawal clause – although it does allow for a slightly longer duration between notification and withdrawal – so states retain flexibility to denounce the treaty even where the intention of the treaty is outright disarmament.[172]

Figure 2.1 Variations in length of membership before member states can issue notification of withdrawal according to treaty type

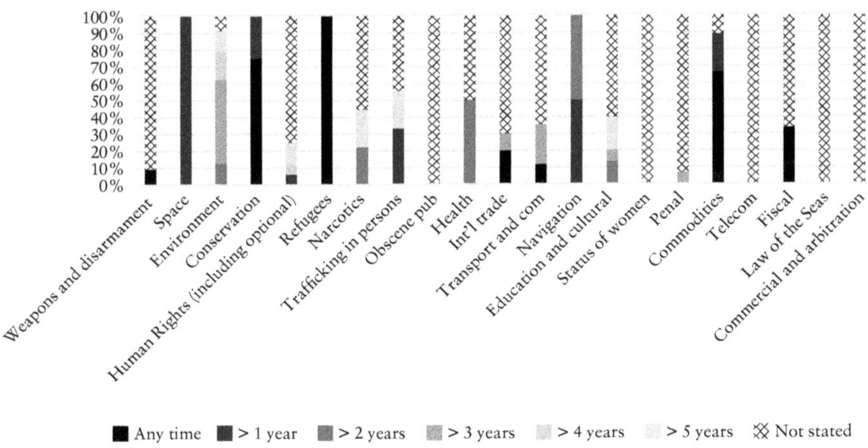

[169] ibid 109–10.

[170] See den Dekker and Coppen (n 61).

[171] See 2005 Review Conference of the Parties to the Treaty on the Non-Proliferation of Nuclear Weapons, 'Working paper on article X (NPT withdrawal) submitted by Australia and New Zealand' (28 April 2005) NPT/CONF.2005/WP.16. The Preparatory Committee for the 2020 review conference also did not engage with any issues of duration, either the time to withdrawal or the time from notice to withdrawal – Preparatory Committee for the 2020 Review Conference of the Parties to the Treaty on the Non-Proliferation of Nuclear Weapons, 'Addressing "Vienna issues": the Comprehensive Nuclear-Test-Ban Treaty; compliance and verification; export controls; cooperation in the peaceful uses of nuclear energy; nuclear safety; nuclear security; and discouraging withdrawal from the Treaty on the Non-Proliferation of Nuclear Weapons' (15 March 2017) NPT/CONF.2020/PC.I/WP.2, paras 64–66.

[172] Treaty on the Prohibition of Nuclear Weapons (adopted 9 August 2017, entered into force 26 October 2020) CN.475.2017.TREATIES-XXVI-9, Art 17.

Equally, the duration of the time from ratification to issuing a denunciation of the treaty can help lock in the treaty's provisions and help cement the benefits that it wishes to create. It is no coincidence that environmental treaties have the longest duration periods, as shown in Figure 2.1. Environmental treaties – as opposed to conservation treaties, which prohibit particular courses of conduct, such as hunting an endangered species – are resolution treaties in that their legal obligations require a state to adopt an action plan to achieve a measurable aim, for example the Montreal Protocol requires signatory states to reduce omissions of substances damaging the ozone layer.[173] Ratification of environmental treaties by states is often driven by a complex range of factors but, as one influential study on the matter concluded, reputational concerns, along with cooperation, are a significant factor in shaping state choices, following a rational choice theoretical framework.[174] After coming to office in 2001, the administration of President George W Bush took the decision not to ratify the treaty and to cease attempts to meet carbon reduction targets, which was not a withdrawal under Article 27 of the Kyoto Protocol (its withdrawal clause), but crucially undermined the collective cooperation on climate change.[175] A major factor behind the design of the withdrawal clause in the Paris Climate Change Agreement was the need to future-proof it against future changes of government in signatory states, out of concern that a change in government could lead to a sudden change in climate change policy, and hence lead to the Agreement's aims being at the mercy of uncertain political events in signatory states.[176] Article 28(1) of the Paris Agreement specified that a party might only withdraw 'after three years from the date on which this Agreement has entered into force for a Party', and there was a further specification that it would take one year from notification to the depository to the withdrawal's becoming effective.[177] For the US and the outgoing Administration of President Barack Obama, who ratified the Paris Agreement by executive action in 2016 during the last year of his presidency, there was an express intention to lock the next political administration into climate change commitments.[178] President Obama's successor, Donald Trump, announced his

[173] MJ Durkee, 'Persuasion Treaties' (2013) 99 *Virginia Law Review* 63, 64.

[174] J Timmons Roberts, BC Parks and AA Vasquez, 'Who Ratifies Environmental Treaties and Why? Institutionalism, Structuralism and Participation by 192 Nations in 22 Treaties' (2004) 4 *Global Environmental Politics* 22.

[175] M Phillipson, 'The United States' Withdrawal from the Kyoto Protocol' (2001) 36 *Irish Jurist* 288.

[176] Christina Voigt 'Institutional arrangements and Final Clauses' in D Klein et al (eds), *The Paris Agreement on Climate Change: Analysis and Commentary* (Oxford University Press, 2017) 352–374 at 370–71; see also L Kemp, 'US Proofing the Paris Climate Agreement' (2017) 17 *Climate Policy* 86.

[177] Paris Agreement (opened for signature 12 December 2015) 3156 UNTS.

[178] Obama used his executive powers to ratify the treaty rather than send it to the US Senate for ratification, in part because at the time there was an anti-climate change consensus in the Senate. He was able to do this because these were no fresh obligations under US law, only extended provisions of an earlier ratified treaty; J Durney, 'Defining the Paris Agreement: A Study of Executive Power and Political Commitments' (2017) 11 *Carbon & Climate Law Review* 234.

intention to withdraw from the Agreement in his first year in office, but it was only in late 2019 that he was able to formally denounce the treaty because of the duration limits imposed by Article 28.[179] The longer waiting times in withdrawal clause push back against a state that is opportunistically committing to an environmental treaty because of the benefits on the international plane, but who withdraws shortly afterwards due to the domestic cost (political and material) of implementing reductions in line with the treaty. Here, the duration provisions of the withdrawal clause are again mediating between the demands for certainty on the international plane and the volatility of domestic politics.

B. The Time from Notification to Exit

Regulating the period of time from notification of an intention to withdraw to the time of actual withdrawal is also vital for the preservation of the principle of good faith, as outlined in section II. In *Nicaragua v United States*, the ICJ's conclusion that the six-month period from notification to withdrawal applied to a declaration having similar effect could be read in part as a protection of the Court as an institution, preventing states from withdrawing from jurisdiction to avoid an adverse judgment.[180] A clause imposing a period until withdrawal is fairly common in treaties involving an enforcement mechanism, and may be complemented by a provision requiring the states to comply with ongoing proceedings against them. For example, under Article 127 of the Rome Statute of the ICC, withdrawals take a year to come into effect and a withdrawal 'shall not affect any cooperation with the Court in connection with criminal investigations and proceedings'.[181] As chapter 3, this helps protect the authority of a judicial tribunal as an institution; and even where there is a lack of clarity, it is presumed that the time between denunciation and the withdrawal's coming into effect should be treated like any other period of treaty membership. When Russia withdrew from the ECHR in March 2022, as a result of the Council of Europe's response to the invasion of Ukraine, it was still bound as a member of the Convention until September 2022.[182]

[179] L Friedman, 'Trump Serves Notice to Quit Paris Climate Agreement' *New York Times* (5 November 2019) at www.nytimes.com/2019/11/04/climate/trump-paris-agreement-climate.html.

[180] *Nicaragua v US* (n 74).

[181] Rome Statute of the International Criminal Court (adopted 17 July 1998, entered in force on 1 July 2002) 2187 UNTS 3854 Art 127.

[182] Committee of Ministers 'Russia ceases to be a Party to the European Convention on Human Rights on 16 September 2022' Council of Europe (23 March 2022) at www.coe.int/en/web/portal/-/russia-ceases-to-be-a-party-to-the-european-convention-of-human-rights-on-16-september-2022 (last accessed 20 September 2022).

Figure 2.2 Variations in time between issuing of notification of denunciation and actual exit date according to treaty type

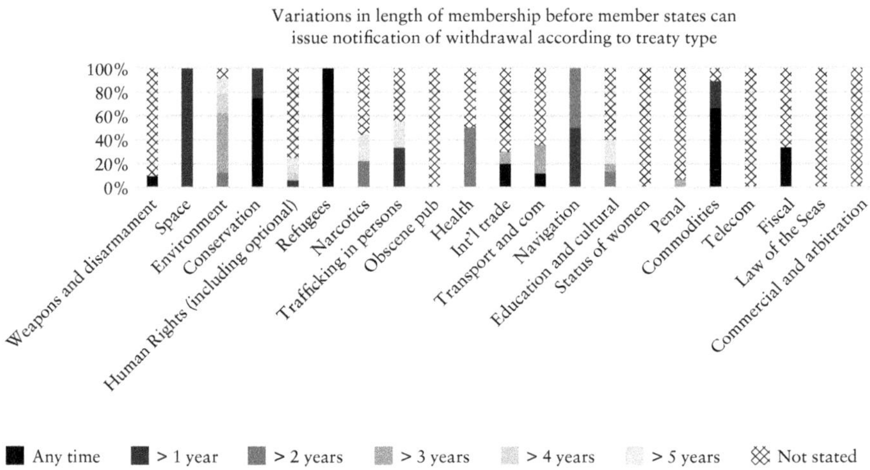

When aggregating the different lengths of time between notice of denunciation and withdrawal's becoming effective by treaty type, what is noteworthy is that there is a strong clustering around the one-year mark – 50 per cent of the treaties in the sample had a one-year duration period following denunciation (see Figure 2.2). This herding is far more pronounced than in relation to the duration period between accession and permission to make a notification – described in section IV.A. Part of this is design-related, as a crucial function of the depository in accepting notification (see section III of this chapter) is to inform other states about the impending withdrawal so that they may respond accordingly.[183] In an age when communications were more primitive, a one-year period would offer sufficient time for this process and for any issues, such as outstanding obligations, to be resolved. It is therefore unsurprising that the duration of one year became fairly standardised, because of the stability it generated, both in terms of ensuring that the withdrawing state discharged its obligations and in terms of recognising and giving effect to its decision to terminate its legal obligations. One area of divergence, however, is weapons control treaties, most of which have duration provisions stipulating less than one year. Again, the motivation behind this relates to the general need to encourage commitment to those regimes managing weapons control, and to the promotion of disarmament norms and general international stability that they promote, and the need to promote relative flexibility over a sensitive area of sovereign interest.[184]

[183] Villiger (n 104).

[184] See den Dekker and Coppen (n 61); L Tabassi and O Elias, 'Disarmament' in M Bowman and D Kritsiotis (eds), *Conceptual and Contextual Perspectives on the Modern Law of Treaties* (Cambridge University Press, 2018) 578–620, 582–83.

The relative scarcity of instantaneous withdrawal – less than 1 per cent of all treaties in the sample with a withdrawal clause allow expressly for instantaneous withdrawal – highlights an important legal principle: the notification of withdrawal under a withdrawal clause is not technically the moment of withdrawal. This point was made in Advocate General Sanchez-Bordona's Opinion in *Wightman* and by the CJEU in its decision in *Ministry of Justice v RO*, both of which noted, in the context of Article 50 TEU (with the obvious caveat about the constitutional nature of the EU law – see section II), that there was a distinction between 'withdrawal' and 'intention to withdraw'.[185] Such a distinction allowed for a metaphorical 'course correction' when a state had denounced the treaty and not yet withdrawn, and the Advocate General's Opinion in *Wightman* referenced a couple of other examples in support of this position.[186] Article 54 does not mention a state's intention to withdraw – it refers to withdrawal as a process – and specifically requires withdrawal 'in conformity with the provisions of the treaty', with the general assumption being that attempts at withdrawal that are not in conformity with the terms of the treaty will be of no legal effect under Article 54.[187] A lawful notice of denunciation (one that fulfils the first duration requirement set out in this section) is the start of the process of withdrawal, not its realisation, and the overwhelming prevalence of the second duration period in withdrawal clauses is indicative of general state practice in recognising two distinct points in time – notice of withdrawal and effectiveness of withdrawal.

CONCLUSION: THINKING ABOUT WITHDRAWAL CLAUSES

One striking thing about withdrawal clauses is how similar they are to one another; the matters discussed in sections III and IV of this chapter are the main scope of variance between different withdrawal clauses. Whilst the time and nature of the notification might vary, the form and direction of withdrawal clauses are more or less the same: a state needs to notify the depository at, or after, a specific time that it wishes to leave, and then at a specified time it will leave. Additional requirements, such as substantive notification requirements, are best understood as evidence of a process of rational design – they are best explained as evidence of an attempt to resolve the cooperation and collaboration problems between states at the time of treaty formation.[188] However, these explanations relate to the commitment stage of an international agreement,

[185] This point is made by M Fitzmaurice and P Merkouris *Treaties in Motion: The Evolution of Treaties from Formation to Termination* (Cambridge University Press, 2020) 291: *Wightman* (n 145); Case C-327/18 – PPU, *Minister for Justice and Equality v RO* [2018] ECLI:EU:C2018:733.

[186] Case C-621/18 *Andy Wightman and Others v Secretary of State for Exiting the European Union* ECLI:EU:C:2018:999, Opinion of AG Campos Sanchez-Bordona, paras 99–101.

[187] T Geigrich, 'Termination of or withdrawal from a treaty under its provisions or by consent of the parties' in O Dörr and K Schmalenbach (eds), *Vienna Convention on the Law of Treaties* (Springer, 2012) 1023.

[188] Koremenos and Nau (n 168).

when a state is considering taking on international legal obligations by ratifying a treaty, and an exit clause can, as noted in chapter 1, offer an incentive for commitment because of the existence of this escape hatch over those commitments.[189] Theoretical work by Koremenos and Meyer has established how these commitments offer the prospect of future bargaining for a state party and an insurance provision against further changes of circumstances, and the promise of political autonomy.[190]

However, no one theoretical template described in this chapter offers a comprehensive explanation as to why a state, when it has decided to leave a legal regime, is incentivised to comply with the provisions of a withdrawal clause. All of the theoretical templates offer various explanations, which can be persuasive, about why a withdrawal clause might affect a state's behaviour in relation to individual elements of a withdrawal clause. Yet, at the same time, there are limitations in all of these explanations that all revolve around the same point: a withdrawal clause is a provision for terminating obligations, and the general theories of compliance in relation to legal obligations run into the same problem – that all of the theoretical models relate to obligations that, for the most part, are terminated by a withdrawal clause. Having taken the decision to withdraw, what causes states to act within a set of bounded constraints when withdrawing, as the remaining chapters set out, is more due to the background culture of legalism in the wider international community, shaping procedural adherence to withdrawal clauses. The way in which withdrawal clauses structure time in the withdrawal process and infer the existence of a hierarchy provides a set of expectations about how states ought to act. These expectations create a form of iterability – there is a template for withdrawing from obligations that they set out, which can be repeated. The language of a notification of withdrawal commences and brings that process into being. Stability, which as chapter 1 sets out is a core aim of the law of withdrawal, is therefore created by a withdrawal clause, not because of the empirical record that those clauses encouraging performance but rather because their written structure describes a form of predictable behaviour from a state. In this, withdrawal clauses fulfil a precise legal function by conforming to Philip Allott's definition of law's presupposing 'a society whose structures and systems make possible … the mutual condition of the legal and the non-legal'.[191] The language of a withdrawal clause is precisely about this kind of line-drawing exercise.

[189] See ch 1, section II.

[190] Change of circumstances and the doctrine of *rebus sic stantibus* is set out in more detail in Chapter One.

[191] P Allot, 'The Concept of International Law' in M Byers (ed), *The Role of Law in international Politics: Essays in International Relations and International Law* (Oxford University Press, 2000) 70.

3

Obligations after Withdrawal

INTRODUCTION

As Rosalyn Higgins described it, the international legal system works when the shared belief that the legal act of state consent that happened in a 'then' is relevant to and governs the 'now'.[1] As outlined in chapter 2, when a state successfully engages a withdrawal clause, it is embarking on a process of removing the legal obligations entered into by that state, imposed by the regime from which they are withdrawing. The eventual end point is captured in Article 70 of the Vienna Convention on the Law of Treaties (VCLT),[2] which provides that on the date that denunciation becomes effective, this 'releases the parties from any obligation further to perform the treaty'. Yet in the process of withdrawing from a legal regime a party can incur obligations that may persist after that party has formally left that regime. These can include obligations to pay moneys owed, to continue to allow access to an international tribunal for its citizens in certain cases, or to allow an organisation to carry on investigations. As section I of this chapter describes, it is possible to clearly identify the sources of these legal obligations, but that positivist exercise does not explain why such obligations exists or why the withdrawing state would comply with them. Withdrawal, to use Higgins' framing, is intended to create a 'now' where the withdrawing state is unincumbered by legal obligations it accepted once upon a 'then'. Legal obligations continuing after exit challenge the existence of the 'now' the state is seeking to construct. The existence of such obligations also poses a challenge for various varieties of realist and neo-realist theories that explain obligations under a treaty or as a member of an organisation, and compliance with those obligations in terms of an alignment of interests between the state and the legal regime in question.[3] In the case of withdrawal, the withdrawing state's interests in maintaining obligations after exit may not align with its interests in pursuing the withdrawal in the first place. Equally, this poses a problem for

[1] R Higgins, 'Time and the Law: International Perspectives on an Old Problem' (1997) 46 *ICLQ* 501, 501.

[2] Vienna Convention on the Law of Treaties (adopted 23 May 1969, entered into force 27 January 1980) 1155 UNTS 331 (VCLT) Art 70.

[3] Making this argument, see R O'Keohane, 'International relations and international law: two optics' (1997) 38 *Harvard International Law Journal* 487; for an outline of realist theory on this point, see A Hurrell *On Global Order: Power, Values, and the Constitution of International Society* (Oxford University Press, 2007) 71.

constructivist or social theorists of international obligations, who reason, like Oran Young does, that obligations arise through the 'social institutions' created by states and the 'practices' of those institutions.[4] In the case of withdrawal, a state is deliberately seeking to alter its social status, and has already to an extent internalised that alteration by pursing withdrawal in the first place. A constructivist would likely claim in response that states will continue to observe the rules of international law even if it is not in their interests to do so, because the social question supersedes the precise legal regime in which interaction occurs and instead refers to the broader interactions of states on the international plane.[5]

A more nuanced theoretical picture is required, as the legal obligations on states after exit come from a number of different sources that are themselves often the subject of fierce contestation. Legal principles such as *pacta sunt servanda* have to operate in a climate where a state's interests may have radically diverged from those of the regime from which it wishes to withdraw; its ideological positions about that regime are likely to be evolving and the social identity of that state may be in flux. This complex political reality poses challenges for realist, liberal and constructivist explanations of legal obligations, requiring new theoretical explanations. Samuel Barkin's attempt to fuse realist and constructivist theories focuses on the non-idealist motivation behind the social construction of the international order, examining 'the way in which power structures affect patterns of normative change in international relations and, conversely, the way in which a particular set of norms affect power structures'.[6] Understanding the role of power structures in the wider international order is particularly important in these cases, as the persistence of obligations, and in many cases compliance with those obligations, belies the idea of the international system as a truly anarchic order with legal obligations mainly arising out of an alignment of interests between states. It also supports some arguments about the role of power made by world systems theorists, who take a longer historical view of the evolution of power in the international system and situate the role of transnational forces, in particular the role of capital, as playing a decisive role in the structure of international society.[7] Alongside this general theoretical framework it is important to acknowledge the growing dominance of rights-based arguments transcending the fact of formal obligation, a phenomenon that, Anne Peters notes, exerts a series of 'pull' factors on individuals and governments, and hence on states in their international interactions.[8]

[4] O Young, *International Cooperation: Building Regimes for Natural Resources and the Environment* (Cornell University Press, 1989) 5–12.

[5] A Arend, *Legal Rules and International Society* (Oxford University Press, 1999) 131; JG Ruggie, 'What Makes the World Hang Together? Neo-Utilitarianism and the Social Constructivist Challenge' (1998) 52 *International Organization* 855.

[6] S Barking, 'Realist Constructivism' (2003) 5 *International Studies Review* 325, 337.

[7] I Wallerstein, *World-systems Analysis: An Introduction* (Duke University Press, 2004) 1–6.

[8] A Peters, *Beyond Human Rights: The Legal Status of the Individual in International Law* (Cambridge University Press, 2016) 534–37.

Although critical theorists have often argued that the deployment of rights in this manner points towards an implicit hierarchy in international law, or a transnational cosmopolitanism, there is another important dimension to the individual rights often at issue in treaty withdrawal.[9] They operate, as illustrated below, as a form of a generalised sovereign constraint on decision making by states, whereby an individual within the withdrawing state or individual interests outside the state claim as a matter of international law that the withdrawing state should respect their rights even though it has terminated, or is in the process of terminating, the formal legal obligations creating those rights. What ties together the different rights described in this chapter, which emerge from disparate sources of law – from investment treaties to human rights instruments – is the idea that the protection of those rights assumes importance because they underpin the norms of a wider international society. The idea of an international society is one often associated with the English school of international relations theory, which maintains that international law provides a normative framework for the operation of an international society.[10] Under this theoretical framework, even after the instrument imposing formal legal obligations in respect of rights or obligations has been departed from, those regimes maintain their 'pull factor' because of their importance within wider international society.[11] International society is not a rigid construct in this theory; most thinkers in the English school subscribe to a more anarchic picture of international society, underpinned by international legal institutions and doctrines which provide a sense of order.[12] Of great importance is the concept outlined in chapter 1, which will be further explored in chapter 5, that is, the general sense of stability that acts as underpinning for international society and as a 'pull factor' for complying with withdrawal clauses. For a number of theorists of the English school, compliance with international law occurs because it helps with the ordering of an otherwise anarchic international society.[13] As will be shown, the framing of obligations after exit as being necessary for wider stability in the

[9] For examples of these arguments, see D Otto, 'Rethinking universals: opening transformative possibilities in international human rights law' (1997) 18 *Australian Yearbook of International Law* 1; R Fine, 'Cosmopolitanism and human rights: radicalism in a global age' (2009) 40 *Metaphilosophy* 8; C Douzinas *Human Rights and Empire: The Political Philosophy of Cosmopolitanism* (Routledge, 2007) ch 1.

[10] P Wilson, 'The English School's approach to international law' in C Navari (ed), *Theorising International Society: English School Methods* (Palgrave Macmillan, 2009) 167–188, 168.

[11] Abbott situates the English school in constructivist theory in making this point: K Abbott, 'International Relations Theory, International Law, and the Regime Governing Atrocities in Internal Conflicts' (1999) 93 *American Journal of International Law* 361, 367–68. However, others have stressed the way the English school actually engages in 'a conversation between different theoretical positions': T Dunne, *Inventing International Society: A History of the English School* (Palgrave, 1998) 8.

[12] For a summary, see B Buzan, *An Introduction to the English School of International Relations: The Societal Approach* (Polity, 2014) 12–20.

[13] B Devlen, P James and Ö Özdamar, 'The English School, International Relations, and Progress' (2005) 7 *International Studies Review* 171, 177–78.

international system provides a powerful normative justification for continued compliance with those obligations. There is a rich theoretical literature on the English school of international relations, and the purpose of this chapter is not to take a position in that work but to show how it helps plug a gap in explanations about what the justification is for compliance with withdrawal clauses beyond the moment of withdrawal. It is important to distinguish between the way in which withdrawal clauses protect rights beyond exit and the way in which they may attempt to project the power of institutions beyond the moment of withdrawal. Before that, however, it is necessary to analyse the sources of the law on obligations beyond the moment of the withdrawal.

I. THE SOURCES OF LAW FOR OBLIGATIONS ON EXIT

It is helpful to see obligations imposing themselves on states at the moment of withdrawal in two ways. First, there are obligations specifically contained in withdrawal clause themselves that relate to breaches of other obligations under the treaty or continuing obligations after exit. The obligation on the state following exit arises because the withdrawal clause itself contains provisions sometimes referred to as 'sunset' (which deal with legal obligations on departure) or 'savings' provisions (which deal with ongoing legal obligations). Second, there is a general obligation in relation to the consequences of continuing breaches of obligations on the part of the withdrawing state, which means that even if a state withdraws from the regime creating an obligation, it is still responsible for any ongoing consequences. These obligations arise regardless of the provisions of an exit clause and are rooted in the fact of the original obligation. This engages the law of state responsibility as defined in the 2001 Draft Articles on Responsibility of States for Internationally Wrongful Acts (ARS), which, whilst not formally binding, is an authoritative synthesis of the law of state responsibility often relied on by international tribunals.

A. Obligations within Withdrawal Clauses

Strictly speaking, withdrawal clauses are no different from any other treaty provision: Article 54 VCLT provides that withdrawal must take place in 'conformity with the provisions of the treaty'. It does not stipulate that there any special rules applying to these provisions, nor do any other articles of the VCLT dealing with exit suggest that those governing withdrawal should be any different from other provisions in a treaty, meaning that the rules on *pacta sunt servanda* apply to this as to any other provision.[14] Article 1 of the League of

[14] SI Lekkas and A Tzanakopoulos, 'Pacta sunt servanda versus flexibility in the suspension and termination of treaties' in C Tams, A Tzanakopoulos and A Zimmermann (eds), *Research Handbook on the Law of Treaties* (Edward Elgar, 2014) 337.

Nations Covenant allowed for states to withdraw from the League, provided that all their 'international obligations and … obligations under this Covenant shall have been fulfilled at the time of its withdrawal'.[15] Among legal commentators in the early 1920s, there was some dispute about what this meant, but one common point of agreement was that the departing state was obliged to settle any debts owed to the League.[16] When Costa Rica withdrew from the League of Nations in 1924, it attached a cheque for its membership fees to its letter denouncing the League Covenant.[17] Any failure to meet obligations such as these would be a breach of that obligation, because even though the withdrawing state had taken the decision not to be subject to the legal obligations of the regime from which it was withdrawing, it still, as an administrative unit, consented to the treaty and a clause entailing obligations in the event of withdrawal.[18] It is therefore not really open to a state to say its consent to be bound by the clause had changed due to the fact of withdrawal: that would be a breach of the good faith principle; many obligations upon a state are contingent upon or only come into force when future events occur, and the obligations on a state in a withdrawal clause would be one of them.[19] Article 42 VCLT echoes these principles, saying that the 'validity of a treaty or of the consent of a State to be bound' by it may be 'impeached only through the application of the present Convention' and when read alongside Articles 54 and 56(1)b, which require a state to withdraw in line with a treaty's terms or obtain permission from other parties to withdraw, would indicate that the terms of withdrawal clauses are binding on a state following the act of withdrawal. If treaty exit occurs as a means of safeguarding a state's interest in the light of changing circumstances and the obligations imposed on a state upon exit are incompatible with the change of circumstances that precipitated withdrawal in the first place, it is unlikely that those obligations are going to be fulfilled.[20]

The elaboration of the principle of *pacta sunt servanda* in the VCLT did not tackle these and other dilemmas created by withdrawal. The Waldock Third Report on the Law of Treaties simply stated that 'a treaty is binding upon the parties and must be applied by them in good faith in accordance with its terms', indicating that both the obligations in exit clauses and any breaches of any other

[15] The Covenant of the League of Nations (adopted on 28 June 1919, entered into force 10 January 1920) Art 1.

[16] M Hudson, 'Membership in the League of Nations' (1924) 18 *American Journal of International Law* 436; R Kay Wyllys 'Latin America and the League' (1928) 4 *Social Science* 60, 66.

[17] JJ Burns, 'Conditions of Withdrawal from the League of Nations' (1935) 29 *American Journal of International Law* 40, 44.

[18] A Orakhelashvili, 'The origins of consensual positivism: Pufendorf, Wolff and Vattel' in A Orakhelashvili (ed), *Research Handbook on the Theory and History of International Law*, 2nd edition (Edward Elgar, 2020) 90.

[19] K Schmalenbach, 'Article 26' in O Dörr and K Schmalenbach (eds), *Vienna Convention on the Law of Treaties* (Springer, 2018) 470.

[20] Binder acknowledges that exit can serve as a form of accommodation of changed circumstances, but contends that such cases are rare: C Binder, 'Stability and Change in Times of Fragmentation: The Limits of Pacta Sunt Servanda Revisited' (2012) 25 *Leiden Journal of International Law* 909.

clauses prior to exit are binding on a state.[21] This describes the legitimate expectation on all parties but does not draw any temporal distinction between the moments of entry and exit, which might be politically relevant for the withdrawing state.[22] During the drafting of the VCLT, a paragraph was included that stated that parties to a treaty should refrain 'from any acts calculated to prevent the due execution' of treaty provisions, which would have been relevant for a scenario in which ongoing obligations rooted in the instrument being withdrawn from were in question, but this never made it into the final VCLT text.[23] Instead, provisions such as Article 42 VCLT fix *pacta sunt servanda* in the initial temporal moment of accession and try to restrict disputes about a treaty's obligations after withdrawal to the terms of that treaty itself.[24] An obligation in a withdrawal clause is therefore binding on a state utilising that clause, regardless of the factual circumstances behind the operation of that clause, although this rather strict construction separates the existence of an obligation from the fact of its operation.

Some human rights treaties, such as the International Covenant on Economic Social and Cultural Rights,[25] do not contain a withdrawal clause. Other human rights treaties contain a withdrawal clause with a temporal constraint; for example, the withdrawal clause of the Convention on the Elimination of all forms of Racial Discrimination (CERD) provides that 'denunciation shall take effect one year after the date of receipt of the notification by the [UN] Secretary General'.[26] Other withdrawal clauses have savings or sunset provisions, specifying that a state is required to prevent or resolve a situation that may have been a breach of its obligations under the treaty from which it was withdrawing.[27] A good example is Article 58 of the European Convention on Human Rights (ECHR), which allows for denunciation after a period of five years, which becomes effective six months after the notice of denunciation, but also clearly states that the withdrawing state is not freed of responsibility for 'any act which, being capable

[21] Sir Humphrey Waldock, 'Third Report' [1964] II *Yearbook of the International Law Commission* 7, draft art 55.

[22] R Kolb, *Good Faith in International Law* (Hart Publishing, 2017) 238.

[23] R Gardiner, *Treaty Interpretation*, 2nd edn (Oxford University Press, 2017) 169.

[24] J Klabbers, 'Reluctant Grundnormen: Articles 31(3)(C) and 42 of the Vienna Convention on the Law of Treaties and the Fragmentation of International Law' in M Fitzmaurice, M Vogiatzi and M Craven (eds), *Time, History and International Law* (Brill Nijhoff, 2007) 141–162, 142.

[25] International Covenant on Economic Social and Cultural Rights. (adopted 16 December 1966, entered in force 3 January 1976) 993 UNTS 3).

[26] Convention on the Elimination of all forms of Racial Discrimination (adopted 7 March 1966, entered into force 4 January 1969), 660 UNTS 195 (CERD), Art 21.

[27] For example, see Optional Protocol to the Convention on the Elimination of All Forms of Discrimination against Women (adopted 6 October 1999, entry into force 22 December 2000) 2131 UNTS 83, Art 19; Optional Protocol to the International Covenant on Civil and Political Rights (adopted 16 December 1966, entered into force 23 March 1976) 999 UNTS 171, Art 12 ('Optional Protocol 1 to the ICCPR').

of constituting a violation of such obligations, may have been performed by it before the date at which the denunciation became effective'.[28] The rationale for this is rooted in the principle of good faith, prohibiting a state from benefiting from its breach of obligations by escaping from the legal consequences of the human rights violations it was committing. A similar provision may be found in the withdrawal clause of the American Convention on Human Rights (ACHR), and it is noteworthy that both these provisions require the withdrawing state to prevent the violation itself, not just to permit the consideration of any alleged violation by an international body.[29] The practical effect is to extend the temporal scope of a human rights instrument beyond the moment of withdrawal, as it can commit the withdrawing state to continuing to comply with the decisions of a tribunal or treaty body with respect to violations of rights that occurred whilst the state was a party to the treaty. As the case study below on the Caribbean death penalty shows, the complexity surrounding these clauses emerges when a state expressly seeks to exit in order not to have rights obligations towards an individual or group of individuals.

In the absence of a withdrawal clause imposing these kinds of clear obligations on the withdrawing state, there is greater scope for that state to ignore decisions of the international tribunal of the regime it is leaving. A good example of this is the Protocol to the African Charter on Human and Peoples' Rights on the Establishment of an African Court on Human and Peoples' Rights (the Court Protocol), which allows states to make a declaration saying they will allow the Court to hear individual petitions from individuals and non-governmental organisations (NGOs) in their jurisdiction.[30] As outlined in chapter 2, the Court had held in *Umuhoza v Rwanda* that the withdrawal of a declaration did not terminate individual proceedings, because to so would be contrary to the good faith principle.[31] There is nothing in the text of the Protocol, however, about what a state is required to do in respect of a matter that is ongoing at the time of the withdrawal of a declaration. In 2020, the Côte d'Ivoire withdrew its declaration to the Court Protocol after the African Court

[28] Convention for the Protection of Human Rights and Fundamental Freedoms (European Convention on Human Rights, as amended) (ECHR) (adopted 4 November 1950, entered into force 3 September 1953) CETS 005 Art 58.

[29] McRorty contrasts this with Optional Protocol 1 to the ICCPR (n 27): G McRorty, 'Reservations of Virtue? Lessons from Trinidad and Tobago's Reservation to the First Optional Protocol' (2001) 23 *Human Rights Quarterly* 769, 782; American Convention on Human Rights (adopted 22 November 1969 entered into force 27 August 1979) 1114 UNTS 123 Art 78.

[30] Protocol to the African Charter on Human and Peoples' Rights on the Establishment of an African Court on Human and Peoples' Rights, Art 34(6).The intention behind this was to give states a control mechanism: G Bekker, 'The African Court on Human and Peoples' Rights: Safeguarding the interests of African states' (2007) 51 *Journal of African Law* 151.

[31] *Victoire Ingabire Umuhoza v The Republic of Rwanda* (Merits) App no 003/2014 (ACHPR, 3 June 2016).

ordered the Government to suspend the arrest warrant of Guillaume Soro, a former rebel leader, who was attempting to compete in presidential elections.[32] The Government of the Côte d'Ivoire attacked the decision for being 'political' and creating 'insecurity', making it clear that it was not going to be implementing the decision.[33] Equally, Benin withdrew its Court Protocol Declaration in response to a Court decision on provisional measures in *Ghaby Kodeih v Benin*, a case arising out of series of commercial decisions surrounding loans to construct a hotel.[34] Claiming the decision was causing 'disarray in the business community', the Government refused to implement it and, following a ruling of the Constitutional Court, also held that the provisions allowing individual applications to the Economic Community of West African States (ECOWAS) Court of Justice were also invalid.[35] There had been criticism of some of these Court decisions, but those critics were well aware of the damage to the rule of law more broadly that could be caused by withdrawal from the individual jurisdiction of the Court Protocol.[36] Article 30 of the Protocol says that states 'undertake to comply with the judgment in any case to which they are parties', and even though the Protocol is careful to differentiate between individual cases and other applications, the use of 'any' would indicate that the withdrawing state is still bound to execute the decision.[37]

B. Breaches of Obligations Prior to Withdrawal

As a matter of law, a state is still bound by the terms of a treaty until the moment a denunciation becomes effective, either under the terms of a withdrawal clause or, in cases where there is no withdrawal clause, until an agreement is reached about

[32] *Soro & Others v Côte d'Ivoire* (Provisional Measures Order) App no 12/2020 (ACHPR, 22 April 2020).

[33] IJRC, 'Benin and Côte d'Ivoire to withdraw Individual Access to African Court' International Justice Resource Centre (6 May 2020) at https://ijrcenter.org/2020/05/06/benin-and-cote-divoire-to-withdraw-individual-access-to-african-court/ (accessed 10 July 2021).

[34] *Ghaby Kodeih v Benin* (Ruling) App no 006/2020 (ACHPR, 30 September 2021). There was some doubt about whether it was this decision or the decision in *Sébastian Germain Ajavon v Benin* (Judgment) (Reparation) App no 013/2017 (ACHPR, 2019) that was at issue in Benin's withdrawal: Centre for Human Rights, 'Press Statement: Centre for Human Rights expresses concern about the withdrawal of direct individual access to the African Court by Benin and Côte D'ivoire', Center for Human Rights, University of Pretoria Faculty of Law (5 May 2020) at www.chr.up.ac.za/press-statements/2073-centre-for-human-rights-expresses-concern-about-the-withdrawal-of-direct-individual-access-to-the-african-court-by-benin-and-cote-d-ivoire (accessed 10 September 2021 as are all subsequent links unless stated otherwise).

[35] V Agué, 'ECOWAS Court of Justice: the Constitutional Court of Benin renders a decision with serious consequences' *Rtb* (10 May 2020) at http://ortb.bj/politique/3165-cour-de-la-justice-de-la-cedeao-la-cour-constitutionnelle-rend-une-decision-lourde-de-consequences-au-benin/.

[36] AK Zouapet, '"Victim of its commitment ... You, passerby, a tear to the proclaimed virtue": Should the epitaph of the African Court on Human and Peoples' Rights be prepared?' *EJIL Talk* (5 May 2020) at www.ejiltalk.org/victim-of-its-commitment-you-passerby-a-tear-to-the-proclaimed-virtue-should-the-epitaph-of-the-african-court-on-human-and-peoples-rights-be-prepared/.

[37] African Court Protocol (n 30) Art 30.

withdrawal. Therefore, a breach of a substantive obligation prior to that moment is still a breach. Although there is some contestation about what constitutes a breach of an obligation, it is generally accepted that a state will still be responsible for the consequences of a breach committed prior to the act of withdrawal.[38] The combined effect of both Article 42 VCLT, which requires denunciation to operate under the principles of good faith, and Article 60, which governs termination on grounds of breach, restricting a defaulting party from claiming breach as a ground for denunciation, means that a right to mitigate damages from a breach of a treaty survives a treaty's termination or a state's withdrawal from that treaty.[39] Ultimately the decision to pursue the withdrawing party for the consequences of any breach of obligation will, as Arie David observes, be tempered by political trade-offs: 'parties may often be willing to lose on a particular issue because they perceive that their gains from existing and future international cooperation are greater than the losses they suffer'.[40] By providing a framework dictating the consequences of a breach of an obligation and the circumstances in which a treaty might be suspended or terminated in the event of a breach, Article 60 VCLT creates a common default position, designed to encourage states to avoid a breach of their obligations and use the legal mechanisms within treaty law, such as denunciation, to alter the legal status of their obligations.[41] In respect of withdrawal, the VCLT's framework is reinforced by the law on state responsibility, and in *Gabčikovo-Nagymaros* the International Court of Justice (ICJ) clarified that the determination of whether a treaty is in force is a matter for treaty law; if the obligation is no longer in force then the matter is one for the law of state responsibility.[42] Article 13 of the ARS 2001 establishes that a state is 'bound by the obligation in question at the time the act occurs', which, as the official commentary notes, entails that 'once responsibility has accrued as a result of an internationally wrongful act, it is not affected by the subsequent termination of the obligation'.[43]

There is a two-part justification for this. First, the temporal underpinning of *pacta sunt servanda* requires that states are bound by the commitments they have made in the past, not on their attitude to those commitments once a dispute has arisen – a position outlined by the Permanent Court of Arbitration in the *Islands of Palmas Case*, where it held that a 'juridical fact must be

[38] C Chinkin, 'Non-performance of International Agreements' (1982) 17 *Texas International Law Journal* 387, 388. On the principle of a breach's surviving withdrawal, see MM, Gomaa *Suspension or Termination of Treaties on Grounds of Breach* (Martinus Nijhoff Publishers, 1996) 53–54.

[39] K vin der Decken, 'Validity and Continuance in force of Treaties' in O Dörr and K Schmalenbach (eds), *Vienna Convention on the Law of Treaties* (Springer, 2012) 797–798.

[40] A David, *The Strategy of Treaty Termination; Lawful Breaches and Retaliations* (Yale University Press, 1975) 223.

[41] J Setear, 'Responses to Breach of a Treaty and Rationalist International Relations Theory: The Rules of Release and Remediation in the Law of Treaties and the Law of State Responsibility' (1997) 83 *Virginia Law Review* 1, 23.

[42] *Gabčikovo-Nagymaros Project (Hungary/Slovakia)* (Judgment) [1997] ICJ Rep p. 7, 38.

[43] ILC, 'Report of the International Law Commission on the Work of the 53rd Session' (23 April–1 June 2001 and 2 July–10 August 2001), UN Doc A/56/10.

appreciated in the light of the law contemporary with it'.[44] From what might be termed a conventional rationalist perspective, states have every incentive for the *pacta sunt servanda* doctrine to operate this way and to exert pressure on other states to adhere to the doctrine in the interests of predictability, but also in the interests of establishing trust between state parties.[45] Second, there is a broader interest in maintaining state responsibility for breaches prior to withdrawal in order to maintain a framework of law that can resolve claims made by an injured party. The ICJ recognised in the *Certain Phosphate Lands* case that if Australia's obligations as a League of Nations trustee for Nauru terminated at the end of its trusteeship without its covering the cost of rehabilitating land damaged by phosphorus, this could interfere with 'the legitimate demands of the Nauruan people', and therefore any rights Nauru had to the 'rehabilitation of the lands remained' unaffected by the trusteeship's termination.[46] In his Separate Opinion, Judge Shahabuddeen expressed the view that protecting the interests of Nauru was essential for the equality of states, and that those interests had not been protected while Australia had been in control of the trusteeship because Australia had failed to 'exercise these comprehensive governmental powers so as to regulate the phosphate industry in such a way as to secure the interests of the people of Nauru'.[47] This reasoning placed emphasis on the role of legal obligation over state interests, referring to what those in the English school of international relations termed 'institutions of international society' where, as Hedley Bull argues, states are 'programmed to operate within a framework of established principles'.[48] Obligations for breaches prior to withdrawal persist in part because of the rule orientation of international society, which ensures that they have a life beyond the lifespan of a state's legal commitments.[49] It would be, from the perspective of the English school, in the interests of international society at large that damages arising from breaches of obligations are compensated for because otherwise that would undermine the wider stability of international society which functions to allow states to interact with one another.[50]

These justifications raise a further issue, that is, whether there is a requirement for damage, or a damaged state, to claim for the breach of an obligation

[44] *Island of Palmas (Netherlands/United States of America)*, UNRIAA vol II, 4 April 1928, p. 829, 845.

[45] J Puciato and M Danek, 'A game-theoretic explanation for the emergence of the second-order rule of justice pacta sunt servanda' (2014) 16 *Internetowy Przegląd Prawniczy TBSP UJ* 45.

[46] *Certain Phosphate Lands in Nauru (Nauru v Australia)* (Preliminary Objections, Judgment) [1992] ICJ Rep 240.

[47] ibid, Separate Opinion of Judge Shahabuddeen at 282.

[48] H Bull, *The Anarchical Society: A Study of Order in World Politics*, 4th edn (Palgrave Macmillan, 2012) 133–40.

[49] For a general explanation of the English School and international law, see Wilson (n 9); EM de Souza, 'The View of the English School of International Relations on International Law', presented at the International Studies Association (ISA), New York, 15–18 February 2009.

[50] Mayall describes international society and its rules as being those needed to allow states to 'rub along' together James Mayall, *World Politics: Progress and Its Limits* (Polity Press, 2000) 29.

by the withdrawing state. A broader duty for material compensation exists under the ARS, but as Federica Paddeu outlines, the customary status of this rule is questionable and subject to a number of uncertainties, and it is open for a state to plead justification for causing material damage to another.[51] In *Northern Cameroons*, the newly independent Republic of Cameroon claimed that the UK, whilst administering the League of Nations Trust over the territory, had created a set of conditions that had led to Nigeria's obtaining the northern part of the Cameroons. This dispute was rooted in colonial era politics: the British had invaded Cameroon in 1914 as it was a German colony, and after the First World War had taken over as the colonial administrator of the Trusteeship Agreement for the Territory of the Cameroons, leading to the shaping of two very distinct entities – Southern Cameroon, which was Francophone and controlled by France, and Northern Cameroon, which the British folded into their existing colony of Nigeria.[52] The claim from Cameroon was that the way the trusteeship had evolved under the stewardship of the British had been a breach of their duties whilst acting as trustees. In substance, it was an argument that decades of colonial administration had led to a situation where, upon independence, the population of Northern Cameroon identified more with Nigeria than with Cameroon. In principle the ICJ held that damages were claimable and would not be liquidated by the trust's termination, but the Court was unclear what remedy or cause of action Cameroon was seeking, as the behaviour about which Cameroon was complaining was years of notionally lawful administration, the damage being largely political and not material.[53] Concluding that a breach of treaty involves 'adjudication [of] an actual controversy involving a conflict of legal interests between the parties', the ICJ held that it was not going to take what would amount to 'political action' because, as the Court saw it, 'no question of actual legal rights is involved'.[54] All of the trusteeship agreements shaped and determined the sovereignty of colonial territories and the states they were to become after independence, so in effect this was litigation against the consequences of colonialism.[55] Yet *Northern Cameroons* suffered from the problem that it was premised on the restitution of an extinct legal order, or more accurately a declaration about the behaviour of an extinct legal order, rather than directly restoring tangible material loss.[56]

[51] F Paddeu, *Justification and Excuse in International Law: Concept and Theory of General Defences* (Cambridge University Press, 2018) 78–81.

[52] For a historical overview of this, see M Njeuma, 'Reunification and Political Opportunism in the Making of Cameroon's Independence' (1995) 41 *Paideuma: Mitteilungen zur Kulturkunde* 27.

[53] *Northern Cameroons (Cameroon v. United Kingdom)* Preliminary Objections, Judgment of 2 December 1963: I.C. J. Reports 1963, p. 15."

[54] ibid p.37.

[55] A Anghie, *Imperialism, Sovereignty and the Making of International Law*, 2nd edn (Cambridge University Press, 2007) 115–23.

[56] H Ascensio, 'Article 70' in O Corton and P Klein (eds), *The Vienna Conventions on the Law of Treaties: A Commentary*, vol 1 (Oxford University Press, 2011) 1603.

However, as Crawford argues, following on from the *SS Wimbledon* decision and the voluntarist philosophy of international obligation it engendered (described in chapter 1), it has long been accepted that a state may bind itself in theory to obligations of all sorts, and there is no obvious reason why damage needs to be a prerequisite of a claim for a breach of an obligation.[57] The *Rainbow Warrior* arbitration arose from the political consequences stemming from the bombing of a Greenpeace ship in Auckland harbour in 1985 by agents of the French Direction générale de la Sécurité extérieure (DGSE), which, after protracted political battles and threats of retaliation, led to an agreement between New Zealand and France about the future of the agents involved in the bombing.[58] The arbitration between the two countries arose because France had seemingly reneged on the agreement between them by not continuing to detain one of the agents on the Island of Hao. But the French Government maintained that by the time this had happened, the agreement had expired and there was no material injury to New Zealand from failing to detain someone in a particular place.[59] The arbitrators concluded, however, that this did not exempt France from being held responsible for a breach of its obligations committed while they were in force, as the breach itself acquired an existence independent from the treaty that gave rise to the obligation.[60] From a realist perspective, a breach's acquisition of an independent existence makes sense as a means of recognising state interests post-withdrawal, and encourages the withdrawing state to resolve the consequences of any breaches so that the parties are returned to a pre-treaty position and may subsequently strike up appropriate bargains between themselves.[61]

Equally, from the perspective of the constructivist or the English school, remedying the consequences of a breach of obligations prior to withdrawal enables the protection of international society at large or should be done to preserve social relations with other states.[62] Even though proposals to expressly link a breach of obligation to the presence of damage were not included in the final draft of the ARS, a compensatory logic is a strong feature of the decisions described above and in some of the reasoning explaining the theoretical justifications behind those decisions.[63] Compensation as a means of settling disputes

[57] J Crawford, *State Responsibility: The General Part* (Cambridge University Press, 2011) 56. See also *SS Wimbledon,* 1923 PCIJ Rep Series A No 1, 25 (28 June).

[58] *Rainbow Warrior (New Zealand v France)* (Arbitration Tribunal) (1990) 82 ILR 499. For background, see R Thakur, 'A Dispute of Many Colours: France, New Zealand and the "Rainbow Warrior" Affair' (1986) 42 *The World Today* 209.

[59] *Rainbow Warrior* (n 58).

[60] ibid.

[61] E Posner and A Sykes, 'Efficient breach of international law: optimal remedies, "legalized noncompliance", and related issues' (2011) 110 *Michigan Law Review* 243, 286.

[62] For this overview of international as society and why this school of thought might draw that conclusion, see A Linklater and H Suganami, *The English School of International Relations: A Contemporary Reassessment* (Cambridge University Press, 2006) 74–80.

[63] Crawford (n 57) 55–56.

arising from withdrawal can be a way of politically terminating issues post-withdrawal. But there are certain rights and interests for which it is difficult to provide compensation. For example, disputes involving the authority of an institution, such as access to a tribunal, are ones where states may not be subject to the same pressures or behavioural factors as those which involve compliance with an obligation relating to property. In *Ajavon v Benin*, the ACHPR ordered the reinstatement of a radio station that had been closed by the Government as part of its campaign against the claimant, Sebastian Ajavon, and other opposition figures.[64] The Government had also excluded his supporters from elections in May 2020, and in April 2020 the African Court ordered them to be suspended.[65] This ruling was made after Benin had withdrawn from the Optional Protocol, and although the proceedings were able to continue, the Government ignored the Court order and the elections went ahead anyway.[66] These were both violations of rights and breaches of the withdrawing state's obligation's in relation to the execution of Court judgments but, given the nature of the remedy required, would not be susceptible to compensation.

II. THE RIGHT TO A HEARING AFTER EXIT

One of the ways in which withdrawal clauses aim to prevent the sort of situation described in section I, where the withdrawal of a declaration for a protocol on adjudication has the effect of terminating the jurisdiction of a tribunal, is to insert a savings or survival provisions into a withdrawal clause.[67] These can preserve access to a tribunal after withdrawal becomes effective, for matters brought to that body prior to the date of a withdrawal becoming effective. There is a broader rights-based argument at work in situations where these clauses are used. The right of access to tribunals or adjudication is bound up in the broader concept of a right to a fair trial or the right to a hearing. Access to justice is central to a conception of international law founded on the rights of the individual, rather than the rights of states, which since 1945 has been at the core of international law, with emphasis on human rights, as defined by

[64] *Sébastian Germain Ajavon v Benin* (Judgment) (Reparation) App no 013/2017 (ACHPR, 2019). For factual context, see Agence France-Presse, 'Benin Opposition Radio Sacks Staff After License Pulled' *VOA News* (23 January 2020) at www.voanews.com/press-freedom/benin-opposition-radio-sacks-staff-after-license-pulled.

[65] SH Adjolohoun, 'A crisis of design and judicial practice? Curbing state disengagement from the African Court on Human and Peoples' Rights' (2020) 20 *African Human Rights Law Journal* 1, 12.

[66] JE Abatan and M Matongbada, 'Benin's local elections further reduce the political space' Institute for Security Studies (27 May 2020) at https://issafrica.org/iss-today/benins-local-elections-further-reduce-the-political-space.

[67] S-I Lekkas and A Tzanakopoulos, 'Pacta sunt servanda versus flexibility in the suspension and termination of treaties' in C Tams, A Tzanakopoulos and A Zimmermann (eds), *Research Handbook on the Law of Treaties* (Edward Elgar, 2014) 312–340, 337–38.

the Universal Declaration of Human Rights, and a panoply of other individual protections in areas as diverse as refugee law and international investment law. Trindade frames the issue thus: if the 'process of formation and application' of international law has ceased to be a monopoly of states then the recognition of an individual's rights as a subject of international law 'ought to correspond to the procedural capacity to vindicate them at [the] international level'.[68] This provides a principled, rather than merely formal-legal, justification for obligations protecting rights and interests to continue after the moment of withdrawal. The two very different examples in this section, one looking at the rights of investors to access international arbitration and the other relating to prisoners on death row, show the utilisation of this reasoning. It also reflects one of the arguments of the English school of international relations theory, that international society is underpinned by certain fundamental principles of cooperation.[69] Leading theorists of this school, such as CE Manning, argued that international law itself was ultimately subordinate to international political forces, but that certain 'shared diplomatic assumptions' helped underpin international society.[70] Hedley Bull developed this further when he described the existence of rules of coexistence between states, which included the regulation of agreements between states.[71]

The existence of a right to a fair hearing at an international tribunal could arguably be one of those principles, and certainly serves the facilitative function of ensuring that the regulation of basic interactions, such as human rights and commerce in the case studies that follow, can continue. This does not need to be particularly well developed; as Manning argues, rights claims can turn into something of a 'myth', gaining most of their value as a 'war cry against those who can be charged with their violation'.[72] The more important thing, Manning clarifies, is that the basic principles of law underpinning international society are recognised as providing the 'rules of the game' in international society, creating both a moral obligation on states to comply with the law and an expectation of deference to the law.[73] Access to courts and tribunals, where there is an expectation that such a right exists, is a principle that has both the moral aim of protecting the rights of the individual, but also value as a means of ensuring stability in international law. The precise way in which this is protected in withdrawal clauses with savings or sunset provisions is to ensure that a state's decision to withdraw does not in and of itself lead to the extinction of an existing right of access to a tribunal, so a state cannot use withdrawal to effectively

[68] AAC Trindade, *The Access of Individuals to International Justice* (Oxford University Press, 2011) 5–6.

[69] Linklater and Suganami (n 62) 44–52.

[70] CAW Manning, 'The Legal Framework in a World of Change' in B Porter (ed), *The Aberystwyth Papers: International Politics 1919–1969* (Oxford University Press, 1972) 301–335 318.

[71] H Bull, *The Anarchical Society: A Study of Order in World Politics* (Macmillan, 1977) 67–70.

[72] Manning (n 70) 317.

[73] ibid 328–29.

stay proceedings, deny other rights without warning, or behave in bad faith in relation to existing proceedings, as there is an obligation that continues after denunciation and potentially past the moment of withdrawal. The legal basis for sunset clauses is set out in Section I, but beyond the obligation, the practical question of whether they are complied with by the withdrawing state is bound up in the politics of the withdrawal in question.

A. Investment Arbitration

The International Centre for Settlement of Investment Disputes (ICSID) Convention has been ratified by 153 states, and in 1966 the International Centre for the Settlement of Investment Disputes was set up as one of the organisations of the World Bank Group by the Washington Convention on the Settlement of Investment Disputes between States and Nationals of Other States. Alongside the New York Convention, which requires foreign states to recognise arbitral awards and enforce them, it is part of the United Nations Commission on International Trade Law (UNCITRAL) system of disputes.[74] Although it does not provide any substantive rules on the protection of investments, what the ICSID Convention does is to create a procedural framework for the resolution of investment disputes that allows the foreign investor, an individual or a company, to be able to take the host state of their investments to an international dispute resolution body – often referred to as 'the Centre' in ICSID parlance. This creates certainty for the investor, but also allows states to market themselves as open to inward investment and, as Eric De Barbandere argues, fulfils a public international law function, not just a private law function, by allowing a form of dispute resolution mechanism over matters that might otherwise lead to inter-state disputes.[75] The jurisdiction of ICSID and other arbitration bodies is based on the consent of parties, either by their specifying their consent to arbitration in a contractual agreement between the investor and the host state, or by a general legislative provision in the host state allowing for ICSID or other international arbitration, or with a Bilateral Investment Treaty (BIT) between the host state and the investor's home state allowing for arbitration in the event that a dispute arises, with the last of the three being the most common way in which consent to jurisdiction is established.[76] Sometimes this can be expressed in terms that are not expressly clear, for example the UK-Soviet BIT contained a clause saying that in the event of a dispute

[74] C Montineri, 'International Commercial Arbitration' in S Chesterman et al (eds), *The Oxford Handbook of United Nations Treaties* (Oxford University Press 2019) 583–565, 585; Convention on the Settlement of Investment Disputes between States and Nationals of Other States (adopted 18 March 1965, entered into force 16 October 1966) 575 UNTS 159.

[75] E De Brabandere *Investment Treaty Arbitration as Public International Law: Procedural Aspects and Implications* (Cambridge University Press, 2014) 49–54.

[76] C Schreuer, 'Investment Arbitration' in C Romano, K Alter and Y Shany (eds), *The Oxford Handbook of International Adjudication* (Oxford University Press, 2015) 295–315.

that had not been settled amicably, it should 'be referred to international arbitration if either party to the dispute so wishes', which the Russian (by this time the post-Soviet) Government contended did not constitute an offer to arbitrate.[77] The Arbitral Tribunal, however, held this was 'language which is found often in BITs' and used by many other states, and which has generally been 'interpreted as a binding consent to arbitration'.[78]

Article 71 of the ICSID Convention allows states to denounce the Convention, with withdrawal coming into effect six months after the notice of denunciation. Article 72 provides for the survival of the right of access to arbitration by stating that a notification under Article 71 'shall not affect the rights or obligations arising out of consent to the jurisdiction of the Centre given by one of them before such notice was received by the depositary'.[79] As Frédéric Sourgens notes, various attempts at drafting a regime of investment protection had been attempted following the end of World War Two, and the Organization for Economic Cooperation and Development (OECD) Draft Convention on the Protection of Foreign Property contained a provision that protected access to the jurisdiction of an arbitral tribunal for a period of five years after the revocation of a declaration, consenting to arbitration in respect of claims arising out of, or in connection with, rights acquired while the declaration was valid.[80] When the ICSID Convention was being drafted, one of the Convention's central aims was to ensure that private contractual terms, on which an investor might rely as the basis for making future commercial decisions, were given an explicit basis in public international law.[81] Article 72 was a mechanism for securing that overall aim of the Convention, and there is evidence from the discussions at the time of drafting that access to arbitration, and the protection of rights to arbitration of matters under consideration at the time of withdrawal, was intended to continue after withdrawal.[82] However, Article 72 only applies in the event that consent has been given to arbitration and also secures the rights of investors engaged in a dispute beyond the six-month period referred to in Article 71. Once consent is given, there is a duty to comply with an award and a duty to refrain from resorting to other remedies, including diplomatic protection, so Article 72 implies obligations continuing beyond the moment of withdrawal.[83]

[77] *RosInvest v Russia* (Award on Jurisdiction) Arbitration V 079/2005 [1 October 2007] paras 58–59.

[78] ibid para. 72.

[79] ICSID, Art 72.

[80] F Sourgens, 'Keep the Faith: Investment Protection Following the Denunciation of International Investment Agreements' (2012) 11 *Santa Clara Journal of International Law* 335.

[81] ibid. See also De Brabandere (n 75).

[82] C Tietje, K Nowrot and C Wackernagel, 'Once and Forever? The Legal Effects of a Denunciation of ICSID' Institute of Economic Law Transnational Economic Law Research Center (TELC), *Essays on Transnational Economic Law*, No 74 (March 2008) at https://institut.wirtschaftsrecht.uni-halle.de/sites/default/files/altbestand/Heft74.pdf, 17–18.

[83] C Schreuer, 'Denunciation of the ICSID Convention and Consent to Arbitration' in M Waibel et al, *The Backlash against Investment Arbitration: Perceptions and Reality* (Wolters Kluwer Law & Business, 2010) 353–368, 363.

Given that investment law was built around the concept of consent, Schurer argues, survivability under Article 72 must be perfected through acceptance by the investor before the date of the denunciation. A general offer of consent, say in a state's domestic legislation, would need to be followed up with a declaration in writing by an investor that it was going to avail itself of that offer in order for the provisions of Article 72 to apply.[84]

In May 2007, the Bolivian Government announced it was withdrawing from the ICSID Convention. This began a series of withdrawals, with Ecuador announcing its withdrawal in 2009 and Venezuela in 2012. These individual acts of withdrawal were in the context of the promotion and establishment of a 'Bolivarian Alternative for Latin America and the Caribbean' (*Alternativa Bolivariana para la América Latina y el Caribe* – sometimes known as ALBA).[85] Although greeted with some scepticism and questions about what it actually meant substantively, ALBA was a response to the Free Trade Area of the Americas, launched in 1994 at the Summit of the Americas and aimed at creating a new free trade agreement across the Americas by 2005. A specific concern about the proposed Free Trade Area raised by Venezuela at the Summit of the Americas in 2001, was the way in which this model of free trade agreement gave preferential treatment to investors.[86] There were other broader economic arguments rooted in the historical experience of the region as a result of colonialism, with which the economic power imbalances between north and south were associated.[87] Even if there was a lack of clarity about what ALBA would look like, the scepticism surrounding investment protection of the sort facilitated by the ICSID Convention was clear enough. In this context, the protection of the rights of investors could easily come into tension with the broader aims behind withdrawal, even though at the ALBA Extraordinary Summit in June 2009 the joint declaration stated that 'a working group [of the Council of Ministers for ALBA] would elaborate the proposed creation of a Regional Instance for Dispute Resolution'.[88] In October 2007, ETI Europe, a

[84] This was the subject of some debate. Some noted that only the word 'consent', not 'perfected consent', was included in the provision; see E Gaillard; 'The Denunciation of the ICSID Convention' (2007) 5 *Transnational Dispute Management* at www.transnational-dispute-management.com/article.asp?key=1074 (accessed 16 March 2022). See also Schreuer (n 83).

[85] A Tzanakopoulos, 'Denunciation of the ICSID Convention under the General International Law of Treaties' in R Hofmann and C Tams (eds), *International Investment Law and General International Law: From Clinical Isolation to Systemic Integration?* (Nomos Verlagsgesellschaft, 2011).

[86] P Kellogg, 'Regional Integration in Latin America: Dawn of an Alternative to Neoliberalism?' (2007) 29 *New Political Science* 187; H Yaffe, 'The Bolivarian alliance for the Americas: An alternative development strategy' (2011) 3 *International Journal of Cuban Studies* 128.

[87] On the broader economic aims of the movement, see A Cusak, *Venezuela, ALBA, and the Limits of Postneoliberal Regionalism in Latin America and the Caribbean* (Palgrave Macmillan, 2013) 93–118.

[88] Published in M Sarmiento, 'The Bolivarian Alliance for the Peoples of Our America Trade Treaty (ALBA-TCP) and the creation of a Centre for the settlement of investment disputes' (30 November 2015) at https://papers.ssrn.com/sol3/papers.cfm?abstract_id=2702419 (accessed 16 March 2022).

European telecoms company with a beneficial owner in Italy and an individual claimant from the Netherlands, made a request for arbitration in respect of alleged breaches of a BIT.[89] The claimants' case was that they had perfected consent by a letter three days prior to the notice of denunciation by Bolivia. The Bolivian Government rejected this, arguing that the claimants had only perfected consent through their letter to the Centre on 12 October, months after Bolivia had denounced the Convention, and that as a consequence, Article 72 of the ICSID Convention did not apply.[90] It dismissed the earlier letter, saying that it did not mention the Centre and was not an effective request for arbitration. However, the Centre accepted the registration of the dispute and the matter proceeded, with Bolivia reportedly agreeing to settle the case for $100 million even though there was never any formal published hearing adjudicating the rights of the different parties.[91] This may have suited all parties to the dispute; the claimants managed to emerge with compensation for some of their losses and the President of Bolivia, Evo Morales, was able to claim the conclusion of the case as a political win because he had stood up to large multinational corporations.

More clarity was given in an arbitration involving Venezuela, where the arbitrators found that Article 72 of the ICSID Convention related to 'consent to the jurisdiction of the Centre given before the notice of denunciation by that State was received by the depositary', firmly linking the survivability of rights to arbitration at the Centre to consent prior to denunciation.[92] At a conceptual level, what the multilateral regime under the ICSID Convention does, Peters argues, is allow a claimant (usually a corporation or investment group) to become the holder or owner of a set of secondary rights under international law entitling the claimant to access to arbitration, or to claim for damages arising from breaches of obligations.[93] The survivability of rights of investors is also another way of acknowledging that under the ARS, a breach of an obligation continues regardless of the status of the source of that obligation, and BITs can have their own survivability clauses that can protect rights after a treaty's termination.[94] Yet the concept of the individual investor as a rights holder is one that reflects the

[89] The case was *ETI Euro Telecom International NV v Republic of Bolivia* ICSID Case no ARB/07/28 Request for Arbitration (12 October 2007).

[90] Letter from the Bolivian Embassy to the Secretary-General of the International Centre for the Settlement of Investment Disputes, 'RE: Request for Arbitration filed by ETI Euro Telecom International, NV' (29 October 2007) at www.italaw.com/sites/default/files/case-documents/italaw10207.pdf (accessed 18 March 2022).

[91] N Kownacki, 'Prospects for ICSID Arbitration in Post-Denunciation Countries: An Updated Approach' (2010) 15 *UCLA Journal of International and Foreign Affairs* 529, 558–559.

[92] *Transban Investments Corp v Bolivarian Republic of Venezuela*, ICSID Case No ARB/12/24, Award (22 November 2017) paras 83–84.

[93] Peters (n 8) 346–47.

[94] A Reinisch and S Mansour Fallah, 'Post-Termination Responsibility of States? The Impact of Amendment/Modification, Suspension and Termination of Investment Treaties on (Vested) Rights of Investors' (2022) *ICSID Review – Foreign Investment Law Journal* 1.

broader shift in international investment law to recognise the procedural nature of stability, going beyond the simply functional towards one that underpinned the broader structure of inter-state commercial activity. Stability, however, is a form of privileging certain types of states, namely, those who have capital or capital holders. This has fed into criticisms of international investment law for being favourable to capital-exporting states, and that procedural aspects of the law, such as arbitration's relative lack of transparency, were a reflection of this underlying privilege.[95] Another way of understanding the survival of rights is as part of what Sabine Frerichs and Rich James call the international law of property, which both creates and protects property rights on the transnational plane, covering both tangible and intangible property.[96] Treaties like the ICSID Convention, in Frerichs and James's analysis, would be part of 'universalising' property rights beyond the nation state that was essential for the development of an advanced market society.[97]

B. The Death Penalty in the Caribbean

In the late 1990s, following the decision of the Judicial Committee of the Privy Council in *Pratt and Morgan v Attorney-General for Jamaica*, a number of Commonwealth Caribbean nations, who were under the appellate jurisdiction of the Privy Council and retained the death penalty, began to withdraw from international human rights instruments.[98] *Pratt and Morgan* did not strictly speaking abolish capital punishment, but it did find that detention on death row amounted to inhuman and degrading treatment, and limited the time someone could spend on death row to five years, presenting an avenue for convicted murders on death row to delay their executions with challenges to human rights bodies.[99] Jamaica had not actually executed anyone for nearly a decade when, in October 1997, it withdrew from Optional Protocol 1 to the International Covenant on Civil and Political Rights (ICCPR), which allowed for individual

[95] For summaries of this line of critique, see K Supnik, 'Making amends: Amending the ICSID Convention to reconcile competing interests in international investment law' (2009) 59 *Duke Law Journal* 343; K Hobér, 'Investment Treaty Arbitration and Its Future -- If Any' (2015) 7 *Yearbook Arbitration and Mediation* 58.

[96] S Frerichs and R James, 'Correlated ownership: Polayni, Commons and the property continuum' in M Hirsch and A Lang, *Research Handbook on the Sociology of International Law* (Edward Elgar, 2020) 62–85.

[97] ibid 77.

[98] For the authoritative history on this, see L Helfer, 'Overlegalizing Human Rights: International Relations Theory and the Commonwealth Caribbean Backlash against Human Rights Regimes' (2002) 102 *Columbia Law Review* 1832.

[99] *Pratt and Morgan v Attorney-General for Jamaica* [1994] 2 App Cas 1 (PC, 1993); J Harrington, 'The Challenge to the Mandatory Death Penalty in the Commonwealth Caribbean' (2004) 98 *American Journal of International Law* 126.

petition to the Human Rights Committee (HRC) from applicants complaining of rights violations under the ICCPR.[100] From the Jamaican Government's perspective, convicts taking cases to the HRC made it difficult to resume executions in Jamaica, a position that commanded a significant degree of public support in the country, and many Jamaican politicians were open in their contempt for international human rights institutions.[101] Yet the HRC had also provided an important bulwark for individual rights in capital punishment cases; most notably, in one instance hearing a petition from a man who had been convicted of murder and sentenced to death whilst being denied a lawyer at his trial, despite repeatedly requesting one.[102] Under the provisions of Article 12 of the Optional Protocol, Jamaica was still required to cooperate with the HRC in relation to petitions filed before the denunciation became effective on 23 January 1998. In *Freemantle v Jamaica*, a case involving a death row inmate claiming there had been political bias in his conviction, the state had not been cooperative with the Committee. The HRC had to remind the Jamaican Government that when it became a party to the Optional Protocol it 'recognized the competence of the Committee to determine whether there has been a violation of the Covenant'.[103] Compliance with the terms of Article 12 was part of this commitment, as the Committee was to remind Jamaica on a number of occasions.[104] The Jamaican Government's lack of cooperation came from the same political place as its withdrawal; it was boxed in between public demands for tough action on crime and a requirement to fulfil international obligations, so it opted for non-cooperation with the HRC, but crucially did not resume executions.[105] Along with other Caribbean states, in 2000 it attempted to re-accede to the Optional Protocol whilst introducing reservations specifically to preclude petitions from death row inmates, but these reservations were strongly opposed by other European nations keen to promote an international anti-death penalty norm.[106] At the time of writing, the death

[100] Optional Protocol 1 to the ICCPR (n 27); 'Optional Protocol to the International Covenant on Civil and Political Rights: Denunciation by Jamaica' (5 December 1997) CN461.1997. TREATIES-3-II.

[101] Amnesty International, 'State Killing in the English-Speaking Caribbean: A Legacy of Colonial Times', AI Index: AMR 05/003/2002 (April 2002). There was a rich tradition of legal challenges to the death penalty in Jamaica, but it was often politically expedient to attack international bodies: J Campbell, 'Murder appeals, delayed executions, and the origins of Jamaican death penalty jurisprudence' (2015) 33 *Law & History Review* 435.

[102] *Robinson v Jamaica*, Communication no 223/1987, UN Doc CCPR/C/35/D/223/1987 (1989); see also N Schiffrin, 'Jamaica Withdraws the Right of Individual Petition Under the International Covenant on Civil and Political Rights' (1998) 92 *American Journal of International Law* 563, 565.

[103] *Freemantle v Jamaica*, Communication no 625/1995, UN Doc CCPR/C/68/D/625/1995 (2000) para 10.

[104] For details of the relevant communications, see G Naldi and K Magliveras, 'Human Rights and the Denunciation of Treaties and Withdrawal from International Organisations' (2013) 33 *Polish Yearbook of International Law* 95, 107.

[105] Harrington (n. 99).

[106] L Helfer, 'Not fully committed-reservations, risk, and treaty design' (2006) 31 *Yale Journal of International Law* 367, 371–72.

penalty remains law in Jamaica, but no execution has taken place since 1988. Significantly, in 2011 a reform was made to the Jamaican Constitution to take account of the *Pratt and Morgan* ruling, and by the mid-2010s the number of prisoners on death row had dwindled to around five convicts, when 20 years earlier, prior to *Pratt and Morgan*, there were nearly 200.[107]

Trinidad and Tobago had joined Jamaica in denouncing Optional Protocol 1, with its then Attorney-General commenting that 'the legality of the death penalty was an essential condition of Caribbean participation in human rights regimes'.[108] A few months after Jamaica's withdrawal from the Optional Protocol became effective, Trinidad and Tobago withdrew from both it and the ACHR on the same day. As far as the Government was concerned, given that following *Pratt and Morgan*, staying on death row was recognised as a form of inhuman and degrading treatment, it was appropriate to limit the time of death row and remove avenues for challenging domestic decisions at international tribunals that might delay prisoners' execution.[109] After denouncing the Convention, but prior to 28 May 1999 when the withdrawal became effective, 20 Trinidadian citizens on death row brought cases against Trinidad and Tobago, and the Court affirmed its jurisdiction to hear these cases. On 4 June 1999, less than a week after the withdrawals from both bodies had become effective, Trinidad and Tobago restarted executions, hanging nine convicts over the course of a week. There was no doubt that this was an enormously popular move in Trinidad and Tobago; a poll run by one local newspaper showed 80 per cent support for the executions, another newspaper ran a front-page headline saying 'Time's Up!' the day before the executions.[110] One of the executed men – Joey Ramiah, a hitman for one of the leading drug dealers in the Caribbean, who had been convicted of murdering an entire family, was one of the claimants in the case pending before the IACtHR. Two years later, in *Hilaire et al v Trinidad and Tobago* the Court held that Ramiah's execution was a violation of his right to a fair hearing and right to life, and ordered the payment of $50,000 compensation to his widow.[111] The decision was, notionally, not anti-death penalty as it was rooted in the structure

[107] 'Jamaica's Compliance with the International Covenant on Civil and Political Rights: Death Penalty and Death Row Conditions', Submitted by Advocates for Human Rights a non-governmental organization in special consultative status with ECOSOC and The Greater Caribbean for Life for the 116th Session of the United Nations Human Rights Committee (7–31 March 2016) available at < https://www.theadvocatesforhumanrights.org/Res/jamaica_list_of_issues_iccpr_death_penalty_january_2016.pdf. >.

[108] E Rediker, 'Courts of Appeal and Colonialism in the British Caribbean: A Case for the Caribbean Court of Justice' (2013) 35 *Michigan Journal of International Law* 213, 238.

[109] Human Rights Watch, 'HRW and CEJIL Call on Trinidad and Tobago to Reconsider Withdrawal from the American Convention on Human Rights' Human Rights Watch (1 July 1998) at www.hrw.org/news/1998/06/01/hrw-and-cejil-call-trinidad-and-tobago-reconsider-withdrawal-american-convention.

[110] D Usborne, 'Trinidad three hanged despite pleas' *The Independent* (4 June 1999) at www.independent.co.uk/news/trinidad-three-hanged-despite-pleas-1098205.html.

[111] *Hilaire Constantine and Benjamin et al v Trinidad and Tobago*, Inter-Am Ct HR (Ser C) N 94 (2002).

of Article 78, which envisaged some ongoing protection of the Court and the rights contained within the ACHR following the act of denunciation. This was consistent with the ACHR, which, like the ECHR (prior to Protocol 13), did not technically prohibit capital punishment. However, the Concurring Opinion of Judge Trindade argued that the execution of Ramiah was evidence of the arbitrary nature of the entire system of mandatory execution.[112] In Trinidad and Tobago it appeared as though the Court was opposing the death penalty, with a report in *Newsday* – one of the leading newspapers in the country – expressing slight astonishment, in an otherwise factual report of the decision, at the idea of paying compensation to the widow of a convicted murderer.[113] Implementation of the decision in *Hilaire*, which included remedies for the other claimants as well, was still in the hands of the Court because, as the Court held, the operation of Article 78 as a sunset provision entailed that denunciation did not relieve the state of its obligations under the Convention, which included the obligation under Article 68 to comply with the Court's decisions.[114] In effect this stretched the authority of the Court beyond the moment of denunciation, as it would have a role in assessing the implementation of any remedies. The Court's view was that it was simply exercising its power under Article 63 ACHR, which provided that the Court should protect rights and authorise compensation where alleged violations of rights had occurred. That provision, the Court held, simply reflected a customary norm in international law and was part of the 'fundamental principles of the law on the international responsibility', implying that the obligation to comply with the Court's decision had an existence independent of the Convention.[115] But the Government of Trinidad and Tobago simply refused to cooperate with the Court. From a rationalist or a realist perspective cooperation no longer had any value, as these were historic issues and the Court had effectively situated itself as a rival political actor within its domestic sphere.[116] In 2015, the Court noted that nearly 12 years had passed without any evidence

[112] Concurring Opinion of Judge AA Cançado Trindade, paras 4–6. This position was also advanced in the Final Written Arguments of the Inter-American Commission on Human Rights.

[113] See 'Inter-American Commission wants Govt to … Pay for Joey Ramiah's hanging?' *Newsday* (21 February 2002); there is only a short extract archived online at www.trinidadandtobagonews.com/forum/webbbs_config.pl?md=read;id=220 (accessed 22 January 2022). The reporting refers to the Inter-American Commission decision even though the Court judgment was handed down that year although the state party had refused to appear at the proceedings – see *Hilaire* (n 110) para 17.

[114] American Convention on Human Rights 'Pact of San Jose, Costa Rica' (adopted 22 November 1969, entered into force 18 July 1978) 1144 UNTS 123, Art 68.

[115] *Cases of Hilaire, Constantine and Benjamin et al. and Caesar v Trinidad and Tobago: Monitoring Compliance with Judgment* (20 November 2015) para 4. This position was later reinforced in the Court's 2020 advisory opinion - see Inter-American Court of Human Rights 'Advisory Opinion requested by the Republic of Colombia in Matters of Human Rights of a State that has Denounced the American Convention on Human Rights and the Charter of the Organisation of American States' (9 November 2020) OC-26/20 paras 76–79.

[116] See Helfer (n 98). Rationalism, or more accurately 'strategic rationality', is critiqued by Reus-Smit as providing an insufficient basis for understanding the binding force of international law in general: C Reus-Smit, 'Politics and International Legal Obligation' (2003) 9 *European Journal of International Relations* 591, 593.

that Trinidad and Tobago was complying with the decision. Warning that the systemic non-compliance in relation to decisions risked the ACHR's protection 'becoming illusory [and] being at the discretion of the internal decisions of a State', the Court referred the issue of non-compliance to the Organisation of American States in hopes of a political resolution.[117] The judgment situated compliance within the context of broader regional stability, supporting the idea that there was a minimum core of rules in the international system, of which access to courts was a crucial component.

III. CONTINUING AUTHORITY AFTER EXIT

The continuance of a legal regime's authority after withdrawal is distinct from the survival of a right post withdrawal. The latter, as this chapter has already laid out, can be justified on the basis of protecting an individual's rights, even though it is premised on the idea that the act of withdrawal has terminated the ongoing legal power of the regime in question. Standing or a hearing at a tribunal can be understood as necessary to protect a right or interest acquired under the instrument from which a state is withdrawing. The former concept maintains that a legal regime will continue to have some degree of authority even after the process of denunciation. Using Joseph Raz's definition of authority as a starting point, authority in international law describes the capacity of international law and legal institutions to place an obligation on state officials to comply with their decisions.[118] As a matter of law, a withdrawal clause may prescribe an ongoing status for an institution in a sunset provision, the assumption being that after denunciation has become effective, there will be decisions with which the withdrawing state would be expected to comply because those decisions would be stemming from a legitimate form of legal power over the withdrawing state.[119] Karen Alter's work on legitimacy in international law distinguishes between the legal formalist approach, which tries to identify the legal source of a regime's claim to authority, from the normative sociological basis of such authority.[120] Whilst there might be a positive legal obligation in place, such as a provision in a withdrawal clause to recognise the authority of an institution, the underlying sociological legitimacy of an institution's authority can be impacted by the mere act of attempting withdrawal. Sociological thinking about institutional legitimacy can be traced back to Max Weber, who defined legitimacy as a form of social action that

[117] *Hilaire* (n 115) 9.

[118] J Raz, 'Authority' in Raz (ed), *Authority* (NYU Press, 1990); B Çalı, *The Authority of International Law: Obedience, Respect, and Rebuttal* (Oxford University Press, 2015) 13–14.

[119] S Besson, 'The Authority of International Law-Lifting the State Veil' (2009) 31 *Sydney Law Review* 343.

[120] KJ Alter, L Helfer and M Madsen, 'International Court Authority in a Complex World' in Alter et al (eds), *International Court Authority* (Oxford University Press, 2018) 3–23, 13–14.

'may be oriented by the actors' in society towards 'a belief in the existence of a "legitimate order"'.[121] Whilst coercion may be in evidence, a legitimate legal order would result in an individual's social action arising independently of that coercion. International courts and tribunals depend on what can be termed 'content independent legitimacy', the idea that a decision is legitimate not because of its substantive content but because it emerges from a legitimate source, which allows the courts and tribunals to issue rulings against states that are complied with.[122] This can develop through a regime's consistency and stability over time, or through appeals to the utility of that institution as a means of resolving a collaboration problem, or through its role in promoting shared inter-state solidarity.[123] The sociological legitimacy of an institution, however, is disrupted by an act of withdrawal as the various ways in which the legal regime maintained legitimacy within the withdrawing state all start to diminish and the internal political climate within that state often increasingly seeks to challenge the authority of that regime.[124]

One way of thinking about why the authority of a regime might persist is to understand the way in which certain regimes exist as part of a constitutional framework in international law.[125] As Samantha Besson argues, a state's role in creating promises does not just relate to its own interests but also has an impact on the wider framework of international society.[126] This form of reasoning follows the assumption of the English school of international relations about the reliance by international society on a set of.[127] But, from a more critical direction

[121] M Weber, *Economy and Society and Outline of Interpretive Sociology*, vol 1, trs AM Henderson and T Parsons (Free Press, 1968).

[122] Lynn Donsbon 'Legitimacy, institutional power and international human rights institutions: a conceptual enquiry' in A Føllesdal, G Ulfstein and J Karlsson Schaffer (eds), *The Legitimacy of International Human Rights Regimes Legal, Political and Philosophical Perspectives* (Cambridge University Press, 2014) 190–211; A Føllesdal, 'Survey article: the legitimacy of international courts' (2020) 28 *Journal of Political Philosophy* 476.

[123] For literature on all three ways in which the legitimacy of a regime can be generated, see respectively: LM Dellmuth, J Aart Scholte and J Tallberg, 'Institutional sources of legitimacy for international organisations: Beyond procedure versus performance' (2019) 45 *Review of International Studies* 627; Reus-Smit (n 116); D Bodansky, 'Legitimacy in International Law and International Relations' in JL Dunoff and MA Pollack (eds), *Interdisciplinary Perspectives on International Law and International Relations* (Cambridge University Press, 2013) 321–343; K Gorobets, 'Solidarity as a Practical Reason: Grounding Authority of International Law' in European Society of International Law Research Forum, *Solidarity. The Quest for Founding Utopias of International Law*, Catania, Sicily (23–24 April 2020) at https://papers.ssrn.com/sol3/papers.cfm?abstract_id=3548673 (accessed 20 September 2022).

[124] This is discussed in I von Borzyskowski and F Vabulas, 'Hello, Goodbye: When do States Withdraw from International Organizations?' (2019) 14 *The Review of International Organizations* 355.

[125] M Kumm, 'The Legitimacy of International Law: A Constitutionalist Framework of Analysis' (2004) 15 *European Journal of International Law* 907.

[126] Besson (n 119) 360–62 notes this with reference to Waldon's work – J Waldron, 'The Rule of International Law' (2006) 30 *Harvard Journal of Law and Public Policy* 15, 23–25.

[127] Barry Buzan, 'The English School: an underexploited resource in IR.' (2001) 27 *Review of international studies* 471.

this also shows the power of international forces, particularly international capital and the dominant political powers, over states. Yet the principal benefit of constitutionalism from a rationalist perspective – the provision of stability and predictability in international relations – is distinct from legitimacy because, as Ian Clarke points out, it is perfectly possible to conceive of an international order as bringing stability but with very limited legitimacy.[128] If the authority of a regime is envisaged as continuing after exit, it is unlikely to have similar sociological legitimacy as it had when it was in force and will depend on legal obligations upon the withdrawing state under the treaty it is withdrawing from. But this authority can be rendered meaningless unless the state complies with its obligations – as Fitzmaurice famously observed, the authority of international law 'depends on enforcement'.[129] As these two case studies demonstrate, the continuing authority of an international regime, as distinct from the protection of rights to access previously described, depends not so much on the sunset provisions of a given instrument but on the presence of wider coercive forces and frameworks in international society at large, which go beyond the regime from which a state is withdrawing and its legal framework.

A. Inspecting Nuclear Weapons after NPT Withdrawal

In 1991 there were growing concerns in US foreign policy circles that North Korea had invested in a research reactor at the Yonbyong reprocessing plant for refining plutonium.[130] With the Cold War between the USSR and the US winding down, the US withdrew nuclear weapons from South Korea, and following multilateral political pressure, North Korea agreed to a safeguarding agreement with the International Atomic Energy Agency (IAEA). This complemented the Nuclear Non-Proliferation Treaty (NPT), to which North Korea had been a party to since 1985, and meant that the IAEA had the right to ensure that safeguards were applied on all nuclear material in the country and to ensure that this was not being used for weapons production.[131] Article 26 of the safeguarding agreement was a duration clause, which said that it remained 'in force as long as the Democratic People's Republic of Korea is a party to the Treaty (the NPT)'.[132] The provision referring to safeguarding agreements in

[128] I Clark, 'Legitimacy in a Global Order' (2003) 29 *Review of International Studies* 75, 82.

[129] G Fitzmaurice, 'The Foundations of the Authority of International Law and the Problem of Enforcement' (1956) 19 *The Modern Law Review* 1.

[130] A Mack, 'North Korea and the Bomb' (1991) 83 *Foreign Policy* 87.

[131] M Asada, 'Arms control law in crisis? A study of the North Korean Nuclear Issue' (2004) 9 *Journal of Conflict and Security* Law 331.

[132] IAEA Information Circular, 'Agreement of 30 January 1992 between the Government of the Democratic People's Republic of Korea and the International Atomic Energy Agency for the Application of Safeguards in Connection with the Treaty on the Non-Proliferation of Nuclear Weapons' INFCIRC/403 May 1992.

the NPT stated that inspections were for the purposes of ensuring that non-nuclear weapons states were adhering to their obligations under the NPT, although technically safeguarding agreements derived their legal authority from the IAEA statute.[133] The system of inspection had by the early 1990s evolved into a crucial component of the NPT, underpinning one of its aims – to limit the number of non-nuclear states – but safeguarding agreements were still dependent on the agreement of the state in question.[134]

North Korea's attempted withdrawal from the NPT in 1993, it contended, was triggered by mounting fear regarding US actions in South Korea, although, as set out chapter 1, this did not really meet the threshold of 'extraordinary events, related to the subject matter' of the treaty or *rebus sic stantibus*.[135] Four weeks before North Korea announced it was withdrawing from the NPT, the IAEA had tried to carry out inspections of two sites where it was concerned that enrichment activity was being conducted with a view to making weapons. As emergency shuttle diplomacy began in mid-1993 – led by former US President Jimmy Carter – North Korean criticism of the IAEA and the inspections regime increased. Denunciation of the NPT under the terms of Article X did not expressly terminate the safeguards agreement and, as Hans Blix, the head of the IAEA, maintained, there was a legal case that the safeguards agreement had an independent identity.[136] Yet when the Security Council issued a resolution on the mounting crisis on the Korean peninsula in May 1993, it emphasised the importance of the NPT and 'the integral role of IAEA safeguards in the implementation of the treaty'.[137] It is not clear if this was an inadvertent connection of the authority of the two. As Antonio Perez noted in his analysis of the attempted North Korean withdrawal, if inspection rights did survive, this would significantly 'change state's perceptions of the consequences of safeguards termination' following unilateral withdrawal from the NPT.[138] Article X seeks to foreground an idea of voluntarism, framing the right to withdraw in terms of allowing a state to exercise 'its national sovereignty' when 'the supreme interests of its country' are in jeopardy, creating a presumption in favour of sovereign decision making.[139] If IAEA inspections could continue, however, this would

[133] The IAEA was created in 1957 with an independent statute; on this point, see L Rockwood, *Legal Framework for IAEA safeguards* (International Atomic Energy Agency, 2013) 2–3 at www-pub.iaea.org/MTCD/Publications/PDF/Pub1608_web.pdf (accessed 20 May 2021).

[134] R Hooper, 'Strengthening IAEA Safeguards in An Era of Nuclear Cooperation' (1995) 25 *Arms Control Today* 14.

[135] JS Wit, DB Poneman and RL Gallucci, *Going Critical: The First North Korean Nuclear Crisis* (Brookings Institution Press, 2004) 24–25.

[136] A Perez, 'Survival of Rights Under the Nuclear Non-Proliferation Treaty: Withdrawal and the Continuing Right of International Atomic Withdrawal and the Continuing Right of International Atomic Energy Agency Safeguards Energy Agency Safeguards' (1994) 34 *Virginia Journal of International Law* 749. Treaty on the Non-Proliferation of Nuclear Weapons (adopted 1 July 1968, entered in force 5 March 1970) 729 UNTS 161 (NPT) Art X.

[137] UNSC Res 825 (11 May 1993) UN Doc S/RES/825, preamble.

[138] Perez (n 136) 772–73.

[139] NPT Art X.

be a difficult proposition to resolve and give the legal obligation any sense of legitimacy, especially in the heightened climate of tension between the different parties. What ultimately preserved the authority of the IAEA inspections regime was a bargain reached between North Korea and other powers – principally the US – where North Korea would cease its attempted withdrawal from the NPT and agree to inspections in return for significant material aid and assistance to create civilian nuclear power.[140]

North Korea had managed to use the threat of withdrawal as leverage to essentially situate the US as its near exclusive interlocutor, in relation to its nuclear weapons programme, and get material assistance and security guarantees from them. This was an example of what Helfer describes as a bargaining theory in action, as the threat of NPT withdrawal was used again in both 1998 and 2000 to advance North Korea's own interests.[141] The power of the IAEA to inspect became a subject of these negotiations, with its authority becoming increasingly less independent and more associated with the US's own interests. Yet at the time the concern was around the lack of effectiveness of the NPT and its wider promise of stability, especially with the renewal conference scheduled for 1995.[142] The NPT was eventually renewed indefinitely in 1995, and the same year enhanced powers were given to IAEA inspections, but the issue regarding the powers of the IAEA post-withdrawal was not addressed.[143] After North Korea's final withdrawal from the NPT in 2003, continuing inspections from the IAEA became a subject matter for negotiations. In 2005, as part of what was called the Six Party process, North Korea committed to abandoning all nuclear weapons and existing nuclear programmes, and agreed to return to the NPT at an early date, in exchange for economic and security guarantees. In 2006, North Korea undermined this by conducting its first nuclear weapon test, but negotiations in 2007 continued and IAEA inspections were proposed in return for cooperation over denuclearisation.[144]

The IAEA's authority was contingent on the outcome of political negotiations, not rooted in a legal proposition stemming from the obligations that North Korea had whilst it was a party to the NPT. At the Preparatory Committee for the 2005 review conference, France proposed amending Article X of the NPT to require any nuclear materials, facilities, equipment or technology acquired

[140] The political commitment can be found in a letter from President Bill Clinton to Kim Jong Il, which is reprinted in J Minnich, *The Denuclearization of North Korea* (First Books Library, 2002) 106.

[141] On the threats, see S Hecker, 'Lessons learned from the North Korean nuclear crises' (2010) 139 *Dædalus* 44.

[142] D Hendrickson, 'The Recovery of Internationalism: Stemming the Isolationist Impulse' (1994) 73 *Foreign Affairs* 26, 35.

[143] R Hooper, 'Strengthening IAEA safeguards in an era of nuclear cooperation' (1995) 25 *Arms Control* 14.

[144] W Huntly 'Rebels without a cause: North Korea, Iran and the NPT' (2006) 82 *International Affairs* 723, 725.

whilst the withdrawing state was an NPT party to be removed as part of the withdrawal process, as the withdrawing state would have acquired that material whilst subject to a regime of safeguards that it would no longer be subject to as a non-state party.[145] There was no real sense of how this could be practically realised and the conference never properly formed a view on these proposals, but this would have clarified the post-withdrawal position of the state by essentially by-passing the question of a continuing role for inspections. It is difficult not to conclude that entire framework of the NPT and the safeguarding system creates too easy a route for exit for states categorised as non-nuclear states who wish to breach their obligations.[146] An alternative conclusion, however, is to note the relative stability of the NPT in defining a norm against proliferation that has led to only two states either withdrawing or using withdrawal as a form of leverage against the institutions designed to control nuclear power and prevent the acquisition of nuclear weapons. This community-orientated conception of the authority of the NPT and the IAEA can be seen in the way that both are referenced repeatedly in UN Security Council Resolutions on North Korea; yet as realist theorists might note, this is largely a reflection of the power of the US and other states seeking to use both the NPT and IAEA as means of meeting a strategic end.[147]

B. International Criminal Court Investigations

The political impetus behind the creation of the ICC emerged out of the experience of the ad hoc international criminal tribunals in the 1990s, yet technically the ICC was in a weaker position as, rather than Chapter VII powers under the UN Charter, requiring states to cooperate with its authority, it relied on the framework of a treaty with a withdrawal clause as the basis of its legal authority.[148] The *travaux préparatoires* of the Rome Statute do not indicate why a withdrawal clause was considered and included in the final treaty beyond its being simply

[145] G Bunn and J Rhinelander, 'The Right to Withdraw from the NPT: Article X is Not Unconditional' *Disarmament Diplomacy*, Issue No. 79, April/May 2005 available at www.acronym.org.uk/old/archive/textonly/dd/dd79/79gbjr.htm.

[146] R Winters, 'Preventing Repeat Offenders: North Korea's Withdrawal and the Need for Revision to the Nuclear Non-Proliferation Treaty' (2005) 38 *Vanderbilt Journal of Transnational Law* 1499, 1508–12.

[147] For examples of these respective positions in this regard, see S Hamidi, 'Law as discursive resource: the politics of the nuclear/non-nuclear distinction in the Non-Proliferation Treaty' (2020) 26 *European Journal of International Relations* 545. For a case more rooted in power politics, see ZS Davis, 'The Realist Nuclear Regime' in Davis and B Frankel (eds.) *The Proliferation Puzzle: Why Nuclear Weapons Spread (and What Results)* (Routledge, 1993) 79–99.

[148] A Jones, 'Non-cooperation and the Efficacy of the International Criminal Court' in O Bekou and D Birkett (eds), *Cooperation and the International Criminal Court: Perspectives from Theory and Practice* (Brill, 2016) 186, 186–87.

a functional component of almost all multilateral-treaties in the 1990s.[149] Most of the literature in the late 1990s on the politics of the ICC makes no reference to the withdrawal clause, focusing more on the prospects of ratification from powerful states rather than on the prospect that states would withdraw from the Rome Statute. Article 127 makes it clear that withdrawal does 'not affect any cooperation with the Court in connection with criminal investigations and proceedings' relating to the withdrawing state, nor does it 'prejudice in any way the continued consideration of any matter which was already under consideration by the Court prior to the date on which the withdrawal became effective'.[150] This can be broken down into two separate duties on the state. First, a duty to continue investigations commenced prior to the end of the one-year notice period for withdrawal specified in Article 127. This, however, raises a dilemma about the authority of the Court: does 'consideration' of a matter refer to the investigation stage only, or should it be interpreted more broadly so as to include the preliminary examination stage?[151] If it is the latter, this would represent a significant temporal extension of the ICC's authority after withdrawal that can be contrasted with that of human rights courts, such as the ECtHR, where the ECHR's withdrawal clause is far less clear about the authority of the Court after exit.[152] The second duty relates to cooperation in respect of proceedings that are ongoing at the time of withdrawal. On the face of it there is, as Antonio Cassese suggests, a question whether the provisions in Article 127 of the Rome Statute would encompass fresh crimes committed in the one-year period after denunciation but before withdrawal became effective, but as the state is still a party to the ICC Statute during this period, and there is nothing to suggest otherwise in Article 127, it seems likely that this would still apply to crimes committed after denunciation but prior to any withdrawal's becoming effective.[153]

[149] TN Slade and RS Clark, 'Preamble and Final Clauses' in RS Lee (ed), *The International Criminal Court – The Making of the Rome Statute: Issues, Negotiations, Results* (Martinus Nijhoff, 1999) 421.

[150] Rome Statute of the International Criminal Court (concluded 17 July 1998, entered into force 1 July 2002) 2187 UNTS 3, Art 127(b).

[151] 'Consideration' was drawn broadly by the Prosecutor in 2016, who said that it covered a variety of matters prior to an investigation, such as 'jurisdiction, admissibility and the interests of justice' – see OTP, 'Statement of the Prosecutor of the International Criminal Court, Fatou Bensouda, on opening a Preliminary Examination into the situation in Burundi' International Criminal Cour (25 April 2016) at www.icc-cpi.int/Pages/item.aspx?name=otp-stat-25-04-2016 (accessed 20 May 2021).

[152] There is no reference in Art 58 ECHR to the continuing authority of the ECtHR as an institution for enforcing the provision in Art 58(2) that states that denunciation does not release parties from obligations in relation to 'any act which, being capable of constituting a violation of such obligations, may have been performed … before the date at which the denunciation became effective'. It is noteworthy though that in the case of Russian withdrawal the Council of Europe envisaged a clear role for the ECtHR in continuing to hear cases pending before the Court - see Council of Europe 'Resolution on legal and financial consequences of the cessation of membership of the Russian Federation in the Council of Europe.' (23 March 2023) CM/Res(2022)3.

[153] A Cassese, *The Rome Statute of the International Criminal Court. A Commentary* (Oxford University Press, 2002) 171–73.

One way of reading Article 127 is as an attempt to make the ICC operate in a horizontal model of legality, supporting the doctrine of complementarity in Article 17 of the Statute, which allows the Court to operate only in cases where the state is 'unwilling or unable' to prosecute crimes itself, by creating a safety hatch to protect a state's sovereignty in the event of expansion of the Court's powers and the side-lining of this principle.[154] This is, however, somewhat unrealistic, as the withdrawing state could not escape its *jus cogens* obligations – and breaches of obligations considered *jus cogens* often form a part of ICC indictments. Beyond the substantive legal argument, the whole idea of the ICC as an institution operating in a horizontal model of legality has been criticised by some critical theorists of international criminal law as neglecting the way that the ICC's operation reflects dominant structures of political power in international relations.[155] States who are not ICC parties, or who, by virtue of having a Security Council veto, are able exert a decisive influence on the UN Security Council's capacity to authorise an investigation under Article 15 of the Rome Statute, are relatively unaffected by the Court's investigative capacity. The good faith argument discussed in chapter 2 would notionally preclude a state from withdrawal in order to escape the imminent indictment of an individual within its jurisdiction, even though some countries have pursued that exact strategy. The difference is that in these cases, the ICC, a body whose authority a state has disavowed by the act of withdrawing from the Rome Statute, still has authority in a formal legal sense over a state under Article 127; whereas in the case of non-signatories, a group that includes UN Security Council veto holders and some of their client states, the ICC has never had direct authority over them as a state party to the Rome Statute, even though both groups of states could face serious charges relating to international crimes.

Burundi's withdrawal from the ICC highlights some of the tensions surrounding the role of authority inherent within Article 127. Burundi signed the Rome Statute in September 1999 but only deposited its instrument of ratification in 2004, in a ratification process described as slow and opaque, with no real attempt to implement the substantive provisions into domestic law.[156]

[154] Jones (n 146). See also M Bergsmo, 'Occasional Remarks on Certain State Concerns about the Jurisdictional Reach of the International Criminal Court, and their Possible Implications for the Relationship between the Court and the Security Council' (2000) 69 *Nordic Journal of International Law* 87, 99; M Benzig, 'The Complementarity Regime of the International Criminal Court: International Criminal Justice between State Sovereignty and the Fight against Impunity' (2003) 7 *Max Plank Yearbook of United Nations Law* 591, 593.

[155] On horizontality, see T de Souza Dias, 'The nature of the Rome Statute and the place of international law before the International Criminal Court' (2019) 17 *Journal of International Criminal Justice* 507. On critical theory and international criminal law, see T Krever, 'International criminal law: An ideology critique' (2013) 26 *Leiden Journal of International Law* 701.

[156] S *Vandeginste, 'The ICC Burexit: free at last? Burundi on its way out of the Rome Statute' (2016) Analysis & Policy Brief* No 20, Institute of Development Policy and Management, Antwerp Univeristy at https://medialibrary.uantwerpen.be/oldcontent/container2673/files/Publications/APB/20-Vandeginste.pdf (accessed 17 March 2021).

Ratification of the Rome Statute took place in the wider context of democratisation in the country from the mid-1990s onwards.[157] President Pierre Nkurunziza was first elected in 2005 and was constitutionally barred from standing for President for a third term, but in April 2015 he took the decision to stand anyway. Fierce protests erupted, and there was an attempted coup, but this did not stop Nkurunziza from winning the first round of the presidential elections. Vigilante violence, linked to both state forces and the President, led to 240 deaths, and there was little attempt to hold the perpetrators accountable.[158] In November, a UN Security Council Resolution noted that as a party to the Rome Statute, Burundi had 'undertaken obligations to fight impunity for crimes falling within the jurisdiction of the Court'.[159] The ICC Prosecutor opened an investigation into the situation in Burundi in April 2016, echoing the language of the AU's withdrawal strategy. Nkurunziza responded by claiming that the ICC was 'deliberately targeting Africans for prosecution'.[160] The Burundian Parliament voted to withdraw from the Rome Statute in October 2016, becoming the first country to officially leave the ICC one year later.[161] Undeterred, a spokesperson for the opposition said 'what Nkurunziza and his regime must know is that the withdrawal from the ICC does not give them permission to kill the people of Burundi … lawsuits will take their course'.[162]

In late August 2017, two months before the denunciation became effective, the Prosecutor of the ICC began an investigation into the situation in Burundi. In the October decision on the authorisation of the investigation, the Pre-Trial Chamber of the ICC examined in depth the obligations entailed by Article 127.[163] The conclusion it reached on the temporal issue of withdrawal was relatively straightforward – as Article 127 said, denunciation was effective only after one year, and since these proceedings were being brought within that timeframe, the fact of the denunciation was moot as far the Prosecutor's application was concerned. When it came to the authority of the Court beyond the specific issue of authorising an investigation, they clarified that the 'acceptance of the jurisdiction of the Court remains unaffected by a withdrawal of the State' from the

[157] S Mitchell, *Institutional Legacies, Decision Frames and Political Violence in Rwanda and Burundi* (Routledge, 2020) 4–6.

[158] N Ifejika, 'Is Burundi on the verge of return to ethnic conflict?' *BBC News* (2 December 2015) at www.bbc.co.uk/news/world-africa-34987198 (accessed 17 March 2021).

[159] UNSC Res 2248 (12 November 2015) UN Doc S/RES/2248, Preamble.

[160] 'International Criminal Court Probes Burundi 'Crimes Against Humanity, BBC News Africa (9 November 2017) at www.bbc.co.uk/news/world-africa-41932291 (accessed 17 March 2021).

[161] Burundi: Withdrawal, CN.805.2016.TREATIES-XVIII.10, 27 October 2016.

[162] T Whitely and I Ivanov, 'The International Criminal Court, Elite Theory, and African States Withdrawal Notifications: South Africa, The Gambia, and Burundi' (2020) 2 *Undergraduate Scholarly Showcase* 1, 26 at https://journals.uc.edu/index.php/Undergradshowcase/article/view/4160 (accessed 17 March 2021).

[163] *Decision Pursuant to Article 15 of the Rome Statute on the Authorization of an Investigation into the Situation in the Republic of Burundi* (*Burundi Decision*), Pre-Trial Chamber III (PTC III), 25 October 2017, Case no ICC-01/17-X, para 24. Special thanks to my former student Dia Kosali (mentioned in the acknowledgements) for her work analysing this case.

Rome Statute.[164] This extended the jurisdiction of the Court to a period of time significantly after a state withdrew, requiring the state to comply with a range of different decisions from the Court that could trigger a variety of different political problems, but the Court stressed that its jurisdiction 'remains in effect for as long as the investigation lasts'.[165] The Court concluded that Article 127 gives effect to Article 70 VCLT, 'which provides that the termination of a treaty [d]oes not affect any right, obligation or legal situation of the parties'.[166] Interestingly, the decision did not really touch upon the issue of state consent as a basis for the continuing authority of the ICC, which was a key feature of other decisions about obligations arising from the sunset provisions of a withdrawal clause. A potential explanation is that the ICC increasingly sees itself as enjoying a virtual monopoly in the international justice field; and in other areas where its jurisdictional powers are at issue, such as with the doctrine of complementarity, it has, as Valérie Arnould argues, interpreted its powers in a way that 'nearly guarantees its ability to claim jurisdiction'.[167]

The Government of Burundi ultimately simply refused to cooperate with the ICC, claiming that the ICC was acting 'ultra vires' in interpreting Article 127 in this way.[168] There was no real merit to this claim, and it was little more than a legal veneer disguising a political attack on the ICC. The Kenyan Government had threatened withdrawal whilst withholding cooperation, which had resulted in the leading case in relation to post-election violence in 2014.[169] Although not formally withdrawing and refusing cooperation might seem like an appealing strategy for a state – especially given that at the time of writing there have been no further developments in relation to the situation in Burundi in four years – such actions were outside the scope of Article 127. It also significantly weakened the ICC's authority as an international court and as an international actor more generally, as identified by some of the literature on ICC withdrawal, which situates this within a broader crisis of authority for the Court.[170] Even though the UN Security Council has the power to refer cases to the ICC, there is no express power regarding the Court's capacity to request support in relation to

[164] ibid.

[165] ibid para 26.

[166] ibid para 25.

[167] V Arnould, 'A Court in Crisis? The ICC in Africa, and Beyond' *Egmont Paper No 93* (May 2017) at http://aei.pitt.edu/id/eprint/87212.

[168] K Lessing, 'Evading Jurisdiction: How to Hold Burundi Accountable for Human Rights Violations after Withdrawal from the International Criminal Court' (2019) 33 *Notre Dame Journal of Law Ethics & Public Policy* 511, 520.

[169] L Helfer and AE Showalter, 'Opposing international justice: Kenya's integrated backlash strategy against the ICC' (2017) 17 *International Criminal Law Review* 1; SD Mueller, 'Kenya and the International Criminal Court (ICC): politics, the election and the law' (2014) 8 *Journal of Eastern African Studies* 1.

[170] For examples, see Arnould (n 165); S Vasiliev, 'The Crises and Critiques of International Criminal Justice' in K-J Heller (ed), *The Oxford Handbook of International Criminal Law* (Oxford

compliance, and this has not arisen as the subject matter of a Security Council resolution. The ICC's continuing authority after withdrawal remains largely contingent upon a state's willingness to comply with its obligations under the Rome Statute. In cases of withdrawal from the ICC, this runs into what Christian Reus-Smit calls the problem of interiority: consent is identified as the source of authority, but from the withdrawing state's perspective, consent is effectively undone by the act of withdrawal, leading to sunset provisions depending on the identification of norms outside the legal system or wider social pressures in international society to ensure compliance.[171] The problem of interiority is compounded by the fact that governmental leaders are, when withdrawing from the ICC, sometimes seeking, to avoid their own individual criminal liability.[172] It is hard in these precise circumstances for the authority of an institution, which, as Başak Çalı argues, involves the political and governmental elites of the state acting as though they ought to comply with an international obligation, to persist after withdrawal from the ICC.[173]

CONCLUSION: OUTSIDE THE MACHINE

At the start of 2022, to say Russia had been a recalcitrant member of the Council of Europe would have been an understatement: it had previously been subject to special measures following its actions in separatist regions of Ukraine; it was the subject of inter-state applications to the ECtHR; and there were nearly 2,000 court judgments Russia had yet to execute. Then, on 24 February 2022 that took on a whole new dimension as Russia launched an invasion of Ukraine that attracted international condemnation and political isolation. The very next day the Council of Europe suspended Russia, and few weeks later, on the same day that the parliamentary assembly of Council of Europe was about to expel Russia, the Russian Foreign Minister sent a notification of denunciation of the ECHR to the Council's headquarters in Strasbourg.[174] It was later clarified by the ECtHR that Russia would, following the terms of Article 58, be bound by the ECHR until September 2022. But the question was whether Russia would actually comply with these obligations and implement the outstanding judgments against it. At the end of March 2022 the prospects were not looking good, as the former ECtHR judge Angelika Nußberger argued there was a sense of

University Press 2020) 626–651; K Magliveras, 'The Withdrawal of African States from the ICC: Good, Bad or Irrelevant?' (2019) 66 *Netherlands International Law Review* 419.

[171] Reus-Smit (n 116) 600.

[172] M Cherif Bassiouni, 'Concerning the ICC Withdrawal Problem' in RH Steinberg (ed), *The International Criminal Court: Contemporary Challenges and Reform Proposals* (Brill Nijhoff, 2020) 115–119.

[173] Çalı (n 118).

[174] It was not at all clear whether it was the Parliamentary Committee of the Council of Europe's decision to effectively expel Russia or the receipt of a notice of denunciation which actually triggered

'the machine departing'.[175] Outside, or after, the 'machine' of political pressure and action by an international organisation, obligations may exist and may as a matter of law continue, but the departure of the 'machine' renders their realisation more fragile. On 16 September 2022, Russia was formally outside the mechanism of the ECHR; on that day there were over 13,000 applications to the Court in Strasbourg relating to human rights violations allegedly committed by Russia still pending, nearly one-quarter of all applications to the Court.[176] Technically, these can continue to be processed and heard by the Court, but it would ultimately be largely symbolic if some of these applications led to a finding of violations against the Russian Federation given its appalling record on non-compliance and a 2015 law to specifically allow Russian domestic courts to refuse to follow ECtHR rulings. Work that the Committee of Ministers had been doing to supervise the execution of judgments and the broader protection of rights had for a number of years failed to make much of impact, with some suggesting that the case for expulsion from the Council of Europe was strong.[177] 'Outside the machine', however, even the mechanisms that had ceased to function were now not available; the sunset provisions in Article 58 ECHR were obligations some legal commentators simply assumed would cease to function after Russia denounced the ECHR in March.

In some cases, as detailed in the final section of the chapter, absent the framework of a legal regime, the issue of whether obligations are complied with becomes inexorably intertwined with the political power behind the regime in question. This can also be relevant for the realisation of rights: as chapter 5 notes, the connection between ICSID membership and access to World Bank credit provides additional features beyond a BIT to encourage the withdrawing state's compliance with its obligations after withdrawal. Human rights courts, however, do not have the same kind of infrastructure surrounding them. The institutions of wider international society describes the set of laws built to enable basic interactions between states. Bull, one of the leading theorists of the English school of international relations, attempted to carve out a distinction

Russia's exit, both of which occurred on 15 March 2022. The Council of Europe's Committee of Ministers resolutions referred to it in terms of its procedure for ceasing membership – Council of Europe 'Resolution on legal and financial consequences of the cessation of membership of the Russian Federation in the Council of Europe.' (23 March 2023) CM/Res(2022)3. For an analysis of the precise chronology in February and March 2022 see P Leech 'A Time of Reckoning? Russia and the Council of Europe' Strasbourg Observer 17 March 2022, https://strasbourgobservers.com/2022/03/17/a-time-of-reckoning-russia-and-the-council-of-europe/.

[175] Taken from author's notes at 'Russia and the future of the Council of Europe', School of Law, Middlesex University, London (30 March 2022), recording available at www.youtube.com/watch?v=G30yUSj230o (accessed 20 September 2022).

[176] K Dzehtsiarou, 'What Would Russia's Departure from the Council of Europe Mean for the Strasbourg System of Human Rights Protection?' *ECHR Blog* (11 March 2022) at www.echrblog.com/2022/03/what-would-russias-departure-from.html?m=1 (accessed 20 September 2022).

[177] K Dzehtsiarou, 'The Closing Door in Strasbourg: An Interview with Kanstantsin Dzehtsiarou on the Council of Europe's suspension decision' *Völkerrechtsblog* (26 February 2022) at https://voelkerrechtsblog.org/the-closing-door-in-strasbourg/ (accessed 30 March 2022).

between an international system, where states would be in regular contact with one another allowing them to make calculations about one another's behaviour, and international society, which was a group of states consciously forming over common values with institutional structures.[178] This was subsequently criticised for lacking a coherent distinction between the two concepts, but the English school generally coalesced around the idea that there existed a framework for international society defined by rules and institutions.[179] The analogy, discussed by Bull, of diplomatic relations is arguably analogous to the law of withdrawal. In both, there was a strong foundation in state practice and customary law, the codification of the principles into treaty law was designed to clarify norms and create stability in the wider international system and there is a clear sense of reciprocity, leading to predictable behaviour by state parties in their interactions. The law of withdrawal in this respect creates boundary norms for international society at large, incentivising states when terminating their legal obligations to pursue behaviour that is broadly predictable. In a similar vein, the law of diplomatic relations helps create a set of parameters for ongoing state interaction, even when there may be rising political tensions and hostility between states.

But this behaviour relates more to the procedural process of withdrawal described in chapter 2; in relation to the obligations in sunset provisions, state behaviour is far more mixed and dependent upon structural political conditions surrounding individual interests. When the 'machine' is departing, the institutional legitimacy factors of the departing regime can be rendered suspect in the eyes of the domestic political actors in the withdrawing state. Therefore, there is often a need for an external set of political factors or incentives to drive compliance with the substance of sunset provisions. Withdrawals are too disparate and infrequent to supply the data for a detailed study of sunset provisions, but what the above examples show is the distinction between the procedural and the substantive in terms of compliance with a withdrawal clause.

[178] Bull (n 48) 10.
[179] Linklater and Suganami (n 61) 57–59.

4

Non-Withdrawal: The Role of Rights

INTRODUCTION

'THOSE WHOM THE persecutor had designated the scum of the earth ... Jews, Trotskyites etc,' the German philosopher Hannah Arendt wrote, in one of the most moving passages in twentieth-century philosophy, 'were received as scum of the earth everywhere ... when unidentifiable beggars, without nationality without money ... crossed their frontiers'.[1] In *The Origins of Totalitarianism*, Arendt was both analysing the experience of Jewish refugees from the Nazis and relating her own experience in the late 1930s. In her analysis, the presence of these stateless refugees at the edge of destitution and helplessness was 'like a practical demonstration of the totalitarian movements' cynical claims that no such thing as inalienable human rights existed'.[2] Rightly famous for the expounding the concept of the 'right to have rights', Arendt identified the failure, or the false promise, of international institutions and 'every attempt by international conferences to establish some legal status for stateless people', because 'no agreement could possibly replace territory to which an alien, within the framework of existing law must be deportable'.[3] Arendt scholars have noted that her focus was on how human rights were tied to national sovereignty, and the question of national emancipation, and she was critical of what she called 'world government'.[4] Yet in the introduction to *The Origins*, Arendt claimed that the experience of totalitarianism and antisemitism 'have demonstrated that human dignity need a new guarantee which can only be found in a new political principle, a new law on earth'.[5] It was fairly unclear what this was, and a common critique of Arendt was that her thought crystallised around events rather than presenting a normative sketch of how

[1] H Arendt, *The Origins of Totalitarianism*, 3rd edn (Harcourt Books, 1976) 296–298.

[2] ibid.

[3] ibid 284.

[4] For an exploration of this, see S Parekh, *Hannah Arendt and the Challenge of Modernity: A Phenomenology of Human Rights* (Routledge, 2008) 12; P Birmingham, *Hannah Arendt & Human Rights: The Predicament of Common Responsibility* (Indiana University Press, 2006) 43.

[5] Arendt (n 1) xi.

the world should be.[6] But by the 1950s, international law was starting to rise to the challenge of preventing rightlessness: the Nuremberg and Tokyo trials presumed that there was a category of rights that applied to all humanity, and the development and identification of *jus cogens* norms presumed there was a set of rights that existed independently of express commitment on the parts of states.[7]

The doctrine of non-withdrawal was part of this picture – fundamental rights existed independently of state consent and the removal of consent by withdrawal from a treaty under which rights were codified and obligations placed on the withdrawing state could not allow states to escape from their obligation to protect fundamental rights. Yet the doctrine of non-withdrawal did not emerge expressly as a means of rights protection; instead, non-withdrawal comprised a disparate set of principles designed to maintain international stability, prevent states from reengaging on their commitments and protect property interests. The doctrine of non-withdrawal – as it is referred to here – describes two separate legal concepts, both of which had their origins in customary law and both of which are covered by separate provisions in the VCLT. First, when a treaty contains no withdrawal clause, Article 56 VCLT requires a party wishing to withdraw to demonstrate that 'the parties intended to admit the possibility of denunciation' or show that 'a right of denunciation or withdrawal may be implied by the nature of the treaty'.[8] This limits the right of withdrawal to the terms of a treaty or mutual consent between the parties and, as section I of this chapter argues, effectively restricts state decision making in the interests of broader stability in the international system at large. The development of a principle orientated toward the maintenance of stability into a mechanism for rights protection came, as section II outlines, as part of a general rise in what may be termed 'rights transcendency' in international law in the late twentieth century. The second legal concept in the doctrine of non-withdrawal, the doctrine of acquired rights, also relates to the protection of rights but from a different direction. Article 70 VCLT provides that unless the parties agree otherwise, the withdrawal of a state 'does not affect any right, obligation or legal situation of the parties created through the execution of the treaty prior to its termination'.[9] Originally, this was a principle that emerged in customary international law, that the termination of a treaty, say in the event of a war between the parties, did not mean that property and rights to property

[6] D Whitehall, 'Hannah Arendt and International Law' in A Orford and F Hoffmann (eds), *The Oxford Handbook of the Theory of International Law* (Oxford University Press, 2016) 233.

[7] F Morrison, 'The Significance of Nuremberg for Modern International Law' (1995) 149 *Military Law Review* 207; MC Bassiouni, 'Nuremberg: Forty Years After' (1986) 80 *Proceedings of the ASIL Annual Meeting* 59.

[8] Vienna Convention on the Law of Treaties (adopted 23 May 1969, entered into force 27 January 1980) 1155 UNTS 331 (VCLT) Art 56(1).

[9] Art 70(1)(b) VCLT.

acquired under the terms of that treaty automatically expired; nevertheless, as is explored in section III, there have been attempts to expand this to a broader doctrine of rights protection.[10]

Even though the legal doctrines respectively described in Articles 56 and 70 VCLT are distinct from one another, they can be placed together under the general banner of non-withdrawal, as from the perspective of the withdrawing state the two have a degree of similarity. Withdrawal is an act where the state intends to terminate legal obligations and cease cooperation with a regime – it means to stop having a set of legal obligations. Both Article 56 and Article 70 effectively stymie that end goal. From a realist perspective, cooperation with a legal regime exists either to resolve a coordination problem or to gain an advantage for the state, and the decision to commence withdrawal either terminates or substantially weakens the basis of cooperation with legal obligations.[11] Non-withdrawal therefore acts as a means of blocking the realisation of a state's interest and continuing obligations even after incentives for cooperation have ceased. Equally, from a constructivist perspective, a state's withdrawal changes the relational aspects of its identity as it is no longer interacting in the same way with other states and international legal regimes, altering the basis of cooperation and inter-state practice.[12] Non-withdrawal aims to freeze the status quo of a state's obligations, regardless of any political changes in behaviour on the part of that state. A state is still obliged to protect rights, even if it wants to withdraw from the instrument containing them. This differs from what was described in the last chapter: non-withdrawal describes near-permanent legal obligations, rather than ones that arose from breaches of the treaty before denunciation or which are safeguarded in a withdrawal clause by sunset provisions. To understand non-withdrawal requires a more nuanced conception of realist thinking about obligation and an understanding of liberal theories of international obligations.

I. STABILITY AND THE PRINCIPLE OF NON-WITHDRAWAL

Article 56 VCLT is an attempt to codify a general principle of treaty law that can be traced back almost a century before the Treaty. Its construction, with the requirement to examine the intention of state parties and the nature of the treaty,

[10] S Wittich, 'Article 70: Consequences of the termination of a treaty' in O Dörr and K Schmalenbach (eds), *Vienna Convention on the Law of Treaties* (Springer, 2012); On attempts to expand the doctrine, see P Mindus, *European Citizenship after Brexit: Freedom of Movement and Rights of Residence* (Palgrave, 2017) 62–70.

[11] For this sketch of realist thinking, see B Kingsbury, 'The concept of compliance as a function of competing conceptions of international law' (1997) 19 *Michigan Journal of International Law* 345, 350–52.

[12] A Wendt, 'Anarchy is What States Make of It: The Social Construction of Power Politics' (1992) 46 *International Organization* 391; see also A Wendt, 'Constructing International Politics' (1995) 20 *International Security* 71, 74.

aims to balance the need for flexibility in an agreement with the requirement of certainty in international relations.[13] Examining the question of the unilateral termination of treaties in the early 1960s, the International Law Commission (ILC) formulated the position that, absent a withdrawal clause, denunciation should be prohibited, unless the 'character of the treaty' and the 'circumstances of its conclusion or the statements of the parties' indicate that they intended to admit 'the possibility of a denunciation or withdrawal'.[14] The ILC's report went onto argue that this was necessary in 'order to safeguard the security of treaties'; and although there was divergence among the members of the Commission about how exceptions to this general principle ought to be constructed, the purpose behind it – the promotion of stability – was well understood.[15] Examples of such treaties listed in the ILC report were the Charter of the United Nations and the 1961 Vienna Convention on Diplomatic Relations, although it is worth noting that following this report, the overwhelming majority of treaties now contain a withdrawal clause.[16]

The emphasis the ILC's report placed on the intention of parties supports an understanding of international obligation from the perspective of liberal theorists (on which more below) and from constructivists, both of whom would argue that the absence of a withdrawal clause reflects broader underlying social conditions or state practice.[17] The broader theoretical question of why, from a realist or rationalist perspective, a state would commit to a treaty without a withdrawal clause can be answered by examining the assumptions that realists make about the nature of the international system. Realist presumptions about the anarchic nature of the international system owe a lot to the thinking of Thomas Hobbes, whose theorising about sovereignty and the state of nature in the seventeenth century was important for the conception of international politics as a game between sovereign states.[18] The absence of a common hierarchical figure creates an anarchical environment where war is common, and international law creates the framework for a series of collaboration games between

[13] T Giegerich, 'Article 56: Denunciation of or withdrawal from a treaty containing no provision regarding termination, denunciation or withdrawal' in Dörr and Schmalenbach (eds) (n 10) 1039.

[14] ILC, 'Report of the International Law Commission covering the work of its fifteenth session' (6 May–12 July) UN Doc A/5509, 200.

[15] ibid 201.

[16] ibid. On the point regarding the majority of treaties and withdrawal clauses, see ch 2; and L Helfer, 'Terminating Treaties' in DB Hollis (ed), *The Oxford Guide to Treaties* (Oxford University Press, 2012) 648.

[17] For an example of liberal theorists making an argument about the underlying social conditions, see A-M Slaughter, 'A Liberal Theory of International Law' (2001) 94 *Proceedings of the ASIL Annual Meeting* 240. For an example of Constructivist theory making this point, see T Risse, '"Let's Argue!": Communicative Action in World Politics' (2000) 54 *International Organization* 1.

[18] For an overview of work on Hobbes and the realist theory of international relations, see AN Yurdusev, 'Thomas Hobbes and international relations: from realism to rationalism' (2006) 60 *Australian Journal of International Affairs* 305. Smith centralises Hobbes's work in realist thought, saying that his 'analysis of the state of nature remains the defining feature of realist thought': M Smith, *Realist Thought from Weber to Kissinger* (Louisiana State University Press, 1986) 13.

states designed to reduce the outbreak of conflict – a theoretical framework that, as one of the most famous realists, Hans Morgenthau, puts it, is close to the 'stock in trade' of international relations theory.[19] Yet, as Michael Williams argues, the important detail of Hobbes's thinking is not that he bases his political vision on the assumption of materially self-interested actors operating in a state of anarchy, but rather that he seeks to create materially self-interested actors.[20] This is important, as what Hobbes is proposing is not an abstract methodological or ontological set of assumptions but instead an argument about how subjects ought to behave. When applied on the international plane, it is a theory about how individual sovereign entities should share 'the same understanding of political order, the same commitment to a politics of limits and the same constraints on their actions'.[21] Some realists would therefore not necessarily have a problem with the fact that an instrument such as the UN Charter had no withdrawal clause, as the instrument was part of an underlying political order that constrained states in order to create international stability and maximise their interests and power. Arguments about stability, especially in the context of UN Charter, as shown in section I.B, can be heavily contextual, but there is a detailed history to the doctrine that it is important to trace first, to illustrate the importance of stability to the principle of non-withdrawal.

A. The Absence of a Withdrawal Clause: Origins and Assumptions

The 1870s was a period when international law was becoming increasingly formalised, and the rights of states surrounding the termination of treaties were becoming more conditional.[22] Most notably in 1871, when, in response to an earlier attempt by the Russian Government to withdraw from the 1856 Treaty of Paris on the neutralisation of the Black Sea – a treaty with no withdrawal clause – a fresh treaty was concluded at a great power conference, with a declaration alongside it clarifying the 'essential principle' that no state could 'liberate itself from the engagements of a treaty' without the consent of other parties.[23] This should be seen more broadly in the context of mid- to late nineteenth-century international treaty law, fostering a system of state interaction that aimed at preserving the balance of power between the European nations, with the creation

[19] M Williams, 'Hobbes and international relations: a reconsideration' (1996) 50 *International Organization* 213; H Morgenthau, *Scientific Man Versus Power Politics*, 3rd edn (University of Chicago Press, 1974).

[20] M Williams, *The Realist Tradition and the Limits of International Relations* (Cambridge University Press, 2005) 33.

[21] ibid 46.

[22] Q Wright, 'Validity of the Proposed Reservations to the Peace Treaty' (1920) 20 *Columbia Law Review* 121, 132.

[23] See WE Mosse, 'The End of the Crimean System: England, Russia and the Neutrality of the Black Sea, 1870–1' (1961) 4 *The Historical Journal* 164.

of certainty in treaty law being part of that overall process.[24] This doctrine was revisited on a number occasions to emphasise that withdrawal needed to take place either with the express consent of other parties or with the implied consent of other parties, through a withdrawal clause included in the treaty and designed for the purposes of withdrawal.[25] By the early twentieth century the Prime Minister of Bavaria was able to inform the Bavarian parliament that in the absence of a treaty provision allowing denunciation, an extradition treaty with Russia, which the parliamentarians claimed was not being honoured as Russia was harbouring German fugitives, could not be denounced.[26] In a 1911 survey of treaty law, Theodore Ion noted the distinction between treaties of 'a permanent character' and treaties that could be 'abrogated or denounced by their parties'; examples of the latter included commercial treaties.[27] Lasa Oppenheim, writing in 1905, argued that withdrawal was possible, provided the treaty in question was 'not such as are concluded for ever'.[28]

Attempts to codify the law of treaties focused both on the presence of a withdrawal clause as evidence of the drafting party's intentions and the overall nature of the treaty. The 1928 Havana Convention on the Law of Treaties stated that only those treaties 'whose denunciation may have been agreed upon and those establishing rules of international law, can be denounced [and] only in the manner provided thereby', seemingly precluding denunciation of a treaty without a withdrawal clause.[29] A few years later, JL Brierly, in his textbook on the *Law of Nations*, confessed that the issue of termination of treaties without a withdrawal clause was 'one of the most complicated problems of practical importance in the law of treaties', but he endorsed the underlying premise of the Havana Draft that there is 'no general right of denunciation of a treaty of indefinite duration'.[30] Tobin's survey of treaty termination in 1933 made passing reference to treaties without withdrawal clauses, concluding that they might be necessary for the promotion of 'stability'.[31] The Harvard Draft Convention on the Law of Treaties in 1935 envisaged two scenarios in Article 33 – either there was a denunciation clause or consent needed to be given for withdrawal – and Article 34 explicitly stated that a treaty could be denounced 'only when such

[24] A Lev, 'The Transformation of International Law in the 19th century' in A Orakhelashvili (ed), *Research Handbook on the Theory and History of International Law* (Edward Elgar, 2011) 125.

[25] For a general description of how the law on denunciation operated in the early 20th century, see W Heicher and C Eagleton, 'Problems of International Legislation' (1933) 8 *Temple Law Quarterly* 505.

[26] American Society of International Law, 'Article 34. Denunciation' (1935) 29 *American Journal of International Law* 1173.

[27] TP Ion, 'Sanctity of Treaties' (1911) 20 *The Yale Law Journal* 268, 274.

[28] L Oppenheim, *International Law: A Treatise*, vol 1, 3rd edn (Lawbook Exchange, 2005) 688.

[29] American Society of International Law, 'Appendix 1. Convention on Treaties: Adopted at the Sixth International Conference of American States at Havana 20 February 1928' (1935) 29 *American Journal of International Law* 1205.

[30] JL Brierly, *The Law of Nations*, 2nd edn (OUP 1936) 201.

[31] H Tobin, *The Termination of Multipartite Treaties* (Columbia University Press, 1933) 200.

denunciation is provided for in the treaty or consented to by all other parties'.[32] In terms of theorisation as to why this was necessary, again the emphasis was heavily on stability, with the commentary to Article 34 noting that in some cases denunciation 'will have the effect of disturbing the equilibrium of rights and obligations as between the other parties'.[33] Realist theory, as it developed after the First World War, was concerned with analysing how great-power politics had resulted in the outbreak of war, but crucially it was not simply diagnostic or involved in making presumptions about how states would behave on the anarchical international plane; it was also prescriptive, outlining the way in which states ought to act.[34] It is essential to read the commitment to stability in the commentary on denunciation clauses in this context; reining in the capacity of states to treat denunciation as a unilateral act was a means of promoting stability.

The ILC began discussing the harmonisation of treaty law in 1949, and in some of its early work on the matter it aimed either to build on the Harvard Draft or shadow diplomatic practice on a given issue.[35] The Second Report on the Law of Treaties by Gerald Fitzmaurice directly referred to the implied will of the parties, noting it was 'always open to the parties to make express provision for termination'.[36] This allows Fitzmaurice to inductively reason, in the 'absence of such provision or agreement [a withdrawal clause], that they did not intend to allow it'.[37] Intention was about what the parties specifically intended in relation to withdrawal, but also about what the parties intended as to the nature of the treaty, and Fitzmaurice lists a series of treaties that by their nature would not be presumed to be susceptible to withdrawal unless explicit provision was made.[38] Writing in 1961, Lord McNair made a similar conclusion about the relationship between intention and subject matter, arguing that intention could be 'inferred from … the nature of the subject-matter' and that it was possible to envisage a treaty from which parties did not intend a right of withdrawal because it lacked an 'implied term giving a party the right to terminate it unilaterally by denunciation'.[39] The position of both McNair and Fitzmaurice is reflected in Article 56 VCLT with the two principles it contains: first, the intention of parties must be identified; and, second, the nature of the treaty had to imply the possibility of withdrawal. Some scepticism has been expressed about the nature of a treaty as a guide to its capacity to be denounced, because it could weaken

[32] American Society of International Law (n 26).
[33] ibid 1176.
[34] S Krasner, 'Realist Views of International Law' (2002) 96 *Proceedings of the ASIL Annual Meeting* 264.
[35] This was seen as an act of conservativism by some commentators; see OJ Lissitzyn, 'Efforts to Codify or Restate the Law of Treaties' (1962) 62 *Columbia Law Review* 1166, 1205.
[36] GG Fitzmaurice, 'Second Report on the Law of Treaties' (1957) II *Yearbook of the International Law Commission*, UN Doc A/CN.4/107, 38.
[37] ibid.
[38] ibid 39.
[39] A McNair, *The Law of Treaties* (Clarendon Press, 1961) 493.

the principle of *pacta sunt servanda* and is a test so open and poorly defined that it could be abused by the withdrawing state.[40] In the *South West Africa Advisory Opinion* in 1971, the ICJ had to determine whether League of Nations mandates issued in 1920 to the Government of South Africa, which its Government were using to authorise their continuing occupation of Namibia (which also meant the imposition of apartheid in Namibia), could be terminated.[41] The South African Government insisted that the absence of a termination clause in the mandates meant this was not possible. The ICJ held that the 'silence of a treaty as to the existence of such a right [termination] cannot be interpreted as implying the exclusion of a general principle of international law' and concluded, examining the intent of the mandates at the time of drafting, that the possibility of termination had not been expressly excluded.[42] Although criticised for in essence suggesting that a customary right existed to withdraw in the event of breach, the ICJ's exploration and construction of the original intention of the parties was a means of examining what the absence of a withdrawal clause entailed.[43] Ultimately, the rule contained in Article 56(1) VCLT can be understood as two ways of asking the same question: What did the parties originally consent to when drafting the treaty?

Yet focusing on the original intent of parties as to whether a right of withdrawal exists raises four specific problems. First, the way in which the intent of the contracting parties is recorded is not always clear; and more generally, the relative weight to be assigned to the original intent of the parties on any issue is a matter of considerable doctrinal dispute among legal scholars.[44] At the Vienna Conference, amendments were proposed suggesting that withdrawal should only be prohibited where 'it is established beyond doubt' that the parties intended to prohibit withdrawal, or that there should be a written statement from the parties about their intentions or that intention should be determined in 'the light of all the circumstances of the case'.[45] All of these options were aimed at clarifying the nature and scope of a state's intention, but instead what was settled on was the more opaque reference to the 'character' of treaties found in the final text of Article 56. This level of doctrinal uncertainty makes it difficult to say with any degree of certainty, from a constructivist viewpoint, that there

[40] AW Rudzinski, 'Review: Denunciation of International Treaties. By Maria Frankowska' (1977) 71 *American Journal of International Law* 805.

[41] *Legal Consequences for States of the Continued Presence of South Africa in Namibia (South West Africa) notwithstanding Security Council Resolution 276 (1970)* (Advisory Opinion) [1971] ICJ Rep 16.

[42] ibid 47–48.

[43] H Briggs, 'Unilateral Denunciation of Treaties: The Vienna Convention and the International Court of Justice' (1974) 68 *American Journal of International Law* 51, 55.

[44] O Ilyinskaya, 'Revisiting the Termination of Treaties Containing No Provisions on Termination, Denunciation or Withdrawal' (2018) 5 *Kutafin University Law Review* 317, 319.

[45] United Nations Conference on the Law of Treaties, First and Second Sessions Official Records (Vienna, 26 March–24 May 1968 and 9 April–22 May 1969) A/CONF.39/11/Add.2, 70.

is evidence of construction of a state's identity or, taking a realist/rationalist perspective, that there is a basis for determining state interest or the parameters of a collaboration game.[46]

Second, if collective intention is the key factor in determining whether withdrawal is possible in the absence of a withdrawal clause, there is a question as to the extent to which a state can dissent from the consensus. For example, the US, in 1948, on accession to the World Health Organization (WHO) – whose legal framework does not contain a withdrawal clause – entered a reservation on the right to withdraw, following a specific request from the US Congress to that effect.[47] This was criticised strongly by Christakis as being detrimental to the principle of the sovereign equality of states, but the US reservation reflected the political position of a member state and represented a divergent view about the nature of the treaty.[48]

Third, the absence of an express withdrawal clause does not mean that it is not possible to effectively withdraw from legal obligations. As Dörr notes, the arguments around Article 56 VCLT do not really apply in cases where states withdraw a declaration under a dispute resolution protocol or a protocol allowing individual petition to an international court or tribunal.[49] Silence in these cases is simply taken as granting permission to terminate the jurisdiction of the tribunal by withdrawal of a declaration, even though that is, as argued in the preceding chapters, an alteration of legal obligation and a destabilising feature of legal regimes more broadly.

Fourth, it is sleight of hand to talk about the intentions of the parties when in fact it is a reference to the original parties, or the parties involved in the drafting. As is often the case with multilateral treaties, parties come along to the treaty after it has been opened for signature. In 1971, when Senegal attempted to withdraw from the 1958 Geneva Convention on Fishing and Conservation of the Living Resources of the High Seas, a treaty that did not have a denunciation clause, the Senegalese highlighted a division of opinion among the states who had drafted the Convention. The minority position among the drafting parties was that a customary right to withdraw from the treaty existed.[50] As a matter of law, though, as the Office of Legal Affairs of the UN concluded, a state party was no longer entitled to rely on the minority position among states that had

[46] For a deeper description of these positions, see C Reus-Smit, 'The politics of international law' in C Reus-Smit (ed), *The Politics of International Law* (Cambridge University Press, 2004) 17.

[47] N Feinberg, 'Unilateral Withdrawal from an International Organization' (1963) 39 *British Yearbook of International Law* 189, 202–03.

[48] ibid. T Christakis, 'Article 56' in O Corten and P Klein (eds), *The Vienna Conventions on the Law of Treaties: A Commentary* (Oxford University Press, 2011) 1269.

[49] O Dörr, 'Codifying and Developing Meta-Rules: The ILC and the Law of Treaties' (2006) 49 *German Yearbook of International Law* 129, 152.

[50] D Bardonnet, 'La dénonciation par le Gouvernement sénégalais de la Convention sur la mer territoriale et la zone contiguë et de la Convention sur la pêche et la conservation des ressources biologiques de la haute mer, en date du 29 avril 1958 à Genève' (1972) 18 *Annuaire français de droit international* 123.

drafted the Convention.[51] At the time of the first UN Conference on the Law of the Sea, held in Geneva in the spring of 1958, Senegal was two years away from achieving independence from France and was not formally, as an independent state, able to participate in the proceedings that led to the codification of the law.

In his 1963 report, Sir Humphrey Waldock, the ILC's Special Rapporteur on the law of treaties, disagreed with Fitzmaurice that there was a presumption against exit from treaties without a withdrawal clause, and instead argued that the presumption against withdrawal related to the treaty's function.[52] Waldock's case was in essence one of character, but looking at function rather intent, making clear that treaties such as a 'commercial or trading treaty' or 'a treaty for technical co-operation in economic, social, cultural, scientific, communications' could not be presumed to be treaties that could not be withdrawn from because of their lack of withdrawal clauses.[53] However, treaties such as those 'establishing a boundary between two States', or treaties such as a 'treaty of peace, a treaty of disarmament, or for the maintenance of peace … or effecting a final settlement of an international dispute' would not be capable of being withdrawn from unless there was a withdrawal clause.[54] From Waldock's perspective, assessing the permanence of the legal structure created gave the best guide to understanding the nature of treaties. Great emphasis was placed on factors relating to stability, with Waldock noting that the creation of general rules on non-withdrawal should be guided by the promotion of 'reasonable stability to the relations set up by the varying kinds of treaty'.[55] He even expressed it as 'regrettable' that state practice in relation to treaties of 'arbitration, conciliation or judicial settlement' clearly recognised that they could be withdrawn from, even where there was no withdrawal clause.[56] Stability and permanence, whilst potentially synonymous, are crucially distinct, as a treaty without a withdrawal clause that creates a notionally permanent structure could fall into disuse, and then it could be in the interests of stability to allow withdrawal from that treaty. As Waldock concludes, the general principle is that in 'a rapidly changing world' outside of what he termed 'permanent' types of treaties, most treaties were either time-limited or included a denunciation clause.[57] Stability is central to both Waldock and Fitzmaurice's reports, especially as they sought to grapple with a doctrine that state practice clearly indicated existed but raised tensions with existing understandings of treaty obligations. The pursuit and maintenance of international stability provided a justificatory rationale for the doctrine of non-withdrawal as well as a framework for identifying its existence.

[51] ibid 150–51.
[52] This is explored by Helfer (n 16).
[53] Sir Humphrey Waldock, 'Second report on the law of treaties, by Sir Humphrey Waldock, Special Rapporteur' (1963) II *Yearbook of the International Law Commission*, UN Doc A/CN.4/156, 64.
[54] ibid.
[55] ibid 69.
[56] ibid 68.
[57] ibid 70.

B. The UN Charter

The arguments about the UN Charter and the capacity of states to leave the UN provide an interesting case study of how pervasive stability-based reasoning is in arguments around non-withdrawal. In November 1919, the US Senate accepted a series of resolutions proposed by the Senate Committee on Foreign Relations, one of which safeguarded the unconditional right of the US to withdraw from the League of Nations.[58] The British Foreign Office objected, they were sceptical that this argument would have any legal basis.[59] Yet in the drafting of Article 1 of the League Covenant, the right of states to withdraw was recognised, subject to the completion of their obligations to the League.[60] As a report to the US Congress noted, 'the right of withdrawal is given to each member of the league in its own uncontrolled discretion as not even a reason for withdrawal need be alleged'.[61] Due its own domestic politics, the US was the country involved in the drafting of the Covenant probably most concerned about the capacity to withdraw. In 1926 they put forward a fairly similar argument around the drafting of the Statute of the International Court of Justice, insisting on a unilateral right to withdraw regardless of any provision in the treaty.[62] President Wilson, the architect of the League, in late 1919 was exhausted from the domestic political travails of trying to get support for the League and from having to broker peace between the European powers; as his biographers now know, he had also been severely incapacitated personally by the influenza pandemic earlier that year. This biographical note helps contextualise why most of his speeches on state behaviour at this time appear almost naively utopian, especially in light of the Great War, which had preceded them, as he assumed that states would be constrained from withdrawing 'by the influence of the public opinion of the world'.[63]

Given what happened 15 years later, as Japan and then Italy simply withdrew from the League whilst committing acts of aggression, when states were tasked with drawing up the legal framework for the UN in 1945 there was a strong reluctance to include a withdrawal clause. The collective assumption from sources at the time appeared to be that withdrawal from the League of Nations was a crucial reason why the League had failed.[64] In retrospect this

[58] Wright (n 22) 127–28.

[59] K Magliveras, 'The Withdrawal from the League of Nations Revisited' (1991) 10 *Penn State International Law Review* 25, 28.

[60] The Covenant of the League of Nations (adopted on 28 June 1919, entered into force 10 January 1920) Art 1.

[61] 'Memorandum on interpretation of withdrawal 4', 66th Congress, 1st Session 4 August 1919, 3; JJ Burns, 'Conditions of Withdrawal from the League of Nations' (1935) 29 *American Journal of International Law* 40, 47.

[62] Feinberg (n 47) 195.

[63] Burns (n 61) 48.

[64] Goodrich noted that withdrawal from the League was meant to be dependent on certain conditions that were 'not enforced in practice': LM Goodrich, 'From League of Nations to United Nations' (1947) 1 *International Organization* 3, 11; Potter described the lack of a withdrawal clause

view makes sense, but the capacity of states to withdraw was not highlighted as much in literature from the 1930s as it later was, with more of the blame for the League's failure being placed on great-power politics.[65] A Uruguayan proposal at the conference to terminate the right to withdraw altogether was rejected. The Soviet delegate to the conference took the view that it was not possible to 'condemn beforehand the grounds on which any state might find it necessary to exercise its right of withdrawal from the Organization', asserting a voluntarist contention about international law that saw obligations under the Charter in an ostensibly realist light.[66] Instead, the drafting committee agreed to adopt an interpretative declaration that stated that the 'Charter should not make express provision either to permit or to prohibit withdrawal from the Organization'. Hans Kelsen was of the view that this was not conclusive that there was an intention to withdraw.[67] But the next part of the declaration muddied the waters by saying that in 'exceptional circumstances', if a member state felt 'constrained to withdraw', it was 'not the purpose of the Organization to compel that Member to continue its cooperation in the Organization'.[68] An almost passive-aggressive line, saying that the withdrawing state would 'leave the burden of maintaining international peace and security on the other Members', again seemed to point to the fact that drafters did not expect states to withdraw from the UN.[69]

However, John Foster Dulles, an advisor to the American conference delegation (and later US Secretary of State), was of the view that there was a right to withdraw under the Charter for two reasons. First, Dulles argued 'there was no provision either to allow withdrawal or to veto withdrawal', which mean that it 'followed, as a matter of law, that there was a right of withdrawal'.[70] A recent analysis is quite sceptical of this reasoning, noting that 'there is no provision in the Charter which authorizes Security Council or the General Assembly to release a state from membership' so it is far from clear that one can infer that a

in the UN Charter as an advance on the League Covenant – P Potter, 'The United Nations Charter and the Covenant of the League of Nations' (1945) 39 *American Journal of International Law* 546, 550.

[65] For examples, see A Zimmern, 'The Testing of the League' (1936) 14 *Foreign Affairs* 373; R Fosdick, 'Stabilization of Peace Through the League of Nations' (1935) 16 *Proceedings of the Academy of Political Science* 72.

[66] UNCIO, Verbatim Minutes of the Ninth Plenary Session, 25 June 1945, Doc 1210 P/20, 9. Soviet theories of international law were highly positivist and steeped in realist presumptions – see B Bowring, 'Positivism versus self-determination: the contradictions of Soviet international law' in S Marks (ed), *International Law on the Left: Re-examining Marxist Legacies* (Cambridge University Press, 2008) 133.

[67] H Kelsen, 'Withdrawal from the United Nations' (1948) 1 *Western Political Quarterly* 29.

[68] Ibid. See also US Senate Committee on Foreign Relations, 'Review of the United Nations Charter: A Collection of Documents, Subcommittee on the United Nations Charter', 83rd Congress, Doc 87 (United States Government Printing Office, 1954) 66.

[69] Ibid, US Senate.

[70] United States Congress-Senate Committee on Foreign Relations, 'Hearings before the Committee on Foreign Relations', 79th Congress, 1st Session on the Charter of the United Nations for the Maintenance of International Peace and Security, submitted by the President of the United States, 2 July 1945 (United States Government Printing Office, 1945) 647.

right to withdraw is implied by the presence or absence of any other provisions in the Charter.[71] The second strand of argument used by Dulles was that 'the agreement was not of a type which in any sense merged the member states into a new government … under which they give up any of their independence', foreshadowing the nature of the treaty test eventually incorporated into Article 56 VCLT.[72] There are two important points in response to this: (i) the UN Charter quite clearly did create a new and distinct type of international organisation, as the ICJ was later to hold in the *Reparations for Injuries* decision, which enjoyed privileges and immunities and some degree of authority over individual states on important questions of international stability;[73] (ii) bar the World Health Organization, all of the other multilateral frameworks that were created after the creation of the UN included withdrawal clauses in their legal frameworks.[74] It is very difficult to conclude that there was any intention among the UN founders to allow states to, using the terminology of chapter 1, unilaterally withdraw from the UN as of right derived from the voluntarist understanding of international law or as a means reflecting the political preference of the state in question. Equally, as some have argued, there is no obvious reading of the Charter that automatically supports the idea of withdrawal in light of changing circumstances.[75]

When Indonesia threatened to withdraw from the UN during the 1964 Christmas holidays, its stated reasons were that the election of Malaysia to the UN Security Council necessitated Indonesia's withdrawal from the organisation.[76] The British territory of Malaya had become independent in 1957, around a decade after Indonesia became independent. In 1963, the Federation of Malaya, as it was known, became the Federation of Malaysia, incorporating a number of territories, including Borneo.[77] As the Indonesian Government saw it this was directly contrary to Indonesia's own security interests, and threatening UN withdrawal was one of a variety of different diplomatic initiatives the country pursued in its political moves against the newly formed state. In January 1965, a letter was sent to the UN Secretary General from the Indonesian ambassador, accusing the UN of 'neo-colonialism' in accepting the formation of '"Malaysia" … this feeble and highly controversial new "State" … [a] tool of British Colonialism'.[78]

[71] S Sharma, 'Withdrawal from United Nations' (11 December 2016) at https://ssrn.com/abstract=2883698.

[72] US Congress-Senate Committee (n 70).

[73] *Reparations for injuries suffered in the service of the United Nations* [1949] ICJ Rep 179.

[74] Feinberg (n 47).

[75] M Paczek, 'On (In)Admissibility of Unilateral Withdrawal from the United Nations' (2018) 12 *Ius Novum* 117, 122–23.

[76] W Harris, 'Legal Aspects of Indonesia's Withdrawal from the United Nations' (1965) 6 *Harvard International Law Club Journal* 172.

[77] For a contemporary account of this dispute, see GMcT Kahin, 'Malaysia and Indonesia' (1964) 37 *Pacific Affairs* 253.

[78] The emphasis on Malaysia is taken from the original document – 'Letter dated 20 January 1965 from the First Deputy Prime Minister and Minister for Foreign Affairs of Indonesia addressed to the Secretary-General UN Doc S/6157' (21 January 1965) 21.

Later that month the Indonesian flag ceased flying outside the UN headquarters and its offices were vacated.[79] Writing in April 1965, Francis Livingston noted that in no way could Indonesia's declaration of withdrawal have arisen in response to 'exceptional circumstances' as set out in the 1945 interpretive declaration, and 'even more remote' was the possibility of claiming that the situation 'falls within the scope of the doctrine of *rebus sic stantibus*'.[80] But rather than engage with legal argument, the UN Secretary General's office simply treated this as occupying a new category of non-cooperation. A letter from UN Secretary General U Thant in February 1965 simply expressed 'regret' and a hope that Indonesia 'will resume full cooperation with the United Nations'.[81] As a practical matter, Indonesia was not seated at the UN for just over 18 months, was exempted from budgetary contributions, and replacements for representatives from Indonesia were found on various committees.[82] Eventually Indonesia was re-seated with the Secretary General stating, that it reflected 'a general consensus that a cessation of co-operation was involved, not a withdrawal'.[83] A distinction can be drawn between this episode and the attempts to challenge South Africa's UN membership, leading to the rejection of South Africa's credentials in 1974, as the South African Government wished to remain a member of the UN whereas most other states saw it as an illegitimate government because of apartheid.[84]

The substantive legal challenge to Indonesia's attempted withdrawal, in the letters from the British and Italian ambassadors to the UN Secretary General, focused on the principle of stability. As Schwelb notes, in a commentary published prior to the UN Charter's adoption the UK Government had concluded that states 'were not allowed to withdraw from the organization', going on to describe this as a 'great innovation … necessary [if] the Organization was to be able to adapt itself to the rapidly changing world'.[85] In 1965, the British ambassador to the UN wrote a letter intended to be 'without prejudice to their [Indonesia's] views' on the legality of withdrawal, arguing that a principle binding on all states was the duty 'to settle their international disputes by peaceful means'.[86] Going further, and almost ignoring the 'without prejudice disclaimer', the letter contended that the principles of Article 2 of the UN Charter were binding on

[79] T Longspecial, 'Indonesian Explains UN Withdrawal' *New York Times* (New York, 5 January 1965) 3.

[80] F Livingstone, 'Withdrawal from the United Nations: Indonesia' (1965) 14 *ICLQ* 637, 641.

[81] 'Letter Dated 26 February 1965 From the Secretary-General to the First Deputy Prime Minister and Minister for Foreign Affairs of Indonesia', UN Doc Nos A/5899 & S/6202 (28 February 1965).

[82] E Schwelb, 'Withdrawal from the United Nations: The Indonesian Intermezzo' (1967) 61 *American Journal of International Law* 661.

[83] YZ Blum, 'Indonesia's Return to the United Nations' (1967) 16 *ICLQ* 522, 530.

[84] A Duxbury, *The Participation of States in International Organisations: The Role of Human Rights and Democracy* (Cambridge University Press 2013) 117.

[85] Schwelb (n 82).

[86] 'Letter dated 8 March 1965 from the Permanent Representative of the United Kingdom of Great Britain and Northern Ireland to the United Nations Addressed to the Secretary-General', UN Doc A/5910 (8 March 1965).

all states regardless of UN membership. The Italian ambassador's letter, in a similar vein to the British ambassador's letter, argued that some obligations persisted regardless of UN membership, saying that it was to be 'assumed that such obligations stand regardless of whether the state continues to be part of the organization or not'.[87] Although the Italian letter went further than the British one, arguing that the lack of a withdrawal clause was significant, and criticising the declaration, the bulk of it concerned the principle that obligations under the UN Charter persisted in and of themselves in order to promote international peace and security and maintain the principles of the UN Charter. There are two potential readings of this. First, there exists an underlying system of international law that states have an interest in promoting outside of their own interests. This is in line with the theoretical framework of realism developed by Jonathon Charney, who maintains that state interest is broader than simple self-interest in an anarchic world, and that stable institutions help promote state interests.[88] It is also the position of the English school of international relations outlined in the preceding chapter, which maintains that there is an international society with certain normative values and institutions, rather than an anarchic society with various clashing forms of self-interest.[89] Second, it could be argued, following the work of constructivist theorists, that these letters are an attempt to articulate and shape the social identities of states.[90] Broader state practice over UN withdrawal, in particular the interpretative declaration, seems to point towards a collective identity shaped by the UN Charter. Louis Sohn's 1964 survey of expulsion from international organisations and the UN Charter noted in its conclusion that 'the future of mankind depends in a large sense on the maintenance of this constitutional unity and on the integrity of the constitutional instruments which form [the UN's] foundation'.[91]

Both interpretations have merit, but both theoretical frameworks are also an attempt to articulate an explanation of why stability ought to be maintained regardless of state action. The absence of a withdrawal clause was not so much evidence of collective intention about the impossibility of withdrawal – there were clearly different schools of thought about the merits of withdrawal during the drafting process; rather, non-withdrawal was more an identification of a shared interest in stability that was of sufficient gravity to preclude unilateral action.

[87] 'Note Verabale Dated 13 May 1965 from the Permanent Representative of Italy to the United Nations Addressed to the Secretary-General', UN Doc S/6356 (17 May 1965).

[88] J Charney, 'Universal International Law' (1993) 87 *American Journal of International Law* 529, 532–33.

[89] S Lechner, 'Anarchy in International Relations' (2017) *Oxford Research Encyclopaedia of International Studies* at https://oxfordre.com/internationalstudies/view/10.1093/acrefore/9780190846626.001.0001/acrefore-9780190846626-e-79 (accessed 24 August 2022).

[90] Wendt Constructing International Politics' (n 12); Reus-Smit (n 14).

[91] LB Sohn, 'Expulsion or Forced Withdrawal from an International Organization' (1964) 77 *Harvard Law Review* 1381, 1423.

II. RIGHTS TRANSCENDENCY

The stability principle described in section I is both a refinement of the 'nature' limb in Article 56 VCLT and a justification of the principle of non-withdrawal. The idea of rights transcendency is related to the principle codified in Article 56, although it was hinted at in the arguments over withdrawal from the UN Charter, as it maintains that there are certain rights, and obligations concerning those rights, that cannot be withdrawn from. There is a fairly well-established set of principles in international law that peremptory norms transcend other obligations, which is another form of rights-transcendent legal principle. This does not by implication mean that human rights treaties or treaties that involve rights protection cannot be withdrawn from in any circumstances, but it helps bolster arguments about the nature of a treaty, so that when such a treaty lacks a withdrawal clause there are ancillary reasons justifying non-withdrawal. Rights transcendency as an argument, as illustrated in the case study on North Korea in section II B, is a means of appealing to a hierarchy of norms in international law and trying to ground stability in values beyond notional inter-state practice.

A. The Principle of Rights Transcendency and Non-Withdrawal

The idea behind rights transcendency can intellectually be traced back to the works of Immanuel Kant and the idea, as Fernando Teson puts it, that 'international law requires respect for human rights because the just civic society is the ultimate goal of all political arrangements'.[92] Developing this further, Teson elsewhere argues that there are limits to the doctrine of state consent when it comes to human rights commitments, saying that state consent 'must be seen and interpreted in light of the principles of international justice that would result from a hypothetical, original contract' in the international community, involving not only states in a hypothetical original position but also the people living within states.[93] This is almost neo-Rawlsian in its use of an original-position analysis, although, as Anthony D'Amato notes in his study of John Rawls' work on international law, it is not clear to what extent Rawls' theory of the equality of nations supports this precise conclusion.[94] Nevertheless, the idea

[92] FR Tesón, 'The Kantian Theory of International Law' (1992) 92 *Columbia Law Review* 53, 55.

[93] FR Tesón, 'International Obligation and the Theory of Hypothetical Consent' (1990) 15 *Yale Journal of International Law* 84, 109.

[94] A D'Amato, 'International Law and Rawls' Theory of Justice' (1975) 5 *Denver Journal of International Law & Policy* 525. Rawls' original position is a thought experiment that imagines a situation wherein people are without information that enables them to tailor principles of justice favourable to their personal circumstances, an 'original position', and from this position would reason that there are certain universal basic social goods that ought to apply to everyone. For more information, see 'Original Position' in *Stanford Encyclopaedia of Philosophy* (3 April 2019) at https://plato.stanford.edu/entries/original-position/#:~:text=Rawls's%20original%20position%20is%20an,favorable%20to%20their%20personal%20circumstances.

of reaching beyond the boundary of the state and focusing on the individual as the ultimate bearer of rights outside of political communities has support in cosmopolitan theory. Cosmopolitan theory emphasised the idea of humanity as a higher principle and regarded the protection of humanity as transcending national boundaries.[95] Human rights law is a manifestation of this basic ideal although, as critics have pointed out, humanity itself is not a value-neutral proposition and cosmopolitanism is predicated on a particular set of ideological assumptions about international law and the state.[96]

Rights-transcendent reasoning is central to both the justification and the operation of peremptory norms. In the Advisory Opinion on *Reservations to the Convention on Genocide*, the ICJ was tasked with addressing the question of whether a reserving state could make a reservation to the Convention to which other parties object, but in analysing the question examined the binding nature of obligations.[97] There were, the Court concluded, principles 'recognized by civilized nations as binding on States, even without any conventional obligation'; in these cases there was 'one common obligation' binding on all states.[98] This was a significant moment in the development of the doctrine of peremptory norms, or *jus cogens*, customary legal norms that were binding on states regardless of formal obligation, overriding legal obligations to the contrary.[99] Peremptory norms had in fact been identified from the beginning of the twentieth century in international legal scholarship; in 1937, Alfred von Verdross argued that peremptory norms represented an 'ethical minimum' for all states that were members of the international community.[100] References to the law of civilised nations in Article 38 of the Statute of the Permanent Court of International Justice (PCIJ) pointed towards a set of transcendent values. In a 1953 ILC report, Hersch Lauterpacht noted that it was accepted that treaties 'cannot contract ... [or] ... violate binding rules of international law'.[101] Such a position is overtly hierarchical, and in fact the ILC Report on Fragmentation in International Law goes so far as to say that 'peremptory norms' is part of the 'vocabulary that gives expression to something like an informal hierarchy

95 D Held, 'Principles of Cosmopolitan Order' in GW Brown and D Held (eds), *The Cosmopolitan Reader* (Polity, 2010) 229; R Fine, 'Cosmopolitanism and Human Rights' (2007) *Law, Social Justice & Global Development Journal* at www.go.warwick.ac.uk/elj/lgd/2007_1/fine (accessed 25 July 2022).

96 C Douzinas, *Human Rights and Empire: The Political Philosophy of Cosmopolitanism* (Routledge-Cavendish, 2007) 134–43; P Cheah, *Inhuman Conditions: On Cosmopolitanism and Human Rights* (Harvard University Press, 2006) 149–52.

97 *Reservations to the Convention on Genocide* (Advisory Opinion) [1951] ICJ Rep 15.

98 ibid 23.

99 M Whiteman, 'Jus cogens in international law, with a projected list' (1977) 7 *Georgia Journal of International and Comparative Law* 609.

100 A von Verdross, 'Forbidden Treaties in International Law' (1937) 31 *American Journal of International Law* 571.

101 *Report on the Law of Treaties by Mr H Lauterpacht, Special Rapporteur*, UN Doc A/CN.4J63 (24 March 1953) 106.

in international law'.[102] There is also some considerable debate about which norms qualify for peremptory status, and using their importance to the international community as a metric for their identification ultimately depends on ideological considerations about the interests of the broader international community.[103] Although there has been extensive debate about the relative hierarchy of peremptory norms, there is an extent to which legal practice has developed an almost default position of assuming the hierarchy of peremptory norms, even though this often proceeds with relatively limited evidence being offered as to the superior status of the specific norm under consideration.[104]

Part of what can be described as the default position on the hierarchical status on peremptory norms is that, because of their wider importance and moral value to the international community, it is not possible for a state to withdraw from them in the way that it is possible to withdraw from a treaty.[105] The justification for this appears to be, according to a 1950 memorandum written by Professor Vespasian Pella at the request of the UN secretariat, that the violation of peremptory norms would be acts that 'endanger the peaceful coexistence of nations'.[106] The community-orientated significance of peremptory norms is repeatedly highlighted by authors such as Daniel Costelloe and William Conkilin, who argue that they are norms necessary for the conduct of international relations and underpin international law.[107] Curtis Bradley and Muti Gulati, in their influential study on withdrawal from custom, argue that the prohibition on withdrawing from customary international law in general was a modern positivist construction, and in the eighteenth and nineteenth centuries, withdrawal from custom was a relatively common practice.[108] Their

[102] ILC, *Report of the Study Group on the Ornamentation of International Law at the Fifty-Eighth Session of the International Law Commission* 2006, UN Doc A/CN.4/L 682 (Koskenniemi Report), para 327.

[103] G Christenson, 'Jus Cogens: Guarding Interests Fundamental to International Society' (1988) 28 *Virginia Journal of International Law* 585, 589. Kadelbach argues that the 'history of the codification projects and the concrete shape *jus cogens* has assumed in their results can best be brought in line with the case-law if both are taken as an expression of core values of the international legal order': S Kadelbach, 'Genesis, Function and Identification of Jus Cogens Norms' (2015) 46 *Netherlands Yearbook of International Law* 147, 165.

[104] D Shelton, 'Normative Hierarchy in International Law' (2006) 100 *American Journal of International Law* 291, 292; JHH Weiler and AL Paulus, 'The Structure of Change in International Law or Is There a Hierarchy of Norms in International Law?' (1997) 8 *European Journal of International Law* 545, 559.

[105] A Bianchi, 'Human Rights and the Magic of Jus Cogens' (2008) 19 *European Journal of International Law* 491, 507; see also P Robinson, 'Affirming the international rule of law' (2012) 1 *European Human Rights Law Review* 32, 34.

[106] Memorandum Concerning a Draft Code of Offences against the Peace and Security of Mankind, UN Doc A/CN/4/39 (1950) 17.

[107] D Costelloe, *Legal Consequences of Peremptory Norms in International Law* (Cambridge University Press, 2017) 53; W Conklin, 'The peremptory norms of the international community' (2012) 23 *European Journal of International Law* 837, 840.

[108] C Bradley and M Gulati, 'Withdrawing from International Custom' (2010) 120 *Yale Law Journal* 202.

project, as they explain it elsewhere, was to address what they saw as 'the failure to adapt exit rights to the new system' of customary international law.[109] They do acknowledge the 'special status' of peremptory norms, and whilst being sceptical about the binding nature of customary international law they are prepared to acknowledge that in certain limited circumstances, where 'certain fundamental rights of individuals' as opposed to 'interstate issues' are involved, there are binding norms on states.[110] Even though some states do violate peremptory norms, as is the case with customary international human rights law, the existence of violations does not negate the universality of the norm if, as Brian Lepard argues, state practice is conceived of as a statement about what is desirable practice for all states in terms of rights protection in light of the interests of the 'global community of states'.[111] As peremptory norms are framed as being crucial to the protection of the rights of individuals and the wider interests of the international community, the fear is that were a right of withdrawal to be in any way contemplated, it would be in essence permitting states to carry on abusing their own citizens.[112] This, however, relates to the norms or specific practices contained in those norms, not to the instruments or legal regimes containing the rights themselves. The presence of a withdrawal clause in instruments such as the ECHR does not mean that the rights in the Convention do not cover norms that have a peremptory status. Case law from the ECtHR on Article 3 ECHR is relatively clear that the prohibition on torture is a norm the prohibition of which exists as customary norm, and is a practice that states are under a duty to eliminate, even when the act of torture occurs in states outside the Council of Europe.[113]

Furthermore, states, when ratifying instruments protecting or granting an individual right, are engaging in a form of precommitment to a particular course of action, namely, the protection and recognition of individual rights, which ought to preclude the removal of those rights.[114] In *Ivcher-Bronstein v Peru*, when Peru tried to withdraw from the provision of the ACHR giving the IACtHR jurisdiction over individual petitions, the Court made this argument in two different ways, even though this was a case about good faith in withdrawal rather than the absence of a withdrawal clause. First, the IACtHR made the character argument, noting both the nature of the Convention as a human

[109] C Bradley and M Gulati, 'Customary international law and withdrawal rights in an age of treaties' (2010) 21 *Duke Journal of Comparative and International Law* 1, 7.

[110] Bradley and Gulati (n 108) 267.

[111] BD Lepard, 'Toward a New Theory of Customary International Human Rights Law' in BD Lepard (ed), *Reexamining Customary International Law* (Cambridge University Press, 2018) 252.

[112] N Petersen, 'The Role of Consent and Uncertainty in the Formation of Customary International Law' in Lepard (ed) (n 111) 111, 128–29.

[113] *Al-Adsani v United Kingdom* (2002) 34 EHRR 273 [60]–[61].

[114] Peters outlines this argument in some depth; see A Peters, *Beyond Human Rights: the Legal Status of the Individual in International Law* (Cambridge University Press 2013) 417–20.

rights treaty and that the denunciation clause set out how to withdraw from the Convention, the implication being that this was known to the parties at the time of commitment to it.[115] Second, the Court distinguished a 'unilateral juridical act carried out in the context of purely interstate relations', which would include recognition or diplomatic protest, from a 'unilateral juridical act carried out within the framework of treaty law'.[116] The latter would constrain state action within the context of that treaty; again, the implication was that this was justified because the states in question were party to a treaty. As Peters argues, this would mean that the sovereignty-based argument – 'what the state has given the state can take away' (described in chapter 1 as recognising sovereign decision making) – would be secondary to the creation of a stable legal regime of individual rights.[117] This presumes that the pre-commitment of states to certain rights, by virtue of treaty participation, ought to entail the locking in of certain values. There is a slight problem in this reasoning as it veers towards the trap, identified by Joseph Raz, of essentially presuming that human rights are important and should be universal by virtue of their basis in a common humanity.[118] A more powerful justification is given later in Peters' account, where she outlines that the citizens of a state are the 'legitimating point of departure' for the state in international law, as the whole basis of state action and its legitimacy to be recognised as a state on the international plane, is its status as a geographic entity making the co-existence of citizens possible.[119] Once a state has enabled the recognition and protection of rights via an international instrument, there is, as Peters argues, almost a presumption against withdrawal due to the relative lack of agency and participation an individual has in the international legal system and goes so far as to argue that this is part of an international order's guaranteeing a 'right to have rights' in the way outlined and advocated for by Hannah Arendt.[120]

Ultimately, all three strands of argument presented above – teleological cosmopolitanism, the protection of rights considered *jus cogens*, and the theory of pre-commitment – are argumentative mechanisms justifying rights protection that transcends the legal capacity of a state to initiate a withdrawal from its obligations. This is both distinct from and related to the principle codified in Article 56 VCLT. It both describes the nature of the treaty, in line with the second limb of Article 56, and implies a hierarchy in international law where the protection of rights supersedes other legal acts.

[115] *Ivcher-Bronstein v Peru* (Competence) IACHR Series C no 54, [1999] IACHR 9 [50]–[51].
[116] ibid [49].
[117] Peters (n 114) 418.
[118] J Raz, 'Human Rights Without Foundations' in S Besson and J Tasioulas (eds), *The Philosophy of International Law* (Oxford University Press, 2010) 322.
[119] Peters (n 114) 418.
[120] ibid 434–35.

B. North Korea and the ICCPR

This case study is often cited in relation both to withdrawal and the status of peremptory norms because it seems to be the most consistent application of the principles in Article 56 VCLT. The International Covenant on Civil and Political Rights (ICCPR), along with the International Covenant on Economic, Social and Cultural Rights (ICESCR), contains no withdrawal clause. North Korea acceded to the ICCPR in 1981, and its first country report to the Human Rights Committee (HRC), the ICCPR's treaty review body, was considered in 1984. It was not surprising that North Korea had signed up to the ICCPR; other Communist countries, such as Poland and Bulgaria, had acceded to the Convention in the 1970s. Although North Korea's initial report to the HRC was relatively unremarkable, it did not submit its second report, due in 1987. Seventeen separate reminders were issued by the HRC, but North Korea ignored them.[121] As the Cold War ended in 1990–91, North Korea not only grew more outwardly defensive, but it also began to be bracketed as a problem state by other international actors. In 1994, a severe famine took hold of the country, caused in part by, and certainly exacerbated by, governmental mismanagement. To control the population and keep news of the famine under wraps, the Government engaged in a brutal internal campaign of repression.[122] Around this time, Kim Yong Il took over from his deceased father Kim Il Sung as the Supreme Leader of North Korea. After taking power, Kim was determined to pursue a different policy trajectory, with a focus on 'our style of rights', based on the twin pillars of national security and the importance of a strong military. In a 1994 speech he outlined his thinking, arguing that 'human rights can never be realised without the defence of sovereignty … [P]eople under foreign rule can never achieve the fulfilment of true human rights.'[123] Ideologically, this position was ill-disposed to the process of an international body scrutinising the Government's domestic law's and human rights record, and with the nuclear crisis (discussed in previous chapters) going on at the same time, North Korea was intrinsically defensive about its sovereignty.

The catalyst for the rejection of the ICCPR came in 1997, when the Sub-Commission on Discrimination and the Protection of Minorities at the UN Commission on Human Rights issued a resolution 'deploring' the delay of over 12 years in receiving North Korea's country report.[124] But the crucial

[121] El Evatt, 'Democratic People's Republic of Korea and the ICCPR: Denunciation as an Exercise of the Right of Self-Defence' (1999) 5 *Australian Journal of Human Rights* 215.

[122] R Howard-Hassmann, 'State-Induced Famine and Penal Starvation in North Korea' (2012) 7 *Genocide Studies and Prevention: An International Journal* 147.

[123] J Song, *Human Rights Discourse in North Korea: Post-colonial, Marxist, and Confucian perspectives* (Routledge, 2011) 150.

[124] UN Commission on Human Rights, Sub-Commission on Prevention of Discrimination and Protection of Minorities, 'Situation of human rights in the Democratic People's Republic of Korea', E/CN.4/Sub.2/1997/50 (21 August 1997).

part, given North Korea's sovereign defensiveness, was the paragraph criticising the restriction of the rights contained in Article 12 ICCPR, which protected 'the right of everyone to leave any country, including his own, and to return to his country'.[125] Restrictions on movement were considered essential by North Korea for maintaining the regime's security during the famine and to ensure the stability of the Government. In a letter a couple of days later, the North Korean ambassador to the UN announced the Government's intention to withdraw from the ICCPR, claiming this was necessary because of 'the political intrigue of the elements who intend to isolate and stifle our Republic', with a further letter that autumn highlighting the political actions of western powers as being instrumental in the Government's decision.[126] In August 1997, the Chairperson of the HRC, after attempting some behind-the-scenes negotiation to try to get North Korea to change its mind, issued a statement saying that denunciation was a 'process aimed at denying its population the international protection of the rights guaranteed by the Covenant'.[127]

The question then was whether the ICCPR could be denounced – a memo submitted to the UN Secretary General later that month noted that the ICCPR was a treaty that did not contain a withdrawal clause. As far back as 1973, Schwelb had observed that in the 19 years during which the draft Covenants were considered by various organs of the UN, 'no suggestion' had been made about the inclusion of a withdrawal clause.[128] It was therefore difficult to assume that the drafters of the ICCPR left open the possibility of withdrawal. In a letter dated November 1997 from the Secretary General of the UN (acting in his capacity as depository of the treaty), this position was affirmed and all other parties were formally notified, presumably to encourage them to reach a position on whether withdrawal was possible.[129] In December 1997, the HRC issued General Comment 26 on the continuity of obligations, and reading this alongside an aide-memoire written in September 1997 by the UN Secretary General and attached to his November letter, three distinct positions on withdrawal from the ICCPR emerged, based on rights transcendency. First, General Comment 26 says that the ICCPR codifies in treaty form 'the universal human rights enshrined in the Universal Declaration of Human Rights' and was therefore meant to be a permanent treaty.[130] A tougher, more declarative statement of

[125] ibid para 1.

[126] International Covenant on Civil and Political Rights: Depository Notification by the Democratic People's Republic of North Korea, 'Letter from Kim Yong Nam, Minister for Foreign Affairs Democratic People's Republic of Korea' CN.467.1997.TREATIES-10 (Annex) (23 August 1997).

[127] Y Tyagi, 'The denunciation of human rights treaties' (2009) 79 *British Yearbook of International Law* 86, 168.

[128] E Schwelb, 'The Law of Treaties and Human Rights' (1973) 63 *Archiv des Völkerrechts* 1, 25–27.

[129] International Covenant on Civil and Political Rights: Depository Notification by the Democratic People's Republic of North Korea, CN.467.1997 (12 November 1997).

[130] HRC, 'CCPR General Comment No 26: Continuity of Obligations' CCPR/C/21/Rev.1/Add.8/Rev.1 (8 December 1997) para 3.

universalism was advanced in the aide-memoire, which noted that 'human rights treaties express universal values from which no retreat should be allowed'.[131] This straddled both rights transcendency, in highlighting the universalism of rights, and the Waldock argument – directly cited by name in the aide-memoire – that state practice indicated treaties of a permanent character could not be withdraw from.[132] Second, the HRC in General Comment 26 attempted to distinguish the presence of withdrawal clauses in other human rights treaties, saying that 'such treaties in general do not imply an inherent right of denunciation', noting that changes in government or state succession or secession did not terminate the protection of the rights under the Covenant.[133] The aide-memoire made this point too, noting four separate examples of human rights instruments containing withdrawal clauses, before concluding that it was 'difficult to argue that the negotiators of ICCPR somehow overlooked the possibility of explicitly providing for denunciation'.[134] Finally, the HRC specifically evoked an explicitly cosmopolitan universalism when it concluded that the rights in the Covenant 'belong to the people living in the territory of the State party' and that the protection accorded by them 'continues to belong to them', regardless of any action by a state party.[135]

General Comment 26's vision of universalism is a highly positivistic one, linking the universality of human rights to participation in a particular legal regime, and it does not attempt a grounding of universality in any particular philosophical proposition or invoke any abstract notion of humanity.[136] Universality is instead proved in the negative – the absence of the ability to withdraw becomes proof of those norms' universality – an argument that is echoed in some of the literature commenting on both North Korea's attempted withdrawal from the ICCPR and Jamaica's 1997 denunciation of Optional Protocol 1 to the ICCPR.[137] A way of understanding this reasoning is to look at the scholarship on the broader constitutionalising of human rights, which argues that even beyond a state's explicit consent, human rights law is binding upon states because of the importance of human rights to the international community.[138] This argument is given some credence by Tyagi, who notes that the absence of

[131] UN Secretary General, 'Aide Memoire: Denunciation of the ICCPR by the Democratic People's Republic of Korea', CN.467.1997.TREATIES-10 (Annex) (23 September 1997) para 7.

[132] ibid para. 6.

[133] HRC (n 130) para 3.

[134] UN Secretary General (n 131) para 8.

[135] HRC (n 130) para 4.

[136] The abstract nature of the humanity that universalism is founded upon is a common criticism of human rights law. C Douzinas, *Human Rights Human Rights and Empire: The Political Philosophy of Cosmopolitanism* (Routledge-Glasshouse, 2007) ch 3.

[137] I Boerefijn, 'Denunciations of Human Rights Instruments Jeopardise Universal Ratification' (1998) 16 *Netherlands Quarterly of Human Rights* 3.

[138] S Gardbaum, 'Human rights as international constitutional rights' (2008) 19 *European Journal of International Law* 749, 755–57. See also L Henkin, 'Human rights and state sovereignty' (1995) 25 *Georgia Journal of International & Comparative Law* 31.

a withdrawal clause in the ICESCR does not allow states to leave in the event of a fundamental change of circumstances, which, as Tyagi argues, occurred when the Committee on Economic, Social and Cultural Rights (CESCR) was established by the UN's Economic and Social Council in 1985.[139] The escape hatch and the change of circumstances theory of withdrawal (outlined in chapter 1) allow states to respond, shape or limit changes of circumstances by using the prospect of withdrawal as a means of shaping the operation and evolution of a treaty. It is also possible to read this in line with what Frédéric Mégret describes as international human rights law's attempt to redefine sovereignty as something that is supervised on the international plane.[140]

After North Korea's aborted withdrawal in 1997, in the summer of 1999 the HRC again issued a request for North Korea to report. Nothing seemed to happen for a year, then in March 2000 North Korea submitted its long-overdue country report. It glossed over several aspects of human rights protection in the country, reassuring the HRC that '[c]itizens enjoy equal rights in all spheres of state and public activity' and downplayed the number of state-sponsored killings recorded by NGOs in the 1990s by giving assurances that use of the death penalty was limited and only retained out of 'consideration of the special domestic circumstances' in the country.[141] In its concluding observations, the HRC welcomed the 'opportunity to resume the dialogue with the State party after an interval of more than 17 years' and said that it was 'pleased' to see that North Korea had 'recognized the importance of the Committee's task'.[142] This was all aimed at emphasising the importance of the HRC and its reporting as an institution, but that did not stop the HRC from being direct about substantive issues, noting, for example, that despite North Korea's statements on the death penalty, it retained capital punishment for four offences that were 'essentially political offences', and these were 'couched in terms so broad that the imposition of the death penalty may be subject to essentially subjective criteria'.[143] Despite the HRC's underscoring the need for the prompt reporting, that was the last report North Korea made; a 2013 resolution from the Security Council that mentioned cooperation with treaty bodies was ignored, as were investigations from Special Rapporteurs.[144] North Korea did engage with the Universal

[139] Tyagi (n 127) 91.

[140] F Mégret, 'International human rights law theory' in A Orakhelashvili (ed), *Research Handbook on the Theory and History of International Law* (Edward Elgar, 2011) 211.

[141] HRC 'Second periodic report of the Democratic People's Republic of Korea on its implementation of the International Covenant on Civil and Political Rights.' CCPR/C/PRK/2000/2 (4 May 2000) 15, 40.

[142] HRC, 'Consideration of Reports Submitted by States Parties Under Article 40 of the Covenant: Concluding observations of the Human Rights Committee', CCPR/CO/72/PRK (27 August 2001) para 1.

[143] ibid para 13.

[144] Human Rights Council, 'Compilation prepared by the Office of the United Nations High Commissioner for Human Rights in accordance with paragraph 15 (b)', A/HRC/WG.6/19/PRK/2 (24 February 2014).

Periodic Review (UPR) process run by the UN Human Rights Council, being reviewed by other states on its human rights in 2009, 2014 and 2019. In 2009, North Korea rejected recommendations made in its UPR review to bring its criminal justice system and legal procedure into line with its obligations under the ICCPR, despite being reminded that the ICCPR required it to do so.[145] A decade later, in 2019, the North Korean Government did not even mention the ICCPR in its report and was non-committal in relation to recommendations on the substantive rights that had triggered the 1997 dispute.[146] The practical outcome of the rights-transcendent arguments about North Korea's inability to withdraw from the ICCPR was to keep a recalcitrant state inside a legal regime with which, under different leaders over a two-decade period, it had shown little interest in complying. Substantively, there was little distinction between this and a non-compliant regime's refusal to withdraw from a treaty regime.

III. PRESERVATION OF LEGAL STATUS

Preservation of legal status is distinct from what has been outlined in the preceding sections of this chapter. In this instance, withdrawal has occurred, or is in the process of happening, and at issue is whether certain rights or legal statuses are preserved after withdrawal from the legal obligations contained in the treaties. The codification of this doctrine is located in Article 70 VCLT, which provides that the termination of a treaty 'does not affect any right, obligation or legal situation of the parties created through the execution of the treaty', which is intended to make a withdrawal from or termination of treaty non-retroactive.[147] This codifies the customary doctrine of acquired rights, outlined in the section III.A, but the scope of this doctrine has a more limited relevance in relation to the protection of rights more broadly.

A. The Doctrine of Acquired Rights

The concept of acquired rights is derived from municipal law in the Continental legal tradition as a mechanism for prioritising legal stability and predictability.[148] In the Advisory Opinion in *Settlers of German Origin in Poland*, the PCIJ held that civil rights acquired under a treaty must be protected; this included 'contract[s]

[145] Human Rights Council, 'Report of the Working Group on the Universal Periodic Review: Democratic People's Republic of Korea', A/HRC/13/13 (4 January 2010) paras 91.3 and 91.37.

[146] Human Rights Council, 'Report of the Working Group on the Universal Periodic Review: Democratic People's Republic of Korea', A/HRC/42/10 (25 June 2019) paras 126.113 and 126.138.

[147] M Villiger, *Commentary on the Law of Treaties* (Brill, 2009) 872.

[148] KS Sik, 'The Concept of Acquired Rights in International Law: A Survey' (1977) 24 *Netherlands International Law Review* 120, 124.

for the possession or use of property, whether such property be immoveable or moveable'.[149] The 1935 Harvard Draft on the Law of Treaties stated that a treaty's termination 'does not affect the validity of rights acquired in consequence of the performance of obligations stipulated in the treaty'.[150] Commentary on the Draft cited the US Supreme Court case *Society for the Propagation of the Gospel v New Haven*, which held that real estate lawfully purchased under the terms of a treaty survived that treaty's termination.[151] In *Northern Cameroons*, the ICJ held that when a trusteeship agreement was terminated by the UN General Assembly, rights that may have been granted to other states or their nationals would come to an end, but that this did not affect 'property rights which might have been obtained in accordance with certain Articles of the Trusteeship Agreement'.[152] In the *Sapphire* Arbitration Award in 1960, quoting a work by Arnold McNair on the subject, the tribunal concluded, in respect of a dispute over land that was used for oil concessions, that 'rights acquired under concessions is … one aspect of the respect for acquired rights, which is undoubtedly one of the general principles of law recognized by international tribunals'.[153] The 1966 Draft Articles on the Law of Treaties took this slightly further, saying that a treaty's termination did not affect any right, obligation or legal situation of the parties created through the execution of the treaty prior to its termination. This led to some pushback when it was discussed at the ILC, with the Uruguayan jurist Eduardo Jiménez de Aréchaga describing it as 'controversial in municipal law', expressing caution about referring to it in the codification of the law of treaties out of concern that it would 'interpreted to refer to rights acquired by nationals or individuals'.[154]

The relationship of the doctrine of acquired rights to human rights was discussed in the Fourth Report on state responsibility by FV Garcia Amador in 1959, where it was noted that questions were arising as to 'whether rights of a patrimonial nature belong among the human rights and fundamental freedoms' of the sort recognised in the UDHR.[155] Recognition of the right to property in both the UDHR and in the ECHR, as well as what were at the time the draft human rights covenants (later to become the ICCPR and ICESCR), prohibited the arbitrary removal of property. But this did not mean that such rights, if originally acquired under a treaty from which a state then subsequently withdrew, would remain permanent or, perhaps more importantly, could be justified with

[149] *Questions relating to Settlers of German Origin in Poland (Advisory Opinion)* PCIL Series B no 6 36 (1923) para 35.

[150] J Garner, 'Article 33. Termination of Treaties' (1935) 29 *American Journal of International Law Supplement: Research in International Law* 1161.

[151] *Society for Propagation of the Gospel v Town of New Haven*, 21 US (8 Wheat) 464 (1823).

[152] *Northern Cameroon (Cameroon v UK)* (Preliminary Objections) (Judgment of 2 December 1963) [1963] ICJ Rep 15.

[153] *Sapphire International Petroleums Ltd v National Iranian Oil Company* (Arbitral Award of 15 March 1963) (1963) 35 ILR 136, para C.9.

[154] *Yearbook of the International Law Commission*, 1966, vol II, para 64.

[155] ILC Document A/CN.4/U9: International responsibility: Fourth report by FV Garcia Amador, Special Rapporteur, *Yearbook of the International Law Commission* vol 2, para 12.

reference to that treaty. Writing in 1962, Pierre Laliev, observing the way in which both the Soviet Union and newly independent states were keen to nationalise or retain sovereignty over natural resources, noted that the doctrine of acquired rights could well 'stir controversies and create opposition' between the '"rich" and "poor" nations' as an expression of the 'conservatism of the "haves" … as a legal weapon in a world conflict of interests'.[156] Although Laliev was keen to stress that this did not have to be the case, it is possible to see how the doctrine could well conflict with more radical conceptions of human rights that sought to address the material conditions of individuals. It was clear from the writings of others around the same time, such as Francis Nicholson, who argued that 'security of the private property and of the acquired rights of aliens constitutes one of the general legal rules recognized by international law', that one of the doctrine's core functions was protecting the rights of the 'capital-exporting State' from 'nationalist sentiment' – which in the context of the time of writing clearly meant protecting the property of those in western (formerly colonial) states from newly independent governments in post-colonial states.[157]

With respect to rights not directly connected to physical property, the text of Article 70 VCLT is less clear, although it appears that a distinction is drawn between obligations on the state in relation to conduct and action, and those in reaction to a legal situation. Fitzmaurice's framing of the doctrine of acquired rights with reference to examples, noting that 'transfers of territory boundary agreements … or other territorial settlements' would be covered by the doctrine but 'an obligation to refrain from certain things' would not, arguably precluded the application of it to human rights.[158] Elsewhere in Fitzmaurice's report, as already noted, in setting out in which type of treaties the absence of a withdrawal clause would indicate non-withdrawal, treaties establishing a boundary or settling a territorial dispute, public international actions that could delineate or establish a status in relation to private property, were highlighted.[159] The justification, both in relation to acquired rights and the lack of a withdrawal clause, could be predicated on the grounds that these treaties are designed to resolve disputes and create stability, and limiting the category of lawful action to one party is important to maintain that stability. The ILC commentary on an early draft of the VCLT in 1966 was even stronger about the framing of the doctrine. As it was being codified, the ILC in the draft Convention stated that the doctrine only related the 'obligation or legal situation' of state parties through 'execution, and is not in any way concerned with the question of the 'vested interests of individuals''.[160] The report was also careful to distinguish between

[156] P Laliev, 'The Doctrine of Acquired Rights' in Southwestern Legal Foundation. International and Comparative Law Center (ed), *Rights and Duties of Private Investors Abroad* (M Bender, 1965) 167–68.

[157] FJ Nicholson, 'The Protection of Foreign Property Under Customary International Law' (1965) 6 *Boston College Law Review* 391, 397.

[158] Fitzmaurice (n 36).

[159] ibid.

[160] ILC, 'Draft Articles on the Law of Treaties with Commentaries', *Yearbook of the International Law Commission*, 1966, vol II, UN Doc A/CN.4/183, 265.

obligations, such as those arising from sunset clauses in human rights conventions, and breaches of international obligations made prior to the treaty, which would be subject to the law surrounding state responsibility, both of which were discussed in chapter 3.[161] However, its application as a general principle of law has led to its citation in investment arbitration in relation to the preservation of rights. In *Rumeli Telekom v Republic of Kazakhstan*, the arbitral tribunal made it clear, in the context of jurisdiction to ICSID, that a state could not 'take away accrued rights of a foreign investor by domestic legislation abrogating the law granting these rights'.[162] Commentary on this case and other investment arbitration decisions is sceptical that this means the doctrine of acquired rights creates a general constraint on the termination of rights, and it is worth noting that in *Rumeli Telekom* the reasoning on acquired rights was in tandem with a sunset clause.[163] This is why the next case study is so significant, as the rights of EU citizens after Brexit arguably involved both an example of vested individual rights and the creation of a new legal situation.

B. EU Citizens after Brexit

One of the important foundational victories for those campaigning for the UK to leave the EU was achieved in November 2015, when Parliament confirmed that EU citizens living in the UK would not have the right to vote in the forthcoming referendum. The Maastricht Treaty officially created a category of European citizenship in 1993, and citizenship conferred a series of rights on individuals from one Member State who were resident in another Member State, including the right to limited political participation, which lumped together nationality and citizenship without really merging the two.[164] Shortly before the Maastricht Treaty came into force, Advocate General Jacobs, one of the Advocates General of the ECJ, remarked that a national of one Member State who was present in another Member State should be 'treated in accordance with a common code of fundamental values … he is entitled to say "civis europeus sum"'.[165] Citizenship was not just a way of describing a procedural measure, it was a substantive set of rights that was further developed in case law in the mid-1990s and expanded by the 2004 Citizenship Directive.[166] Entailing access to the labour market, most

[161] ibid.

[162] *Rumeli Telekom AS and Telsim Mobil Telekomunikasyon Hizmetleri AS v Republic of Kazakhstan*, ICSID Case no ARB/05/16 Award (29 July 2008) para 335.

[163] T Voon, A Mitchell and J Munro, 'Parting Ways: The Impact of Mutual Termination of Investment Treaties on Investor Rights' (2014) 29 *ICSID Review* 451, 470–71.

[164] E Guild, 'The legal framework of citizenship of the EU' in D Cesarani and M Fulbrook (eds), *Citizenship, Nationality, and Migration in Europe* (Routledge, 1996) 30–55, 32.

[165] Case C-168/91 *Christos Konstantinidis v Stadt Altensteig -Standesamt and Landratsamt Calw - Ordnungsamt* (CJEU, 30 March 1993), Opinion of AG Jacobs, para 4.

[166] CM Rieder, 'The withdrawal clause of the Lisbon Treaty in the light of EU citizenship: between disintegration and integration' (2013) 37 *Fordham International Law Journal* 147.

social benefits and access to public institutions like schools, it meant that by the mid-2000s EU citizens could move their entire lives with ease to another country in the Union and expect a whole set of legal protections as of right from the domestic institutions of that state.[167] Although EU citizenship was later highlighted by Brexit supporters as evidence that the EU, as developed by the Maastricht Treaty, had departed from the concept of a common economic community, the origins of citizenship could be traced back to the 1950s.[168] Winston Churchill, speaking to the Hague Conference in 1948, said that he hoped in future 'men will be proud to say "I am a European" … men of every country will think as much of being a European as of belonging to their native land'.[169] The link between the Union and its citizens was made clear in the 2009 TEU, and case law highlighted that the protection of European citizenship was fundamental to the protection of all rights covered by European law more generally.[170] In 2016, it was estimated that there were over 3 million EU nationals living in the UK and over a million or more UK nationals living elsewhere in the EU, all exercising their right to citizenship.[171] The crucial value of EU citizenship for many of these individuals was regularising their legal status, but as the referendum on the UK's leaving the EU approached, the vast majority of them lacked the right to vote in it.

It is hard to understand the result of the Brexit referendum without acknowledging that hostility to migration from the EU, which used EU citizenship as the legal vehicle for that migration, served as a driver of support for the leave campaign.[172] The accession of eastern European nations in 2004 – around the time of the Citizenship Directive – and the lack of transitional controls on entrants to the UK from the accession states created an association between EU citizenship and the political problems of migration. Yet it was not clear

[167] W Maas, 'The Origins, Evolution, and Political Objectives of EU Citizenship' (2014) 15 *German Law Journal* 797; Council Directive 2004/38/EC of 29 April 2004 on the right of citizens of the Union and their family members to move and reside freely within the territory of the Member States amending Regulation (EEC) No 1612/68.

[168] E Olsen, 'The origins of European citizenship in the first two decades of European integration' (2008) 15 *Journal of European Public Policy* 40.

[169] Address given by Winston Churchill at the European rally in Amsterdam (9 May 1948) at http://www.cvce.eu/obj/address_given_by_winston_churchill_at_the_european_rally_in_amsterdam_9_may_1948-en-19c46889-2c6d-4dba-9371-dc965cd79a6a.html (accessed 19 September 2022).

[170] AG Jacobs argued that the 'seamless protection of fundamental rights under EU law in all areas of exclusive or shared EU competence matches the concept of EU citizenship' – see Case C-34/09 *Gerardo Ruiz Zambrano v Office National de l'Emploi (ONEm)* [2010] ECR I-01177, para 170.

[171] These figures were open to some dispute – BBC Brexit News, 'Reality Check: How many EU nationals live in the UK?' *BBC News* (8 July 2016) at www.bbc.co.uk/news/uk-politics-uk-leaves-the-eu-36745584 (accessed 20 January 2021).

[172] At the level of elite political campaigning there was a fairly clear link between immigration and the vote to leave; see A van der Zwet, 'Brexit, Europe and othering' (2020) 15 *Journal of the Academy of Social Sciences* 517. However, in terms of voting patterns and public, the link between hostility to EU citizens was much less clear and dissipated after the referendum vote; see M Goodwin and C Milazzo, 'Taking back control? Investigating the role of immigration in the 2016 vote for Brexit' (2017) 19 *The British Journal of Politics and International Relations* 450.

what those advocating leaving the EU actually wanted to happen to EU citizens living in the UK after Brexit; during the campaign, the chair of the Vote Leave campaign claimed that Article 70 VCLT would guarantee EU citizens' rights after Brexit, but when pressed was incredibly vague about what this entailed.[173] Most experts at the time disagreed about the status of the VCLT in securing the type of rights entailed by EU citizenship.[174] The promises in relation to migration from the official campaigns supporting Brexit were almost exclusively focused on what the UK would be able to do in the future after the transition period in Article 50 TEU had ended and, despite what some racist elements claimed, there were no clear commitments that would affect EU citizens' status. The general principle of non-retroactivity, referred to in Article 70 VCLT, had an obvious precedent in respect of foreign nationals as, when the Netherlands denounced the Netherlands–Indonesia Union in 1975, which gave a set of rights to Indonesians in relation to migration and residency, these rights were preserved after exit.[175] Greenland officially left the European Community (EC) in 1982, but its citizens were still considered citizens of the EU, whereas the Faroe Islands, whose residents hold Danish nationality, were explicitly excluded from EU citizenship due to a declaration made at the time of their accession to the EC in 1973.[176] After the Brexit referendum, however, the status of EU nationals was not guaranteed by the new Prime Minister, Theresa May, with members of Government describing EU citizens as being a 'card' to play in negotiations with the European Commission.[177]

The European Union Committee of the House of Lords issued a report in December 2016 on acquired rights and Brexit, concluding that acquired rights was 'a very useful label to describe people's expectations' but that the actual doctrine of acquired rights was 'much narrower' than was commonly supposed.[178] Vaughn Lowe QC's view was that the doctrine of acquired rights related principally to property rights of non-nationals where they were 'in circumstances where the enjoyment of those rights was threatened by a foreign State', and most of those giving evidence concluded that acquired rights were difficult to enforce.[179] This view had been articulated by Sionaidh Douglas-Scott

[173] For a contemporary account, see P Worrall, 'Will Brexit lead to mass deportations?' *Channel 4 Fact Check* (20 May 2016) at https://www.channel4.com/news/factcheck/factcheck-brexit-lead-mass-deportations (accessed 3 October 2022).

[174] R Mason, 'EU citizens in UK face Brexit uncertainty' *The Guardian* (15 May 2016) at www.theguardian.com/politics/2016/may/15/eu-citizens-uk-brexit-uncertainty-immigration-status-referendum (accessed 22 July 2022 as are all subsequent links unless stated otherwise).

[175] Sik (n 148) 139.

[176] WT Wooster, 'Brexit and the International Law Prohibitions on the Loss of EU Citizenship' (2018) 15 *International Organizations Law Review* 341.

[177] J Elgot, 'Liam Fox: EU nationals in UK one of "main cards" in Brexit negotiations' *The Guardian* (4 October 2016) www.theguardian.com/politics/2016/oct/04/liam-fox-refuses-to-guarantee-right-of-eu-citizens-to-remain-in-uk.

[178] European Union Committee, *Brexit: Acquired Rights* (HL 2016-17, HL Paper 82) paras 70–71.

[179] ibid paras 60 and 69.

prior to the referendum, who noted that whilst there was a lot of political 'noise' surrounding acquired rights and individuals' derived rights from EU treaties, individuals were not in any real sense parties to the treaties.[180] However, another view, set out by Michael Waibel, was that over the course of EU membership, EU citizens who had exercised their rights in the UK had crystallised their rights.[181] Although not explicitly mentioned in the House of Lords report, Article 50 TEU did not contain a savings clause expressly protecting citizens' rights in the withdrawing state. In common with other Member States, the UK remained a member of the ECHR, and the House of Lords noted that this would offer a variety of protections for EU citizens. Yet whilst Article 8 ECHR could be used to prevent deportations of EU citizens, at the time the House of Lords concluded its report it was still the stated policy of the UK Government to embark on a policy agenda that could entail withdrawal from the ECHR as well.[182] Ultimately, the main guarantor of EU citizens' rights post-Brexit, the House of Lords concluded, would be the protection of rights in a withdrawal agreement of the sort envisaged by Article 50 TEU.[183] Even then, however, there were uncertainties about what would happen to EU citizens if the UK were to withdraw from that, and in the 2020 UK–EU Cooperation Agreement there were no real safeguards that would preserve the rights of EU citizens in the event of its termination or withdrawal.[184]

Ultimately, this was treated as a question for resolution through immigration law processes, and from 2018 onwards, the continuing status of EU citizens in the UK and of British citizens in EU Member States was regularised through various registration systems.[185] UK nationals living in Britain simply lost their EU citizenship at the end of the Brexit transition period on 31 December 2020. Although the idea of a form of associate citizenship for UK nationals who wanted it was mooted, there was some doubt cast on its legality, as EU citizenship had always been held to be contingent on also possessing the nationality of a Member State.[186] Essentially, the issue of EU citizenship became part of a

[180] S Douglas-Scott, 'What Happens to "Acquired Rights" in the Event of a Brexit?' *UK Constitutional Law Blog* (16 May 2016) at https://ukconstitutionallaw.org/2016/05/16/sionaidh-douglas-scott-what-happens-to-acquired-rights-in-the-event-of-a-brexit/.

[181] M Waibel, 'Brexit and Acquired Rights' (2018) 111 *American Journal of International Law* 440, 444.

[182] V Mantouvalou, 'Using EU citizens as bargaining chips is wrong, problematic – and possibly illegal' *LSE Brexit Blog* (19 July 2016) at https://blogs.lse.ac.uk/politicsandpolicy/eu-citizens-as-bargaining-chips/.

[183] House of Lords (n 178) Conclusion, paras 4–9.

[184] For a general discussion see M Karayiğit, 'Post-Withdrawal legal implications of international agreements concluded within the framework of the EU legal order for the withdrawing member state' (2020) 19 *Ankara Avrupa Çalışmaları Dergisi* 153, 161–63.

[185] E Spaventa, 'Mice or Horses? British Citizens in the EU 27 after Brexit as "Former EU Citizens"' (2019) 5 *European Law Review* 589.

[186] M van den Brink and D Kochenov, 'Against associate EU citizenship' (2019) 57 *Journal of Common Market Studies* 1366, 1372.

broader cooperation game, following the logic of rationalist theorists, between the UK and the remaining EU Member States and EU institutions.[187] International law provided a framework for cooperation to take place on a shared matter of interest – the status of former EU citizens both in and out of the EU – and the issue of rights created a political imperative to cooperate rather than creating a continuing legal identity after exit. Human rights law's role in this process was to operate as a notional backstop against failure of the negotiations.

Individual EU citizens were essentially treated as passive recipients of rights, which were granted at the discretion of states, they did not gain any tangible legal legacy from the EU treaties that had for decades provided them with rights.[188] A savings or survival, clause in Article 50 TEU, or some other safeguard in Article 3 TEU might have changed the way this played out during the Brexit process, but it was unlikely that the TEU would have been designed that way, as EU citizenship was jealously safeguarded by Member States given the wide-ranging benefits it provided. Challenges by UK citizens as to whether they retained EU citizenship rights were ultimately unsuccessful. In the Opinion of Advocate General Collins in *Préfet du Gers*, a case brought by a British woman living in France who wanted to exercise her rights as an EU citizen, the loss of the rights of EU citizenship were 'one of the consequences of the sovereign decision of the United Kingdom to withdraw from the European Union'.[189] Beyond a state's being a Member State and being a party to EU treaties, the Advocate General's Opinion went on to reason there was no other source of access to EU citizenship, and there was no consideration of whether any rights had been acquired by the applicant. One NGO responding to the decision argued that this was emblematic of the deterioration since 2015 of the status of EU citizenship, as 'the attention has shifted towards security and EU member states have become more inventive, so to speak, on ways to undermine free movement'.[190] Another way of looking at this is as a direct reflection of an absence of a citizenship law for the EU; since the early 1990s, the EU has possessed a concept of citizenship but no unified law on obtaining or removing that citizenship, leading, as Wooster argues, to acquired rights being awkwardly bolted on to the different legal frameworks codifying EU citizenship.[191]

[187] See, for an overview of this theory, K Raustiala, 'Refining the limits of international law' (2005) 34 *Georgia Journal of International & Comparative Law* 423, 426–29. In terms of the way in which reputation shapes this rationalisation, A Guzman, 'A Compliance-Based Theory of International Law' (2002) 90 *California Law Review* 1823, 1849–50.

[188] Peters (n 114) 411.

[189] Case C-673/20 *Préfet du Gers and Institut national de la statistique et des études économiques* [2022] Opinion of AG Michael Collins at para 70.

[190] C Delpero, 'EU's top court confirms Brits lost EU citizenship because of Brexit' *Europe Street News* (9 June 202) at https://europestreet.news/eu-top-court-confirms-uk-citizens-lost-eu-citizenship-because-of-brexit/#:~:text=The%20Court%20of%20Justice%20of,from%20EU%20citizenship%20despite%20Brexit (accessed 15 September 2022).

[191] WT Wooster, 'Brexit as an Arbitrary Withdrawal of European Union Citizenship' (2022) 33 *Florida Journal of International Law* 96, 122.

CONCLUSION: RISING TO ARENDT'S CHALLENGE

Although not apparent from their highly technical reports in 1957 and 1963, the disagreement between Waldock and Fitzmaurice, about what presumptions could be drawn from the absence of a withdrawal clause in treaties, had a much deeper ideological dimension to it, one that raised a deeper question about the nature of international obligations. Presumptions in international law, as Thomas Frank and Peter Prowes note, are 'a guess about causality or correlation based on the common experience of a community of law'.[192] The 'community of law' to which Frank and Prowes refer describes international courts and tribunals, and the deductive reasoning that they undertook, and a key part of the English theory of international relations, is that there are institutions underpinning the often anarchic nature of international society.[193] Therefore, what was deduced from the absence of a withdrawal clause in a treaty from which a state was trying to withdraw, reflects both assumptions about institutions, such as treaty law, and more broadly the shared values of wider international society. After 1871 and the Black Sea Declaration, the presence of a withdrawal clause in a treaty meant that it was presumed that a lawful unilateral termination of obligations under the treaty was possible, when a state followed the terms of that withdrawal clause.[194] But this presumption by implication involved a further set of presumptions, including that there were certain cases where silence indicated withdrawal was not permitted.

Resolving the question of what the cases were where withdrawal would not be permitted because of the absence of a withdrawal clause, ultimately came down to some form of ideological argument about international law as a system. Assumptions about permanence were about informing system stability, and as chapter 5 makes clear, the stability of the overall international legal system is central to the international rule of law. Looking at the historical context of international treaty law's attempts at codification, the emphasis on permanence after the end of the First World War can be seen as the intellectual counterpart to the emergence of realist theory in international relations as a means of exploring how an international system broke down in the second decade of the twentieth century and then broke down all over again twenty years later. Legal argument, Anne Orford notes, relies on the assembling of the texts and practices of the past into 'persuasive patterns', giving a form of 'narrative whole'.[195] In the context of a world where international institutions' permanence had been conditional, it was persuasive to presume that the absence of a withdrawal clause in the UN

[192] T Franck and P Prows, 'The Role of Presumptions in International Tribunals' (2005) 4 *The Law & Practice of International Courts and Tribunals* 197, 200.
[193] ibid.
[194] Tobin (n 31) 194–95.
[195] A Orford, *International Law and the Politics of History* (Cambridge University Press, 2021) 285.

Charter both reflected the intent of the drafters to prohibit withdrawal and was necessary for the overall stability of the international system. From a realist perspective, such a conclusion is persuasive, in that a form of normative stability can help with the pursuit of individual interests on the part of states and stabilisation of their own power and status; and even though there is a strong diversity of theories in modern realist thought, this conclusion would be fairly common in many of them.[196]

Arendt's challenge, outlined in the Introduction to this chapter, of founding a 'new law on earth', questions in part whether there can be a set of rights that cannot be ignored, which is at the core of rights-transcendent reasoning outlined in section II of this chapter. Individual rights relating to treaty termination had, as section III outlined, a fairly clear antecedent prior to what may be described as the rise of modern international human rights law in the second half of the twentieth century, in the form of the doctrine of acquired rights. Rights-transcendent reasoning, as Joseph Raz synthesised it, involved recognising that there were moral reasons for limiting an exercise of state sovereignty, which in the context of this book meant saying that certain rights could not be withdrawn from.[197] Rights-transcendent reasoning bolstered arguments about both the intent and the character of a treaty, and could from a doctrinal point of view, be used interchangeably with the codification of the test set out in Article 56. Yet in substance this was a legal fiction; the presence of a legal prohibition on withdrawal meant imprisoning a state in regimes and legal obligations with which they had little intention of complying. Rights were transcendent, but not manifested in the case study described in section II of this chapter. Worst of all is that rights-transcendent reasoning can encourage a form of complacency about the power of rights and the institutions that protected them, as illustrated in the case study at the end of section III; there really was nothing to prevent the UK's withdrawal from the notional fallback architecture of human rights law in respect of EU citizens' rights. Arendt's observation about the 'poignant irony' of the discrepancy between the 'efforts of well-meaning idealists' who insist on the construction of inalienable human rights in law and the situation 'of the rightless' in practice seems to encapsulate this predicament.[198] Except that in the specific case of EU citizens, solutions were found, if haphazardly in practice, in part because of what is discussed in the next chapter – the international rule of law and the way in which the law of withdrawal fits into it.

[196] WC Wohlforth, 'Realism' in C Reus-Smit and D Sindal (eds), *The Oxford Handbook of International Relations* (Oxford University Press, 2008) 136–141.

[197] J Raz, 'Human Rights without Foundations' in S Besson and J Tasioulas (eds), *The Philosophy of International Law* (Oxford University Press, 2013) ch 15.

[198] Arendt (n 1) 364.

5

The Law of Withdrawal and the International Rule of Law

INTRODUCTION

IN APRIL 2009, news reports began to emerge about a strange new type of influenza in southern Mexico. It was when the second human infection of H1N1 was detected in California, 130 miles away. that a real sense of panic began. The World Health Organization's international health regulations kicked in shortly afterwards, requiring states to limit travel, start information sharing and work together to track the emerging spread of the virus. Originally conceived in the aftermath of the 2003 SARS pandemic, the regulations were drawn up in 2005 and revised in 2007, and were designed to reduce arbitrary measures at borders and encourage information sharing about outbreaks of infectious diseases.[1] Their legal framework stemmed from the WHO Constitution, which authorised the Organization to negotiate conventions, regulations and recommendations on any public health matter. As one scholar put it, epidemics often created 'irrational fears and discriminatory behaviours' among governments, and when emergencies struck, it was important to ensure that the public-health systems in different countries 'conform[ed] to the rule of international law'.[2] The H1N1 crisis passed a few months later, but shortly after the new decade started in January 2020, reports began to emerge about a new type of virus in the Wuhan region of China. This time, the panic was much worse; information sharing and data about health capacity were patchy and poorly communicated. Commenting in the medical journal *The Lancet* a year later, the members of the Review Committee on the Functioning of the International Health Regulations noted that 'inadequate compliance of states with [the health regulations], particularly on preparedness, contributed to the Covid-19 pandemic becoming a protracted global health emergency.'[3] As Laurence Gostin argued, 'the global

[1] WHO, 'Revision of the International Health Regulations' (23 May 2005) WHA58.3. For a critical analysis, see G Bartolini, 'The Failure of "Core Capacities" under the WHO International Health Regulations' (2021) 70 *ICLQ* 233.

[2] L Gostin 'Influenza A(H1N1) and Pandemic Preparedness Under the Rule of International Law' (2009) 301 *Journal of the American Medical Association* 2376, 2378.

[3] P Aavitsland et al, 'Functioning of the International Health Regulations during the COVID-19 pandemic' (2021) 398 *The Lancet* 1283, 1284.

solidarity envisaged' by the regulations, which required states to adopt a common and shared responsibility to 'collaborate … to the extent possible', had not been followed, and the wider political forces underpinning this collapse risked undermining health law and the international rule of law more generally.[4]

At issue were the specific provisions of the law, requirements on states to adapt their health care systems in a particular way and also, and perhaps more importantly, the idea that international law should rule this emergency and that the random and arbitrary actions of states should be discouraged. This speaks to a wider sense of law as a form of belief system. As Robert Howse and Ruti Teitle argue, a weakening of a belief in politics and economics to provide solutions for global problems has created a situation where law 'has enough positive resonance … to have become a preferred vocabulary for social order and for legitimating decisions of governance'.[5] Writing in a similar vein nearly two decades earlier, Martti Koskenniemi criticised international lawyers for their liberal desire to flee the hard realities of politics, looking to international law as a form escape route.[6] Yet the sense that international law's existence is premised on the solving of complex inter-state problems remains a compelling one for rationalist thinkers in their quest both to explain why international law works and to justify its operation.[7] Equally modern or 'new' realists seeking to nuance earlier realist theorists, who saw international law chiefly as a simple cipher for power politics, instead looked at grounding a theory of international obligation in ensuring predictability and stability.[8] In order for international law to be able to construct a predictable order and a framework to constrain states and solve global problems, there is a growing consensus, at least since the early 1990s, that international law needs to operate within a broader international rule of law.[9] The international rule of law means that international regulations, of the sort described above, which aim to deal with the problem of a global pandemic, gain a more predictable status and operate in a framework that more effectively binds states to particular courses of action.[10]

[4] LO Gostin, R Habibi and BM Meier, 'Has Global Health Law Risen to Meet the COVID-19 Challenge? Revisiting the International Health Regulations to Prepare for Future Threats' (2020) 48 *Journal of Law, Medicine and Ethics* 376, 379.

[5] R Howse and R Teitel, 'Beyond Compliance: Rethinking Why International Law Really Matters' (2010) 1 *Global Policy* 127, 134.

[6] M Koskenniemi, 'The Politics of International Law' (1990) 1 *European Journal of International Law* 4.

[7] R Keohane, 'The Demand for International Regimes' (1982) 36 *International Organization* 325; JK Setear, 'Responses to Breach of a Treaty and Rationalist International Relations Theory: The Rules of Release and Remediation in the Law of Treaties and the Law of State Responsibility' (1997) 83 *Virginia Law Review* 1.

[8] See G Shaffer, 'The New Legal Realist Approach to International Law' (2015) 28 *Leiden Journal of International Law* 189, 202.

[9] H Krieger and G Nolte, 'The International Rule of Law – Rise or Decline? Approaching Current Foundational Changes' in H Krieger, G Nolte and A Zimmerman (eds), *The International Rule of Law: Rise or Decline* (Oxford University Press, 2019) 3–30, 5–6.

[10] Some accounts of the International rule of law place a high virtue on compliance, eg see RE Goodin, 'Toward an International Rule of Law: Distinguishing International Law-Breakers from Would-Be Law-Makers' (2005) 9 *The Journal of Ethics* 255. See also Howse and Teitel (n 5).

In the English/Anglosphere tradition, the rule of law's most notable exponent was AV Dicey, an arch conservative legal scholar who, whilst not inventing the concept of the rule of law, which can be traced back to Cicero and had distinct historical antecedents such as Magna Carta, nevertheless came up with a persuasively simple synthesis. The rule of law, Dicey argued, could be defined by three core features: (i) all laws should be prospective and certain; (ii) all classes should be equally subjected to the law; and (iii) the law should emanate not from any written constitution but from the 'common law (judge-made)'.[11] This was parochially English but nevertheless came to dominate thinking about the concept, even though other legal traditions and concepts, such as *Rechtsstaat*, *Estado de direito* or *état de droit*, played analogous, but not synonymous, roles in other European countries and legal systems.[12] There are a number of references to the rule of law in international instruments such as the European Convention on Human Rights (ECHR), which refers to the governments of European countries as having 'a common heritage of political traditions, ideals, freedom and the rule of law'.[13] The rule of law has also been the subject of numerous international resolutions and declarations, but it is important to distinguish between the promotion of the rule of law, where states seek to export a particular set of ideas and ideological constructs to other states, and the international rule of law, that is, the idea that there is an international framework within which international laws – treaties, judgments, etc – ought to function.[14] The latter concept is important for the law of withdrawal, as it is concerned with the framework within which states operate in their international interactions, rather than with the way that they construct their internal domestic legal systems.

The Declaration on the Rule of Law at National and International Levels, adopted by the General Assembly following a High-Level Meeting of UN Member States in September 2012, is a good starting point, as there was an attempt at a synthesis of different conceptions of the rule of law.[15] The substantive provisions identify three basic features of the rule of law, the first being that international disputes are settled peacefully, echoing provisions in international instruments dating back centuries on the promotion of peace and

[11] AV Dicey, *Introduction to the Study of the Law of the Constitution*, 11th edn (Macmillan Press, 1979) ch IV; B Tamanaha, *On the Rule of Law: History, Politics, Theory* (Cambridge University Press, 2004) 63–65.

[12] European Commission for Democracy Through Law (Venice Commission), *Report on the Rule of Law*, CDL-AD(2011)003rev (Venice, 25 March 2011) at https://rm.coe.int/1680700a61 (accessed 10 September 2022).

[13] A Watts, 'The International Rule of Law' (1993) 36 *German Yearbook International Law* 15, 20; European Convention on Human Rights and Fundamental Freedoms (adopted 4 November 1950, entry in to force 3 November 1953) ETS 5.

[14] I Hurd, 'The International Rule of Law: Law and the Limit of Politics' (2014) 28 *Ethics and International Affairs* 39, 40; N Barber, 'The Rechtsstaat and the Rule of Law' (2003) 53 *University of Toronto Law Journal* 443, 452.

[15] UNGA Res 67/1, Declaration of the High-level Meeting of the General Assembly on the Rule of Law at the National and International Levels (30 November 2012) A/RES/67/1.

underpinning the Hague Convention, the League of Nations Charter and subsequently repeated in numerous other international instruments and international court decisions.[16] Second, that human rights need to be protected, reflecting and protecting norms considered *jus cogens* in international law.[17] Finally, the importance of 'fair, stable and predictable legal frameworks' was emphasised in the Declaration, in part to ensure 'equitable development, economic growth and employment', but also simply as a general public international good.[18] Other accounts of the international rule of law emphasise different features of the rule of law, but almost all of them focus on the issue of stability and the preservation of various rights.[19] Some, such as Simon Chesterman, highlight how the international rule of law is more about protecting the functioning of the international order than simply a reflection of the legal status quo, and in this context emphasis on doctrines, such as sovereign equality, are important in the promotion of the international rule of law.[20] Others, such as Mattias Kumm, argue that the precise features of the international rule of law are less important than is the assumption that states' interactions 'are to be ruled by law' and that inter-state cooperation is facilitated, allowing international law to shape dialogue between states.[21] The intention, as Kumm puts it, is not that states are ruled by 'good' law but that they are ruled by a framework of law and are constrained by clearly agreed rules.

The withdrawal of a state from a legal regime, following the legal principles of withdrawal, is not necessarily incompatible with the international rule of law and at some level is a fundamental feature of it. However, the practical reality of many incidents of withdrawal detailed so far in this book is that they can pose a challenge to the international rule of law. When a state withdraws from a legal regime, there may, in a fashion akin to the politics of the Covid-19 pandemic, be internal politics in states that incentivises the breaking of international obligations. There also may, in a fashion similar to the legal regime surrounding the response to pandemics, be harm caused to other states caused by the withdrawing state's not complying with legal obligations. Furthermore, there is a sense that if all states acted in their own interests, the coordination problems, which rationalist theory maintains international law exists to solve, would become irreconcilable. The international rule of law is there, in short, to

[16] ibid Art 4; R Higgins, 'Peaceful Settlement of Disputes' (1995) 89 *Proceedings of the Annual Meeting of the American Society of International Law* 293.

[17] UNGA Res 67/1 (n 15) Art 5. On the general point of *jus cogens*, K Parker, 'Jus Cogens: Compelling the Law of Human Rights' (1988) 12 *Hastings International & Comparative Law Review* 411.

[18] UNGA Res 67/1 (n 15) Art 8.

[19] See, eg, S Wheatley, 'A Democratic Rule of International Law' (2011) 22 *European Journal of International Law* 525; J Waldron, 'Are Sovereigns Entitled to the Benefit of the International Rule of Law?' (2011) 22 *European Journal of International Law* 315.

[20] S Chesterman, 'An international rule of law?' (2008) 56 *The American Journal of Comparative Law* 331.

[21] M Kumm, 'International Law in National Courts: The International Rule of Law and the Limits of the Internationalist Model' (2003) 44 *Virginia Journal of International Law* 19, 22–23.

ensure that even if there is rule breaking, there is a sense of an overarching legal framework that differentiates those states who are acting lawfully from those who are not, thereby in turn reinforcing the law itself. Maintaining a sense of constraint when a state is seeking to free itself from its obligations is difficult, as chapter 3 has outlined, but that sense of obligation, as this chapter argues, is vital for the international rule of law. It means that in a moment of potential crisis for the law's authority, as legal obligations cease, a rule-bound order dictating how states act maintains the wider international rule -bound system. The law of withdrawal does this by helping underpin the overall 'public good' of stability in international law, but this does not necessarily extend as far as underpinning other wider aims and goods associated with the international rule of law.

I. STABILITY GOODS, THE INTERNATIONAL RULE OF LAW AND WITHDRAWAL

Stability is at the core of many theories of the rule of law, with theorists as diverse as Dicey, Friedrich Hayek and Joseph Raz all acknowledging it as a core attribute.[22] Because of international law's lack of a hierarchical structure, some theorists, such as HLA Hart, have doubted the existence of an international rule of law more generally.[23] But this lack of hierarchical structure has not prevented arguments that stability is an essential feature of certain international legal doctrines. To illustrate, take the following two examples. Writing in 1950, DN Johnson argued that the doctrine of acquisitive prescription – where claims to title over territory not heard within a reasonable time were determined to have lapsed – was essential to 'preserve international order and stability', and that most scholars identified 'stability' as the basis for the rule of acquisitive prescription.[24] The World Trade Organization's (WTO) waiver regime allows for waivers of any obligation under WTO agreements, which, although subject to a set of precise rules governing their operation, at the same time notionally allow different legal standards.[25] One of the core justifications for allowing flexibility in this area, Isabel Feichtner argues, is the promotion of trade liberalisation through a legal framework that is aimed at overall stability in the international trading system.[26] Stability can become almost self-justificatory

[22] S Beaulac, 'The Rule of Law in International Law Today' in G Palombella and N Walker (eds), *Relocating the Rule of Law* (Bloomsbury Publishing, 2008) 197–224, 205–06.

[23] For an overview and critique of Hart's theory, see M Payandeh 'The Concept of International Law in the Jurisprudence of HLA Hart' (2011) 21 *European Journal of International Law* 967.

[24] D Johnson 'Acquisitive prescription in international law' (1950) 27 *British Yearbook of International Law* 332.

[25] M Matsyshita et al, *The World Trade Organization: Law, Practice and Policy*, 3rd edn (Oxford University Press, 2015) 15–17.

[26] I Feichtner *The Law and Politics of WTO Waivers: Stability and Flexibility in Public International Law* (Cambridge University Press, 2011) 45–47.

in these arguments, allowing the reproduction of international legal authority because international law is implicitly positioned as saving the international system from instability or 'crisis'.[27]

The justification of individual international legal doctrines on the basis that they facilitate stability between states, or protect particular aspects of international society such as the international trading system, is distinct from the rule of international law's capacity to promote the stability of international law as a legal system. This is about providing a framework, for facilitating a shared understanding about what functional legal norms are and how they ought to operate to encourage a practice of legality among states.[28] For example, in relation to *pacta sunt servanda*, formal legal rules contained in the Vienna Convention on the Law of Treaties (VCLT) aim to provide a framework for distilling a state's will at a particular point of time and provide a justification for constraining a state's future actions. As a consequence, a treaty provides a form of stability, regardless of whether it restricts the use of chemical weapons or facilitates trade in computers.[29] The stability created by the doctrine of *pacta sunt servanda* relates not just to the substantive effects of the treaty in question – that is, an arms reduction treaty creating stability by controlling the numbers of a particular type of missile – it also relates to the system of international law as a whole. A state complying with a weapons treaty, because, say, it has an obligation to do so, promotes the stability of the international legal system as a rule-bound international system by being yet another example of a state that is complying with its obligations. This can be termed a 'stability good' – a form of public good in international law that is part of the form of international law as a system of law. It is both a product of and a justification for the rule of international law. As Daniel Bodansky notes, international law does not strictly speaking recognise a category of 'global public goods' or 'international goods', but does recognise certain international community interests, such as *erga omnes* obligations – obligations owed to the international community as a whole.[30] The protection of the community interest of stability and predictability in the international legal system is central to the rule of international law, and in debates about law ascertainment, such as the role of 'soft law' in international law, preserving 'stability' is as a vital component of the rule of international law.[31]

[27] J d'Aspremont, 'Send back the lifeboats: confronting the project of saving international law' (2014) 108 *American Journal of International Law* 680.

[28] SJ Toope, 'International law and the practice of legality: Stability and change' (2018) 49 *Victoria University of Wellington Law Review* 429, 435.

[29] In a sense this is an expression of state will and consent – see V Pergantis, *The Paradigm of State Consent in the Law of Treaties* (Elgar International Law, 2017) 99–103.

[30] D Bodansky, 'What's in a Concept? Global Public Goods, International Law, and Legitimacy' (2012) 23 *European Journal of International Law* 651, 653; *Barcelona Traction, Light and Power Company, Limited (Belgium v Spain)* [1970] ICJ Rep 3.

[31] C Chinkin, 'Normative Development in the International Legal System' in D Shelton (ed), *Commitment and Compliance: The Role of Non-binding Norms in the International Legal System* (Oxford University Press, 2003) 21–42, 23.

The argument about the production of stability is in essence part of a wider justification for the rule of international law more generally, in that the claim is made that it creates a stable system or framework of expectations on states. Stability and its promotion through the rule of international law can be inherently conservative, in that it fixes the subjects of the rule of law (ie. designates who are and who are not states) and limits the capacity for certain political actions, such as the secession of states, in the interests of stability and the legal framework for recognition of new states heavily favours existing state entities and geographic boundaries.[32] Equally, the maintenance of stability is not necessary value-neutral; by protecting international law as it is and ensuring its predictability, existing hegemonic powers and dominant economic relationships are prioritised.[33] The maintenance of stability also does not mean that exceptions will not be found to certain laws or legal principles, nor that lawyers will not try to work around legal prohibitions. This is common to all legal systems; a criminal defence lawyer in any given domestic legal system, will for example try to find ways round the law or loopholes in the law in the process of defending their client. At the international level, as Jeremy Waldron argues, this demonstrates that there is a legal system in place governing international relations, ensuring the construction of a 'predictable environment' in which states can 'plan their affairs and make … decision[s]'.[34] Stability of the international legal system as a whole has, as chapter 1 of this book sets out, been cited as a justification for the law of withdrawal and the constraining effect it has on states wishing to leave a legal regime. The law of withdrawal is also one of the features that helps create stability within the international rule of law, fulfilling the dual, and self-referential, role of both being created by and helping to justify the rule of international law. To understand how the law of withdrawal helps create stability, thereby underpinning the rule of international law, it is important to examine two concepts that can be described as stability goods – the tangible forms of the more abstract notion of stability.

A. The Creation of Legal Certainty

A common aspect of rule of law theory, noted both by conservative theorists like Friedrich Hayek and by left-critical theorists such as Roberto Unger, is the existence of legal certainty and predictability.[35] At the international level,

[32] See Y Shany, 'Does International Law Grant the People of Crimea and Donetsk a Right to Secede? Revisiting Self-Determination in Light of the 2014 Events in Ukraine' (2014) 21 *The Brown Journal of World Affairs* 233; T Christakis, 'The ICJ Advisory Opinion on Kosovo: has International Law something to say about secession?' (2011) 24 *Leiden Journal of International Law* 73, 81.

[33] See N Krisch, 'International Law in Times of Hegemony: Unequal Power and the Shaping of the International Legal Order' (2005) 16 *European Journal of International Law* 369, 373–75.

[34] Waldron (n 19) 338.

[35] See Tamanaha (n 11) 65–66 and 83 for an in-depth analysis of both thinkers' views of legal certainty.

a 2013 Report from the UN Secretary General noted that the 'rule of law accords predictability' to the actions of states, underpinning 'the responsibility of a state to all individuals within its territory'.[36] A year earlier, the Resolution on the Rule of Law at the National and International Levels had cited predictability as a core feature of the rule of international law.[37] Other international organisations and bodies have also issued declarations citing legal certainty as a central feature of the international rule of law, loosely defining legal certainty as the idea that legal rules guide people's, or states', actions and judges' decisions, and that those rules are internally consistent.[38] Historically, the contract theory of international treaty law meant that, outside principles deemed to be part of the law of nations, treaties were treated as individual bargains; but from the nineteenth century onwards, the creation of permanent multilateral legal regimes, such as the Copyright Union, or international transit regimes, meant that treaties progressed from being bargains to webs of obligations.[39] The increasingly complex international interactions created by these treaties required a doctrine of certainty that extended beyond the trust that states, or more accurately heads of government, had towards one and other and into a networked form of predictability. Some legal regimes, such as those dealing with international financial stability or regional economic organisations, such as the EU, require the implementation of provisions from international law into domestic law, in order for there to be legal certainty at the international level.[40] Even though there are clear organisational aims and advantages to states from becoming party to these treaties, such as facilitating the movement of capital and free trade in goods, they are not dependent on the realisation of those outcomes in order to achieve adherence to those legal principles. However, their legal structures create a sense of certainty in the legal regime and afford state actors a sense of predictability in their interactions with one another in these areas. Human rights regimes, which are designed to create universalised international standards of rights protection for individuals living in diverse and different societies, often face difficulties in balancing flexibility and certainty when it comes to interpretations of substantive rights provisions by states seeking to argue that a particular provision of a treaty must be interpreted in light of their own cultural sensitives.[41]

[36] Report of the Secretary-General, *Strengthening and coordinating United Nations rule of law activities* (2013) United Nations General Assembly Sixty-Eighth session, A/68/213.

[37] UNGA Res 67/1 (n 15).

[38] J Maxeiner, 'Some Realism About Legal Certainty in the Globalization of the Rule of Law' (2008) 31 *Houston Journal of International Law* 27, 40.

[39] AD McNair, 'The Functions and Differing Legal Character of Treaties' (1930) 11 *British Yearbook of International Law* 100, 105.

[40] See F Lupo-Pasini, 'Financial stability in international law' (2017) 18 *Melbourne Journal of International Law* 5, 13; J Raitio, *The Principle of Legal Certainty in EC Law* (Kluwer Academic Publishers, 2003) 6–10.

[41] Y Donders and V Vleugel, 'Universality, Diversity and Legal Certainty: Cultural Diversity in the Dialogue between CEDAW and States Parties' in M Kanetake and A Nollkaemper (eds), *The Rule of Law at the National and International Levels: Contestations and Deference* (Hart Publishing, 2015) 321–352.

Withdrawal was historically seen as a potentially destabilising concept in treaty law, with one writer noting, in a 1917 article in the *American Journal of International Law*, that 'whilst not illegal', unilateral denunciation by a state party was a somewhat 'abrupt' way of ending a treaty.[42] A quest for doctrinal certainty and the creation of real-world stability underpinned the treatment of withdrawal clauses when the rules on treaty law began to be codified in the mid-twentieth century.[43] Withdrawal clauses facilitate legal certainty by creating the expectation that all acts to do with the removal or termination of substantive obligations are legal acts, not acts operating outside the law. Take weapons control treaties: as outlined in earlier chapters, the 1968 Nuclear Non-Proliferation Treaty (NPT) contains a withdrawal clause providing a legal framework for states to leave. When the treaty was being drafted in the late 1960s, this was highlighted as being important for states that did not possess nuclear capacity and were dependent on the security guarantees of those states that did possess nuclear weapons.[44] Article X of the Treaty not only provided a predictable and stable framework for states to withdraw, regulating withdrawing states' actions, but also helped underpin the stable international order that the NPT sought to create. By giving non-nuclear weapons states a means to withdraw if the nuclear powers did not fulfil their responsibilities, such as guaranteeing the security of smaller states, the uncomfortable spectre of more states without nuclear weapons deciding to become armed, now without any lawful restraint, was implicitly raised.[45] This gave incentives for compliance, giving a degree of certainty, and also helped generate stability in the wider world in relations between states when it came to nuclear proliferation. Beyond the NPT, where states have sought to work around the substantive provisions in weapons control treaties, and thus undermine the legal certainty of the treaty, this has been criticised for its general impact on the stability of weapons control regimes. When in 2000 some politicians in the US began considering the creation of a missile defence system that could undermine the substantive provisions of the 1972 Anti-Ballistic Missile (ABM) Treaty, the then Russian Foreign Minister warned that this disrupted the way that the ABM Treaty had made relations between 'nuclear powers, become stable and predictable'.[46] By acting outside the Treaty's legal framework, the

[42] D Myers, 'Treaty Violation and Defective Drafting' (1917) 11 *American Journal of International Law* 538, 545.

[43] See O Lissitzyn, 'Stability and Change: Unilateral Denunciation or Suspension of Treaties by Reason of Changed Circumstances' (1967) 61 *Proceedings of the American Society of International Law at Its Annual Meeting (1921–1969)* 186, 187.

[44] G den Dekker and T Coppeny, 'Termination and Suspension of, and Withdrawal from, WMD Arms Control Agreements in Light of the General Law of Treaties' (2012) 17 *Journal of Conflict & Security Law* 25, 34–36.

[45] ibid. As Dunn notes, without the withdrawal clause it would not have been possible to negotiate the NPT: LA Dunn, 'The NPT: Assessing the Past, Building the Future' (2009) 16 *Non-Proliferation Review* 143, 166.

[46] I Ivanov, 'The Missile-Defense Mistake: Undermining Strategic Stability and the ABM Treaty' (2000) 79 *Foreign Affairs* 15, 17. Treaty on the limitation of anti-ballistic missile systems (adopted 26 May 1972, entered into force 3 October 1972) 944 UNTS 13.

US was creating an 'exceptional circumstance' justifying Russia considering withdrawal from other instruments, such as the Strategic Arms Reduction Treaty.[47] This political dispute was framed in the language of legality, in part because there were legal frameworks in existence for managing uncertainty, change and withdrawal. Operation outside of those frameworks meant that the legal nature of the state's actions compromised both the treaty system and the efficacy of international law as a whole to regulate weapons control.

By providing this link between legal certainty as a formal legal construct and certainty of a state's actions, withdrawal clauses can complement other compliance clauses in an instrument. Drawing on insights from game theory, one study of international environmental treaties argued that environmental treaties needed to be carefully designed to create incentives both to comply and not withdraw in order to prevent the 'free-rider problem', where states remained members of an agreement without taking actions to reduce environmental damage.[48] In this context a withdrawal clause could encourage compliance by the other members by providing a notional escape route for non-compliant states.[49] Although premised on a realist calculation of the individual benefits to states being the core feature of international obligations, this analysis points toward one important aspect of how withdrawal clauses work: they aim to create fixed classes of subjects, of states with and states without legal obligations, thereby underpinning legal certainty. This can have distinct downsides, as if powerful or key state parties remain outside a treaty regime, or there is mass withdrawal from a regime, this significant weakens the overall normative environment in favour of compliance with that treaty, hence encouraging broader uncertainty about the stability of legal regimes, both the specific regime itself and as a general principle in international law.[50] Equally, an act of withdrawal itself can create wider patterns of uncertainty. In March 2021, the Turkish Government withdrew from Istanbul Convention, a Council of Europe treaty on preventing and combatting violence against women. An official statement from the office of the President of Turkey explained that the Convention had been 'hijacked by a group of people attempting to normalize homosexuality', necessitating Turkish withdrawal, and this was fiercely criticised internationally, including by the Committee on the Elimination of Discrimination against Women, who described it as a 'deliberately retrogressive measure'.[51] The Parliamentary Committee of the Council of Europe noted in a resolution on the topic that 'the ratification and denunciation

[47] ibid.

[48] U Wagner, 'The Design of Stable International Environmental Agreements: Economic Theory and Political Economy' (2001) 15 *Journal of Economic Surveys* 377.

[49] ibid.

[50] R Williamson, 'Hard Law, Soft Law, and Non-Law in Multilateral, and Non-Law in Multilateral Arms Control: Some Compliance Hypotheses' (2003) 4 *Chicago Journal of International Law* 59, 62.

[51] These quotations are taken from the definitive account of the episode, B Çali and L Helfer, 'The Gender of Treaty Withdrawal: Lessons from the Istanbul Convention' *EJIL Talk* (28 November 2022) at www.ejiltalk.org/the-gender-of-treaty-withdrawal-lessons-from-the-istanbul-convention/.

of treaties are a matter of national sovereignty', but also went on to say that the decision had been based on misinformation and minimal parliamentary processes, which would undermine 'legal stability and predictability'.[52] The Resolution went on to call for the Venice Commission, the Council of Europe's advisory body on constitutional matters relating to democracy, human rights and the rule of law, to prepare guidelines on 'the modalities that should govern the ratification and withdrawal from Council of Europe conventions'.[53] Other nations had been threatening withdrawal from the Istanbul Convention, and the episode highlighted how the use of an individual sovereign prerogative of withdrawal, and the stated reasons accompanying it, could create wider uncertainty about the protection of human rights more generally.

Fears of a mass exodus of African states from the ICC were, as shown in the preceding chapters, somewhat overblown. However, the withdrawal of Zimbabwe in 2009 from the Southern African Development Community's (SADC) Tribunal Protocol led to a chain of events that significantly weakened the Tribunal and undermined legal certainty in relation to its capacity to enforce its decisions.[54] In this case, the Zimbabwean Government successfully lobbied other states within SADC to reject the proposition that the SADC Tribunal could rule on *Mike Campbell v Zimbabwe*, a case involving land appropriation in Zimbabwe, and order damages against Zimbabwe, and as a consequence urged other states to strip the Tribunal of its human rights jurisdiction.[55] As Erica de Wet noted, this was in part a reflection of a weak rule-of-law culture among SADC member states, but also reflected foundational weaknesses in the structure of the organisation as a whole.[56] A wider uncertainty was created by this episode, both about how far a regional legal order could evolve and to what extent an international tribunal's capacity to order remedies was in fact conditional.[57] Although the claimant in *Campbell* was able to pursue other legal options, this was another example of the absence of clear withdrawal provisions in a jurisdiction protocol, creating broader legal uncertainty as to whether states could pre-emptively withdraw pending a difficult decision. As argued in previous chapters, although this is contrary to the general good faith principle, an

[52] Parliamentary Assembly of the Council of Europe, Resolution 2376 (2021), The functioning of democratic institutions in Turkey, para 8.

[53] ibid.

[54] K Alter, J Gathii, and L Helfer, 'Backlash against international courts in west, east and southern Africa: causes and consequences' (2016) 27 *European Journal of International Law* 293.

[55] *Mike Campbell (Pvt) Ltd and Others v Republic of Zimbabwe* (2/2007) [2008] SADCR 2 (28 November 2008). For the chronology on this, see F Cowell, 'The death of the Southern African Development Community Tribunal's human rights jurisdiction' (2013) 13 *Human Rights Law Review* 153.

[56] E De Wet, 'The Rise and Fall of the Tribunal of the Southern African Development Community: Implications for Dispute Settlement in Southern Africa' (2013) 28 *ICSID Review* 1,18.

[57] CPR Romano, 'Trial and Error in International Judicialization' in CPR Romano, K Alter and Y Shany (eds), *The Oxford Handbook of International Adjudication* (Oxford University Press, 2015) 122–125.

appropriately drafted withdrawal clause can create legal certainty by defining the expected behaviour of states. Even if the terms of a withdrawal clause may not in practice be followed in an individual case, the existence of the expectation in and of itself has value in distinguishing adherence to law and compliance from law breaking and non-compliance by states, contributing to overall legal certainty.[58] In this respect, a withdrawal clause can act to further buttress the rule of international law.

B. The Restriction of Arbitrary Behaviour by State Parties

The constraint of arbitrary power, and the idea that rulers should act within the law, is a common feature of writings on the rule of law, going back several centuries.[59] In the Anglophone tradition, this can be dated back to Henry of Bratton's thirteenth-century treatise *On the Laws and Customs of England*, which said that a king would gain his power not from 'reigning but from ruling well', and would need to 'tempor his power by law' as 'the law of mankind has decreed that his own laws bind the lawgiver'.[60] In the German legal tradition, the concept of *Rechtsstaat* was defined in part by the state's 'having the duty to uphold the law as laid down by the legislature and to ensure that all state activity was conducted according to law'.[61] At the international level similar concepts can be seen: in its *Report on the Rule of Law*, the Venice Commission cited the 'Prohibition of arbitrariness' as one of the core features of the international rule of law, and a number of other declarations on the rule of law at both national and international level highlight the prohibition of arbitrariness.[62] The international rule of law, as it applies to states in their international interactions with other states and with international legal regimes, may be viewed, as Robert Goodin puts it, as a prohibition on 'each state doing exactly as it pleases, or dares without restraint from any internalized normative constraints'.[63] The literal manifestation of this lies inside the decision making of governments, or in the mentality of individual political leaders, who accept that the existence of a legal obligation

[58] For an analysis about the expectation of compliance in international law, see B Simmons, 'Compliance with international agreements' (1998) 1 *Annual Review of Political Science* 75; GW Downs and MA Jones, 'Reputation, Compliance, and International Law' (2002) 31 *The Journal of Legal Studies* 95, 99–101. For a more critical account of the expectations on states, see E Posner, 'Do States Have a Moral Obligation to Obey International Law?' (2003) 55 *Stanford Law Review* 1901.

[59] Stein traces this in R Stein, 'Rule of Law: What Does It Mean' (2009) 18 *Minnesota Journal of International Law* 293, 297–99.

[60] H Bratton, *On the Laws and Customs of England*, vol III (Harvard University Press, 1968) 305–06.

[61] Watts (n 13) 18.

[62] European Commission for Democracy (n 12); R McCorquodale, 'Defining the international rule of law: defying gravity?' (2016) 65 *ICLQ* 277.

[63] Goodin, (n. 10) 228.

will set the parameters of their actions internationally and as a consequence act as though they are constrained by their legal obligations.[64] The rule of law does not need or entail, nor does it even imply, a complete or coherent legal framework, Dencho Georgiev argues; rather, it needs to exist as a social phenomenon where contradictions do occur but there is a continuous process of overcoming those contradictions.[65] Crawford makes a related observation, commenting on the treatment of the rule of international law by the International Court of Justice (ICJ) in *Elettronica Sicula SpA (ELSI) (United States of America v Italy)*, that in essence the prohibition of arbitrariness was not a breach of a specific obligation but the prohibition of actions in an inconsistent manner by a state.[66] So a violation of the rule of law is not just, for example, the failure to carry out the specific terms of an obligation; it would also be accompanied by a set of actions designed to destabilise the operation of a legal regime, or would create a broader precedent that would undermine other legal regimes. The prohibition on arbitrary actions by states in favour of actions within a legal framework helps underpin a series of aims that the rule of international law, or more precisely the aims contained in statements about the rule of international law from both academic or official sources, purports to bring to the wider international system.[67]

The application of this to withdrawal is, on the surface, both straightforward and contradictory. Straightforwardly, the obligations contained in a withdrawal clause need to be adhered to, and a state not adhering to a withdrawal clause, or seeking to undermine or destroy a legal regime on the way out, is engaging in arbitrary behaviour, as by definition it is trying to achieve withdrawal by non-legal actions in a way that undermines the continued existence of those obligations for others beyond the withdrawing state. But withdrawal is a process that has to react and respond on the international level to the changing views of a state at the domestic level, which can often reflect political whims or political anger about the very predictability and stability that international law imposes. During the process of Britain's exit from the European Union (EU) for example, there was a debate in 2017 about whether the process set out in Article 50 of the Treaty of the European Union could just be ignored.[68] Although confined to the margins of political discourse, it gained momentum when politically controversial issues, such as paying remaining contributions and charges to the EU – popularly dubbed the 'Brexit bill' – gained salience. The legal framework of the

[64] Watts (n 13) 15.

[65] D Georgiev, 'Politics or rule of law: deconstruction and legitimacy in international law' (1993) 4 *European Journal of International Law* 1.

[66] J Crawford, 'International Law and the Rule of Law' (2003) 24 *Adelaide Law Review* 3, 8.

[67] WW Bishop, 'The International Rule of Law' (1961) 59 *Michigan Law Review* 553.

[68] This was known as a 'No Deal Brexit'; for a comment on the legality, see H Woolaver 'Could International Law Stop a No-Deal Brexit?' *EJIL Talk* (16 October 2019) at www.ejiltalk.org/could-international-law-stop-a-no-deal-brexit/ (accessed 21 August 2022 as are all subsequent links in this chapter unless stated otherwise).

Treaty tried to prescribe what was and was not arbitrary behaviour, but for those seeking to exit the EU quickly, this was not a question of arbitrariness and the general preservation of the stability of institutions of the EU.[69] For them, this was a question of the law itself taking sides in a political argument and, consequently, fettering the democratic decision making of a government. Although eventually resolved politically, this points to a broader issue, that the definition of what is arbitrary, by virtue of prescribing the actions a state may make or decide, is in and of itself a value statement with a distinct ideological dimension.[70] Protection against arbitrariness therefore becomes a means not only of maintaining the status quo, but also of creating a set of bounded circumstances within which a state can act. In relation to weapons control treaties, such conservatism can be justified in terms of balancing out a variety of interests, and in relation to nuclear weapons it can be seen as a form of pragmatism, dealing with the realities of a world where many states refuse to fully engage in multilateral disarmament.[71] However, when dealing with commercial relationships and the protection of property, the preservation of the status quo can involve taking sides in an area where there is potentially a greater degree of ideological contestation.[72]

An example of this is Bilateral Investment Treaties (BITs), which protect the interest of private investors' capital in host states. These treaties rely on the general framework of international investment law, which through its reliance on and promotion of the arbitration function, as Eric de Brabandere notes, has a public international law character.[73] Decisions from ICSID have made clear that whilst investors may not rely on the terms of a BIT 'as a kind of insurance against the risk of any changes in the host state's legal and economic framework', they are entitled to rely on the specific provisions that the host state has made, including a 'specific legal obligation for the future, such as by contracts, concessions or stabilization clauses', on which an investor is 'entitled to rely as a matter of law'.[74] The whole purpose of this is to ensure a 'predictable framework' for

[69] M Dougan, *The UK's Withdrawal from the EU: A legal Analysis* (Oxford University Press 2021) 60–75.

[70] For an outline of the theory behind this, see A Orford, 'Constituting Order' in A Crawford and M Koskenniemi *The Cambridge Companion to International Law* (Cambridge University Press, 2012) 271, 284–87.

[71] On the concept of stability generated by the NPT, see L Horovitz, 'Beyond Pessimism: Why the NPT Will Not Collapse' (2015) 38 *Journal of Strategic Studies* 126. Jasper's point emphasises this is a highly unequal order: U Jasper, 'Dysfunctional, but stable – a Bourdieuian reading of the global nuclear order' (2016) 4 *Critical Studies of Security* 42.

[72] S Frerichs and R James, 'Correlated ownership: Polanyi, Commons and the property continuum' in M Hirsch and A Lang (eds), *Research Handbook on the Sociology of International Law* (Edward Elgar, 2020) 63.

[73] E de Brabandere, *Investment Treaty Arbitration as Public International Law: Procedural Aspects and Implications* (Cambridge University Press 2014) 11–12.

[74] *EDF v. Romania*, ICSID Case No. ARB/05/13, Award, 8 October 2009, para. 216; *Total S.A. v The Argentine Republic*, ICSID Case No ARB/04/01, Award (27 November 2013) para 117; See more generally of ICSID Centre and stability Katja Gehne and Romulo Brillo 'Stabilization Clauses in International Investment Law: Beyond Balancing and Fair and Equitable Treatment' Research Paper Institute of Economic Law Transnational Economic Law Research Center (TELC)

investment; and the promotion of this form of stability allowed for the rapid expansion of private investment during the 1990s, to the extent that by the year 2000, 50 per cent of all foreign direct investment was through BITs.[75] This made BITs increasingly desirable to states seeking to advance their economic development; and for developing states, signing up to a BIT in the 2000s became a way not just to receive inward investment but also to demonstrate to outside actors their stability as a destination for inward investment.[76] Yet maintaining stability also involved allowing a considerable degree of external examination of a state's own internal economic policies in the arbitration process. For instance, when in 2002 Ecuador decided to change the way it awarded reimbursements of value-added tax (VAT), a foreign company engaged in oil exploration was able to use the terms of a US–Ecuador BIT to engage in international arbitration. In the arbitration it was held that the central question was not whether there was an international legal obligation to refund VAT, but whether the legal and business framework met the requirements of 'stability and predictability'.[77] When interpreting another BIT, the arbitral tribunal focused on the statement in the preamble 'that a stable framework for investment will contribute to maximizing the effective utilization of economic resources and improve living standards', concluding that this was indicative of the parties' intention to provide 'continuous investment protection to investors of the other contracting state'.[78]

The emphasis on stability also carries over into the consideration of the question of consent to arbitration in Article 72 of the ICSID Convention, which preserves the rights of individuals in the event of withdrawal and reinforces the language of Article 25 of the Convention, which prohibits the unilateral withdrawal of consent to arbitration by any party. This prevents an attempted withdrawal of consent by denouncing the ICSID Convention, effectively allowing a prohibition on unilateral acts terminating arbitration.[79] This directly favours the investing state and legal individuals within the investing state, by moving away from a framework where, as Frédéric Sourgens puts it, the host or home state retains discretion to modify the terms under which investment is carried out in its jurisdiction by unilateral action.[80] This is necessary, as Sourgens

No. 143 (March 2017) available at <https://icsid.worldbank.org/sites/default/files/parties_publications/C6106/2021.01.08%20Parties'%20Post%20Hearing%20Briefs/Claimants'%20Post%20Hearing%20Submission/Legal%20Authorities/CL-0281.pdf>.

[75] *Metalclad Corporation v The United Mexican States*, ICSID Case no ARB(AF)/97/1, Award (30 August 2000) para 99; D Swenson, 'Why Do Developing Countries Sign BITS?' (2005) 12 *UC Davis Journal of International Law & Policy* 131, 138.

[76] Swenson (n 75).

[77] *Occidental Exploration and Production Company v The Republic of Ecuador*, LCIA Case no UN3467 (US/Ecuador BIT), Final Award (1 July 2004) para 191.

[78] *Mohamed Abdel Raouf Bahgat v Arab Republic of Egypt*, PCA Case no 2012-07, Decision of Jurisdiction (30 November 2017) para 314.

[79] C Schreuer, 'Denunciation of the ICSID Convention and Consent to Arbitration' in M Waibel et al, *The Backlash against Investment Arbitration: Perceptions and Reality* (Kluwer Law International Law, 2010) 363–64.

[80] F Sourgens, *A Nascent Common Law: The Process of Decisionmaking in International Legal Disputes between States and Foreign Investors* (Brill Publishing, 2009) 62.

explains, because the 'prospective entitlements upon which investors could rely in making long-term decisions' are entirely dependent on the 'stable transnational process of investor-state arbitration'.[81] As another study highlights, the whole process of drafting clauses in investment treaties that notionally present a state with autonomous options is in fact often designed to make it harder for the state to alter its means of escaping its obligations and protect the long-term nature of foreign investment.[82] In *Transban Investments v Venezuela*, the Venezuelan Government, which had withdrawn from the ICSID Convention, argued that the claimant company had not properly perfected consent to arbitration as required by the Convention's withdrawal clause. Responding to this, Transban Investments argued that 'Venezuela's position violated basic principles of legal security', and even though the claimants were ultimately unsuccessful for other reasons, the defendant state's objection to jurisdiction was dismissed.[83] Unilateralism and concern about unilateral conduct need to be seen in the context of a broader set of assumptions about the conduct of states when it came to inward investment, which favoured rule-bound stability and reflected the interests of capital-exporting states.[84]

Prior to South American states' withdrawal from the ICSID Convention in the late 2000s, there was some considerable criticism about how ICSID membership was essential for obtaining World Bank credit.[85] Indeed, attempts to create an alternative regional system of arbitration can be read as an attempt to demonstrate their desire to maintain a rule-based framework, with the Bolivian Government even going so far as to argue, shortly before denouncing the Convention in 2006, that ICSID's decisions were arbitrary, because of their unclear 'methodology' and secrecy.[86] Over course of the next decade, this became a more accepted line of criticism, with the EU Trade Commissioner in 2017 expressing disapproval of investment arbitration for its lack of legitimacy and unpredictability.[87] Direct and indirect uses of the language of arbitrariness, and the attempt to challenge the dominant pro-investor ideological position of international investment law using this language, shows how key a component the prohibition on arbitrary behaviour is to the rule of international law. The ICSID Convention's withdrawal clause supports a particular set of ideological

[81] ibid.

[82] See T Voon and AD Mitchell, 'Denunciation, Termination and Survival: The Interplay of Treaty Law and International Investment Law' (2016) 31 *ICSID Review – Foreign Investment Law Journal* 413; see also F Sourgens, 'Keep the Faith: Investment Protection Following the Denunciation of International Investment Agreements' (2013) 11 *Santa Clara Journal of International Law* 335.

[83] *Transban Investments Corp v Bolivarian Republic of Venezuela*, ICSID Case no ARB/12/24, Award (22 November 2017) para 57.

[84] L Trakman, 'The ICSID Under Siege' (2012) 45 *Cornell International Law Journal* 603, 611–16.

[85] SK Fiezzoni, 'The Challenge of UNASUR Member Countries to Replace ICSID Arbitration' (2011) 2 *Beijing Law Review* 134.

[86] ibid 138.

[87] C Malmström (European Commissioner for Trade), 'Reforming Investment Dispute Settlement', Speech on 27 February 2017 at http://trade.ec.europa.eu/doclib/docs/2017/february/ tradoc_155393.pdf (accessed 3 January 2022).

assumptions about what is and what is not arbitrary, by protecting investors with the creation of legal remedies for them to access in the event of withdrawal, in the interests of preserving a stable international regime.[88]

II. COMMUNITY VALUES, THE INTERNATIONAL RULE OF LAW AND WITHDRAWAL

The rule of international law can be said to be creating a systemic framework of legality that sets out the rules for states to operate in international society. Stability, as a concept, has a status quo bias, which means that part of a withdrawal clause's job in supporting the international rule of law is to help maintain the existence of the status quo constructed by a legal instrument, as was illustrated by the nuclear weapons and BIT examples discussed in section I. Even though the process of withdrawal terminates legal obligations for an individual state, stability in the system overall survives. But theories of the rule of law are not just about the preservation of stability; they often have a distinct moral dimension to them. As Terry Nardine puts it, the rule of international law should be 'a moral idea', implying limits on the means by which governments as well as persons pursue their goals.[89] Value-orientated ends became increasingly important for the rule of law project at an international level, with the ascent of international human rights law as a universal good.[90] But ideas of the rule of law as serving a broader set of values beyond the promotion of stability go back further. As Georg Schwarzenberger noted in a 1939 article, the international community often was underpinned by quasi-Christian theological values, reflected in legal concepts such as the law of nations, and it was the ascent of a positivistic form of international law from the eighteenth century onwards that moved international law away from this value-orientated conception of the rule of law.[91] The date on which Schwarzenberger was writing was significant for his critique, as with the advent of the Second World War there was wider scepticism of positivist international law, the failure of international structures to preserve peace seeming to confirm that something more than formal legal obligation was needed in order for international legal structures to be effective.[92]

[88] McLachlan argues that withdrawals and threats of withdrawal have put investment arbitration reform 'on the table in UNCITRAL': C McLachlan, 'The Assault on International Adjudication and the Limits of Withdrawal' (2019) 68 *ICLQ* 499, 510.

[89] T Nardin, 'Theorising the international rule of law' (2008) 34 *Review of International Studies* 385, 386.

[90] Hurd (n 14); R Teitel, 'Humanity's Law: Rule of Law for the New Global Politics' (2002) 32 *Cornell International Law Journal* 355; D Kinley, 'Human Rights, Globalization and the Rule of Law: Friends, Foes or Family?' (2002) 7 *UCLA Journal of International Law and Foreign Affairs* 239.

[91] G Schwarzenberger, 'The Rule of Law and the Disintegration of the International Society' (1939) 33 *American Journal of International Law* 56.

[92] For examples, see I Jennings, 'The Rule of Law in Total War' (1941) 50 *The Yale Law Journal* 365; Q Wright, 'International Affairs: International Law and the Totalitarian States' (1941) 35 *The American Political Science Review* 738.

Arguments about the thick and thin conceptions of the rule of law are the subject of a vast literature on the rule of law in the domestic sphere, and the position of human rights and arguments about individual welfare feature heavily within this discussion.[93] In the international sphere, as Robert McCorquodale argues, there has been a tendency among theorists on the rule of international law to focus on the 'thick conceptions of the rule of law', which advocate the concept of the rule of law as protecting substantive interests, as opposed to the thin conception of the rule of law, which sees the rule of law as being limited to providing a framework that prohibits practices such as arbitrary rule.[94] McCorquodale's case is that 'order and stability, transparency, good governance, justice and accountability' in international affairs requires that human rights be recognised as part of the rule of law.[95] There is an ongoing debate in the English school of international relations, which mirrors this argument in international legal theory, between pluralists, with a more minimalist conception of international society with institutions focusing on order between states, and solidarists, who argue that protecting values is a core component of international society.[96] Those in the solidarist school would, for example, place a greater emphasis on the promotion and protection of human rights as a key element of international political order than pluralists would.[97] However, more generally human rights has become central to discussions over international stability. Increasingly, political scientists and international relations scholars have recognised that the protection of rights and economic interests within a state is important for that state's ability to continue as a functioning entity.[98] The wider impact on stability in the international system as a result of state collapse was and is considerable, therefore any conception of the international rule of law ought to recognise certain substantive interests, in particular the protection of human rights, as being essential to statehood, even though there may be ideological contestation over which rights are recognised.[99]

[93] For summaries of this literature and the wider debate about different conceptions of the rule of law, see Tamanaha (n 11) 99–113; J Møller and S-E Skaaning, 'Systematizing Thin and Thick Conceptions of the Rule of Law' (2012) 33 *The Justice System Journal* 136.

[94] McCorquodale (n 62) 292–94 discusses both Bishop (n 67) and Watts (n 13) in his analysis.

[95] McCorquodale (n 62) 292–94.

[96] J Williams, 'Pluralism, solidarism and the emergence of world society in English school theory.' (2005) 19 International relations 19; W Bain 'Pluralism and Solidarism' in C Navari (eds.) *International Society: The English School* (Palgrave Pivot, 2021) 95–108.

[97] J Vincent *Human Rights an International Relations* (Cambridge University Press 1986) 92–105.

[98] This was a core tenet in the literature on state failure; see R Jackson, 'Juridical statehood in sub-Saharan Africa' (1992) 46 *Journal of International Affairs* 1. See more generally N Englehart, 'State Capacity, State Failure, and Human Rights' (2009) 46 *Journal of Peace Research* 163; HP Just and G Nolte, 'International Law and the Rule of at the National Level' in M Zurn, A Nollkaemper and R Peerenboom (eds), *Rule of Law Dynamics: In an Era of International and Transnational Governance* (Cambridge University Press, 2012) 48–67.

[99] State collapse and the importance of a functioning system of human rights are linked in some of literature on juridical statehood – see C Clapham, 'Degrees of statehood' (1998) 24 *Review of international Studies* 143 – with some suggesting that respect for human rights is interlinked with the doctrine of recognition, eg C Reus-Smit, 'Human rights and the social construction of sovereignty' (2001) 27 *Review of International Studies* 519.

Discussion of the concept of state failure has been criticised for being part of a broader trend of not recognising the differences between states that were created as a result of colonialism and those that had engaged in colonialism.[100] Yet the legal doctrine of sovereign equality maintains that there is at least a formal legal equality between states.[101] Sovereign equality, or the equal treatment of states before the law on the international plane, is a feature of some early accounts of the rule of international law; Emer de Vattel, in 1749 in the *Law of Nations*, reasoning that 'a dwarf is as much a man as a giant', drew the conclusion that 'a small Republic is no less a sovereign state than the most powerful kingdom'.[102] Both the protection of human rights and the doctrine of sovereign equality are what may be termed community values – concepts that underpin the international community and the international rule of law, providing it with longer-term teleological benefits. In a similar fashion to stability goods, they are both justified and produced by the international rule of law but involve a 'thicker' conception of the rule of law than that described so far. Yet they both sit somewhat awkwardly with the law of withdrawal.

A. Sovereign Equality and Withdrawal Clauses

The 1945 UN Charter founded the UN on the principle of the 'sovereign equality of all its Members', creating what Fassbender described as an impressive principle but one that was in service of an 'ideal type' constitutional order.[103] The 1933 Montevideo Convention was more specific in the way that it defined sovereign equality, clarifying that it meant that states enjoyed 'the same rights and have equal capacity in their exercise' and that these rights 'do not depend upon the power which [the state] possesses to assure its exercise, but upon the simple fact of its existence as a person under international law'.[104] The narrower definition in the UN Charter represented a form of equality premised on equality before the law, not substantive equality in terms of the possession of equal rights and duties but, as Hans Kelsen put it, 'equality of *capacity for* duties

[100] For an outline of this critique, see A Anghie, 'The Evolution of International Law: Colonial and Postcolonial Realities' (2006) 27 *Third World Quarterly* 739.

[101] Roth notes its particular application to 'weak' states: B Roth, *Sovereign Equality and Moral Disagreement: Premises of a Pluralist International Legal Order* (Oxford University Press, 2011) 14–15.

[102] E Vattel, *The Law of Nations or the Principles of Natural Law Applied to the Conduct and to the Affairs of Nations and Sovereigns* (GG and J Robinson, Paternoster-Row, 1797) Preliminaries, para 18 at https://oll.libertyfund.org/title/whatmore-the-law-of-nations-lf-ed (accessed 20 September 2022).

[103] B Fassbender 'Rediscovering a Forgotten Constitution Notes on the Place of the UN Charter in the International Legal Order' in J Dunoff and J Trachtman, *Ruling the World Constitutionalism, International Law and Global Governance* (Cambridge University Press, 2009) 133–147, 138–39.

[104] Montevideo Convention on the Rights and Duties of States (adopted 26 December 1933, entered into force 26 December 1934) 165 LNTS 19, Art 4.

and rights'.[105] Withdrawal clauses do protect and underscore this conception of equality of states, in that all states are notionally able to exit the duties they have assumed under a treaty following the terms of that treaty's withdrawal clause. When Indonesia attempted to withdraw from the UN in 1965, the argument was made that because the UN Charter had no withdrawal clause in it, the principle of sovereign equality as envisaged in the Charter meant that an independent right to withdraw did not exist.[106] Kelsen had expounded on this a decade earlier, when he argued that if 'sovereignty implies the inalienable right of withdraw' then international law exists 'only as long as it pleases'.[107] Whilst someone subscribing to a voluntarist conception of international law could object to the notion that consent could be required to enter a legal regime but not required to exit a legal regime, the UN Charter contained a myriad of legal features that prioritised the formal equality of states and the stability of the international system.[108] Read alongside the definition of sovereign equality in the Declaration on Principles of International Law concerning Friendly Relations and Cooperation Among States, which requires all states to 'comply fully and in good faith with its international obligations', it is relatively straightforward to conclude that compliance with a withdrawal clause, or where there is no withdrawal clause the principles as codified in Article 56 VCLT, is part of the doctrine of equality of states.[109] This gives instrumental reasons for the provision of stability, but also underpins the entire conception of a rules-based international order. As the General Assembly noted when passing the Declaration, ensuring the equality of states is vital for 'promoting the rule of law among nations', and in the Declaration the adherence to legal obligations was associated with the aim to 'live in peace with other States'.[110]

However, the formal juridical equality of states is not the same as substantive equality. In the General Assembly, the Group of 77, consisting mainly of newly independent states from Africa and Asia who had experience of living under colonial rule, pushed for a more substantive conception of sovereign equality that addressed the material inequalities between states. This led to instruments such as the Declaration on the Establishment of a New International Economic Order, which linked 'sovereign equality' to correcting 'inequalities' and providing 'redress [for] existing injustices ... to eliminate the widening gap between the

[105] H Kelsen 'The Principle of Sovereign Equality of States as a Basis for International Organization' (1944) 53 *The Yale Law Journal* 207, 209 (emphasis added).

[106] F Livingstone 'Withdrawal from the United Nations: Indonesia' (1965) 14 *ICLQ* 637, 642.

[107] H Kelsen, *The Law of the United Nations; A Critical analysis of its Fundamental Problems*, 2nd edn (Lawbook Exchange, 2000) 126.

[108] For an outline of voluntarist thinking and the theory of state consent, see ch 1. Some histories have pointed out that equality was much more of a formal legal concept than anything substantive, eg C Webster 'The Making of the Charter of the United Nations' (1947) 32 *History* 16.

[109] Declaration on Principles of International Law concerning Friendly Relations and Cooperation among States in accordance with the Charter of the United Nations, UNGA RES /2625(XXV) (24 October 1970), Preamble, para (f).

[110] ibid Preamble.

developed and the developing countries'.[111] The inclusion of withdrawal clauses has been supported by some states as a means of ensuring sovereign equality. During the Sea-Bed Commission hearings in 1973, which were working towards a Convention intended to 'deal with all matters relating to the Law of the Sea', the Representative of Spain said that 'the omission of a denunciation or withdrawal clause from a treaty was usually the result of pressure on the part of a stronger State against the weaker party'.[112] There was also a sense, reflected in other states' contributions to the discussions at the Sea-Bed Commission, that the absence of a withdrawal clause would be used to represent a particular consensus on legal norms, which was subject to change and could be detrimental to new states, particularly post-colonial states who had not been able to play as big a role in shaping international legal norms as other states.[113]

Withdrawal clauses, by treating all states equally in a formal sense, does not recognise the relative material inequalities between states and how that may make it more difficult for some states to leave an agreement than others. Withdrawal from the ICSID Convention and denunciation of BITs, in pursuit of a broader economic programme by the withdrawing state, involving policies that would impede foreign investors, would likely still result in arbitration rights being preserved for the parties affected by such actions.[114] This would be of benefit to capital-exporting states but could impede the enactment of a new form of economic policy by the withdrawing states. Although this can be justified in terms of stability and the general preservation of the international economic order, it would also be a reflection, and to some extent the preservation, of existing economic inequalities between states, as those with existing economic advantages and the possession of capital would be in more of a position to benefit, whereas those who were disadvantaged would face a set of policy options constrained by international rules. Another example of this would be the difficulty a Eurozone state, which was indebted or had a relatively small economy, would face on using Article 50 TEU to withdraw from the EU. Writing in 2009, before the Eurozone sovereign debt crisis and Brexit, the then Legal Counsel for the European Central Bank concluded that it was very unlikely that Eurozone membership would survive withdrawal from the EU, but that it was perfectly possible that a country could continue using the euro as a currency, even though this would in practice put the withdrawing state at a significant economic

[111] Declaration on the Establishment of a New International Economic Order, UNGA Res 3201 (S-VI) (1 May 1974), Preamble.

[112] T Christakis, 'Article 56' in O Corten and P Klein (eds), *The Vienna Conventions on the Law of Treaties: A Commentary* (Oxford University Press, 2011) 1251–1278, 1260.

[113] See ch 4. The mandate of the Sea-Bed Commission was, according to its General Assembly Resolution, intended to be 'universal', so some of these concerns reflected a fear that this would not be honoured: UN GA Res 3067 (XXVIII) (16 November 1973).

[114] There is, as noted earlier, some dispute about whether this means that consent to dispute resolution automatically survives; see A Tzanakopoulos, 'Denunciation of the ICSID Convention under the General International Law of Treaties' in R Hofmann and C Tams (eds), *International Investment Law and General International Law: From Clinical Isolation to Systemic Integration?* (Nomos, 2011) 75–93.

disadvantage.[115] Although legally possible to withdraw from the EU, the likely impact of this on all but a couple of states in the Eurozone, would be so vast as to act as a practical constraint on many states' autonomy in terms of considering EU withdrawal in a practical sense, even though in a formal sense that autonomy is preserved by the text of Article 50 TEU.[116] Again, although formal equality is preserved in the withdrawal clause, substantive material inequalities between states significantly limit the ability of all states to use that provision. The doctrine of sovereign equality in the law of withdrawal is one that for the most part supports a thin definition of the rule of law, focusing on the formal legality and the capacity to leave as a juridical rather than a practical concept.

B. The Protection of Human Rights and Withdrawal

The protection of rights, or the rights conception of the rule of law as Ronald Dworkin called it, took the position that an essential component of the rule of law was that 'moral and political rights be recognized in positive law, so that they [might] be enforced upon the demand of individual citizens through courts' in so far as was practical.[117] The increasing centrality of human rights to questions of international law in general led to the idea that human rights, as defined by the Universal Declaration of Human Rights (UDHR) and the subsequent treaties created to bring the rights contained in the Declaration into international law, were part of the constitutional order of international law.[118] Conceptions of the international rule of law often cite the protection of human rights as a core element of it, because of the role that human rights play in protecting the individual.[119] Centring the individual, and individual rights, over the interests of the states is something that is historically situated from the mid-twentieth century onwards. Seldom does an account of the international rule of law not cite the protection of human rights as one of its core features.[120]

[115] P Athanassiou, 'Withdrawal and Expulsion from the EU and EMU: Some Reflections' *European Central Bank Legal Working Paper Series no 10* (December 2009) at www.econstor.eu/bitstream/10419/154664/1/ecblwp10.pdf (accessed 20 October 2022).

[116] It is not entirely clear how a withdrawal from the European Monetary Union and not the EU would work, and to some extent that has deliberately not been explored beyond the general invocation of the powers of potential expulsion – see H Hofmeister, 'Goodbye Euro: Legal Aspects of Withdrawal from the Eurozone' (2011) 18 *Columbia Journal of European Law* 111. See, on this more generally, JC Dammann, 'The right to leave the Eurozone' (2012) 48 *Texan International Law Journal* 125.

[117] R Dworkin, *A Matter of Principle* (Harvard University Press, 1985) 11–12.

[118] S Gardbaum, 'Human Rights and International Constitutionalism' in J Dunoff and J Trachtman (eds), *Ruling the World Constitutionalism, International Law and Global Governance* (Cambridge University Press 2009) 237.

[119] Waldron (n 19) 323; Chesterman (n 20) 345; McCorquodale (n 62).

[120] See R Peerenboom, 'Human rights and rule of law: What's the relationship?' (2004) 36 *Georgia Journal of International Law* 809; E Criddle and E Fox-Decent. 'Human rights, emergencies, and the rule of law' (2012) 34 *Human Rights Quarterly* 39; J Crawford, 'International Law and the Rule of Law' (2003) 24 *Adelaide Law Review* 3.

The way in which peremptory norms entail the protection of certain rights over other legal obligations is justified on the basis that the protection of these rights is an essential interest of the international community.[121] There is, however, the broader issue of interpretation in the question of rights, as, to become operative in society, rights require interpretation in a particular context, which means that institutions sitting above the state need to make determinations about the precise meaning and application of rights in a given context. In cases such as *Kadi v the Council of the European Union*, where the rights to a fair hearing, contained in EU law, were held to trump the requirement to sanction an individual who had been listed as a suspected terrorist by the UN Security Council, the role of international courts in protecting the international rule of law is relatively clear, as it is about the demarcation of different sources of authority and the recognition of the importance of rights.[122] However, interpretations of rights where there are complex social or political questions can come into tension with domestic authorities who have the mandate to resolve such issues, or result in the calling into question of the legitimacy of international bodies tasked with interpreting rights.[123] The rise of opposition from states to the international human rights bodies in the 2010s understandably raised broader concerns about the international rule of law more generally.[124]

The law of withdrawal fits into this broader picture in a somewhat complex fashion, as notionally, human rights protection is preserved as a matter of law but the institutional framework of human rights protection is weakened by withdrawal. As outlined in the previous two chapters, a central part of the interpretation of the rights of individuals protected by withdrawal clauses rests on both the doctrine of *pacta sunt servanda*, and the rights implicitly or explicitly saved by withdrawal clauses, as well as the general principle of rights transcendency. In spite of practical issues with its enforcement, the doctrine of peremptory norms allows a language of legality to survive the withdrawal or suspension of treaty obligations.[125] This means that the preservation of human rights as a component of the international rule of law is possible even where the law of withdrawal allows for escape from the legal regimes protecting rights, but the absence of a forum to adjudicate and ultimately protect rights is one

[121] D Costelloe, *Legal Consequences of Peremptory Norms in International Law* (Cambridge University Press, 2018) 20–24.

[122] Cases C-402/05 P and C-415/05 P *Yassin Abdullah Kadi and Al Barakaat International Foundation v Council of the European Union and Commission of the European Communities* [2008] ECR II-3533.

[123] Feichtner (n 26) 9.

[124] See specifically J Ikenberry, 'The end of liberal international order?' (2018) 94 *International Affairs* 7; see in general L Hooghe, T Lenz and G Marks, 'Contested world order: The delegitimation of international governance' (2019) 14 *The Review of International Organizations* 731.

[125] See Dubois who notes, 'the ability of … peremptory norms to trump treaties should render the positivist uncomfortable … the most distinguishing characteristic of peremptory norms is their non-derogability': D Dubois, 'The Authority of Peremptory Norms in International Law: State Consent or Natural Law?' (2009) 78 *Nordic Journal of International Law* 133, 138.

that creates difficulties.[126] The preservation of the right of access to courts and tribunals is one that has been deemed central to the protection of human rights and to protection of the international rule of law. In *Golder v UK*, a European Court of Human Rights case involving the rights of a prisoner who had been prohibited from communicating with his Member of Parliament or solicitor, the Court held that it was impossible to 'conceive of the rule of law without there being a possibility of having access to the courts'.[127] The explanation was couched in the language of stability goods, with the ECtHR warning about the 'danger of arbitrary power' if access to the courts was restricted, but also justifying access to courts in terms of the 'common heritage of political traditions, ideals, freedom' that lay behind the ECHR.[128] Withdrawal from court protocols or outright withdrawal from a legal regime with a court or tribunal attached to it allows for a de facto restriction of this right.

Furthermore, the interpretative function of the courts is important in establishing whether or not practices are compatible with human rights law; as Rosa Brooks notes, one of the issues with drone warfare from a rule-of-law perspective is not that it can 'be easily categorized as blatant instances of rule-breaking' but that it defies easy legal categorisation.[129] Part of the role of courts is helping to order the boundaries of rights, as well as providing a remedial function. Withdrawal from a tribunal or treaty body's jurisdiction is in a way a component of the wider practical problem of the enforcement and protection of human rights in international law dating back to the UDHR, which, as Hersch Lauterpacht observed, had 'no legal force' and 'only inconsiderable moral authority'.[130] But it is also a practical problem directly created by the law of withdrawal by allowing states to exit regimes that preserve the capacity for human rights to be enforced, and is also not just a problem confined to human rights law but applies to any withdrawal by a state from a jurisdictional protocol without the protection of a withdrawal clause. Scepticism has surrounded the possibility of the 'immediate effect' of withdrawals from the optional protocols on the jurisdiction of tribunals because of the impact this would have on the wider framework of good faith in the rule of law. As Robert Kolb noted in relation to this practice at the ICJ, even if it were argued that the 'principle of the rule of law is weak in general international law', there was an imperative to protect the international courts to stop the 'weakness of the basis of [their] jurisdiction'.[131] Good faith in these cases, though, requires more than

[126] See the discussion surrounding EU citizens following a no-deal Brexit in ch 4.

[127] *Golder v UK* (1976) 1 EHRR 524 [34].

[128] ibid.

[129] R Brooks, 'Drones and the International Rule of Law' (2014) 28 *Ethics & International Affairs* 83, 83.

[130] H Lauterpacht, *International Law and Human Rights* op cit; MA Glendon, 'The Rule of Law in the Universal Declaration of Human Rights' (2004) 2 *Northwestern Journal of International Human Rights* 2, 11.

[131] R Kolb, *Good Faith in International Law* (Hart Publishing, 2017) 238.

mere acquiescence with the obligation to participate in court proceedings; it requires acceptance of a decision and implementation, which is rendered politically difficult if, as illustrated in earlier chapters, the withdrawing state has made the legitimacy of a tribunal central to its justification for withdrawal. The law of withdrawal therefore continues to acknowledge the importance of human rights as a set of norms in the international rule of law, seemingly underpinning thick conceptions of the international rule of law, but this does not necessarily translate to ensuring the protection of human rights in a practical sense.

III. COMPLIANCE WITH WITHDRAWAL CLAUSES AND THE INTERNATIONAL RULE OF LAW

The question of why states comply with international law is both separate from and central to the rule of international law.[132] It is separate in that compliance as a subject matter focuses on state behaviour, rather than on the substance of obligation, leading some to argue that compliance struggles to exist as a free-standing concept.[133] As Andrew Guzman observes, it is difficult to construe a theory of international law that neglects compliance, because compliance is what gives the substantive terms of a treaty a tangible existence, and the principle that international obligations should be complied with says nothing about why they are complied with.[134] More basically, as Trevor Purvis puts it, whilst it would be wrong to simply 'reduce the rule of law to compliance', without compliance with legal obligations the entire concept of the 'rule of law is nothing but an aspiration'.[135] Compliance does not mean full implementation of a treaty's substantive provisions: many treaties have provisions that it takes a long time to fully realise, or are about regulating an on-going set of behaviours of the state in question, therefore compliance is instead best understood as a form of identity of or conformity with a specific rule from the state in question.[136] Thus, identifying how compliant a state is, is a question of examining how its actions are justified in accordance with rules. Yet, even then, because the international

[132] For an explanation of compliance and international law as a system see K Alter, 'Do International Courts Enhance Compliance with International Law?' (2003) 25 *Review of Asian and Pacific Studies* 51, 53–54; A d'Amato, 'Is international law really "law"?' (1984) 79 *Northwestern University Law Review* 1293, 1296–297.

[133] B Kingsbury, 'The concept of compliance as a function of competing conceptions of international law' (1997) 19 *Michigan Journal of International Law* 345.

[134] A Guzman, 'A compliance-based theory of international law' (2002) 90 *California Law Review* 1823, 1834.

[135] T Purvis, 'Looking for Life Signs in an International Rule of Law' in A Bartholomew (eds), *Empire's Law: The American Imperial Project and the 'War to Remake the World* (Pluto Press, 2006) 110–137, 113.

[136] K Raustiala and A-M Slaughter, 'International law, international relations and compliance' in W Carlsnaes, T Risse and B Simmons (eds), *Handbook of International Relations* (Sage Publications, 2002) 539.

system does not have an executive or courts, like a state does in its domestic sphere, the international legal system's ability as a system to self-correct or respond to the actions of states means that precise definitions of what legal terms are and what it means to comply with them are difficult to determine in every single case.[137] It therefore becomes something of a prevailing and generalised sentiment that states must or ought to act in compliance with the law.[138]

Many writers on the rule of law, dating back to AV Dicey, have argued that the rule of law was based on a set of habits that lived within societies.[139] Theoretical models to explain compliance with international law were predicated on an iterative or managerial conception of international law, such as Chayes and Chayes' argument in *The New Sovereignty*, which maintained that an 'iterative discourse' between parties to a treaty or members of an organisation to create a cooperative environment favours compliance.[140] 'Persuasion' was at the centre of Chayes and Chayes' account of managerialist thinking about compliance, and ideas about persuasion also featured in other theoretical accounts that looked at the socialisation of states as a core factor in compliance.[141] Constructivist accounts of compliance attempt to explain how a state's identity and identity formation can be used in a process of interaction between a state and a legal regime.[142] Compliance with the substantive provisions of international law, constructivists argue, does not require a continuous or conscious process of persuasion but emerges out of the way in which a legal regime structures interactions between state parties and a legal regime's institutions.[143] Non-compliance, by the same token, undercuts what Thomas Franck dubbed the 'compliance pull' of international law, because it not only results in weakening interactions between states, encouraging some states potentially not to interact with others or to free-ride on their international commitments, but also directly challenges the assumption that states must comply with international law.[144]

[137] JK Cogan, 'Noncompliance and the International Rule of Law' (2006) 31 *The Yale Journal of International Law* 189, 190.

[138] ibid.

[139] S Humphreys, *Theatre of the Rule of Law: Transnational Legal Intervention in Theory and Practice* (Cambridge University Press, 2010) 32–35.

[140] A Chayes and A Chayes, *The New Sovereignty: Compliance with International Regulatory Agreements* (Harvard University Press, 1995) 143.

[141] ibid 25. See also R Goodman and D Jinks, 'International law and state socialization: Conceptual, empirical, and normative challenges' (2004) 54 *Duke Law Journal* 983. There is a case that this chiefly relates to particular types of treaties where states have resolved to act, such as environmental treaties, which 'anticipate domestic implementation through regulation of private actors'; see M Durkee, 'Persuasion Treaties' (2013) 99 *Virginia Law Review* 63, 67.

[142] See specifically J Brunnée and S Toope, *Legitimacy and Legality in International Law: An Interactional Account* (Cambridge University Press, 2010). More generally see N Onuf, 'Constructivism: A User's Manual' in V Kubálková, N Onuf and P Kowert (eds), *International Relations in a Constructed World* (Routledge, 2005) 58–78.

[143] Brunnée and Toope (n 142); H Cohen, 'Can International Law Work? A Constructivist Expansion' (2009) 27 *Berkley Journal of International Law* 636.

[144] T Franck, *The Power of Legitimacy Among Nations* (Oxford University Press, 1990) 41; Cogan (n 135) 205–04.

Interactions in the above analysis occur both inside the specific international regime in question and in the international system at large. In *The Anarchical Society*, Hedley Bull put forward three motivations for compliance: first, states believe it is in their own interests (either instrumentally or for the projection of values) to comply; second, states can believe they are or will be coerced into compliance; and, third, states anticipate or experience reciprocal action by other state parties.[145] Bull's focus was on state motivation in the context of a wider international society, although he was careful to dismiss the idea that compliance was only for 'ulterior motives'.[146] Realist and rationalist theories of compliance, which respectively focus either on assumptions about states' behaving as actors in pursuit of their own interests, or on the assumption that states pursue cooperation and collaboration games with one another, also give accounts of compliance very much shaped by the international climate – what Bull might call international society, created by international law.[147] The globalisation of legalism, as Christopher May terms it, describes the growth both of the number of legal regimes and the way in which international courts make a complex system of determinations, effectively legalising and authorising political structures and decisions.[148] Compliance with international obligations is a broader part of this legalism, as it creates the predictability of interactions but is also self-reinforcing – a state complies with its obligations because there is an expectation to do so, and each act of compliance further entrenches the general expectation of compliance. Legalism, or a state's acting legally, then becomes synonymous with the legitimacy of a state's action, because the state is acting in accordance with broadly accepted international legal principles.[149] As one former ICJ judge puts it, states must 'act in compliance with the law, and in particular with international law … that is the underlying condition for the legitimacy of their action'.[150] Compliance therefore serves part of the operational framework within which a state calculates its self-interest or engages in collaboration, because compliance bestows legitimacy. Non-compliance is punished by the bestowing of illegitimacy on the non-compliant state and its actions, which in turn has reputational consequences for the state in question.[151]

The very fact of withdrawal itself can occur as a result of actual or anticipated non-compliance with substantive provisions. When Canada withdrew from the Kyoto Protocol in 2011, it had for some years been questioning whether

[145] H Bull, *The Anarchical Society: A Study of Order in World Politics*, 2nd edn (Macmillan, 1995) 133–34.

[146] ibid.

[147] Kingsbury (n 131).

[148] C May, *The Rule of Law: The Common Sense of Global Politics* (Edward Elgar, 2014) 58–61.

[149] On the concept of legalism and legitimacy, see I Hurd, 'The empire of international legalism' (2018) 32 *Ethics & International Affairs* 265, 268–71; R West, 'Reconsidering Legalism' (2003) 88 *Minnesota Law Review* 119, 126–30.

[150] G Guillaume, 'Terrorism and International Law' (2004) 53 *ICLQ* 537, 548.

[151] R Brewster, 'Unpacking the State's Reputation' (2006) 50 *Harvard International Law Journal* 231.

the Protocol could be made to work, both at the international level and in terms of Canadian politics and the economy.[152] Aware that if Canada remained party to the Protocol it would eventually face fines for non-compliance, it was the Canadian Government's position that withdrawal was the act that would be most consistent with both its own internal political position and its wider desire to be norm compliant on the international plane.[153] There was some support for a different approach to climate change regulation within the domestic Canadian sphere, and later, after a change of government, Canada was to support other climate change initiatives.[154] Yet many other withdrawals do not necessarily occur in such relatively benign circumstances, and compliance with the terms of withdrawal clauses themselves can be in question. Compliance with a withdrawal clause, as set out in chapters 2 and 3, poses some challenges for theoretical understandings of why states comply with obligations. Sometimes compliance may be instrumental; for example, in the event that that negotiations are either practically necessary or structured into a withdrawal clause, compliance with the law of withdrawal can help the withdrawing state build trust for future negotiations whilst at the same time signalling the seriousness of its intention in those negotiations that the withdrawal be final.[155] Seen in the wider context of international legalism, compliance with a withdrawal clause, even if only partial, is a means of demonstrating the withdrawing state's commitment to general rule-bound legalism whilst objecting to, and ultimately rejecting, the specific obligations of the legal regime from which the state is withdrawing. The terms of a withdrawal clause are what Fleur Johns calls a means of making illegality in international law, as they denote, by 'legal crafting', conduct that is 'forbidden' or 'defiant'.[156] The citation of a withdrawal clause and compliance with its terms – again even if only partial, such as keeping to a duration provision between notification of denunciation and the cessation of legal obligations – is a means by which a state may demonstrate its adherence to a broad notion of legalism and legality of action.

Yet withdrawal clauses can also provide a cover for broader non-compliance on a state's part, as by threatening withdrawal and implying that it is going to invoke a denunciation clause (a lawful act), the state can at the same time engage in non-compliance with a legal regime (a non-lawful act). This was what the Dominican Republic did after threatening to withdraw from the American Convention on

[152] Associated Press. 'Canada pulls out of Kyoto protocol' *The Guardian* (13 December 2011) at www.theguardian.com/environment/2011/dec/13/canada-pulls-out-kyoto-protocol.

[153] B Curry and S McCarthy, ' Canada formally abandons Kyoto Protocol on climate change' *The Globe and Mail* (12 December 2011) at www.theglobeandmail.com/news/politics/canada-formally-abandons-kyoto-protocol-on-climate-change/article4180809/.

[154] For a comprehensive account, see CV Ramos Fjellvang, 'Why did Canada withdraw from the Kyoto Protocol? A case study' (Masters Thesis, Department of Political Science University of Oslo) at www.duo.uio.no/bitstream/handle/10852/40357/_Fjellvang_master_25.pdf, 15–20.

[155] TL Meyer, 'Power, Exit Costs, and Renegotiation in International Law' (2010) 51 *Harvard International Law Journal* 379, 397–400.

[156] F Johns, *Non-Legality in International Law: Unruly Law* (Cambridge University Press, 2013) 10.

Human Rights (ACHR) after a ruling against the Republic in the *Case of the Expelled Dominicans and Haitians v Dominican Republic*, which dealt with the recognition of a policy of restricting citizenship to people of Haitian descent in Dominica.[157] The decision was politically controversial because it meant overturning a domestic court decision, which challenged the constitutionality of the Inter-American Court of Human Rights (IACtHR) under domestic Dominican law, and implementation of the IACtHR's decision in the *Expelled Dominicans and Haitians* case would have fallen along a social fault line in relation to ethnic status in the country.[158] The Government announced that it would withdraw from the ACHR, but four years later had yet to file a notice of denunciation. At the same time, the Government refused to appear before the Court and ceased cooperation with it, effectively cementing the backlash to an individual decision.[159] Instead of clearly demarcating the legal from the non-legal, the anticipation of commencing a legal act in this case triggered the emergence of a legal grey-zone.

In general, a presumption toward legalism can help explain why states would comply with withdrawal clauses. International law often relies on a form of outcasting by constructing a framework that distinguishes the legal from the non-legal in terms of state behaviour. This is intended to substantively marginalise and impose broader existential costs on a state's reputation when it engages in non-legal behaviour.[160] When seen as relating to a broader concept of legalism, outcasting as an idea becomes linked to concept of being lawful or framing actions in the concept of legality in order to facilitate interactions between states, with legalistic actions having more of a horizontal than a vertical nature to them.[161] In the process of withdrawal, legalism on the international plane can conflict with legalism on the domestic plane. Four years before it formally denounced the ACHR, the Supreme Court of Venezuela ruled that a decision of the IACtHR on the arbitrary dismissal of judges was not admissible because the individual interests of the dismissed judges, who were the claimants arguing for their rights, could not prevail over the protection of national sovereignty and the collective will of the people.[162] The Supreme Court went on to recommend

[157] *Case of Expelled Dominicans and Haitians v Dominican Republic* Inter-American Court of Human Rights, IACtHR, Series C no 282 (28 August 2014).

[158] I Skeie, 'A Conflict Transformation Perspective on Efforts to Protect Human Rights of Haitian Migrants and their Descendants in the Dominican Republic' (2014) 44 *Iberoamericana: Nordic Journal of Latin American and Caribbean Studies* 121.

[159] X Soley and S Steininger, 'Parting ways or lashing back? Withdrawals, backlash and the Inter-American Court of Human Rights' (2018) 14 *International Journal of Law in Context* 237.

[160] M Jovanović, *The Nature of International Law* (Cambridge University Press, 2019) 185–87; see also O Hathaway and SJ Shapiro, 'Outcasting: enforcement in domestic and international law' (2011) 121 *Yale Law Journal* 252.

[161] Constitutive models of international law focus less on strict rule adherence, as realist theorists do, and more on how law and legalism shape relationships and interactions; see G Dancy and CJ Fariss, 'Rescuing Human Rights Law from International Legalism and Its Critics' (2017) 39 *Human Rights Quarterly* 1, 3.

[162] The decision of the Venezuelan Court – Sala Constitucional Supremo de Justicica (Venezuela), *Sentencia 1939/2008* – is outlined in Soley and Steininger (n 159).

the denunciation of the ACHR, even though it would have been well aware that withdrawal did not terminate the state's obligations in relation to the case in question.[163] This did not really bother the Venezuelan Government in the years leading up to 2012, when it finally denounced the Convention, because, in the Government's view, the IACtHR was undermining the state's sovereignty and serving right-wing American interests.[164] Legalism, for the Venezuelan Government, under the leadership of Hugo Chavez, involved emphasising the importance of human rights in terms of economic and social rights and the importance of progressive constitutionalism; it did not involve compliance with a body the Government believed to be in the service of its political opponents.[165]

Whilst most states may comply with the procedural features of a withdrawal clause, for example by waiting the length of time required to be a member before denouncing a treaty, this is a version of legalism in service of a relatively thin conception of the international rule of law.[166] States are lawful in terms of their procedural actions in complying with a withdrawal clause to legitimate their decision to withdraw. More substantive commitments, or commitments to preserve rights in a thicker conception of the rule of law, are more easily subject to countervailing arguments about sovereignty or alternative claims about the legality of their actions. It is noteworthy that in both the IACtHR cases, there was a broader argument about the legal status of the Court within the withdrawing state's, or would-be withdrawing state's, jurisdiction, thereby allowing the state to claim that its actions were following an alternative source of law.[167] In 2020, in response to a request from Colombia for an advisory opinion, the IACtHR sought to formalise the principles governing withdrawal from the ACHR, which emphasised rule of law principles.[168] In the Venezuelan case, the country continued a broader practice of ignoring IACtHR decisions, even though they related to fundamental rights notionally recognised in the Venezuelan Constitution.[169] Yet there was no real argument that the state had acted legally on the international plane, in respect of all other aspects of the law of withdrawal.

[163] Art 78(2) of the American Convention contains that obligation – see ch 2. See more generally G Candia, 'Regional human rights institutions struggling against populism: The case of Venezuela' (2019) 20 *German Law Journal* 141, 153.

[164] J Contesse, 'Resisting the Inter-American Human Rights System' (2019) 44 *Yale Journal of International Law* 179, 207.

[165] See Soley and Steininger (n 159); See also J Contesse, 'Conservative governments and Latin America's human rights landscape' (2019) 113 *American Journal of International Law* 375, 376.

[166] See ch 2 for this exploration of the literature.

[167] A Huneeus, 'Courts Resisting Courts: Lessons from the Inter-American Court's Struggle to Enforce Human Rights' (2011) 44 *Cornell International Law Journal* 493.

[168] Inter-American Court of Human Rights 'Advisory Opinion requested by the Republic of Colombia in Matters of Human Rights of a State that has Denounced the American Convention on Human Rights and the Charter of the Organisation of American States' (9 November 2020) OC-26/20 para 139.

[169] HB Leon, 'The Jurisdiction of the Inter-American Court of Human Rights Should Outlive Defection' (2021) *University of Miami Inter-American Law Review* 1, 23.

CONCLUSION: HOW THE LAW OF WITHDRAWAL UNDERPINS THE INTERNATIONAL RULE OF LAW

The international rule of law is difficult to conceive of in the same fashion as the domestic rule of law. This is due to the absence of the equivalent hierarchical authority of a nation state. The international rule of law is best understood more as a framework for authorising and delineating the actions of states.[170] As Kumm and others argue, the precise form of the international rule law is less important than the prevailing assumption that states' interactions 'are to be ruled by law', and in the case of the law of withdrawal this involves creating a legal framework for a particular type of interaction – the termination of legal obligations – to take place.[171] In this context, the law of withdrawal underpins the international rule of law, in that it helps facilitate the existence of a legal framework regardless of the source or nature of an individual legal obligation. If one takes the positivist view that obligations arise from the actions of states, or that entry into a legal regime ought to entail the inverse capacity to free oneself from that regime, the role of withdrawal can be formalised within the positivistic conception of consent, as chapter 1 sets out, in either facilitating a recognition of changed circumstances (*rebus sic stantibus* and related doctrines) or allowing a state party to change its mind regarding its legal commitments.[172] In essence, the formal structure of withdrawal allows these doctrines to operate, delineating legal and non-legal, expressions of a state's will or claims of a change of circumstances. Beyond this, withdrawal can be said to underpin the international rule of law by helping identify the wrongful acts of states and the breach of obligations by a state attempting to withdraw from its legal obligations. It can help recognise states who fall outside the bounds of lawfulness in the process of withdrawal. Looking beyond positivist conceptions of the sources of law, the law of withdrawal is also to an extent used to define the limits of state action by supporting the general principle that *jus cogens* norms exist regardless of conventional obligation.

It is not clear, however, that the law of withdrawal underpins a thick conception of the rule of law. Instead, the conception of the rule of law maintained by the law of withdrawal is one premised on the maintenance of the stability in international law, over and above any broader community goals. It may, as Douglas Guilfoyle has argued, be too difficult to sustain a 'values-orientated international rule of law' similar to that of domestic legal systems, because of the plurality of values in the international system and in operation in different states.[173] Therefore a narrower notion of the rule of law, maintaining 'a

[170] Hurd (n 14).

[171] Kumm (n 21); S Menon, 'The Rule of Law, the International Legal Order, and the Foreign Policy of Small States' (2010) 10 *Asian Journal of International Law* 50.

[172] As well as ch 1, see on the theory of state consent and decision-making in S Besson, 'State Consent and Disagreement in International Law-Making. Dissolving the Paradox' (2016) 29 *Leiden Journal of International Law* 289.

[173] D Guilfoyle, 'The rule of law and maritime security: understanding lawfare in the South China Sea' (2019) 95 *International Affairs* 999, 1001.

thin moral consensus', can help the international rule of law in its function of 'achieving cooperative ends and placing normative constraints on the perceived legitimacy of state policies'.[174] As noted earlier in this chapter arguments about the nature of international society often mirror the arguments about the thick and thin nature of international society, and as Paul Tucker has argued, is that 'except in its thinnest ... the very idea of "international society" can seem to have civilizational undertones'.[175] Discussions about substance of international society, or among international law scholars the thick conception of the rule of law, Tucker argues often draw on the 'history of European customary law, an ICJ statute framed at the moment of maximal American power' and other philosophical ideas from a distinctly western set of traditions.[176] This means that procedural norms in international law often tend to point towards a thinner conception of the rule of law, one which would support what the English school theorists called pluralist conceptions of international society, as this would facilitate interaction at a basic level between states without any necessary commitment to political values beyond the maintenance of stability and order.[177] On the specific issue of withdrawal there is an additional broader dilemma for the international rule of law. The line between lawful and unlawful is blurred, as the withdrawing state is attempting to reduce its legal obligations or, to put it another way, reduce the number and nature of the international laws that constrain its actions. To avoid a fully anarchical international society, of the sort described by some realist theorists, where legal obligations are a reflection of power and interest, the law of withdrawal attempts to structure a system of law whereby the exit from legal regimes is about preserving the stability of that regime and the stability of interactions between states in so far as is possible.[178]

By default, this all gravitates towards a very thin conception of the rule of law, where community values are secondary to the maintenance of the political, physical and material status quo regardless of the change in legal status. Yet it also supports a key tenet of structural realism, of the variety originally proposed by Stephen Krasner, which maintains that international law is merely epiphenomenal of underlying state power and interests.[179] The rule of international law, when it comes to the law of withdrawal, therefore is highly dependent on a sense of interest superseding the moment of withdrawal about the legal regime from which a state has just withdrawn, or is in the process of withdrawing from. Hence, conceiving of stability not just as a process but as a good or property that states enjoy, helps in understanding what the interest is for the withdrawing state

[174] ibid.
[175] P Tucker *Global Discord: Values and Power in a Fracture World Order* (Princeton University Press, 2022) 190.
[176] Ibid.
[177] See Bain (n 96).
[178] SD Krasner, 'Realist Views of International Law' (2002) 96 *Proceedings of the Annual Meeting of the American Society of International Law* 265.
[179] SD Krasner, 'Structural Causes and Regime Consequences: regimes as Intervening Variables' in Krasner (ed), *International Regimes* (Cornell University Press, 1983) 6–7.

in conducting a legal withdrawal. The instability generated by withdrawal can be inflicted on states other than the withdrawing state, and therefore a role the law of withdrawal fulfils is to signal the outer limits of what that harm may be and what a withdrawing state may do in exercising its political decision to withdraw. What Christian Tams describes as the liberal-cosmopolitan approach to understanding the international community, where there is a strong emphasis on individual rights and duties and states are seen as a trustees of the human interests more broadly, is notionally reflected in the terms of withdrawal clauses, such as sunset provisions, and in the assumptions of the law of withdrawal more generally.[180] However, this is not essential for the construction of stability as a good; a relatively stable international system can incorporate the idea that there are states that exist outside of the international community, although this is potentially more problematic in areas such as climate change, where the size of and scale of the outcasted state's activities may create problems.[181] In other areas, though stability incorporates outcasted states, it is telling that the human rights examples in this chapter concern states that were either quite willing for ideological reasons to become 'outcasted' states or occupy a conceptual 'grey-zone' between non-compliance and non-withdrawal. Stability in relation to investment treaties and the broader international commercial system is also compatible with this narrow view. Even though there might not be substantive compliance with the specific elements of a withdrawal clause, especially in connection with individual rights, the parameters that are set about the relative boundaries of legal action and what constitutes a lawful state can be sufficient to ensure systemic stability.

The underpinning of what the law of withdrawal provides to the international rule of law is a set of virtual, yet functional, 'tram-lines'. It provides the rails for the international legal system to operate on; obligations can be formed, and commitments can be made by states, whilst expectations about state behaviour are maintained. In this, the law of withdrawal is one among several different devices in international law generating and maintaining these expectations. Weapons control treaties, for example, use precise legal frameworks with a variety of legal mechanisms in common with the other treaties described in this chapter. Yet, unlike the other treaties discussed, there is no expectation of future litigation in relation to these treaties; but again, like the treaties noted in this chapter, the presence of legal devices within withdrawal clauses controls what state behaviour is legal, and hence legitimate. A withdrawal clause – to stretch the tram metaphor further – is a means of departing from a tram route heading to a particular destination, without crashing the tram car completely off the rails. Stability is therefore maintained – in that the system itself is functional. Yet ultimately stability, and the stability the law of withdrawal gives to the international rule of law, is systemic and not substantive.

[180] C Tams, 'The International Community as a Legal Concept' in J d'Aspremont and S Singh (eds), *Concepts for International Law Contributions to Disciplinary Thought* (Edward Elgar, 2019) 505–523, 509–10.

[181] This argument is made by Durkee (n 141).

Conclusion: The Law of Withdrawal and the Idea of Stability

THE LAW OF withdrawal seeks to structure a series of political arguments about the relationship of states to international legal regimes. The law of withdrawal works – with 'works' being narrowly defined as the creation of a predictable system for terminating legal obligations – because the law of withdrawal in a thin procedural sense regulates the nature and forms of the arguments between the withdrawing state and the regime from which it is departing. As noted in chapter 2, withdrawal clauses are quite formulaic, in part because a lot of withdrawal clauses originate as templates of final clauses for treaties produced by various international organisations.[1] The main substantive requirements are time, both the duration of membership and time from denunciation to completion of withdrawal, and notification, both the location of a notification and – in some very specific cases – a requirement to include substantive comments in the notification. The control of time and the notification process by withdrawal clauses visibly orders the process of withdrawal, notionally generating certainty and effectiveness. By way of conclusion, and to answer this book's basic question, it is important to look at how the law of withdrawal imagines the way that states will act.

I. AUTONOMY AND THE DECISION TO LEAVE

Since 1871, which as chapter four set out is probably the law of withdrawal's starting point, the law of withdrawal has attempted to balance the autonomy of states in making and un-making treaties, with the maintainance of international law as a system. 'Autonomy' here refers to the ability to take actions in relation to the international obligations a state has, rather than the recognition of its own internal system of government and its capacity to govern.[2] Even though, as set out in chapter 1, it is not quite correct to see withdrawal as the simple inverse of state consent, both withdrawal and consent are about the recognition of the autonomy of decision making. As Humphrey Waldock put it, '[t]he power to annul, terminate, withdraw from or suspend treaties, no less than the power to

[1] L Helfer, Terminating Treaties' in D Hollis (ed), *The Oxford Guide to Treaties* (Oxford University Press, 2012) 624–644.

[2] H Hannum and RB Lillich, 'The Concept of Autonomy in International Law' (1980) 74 *American Journal of International Law* 858, 860.

conclude treaties, forms part of the treaty-making power of the state'.[3] Unlike other processes of ending international obligations, such as through the termination of a treaty, the ongoing presence of a legal regime creates a separate and distinct political dynamic. As shown in the case studies in chapter 3, the continued existence of institutions such as the International Criminal Court (ICC) and the European Court of Human Rights (ECtHR), and their continued attempts to exercise authority over a state whilst it is withdrawing and after it has withdrawn, means that the withdrawing state is still negotiating a contested relationship with these institutions.[4] Furthermore, the moral authorising functions that legal regimes such as the ECtHR and the ICC play in international relations, by virtue of protecting rights and administering international justice, make it difficult for the withdrawing state to completely ignore them. Regimes such as the International Centre for Settlement of Investment Disputes (ICSID) play a different kind of authorising function, in that the withdrawing state may face a loss of inward investment or difficulties in obtaining credit. Yet although these costs exist, withdrawal clauses describe a notional autonomy for state parties, with references to the 'decision' of states or that states 'may' take a decision to denounce a treaty.

How substantive this autonomy is may be open to question given the structural constraints on decision making and the relative power of certain norms of international law, but there is no doubt that in a formal sense, withdrawal clauses describe how a state ceases to have legal obligations. Sources of law and legal forms, Jean d'Aspremont argues, are conducive to one another, in that making a legal argument about a source of law helps formalise that source and recognise its constraining role on state action.[5] Reference to a withdrawal clause, implicitly or explicitly, is therefore formalising and affirming of its role as a constraint on the state. The necessity for this, as Waldock put it, was simple: although individual claims or cases for withdrawal not in accordance with a treaty's withdrawal clause might be 'legitimate in themselves' (they might, for example, be made as part of a claim of changed circumstances or invalidity), such an action carried 'definite risks to the security of treaties'.[6] Therefore, even if in practice it might be relatively meaningless to formally convey a notification that a state has withdrawn or is withdrawing from given treaty, it is important, Waldock argues, to ensure 'regularity and certainty in treaty relations'.[7] Waldock's commentary centred on the need for the codification of the principles of the law on treaty withdrawal to

[3] H Waldock, 'Second Report on the Law of Treaties by Sir Humphrey Waldock' (1963) 2 *ILC Yearbook* 36, 85.

[4] Equally, those institutions' juridification, the same juridical power that is called on to deal with questions arising from withdrawal, may also drive withdrawal – see N Kang-Riou and D Rossati, 'The Effects of Juridification on States Exiting International Institutions' (2018) 15 *International Organizations Law Review* 265.

[5] J d'Aspremont, 'Sources of Law in Legal-Formalist Theories: The Poor Vehicle of Legal Forms' in S Besson and J d'Aspremont (eds), *The Sources of International Law* (Oxford University Press, 2017) 365–383, 366–67.

[6] Waldock (n 3) 87.

[7] ibid 86.

ensure the predictability of the overall system of treaty law. In this respect the autonomy of decision making is, as outlined in chapter 1 and expanded upon in chapters 2 and 3, justified in being constrained so as to encourage system stability. Miodrag Jovanović's theory of international law as a system maintains that it is defined in part by its capacity for producing certainty, even though a lot of this capacity is predicated on the maintenance of rules resolving uncertainties rather than on the production of certainty.[8] In tackling the problem of identifying legal systems, Joseph Raz, cautioning against being too dogmatic about rules regarding the recognition of laws, conceded that one of the features of a legal system would be a framework of rules to 'guide human behaviour, help people in planning and deciding on a future course of action'.[9] Raz was ultimately an institutionalist, reasoning that what made systems operate as legal systems was the presence of law-applying institutions, such as courts, in part because of the continuity such institutions were able to bring to the practice of law making.

In effect, the constriction of state autonomy by a withdrawal clause is relatively minimal, with an emphasis on the procedural rather than the substantive, although as chapter 3 demonstrated, pre-withdrawal breaches of duty and sunset clauses can create obligations on a state that may continue after it has withdrawn. The most important principle, though, is that a state's autonomy of action in withdrawal is, according to the law of withdrawal, defined, or system regulated, by international law. In some ways this is similar to entering into a treaty, in that there are rules regarding when and how a state becomes a party to a treaty, and on implementation of the substantive provisions into domestic law, all of which recognises a state's autonomy to acquire legal relations on the international plane but then prescribes how that acquisition is carried out. Yet this is not quite the case with the law of withdrawal, as Hannah Woolaver points out in a study of different domestic court rulings on withdrawal; the interface between the international and domestic legal orders in cases of withdrawal is far more mixed.[10] As set out throughout the book, it is very difficult to assess compliance with the law of withdrawal in the same way that compliance with substantive treaty obligations or institutions is able to be assessed.[11] The question then arises as to what exactly the system stability is towards which the law of withdrawal aims.

[8] M Jovanović *The Nature of International Law* (Cambridge University Press, 2019) 228–31.

[9] J Raz, *The Authority of Law*, 2nd edn (Oxford University Press, 2009) 86.

[10] H Woolaver, 'From Joining to Leaving: Domestic Law's Role in the International Legal Validity of Treaty Withdrawal' (2019) 30 *European Journal of International Law* 73, 83.

[11] There is an extensive literature on measuring compliance in international law, but none of this includes data focused on the period between denunciation and withdrawal's becoming effective: for this literature, see C Hillebrecht, 'Rethinking compliance: the challenges and prospects of measuring compliance with International Human Rights Tribunals' (2009) 1 *Journal of Human Rights Practice* 362; B Simmons, 'Compliance with international agreements' (1998) 1 *Annual Review of Political Science* 75; JE Alvarez, 'Measuring Compliance' (2002) 96 *Proceedings of the Annual Meeting of ASIL* (13–16 March 2002) 209.

II. DEFINING ORDO-STABILITY

The best way of understanding what the law of withdrawal envisages or, to put it another way, to describe what the institution of the law of withdrawal creates in international society, is ordo-stability. Stability in international law is a recurring theme of any analysis of different doctrines of public international law, such as *pacta sunt servanda*, *rebus sic stantibis*, reservations to treaties and a host of other doctrines that would be too many to list here.[12] There is, as chapter 5 set out, a strong relationship between the international rule of law and the production of stability as a form of 'public good' in international society. The prefix 'ordo' in this context is meant as shorthand for 'orthodox', the idea being that the law is envisaging a form of highly orthodox stability. The concept of ordoliberalism in international economics and international organisational law is usually associated with a restraint on public spending, but also the belief that markets were legally constructed entities where risks could be regulated and minimised, and is often cited in relation to the way that German power operates in the EU and Eurozone.[13] A feature of this literature is the emphasis on how this promotes a form of economic stability and risk management, different from its more well-known relative, neo-liberalism, with its focus on the freedom of markets and a lack of regulation.[14] Ordoliberalism led to the development of specific institutional structures at the transnational level in Europe to create regulated markets and preserve a version of economic stability in states within the European Common Market and later the EU.[15]

Ordo-stability is a related idea, in that it describes the intended institutional functions of a withdrawal clause; it envisages a form of stable international order and describes the features of state behaviour necessary to achieve that order. The substance of what that stability entails, though – or, to put it more directly, what is actually being kept 'stable' – is often highly self-referential, with references to stability as a matter of legal form or stability being generated for the system of international law being the most common ways of expressing the meaning of 'stability'. It is necessary to distinguish externally descriptive stability, such as the references to stability that might appear in treaty provisions

[12] For example, see C Binder, 'Stability and change in times of fragmentation: the limits of pacta sunt servanda revisited' (2012) 25 *Leiden Journal of International Law* 909; J Kulaga, 'A renaissance of the doctrine of rebus sic stantibus?' (2020) 69 *ICLQ* 477; C Logan Piper, 'Reservations to Multilateral Treaties: The Goal of Universality' (1985) 71 *Iowa Law Review* 295.

[13] S Bulmer, 'Germany and the Eurozone Crisis: Between Hegemony and Domestic Politics' (2014) 37 *West European Politics* 1244; L Warlouzet, 'The EEC/EU as an Evolving Compromise between French Dirigism and German Ordoliberalism (1957–1995)' (2019) 57 *Journal of Common Market Studies* 77, 80.

[14] K Dyson, *Conservative Liberalism, Ordo-liberalism, and the State: Disciplining Democracy and the Law* (Oxford University Press, 2021) 5–7.

[15] Ernst-Ulrich Petersmann, 'German and European Ordo-Liberalism and Constitutionalism in the Postwar Development of International Economic Law.' In Peter Hilpold (ed.) *European International Law Traditions* (Springer, 2020) 305–332.

concerning recognition, which describe stable countries or governments, from normative systemic stability that is generated by the clauses describing the instrumental functioning of a treaty, such as termination or reservation clauses. The former form of stability, as outlined by Krystyna Marek, involves rules such as the customary principle that the identity and continuity of a state are unaffected by a change in government.[16] These rules describe an object or an external stable situation allowing another external actor to determine what is and what is not a 'stable' entity in international law. The latter form of stability describes how a legal process functions, not referring to an external event or condition of a state deemed stable but rather to how a process should work or a state should act in the future. For example, the rules on reservations in the Convention on the Elimination of all Forms of Discrimination Against Women (CEDAW) contain a version of the object and purpose test, which can be used to challenge states to withdraw reservations that do not meet that standard.[17] This does not, in practice, entail greater scrutiny of a state's performance of its obligations; instead it creates a legalist dividing line between lawful and unlawful state conduct, and for ordo-stability it is the description of this dividing line and its codification that is important.

At the time of the VCLT's drafting, and shortly afterwards, there was a range of scholarship on treaty law and the behaviour of states that described how treaty law, and the doctrines of treaty law eventually codified in parts III–V of the VCLT, was essential to stability in the wider international system. Writing in 1962, Kenneth Carlston, although not directly tackling withdrawal, looked at how treaties helped shaped behaviour, noting that the rule of *pacta sunt servanda* created a set of behaviours in states that, if carried out with a sufficient degree of uniformity, would enable 'us to predict social behaviour'.[18] The need to ensure stability in the legal system surrounded the discussion on treaty denunciation at the 1967 American Society of International Law conference, where they also tried to clarify the rules on *rebus sic stantibus*.[19] But there was concern even at this stage among members of the American Society of International Law about the meaning of stability, with Richard Bilder arguing that the 'resting'

[16] Krystyna Marek *Identity and Continuity of States in Public International Law* (Librarie Droz, 1968) 24–25.

[17] It is worth noting that the use of this test and the regime of enforcing CEDAW more generally is open to numerous problems: Marijke De Pauw, 'Women's Rights: From Bad to Worse-Assessing the Evolution of Incompatible Reservations to the CEDAW Convention.' (2013) 29 Merkourios-Utrecht Journal of International & European Law 51; Liesbeth Lijnzaad, *Reservations to UN Human Rights Treaties: Ratify and Run* (Brill Nijhoff, 1995) 77–79, 89.

[18] Kenneth Carlston *Law and Organization in World Society* (University of Illinois Press, 1962) 111.

[19] This is discussed in ch 1, but see O Lissitzyn, 'Treaties and changed circumstances (rebus sic stantibus)' (1967) 61 *American Journal of International Law* 895. Concerns about stability also permeated the discussion of other issues that might void a treaty, such as the status of jus cogens norms; see E Schwelb, 'Some Aspects of International Jus Cogens as Formulated by the International Law Commission' (1967) 61 *American Journal of International Law* 946, 973.

assumption about the question of why states should comply with treaties depended on the 'fact of formal solemization … of the so-called "stability of the international order"'.[20] Bhek Sinha, writing a year beforehand on unilateral determination due to prior violations of treaties, although very critical of what he saw as the unjust consequences of *pacta sunt servanda* for states who were at a disadvantage due to being party to unequal treaties, was still careful to point out that *pacta sunt servanda* was an 'order function of international law, and therefore a disregard of this norm is deemed to be prejudicial to international legal order'.[21] Hence, Sinha's project, to try to synthesise a framework for different forms of unilateral denunciation, was predicated both on the preservation of order and on achieving justice in the international community. William Reisman, writing in 1969, the year of the VCLT's conclusion, argued that the law of withdrawal and dispute settlement arising from withdrawal was necessary, to ensure that *pacta sunt servanda* was not so rigid that it 'impedes treaty-making and stable international relationships'.[22] Shortly after the VCLT was concluded, Richard Kearney, a member of the ILC and a member of the US delegation to the Conference on Treaties, noted that 'concern remained high over the possible effect upon treaty stability … [in relation to] the invalidity articles'.[23] Writing about the theory of treaty termination in 1975, Arie David argued that the rules of leaving legal obligations depended on 'the [international] community … the web of simultaneity and interdependence' that would eventually institutionalise treaty rules, particularly those on termination and withdrawal, 'in the interests of all those having a part in the community'.[24]

This is just a sample of some of the discussion from contemporary commentators about the concept of stability, but what is striking in the above, and some of the literature described in chapter 5, is how self-referential it is as a concept. Jean d'Aspremont described the self-referentiality of international law as a form of 'justificatory space' where fundamental doctrines of international law can be explained in the context of the wider belief system of international law.[25] His critique was focused on the doctrine of sources and the way that their justification was premised on 'modes of legal reasoning' that ended up referring back to other rules, such as Article 38 of the ICJ statute, to prove the existence of a source of law.[26] Methodologically, ordo-stability has a similar conceit; withdrawal clauses justify their binding nature and their authority over states through the lens of *pacta sunt servanda*. In this there is the implicit

[20] R Bilder, 'Breach of Treaty and Response Thereto' (1967) *Proceedings of the American Society of International Law* (April 1967) 202.

[21] BP Sinha, *Unilateral Denunciation of Treaty Because of Prior Violations of Obligations by Other Party* (Martinus Nijhoff, 1966) 76.

[22] W Reisman, 'Procedures for Controlling Unilateral Treaty Termination' (1969) 63 *American Journal of International Law* 544, 544.

[23] RD Kearney, 'The Future Law of Treaties' (1970) 4 *International Lawyer* 823, 830.

[24] A David, *The Strategy of Treaty Termination* (Yale University Press, 1975) 298.

[25] J d'Aspremont, *International Law as a Belief System* (Cambridge University Press, 2018) 55.

[26] ibid 57–59.

assumption that commitment to those clauses is necessary because of the overall ordering function *pacta sunt servanda* applies to the international legal order. The common form of withdrawal clauses and the repetition in arguments about their interpretation, detailed in chapters 2 and 3, of the doctrine of *pacta sunt servanda* are part of what Werner Wouter describes as the reactualising of the past into the present, which occurs frequently in arguments about state consent.[27] The repetition of the language of stability in withdrawal clauses, as chapter 2 sets out, describing in procedural ways the process of withdrawal, and then the subsequent rearticulation of the language of stability when interpretative communities such as courts or organisations interpret withdrawal clauses (as outlined in chapters 3 and 4), all re-actualises the vision of stability. Ordo-stability becomes self-referential because, as d'Aspremont puts it, it does not require 'empirical or rational demonstration'; it is instead 'deemed to have been irrefutably and transcendentally enunciated'.[28] Both Wouter and d'Aspremont refer to the belief-like structure of international law, and, as discussed in chapter 2, the ordering of time can help structure the very nature of international society. As David Kennedy observed, the belief structure of international law, and its quasi-religious nature, means 'international law appears as a universalist ideology of its own – temporally freed from its origin and context', which it is able to achieve by practices of 'calling forth' doctrines.[29] By being able to implicitly and continually reference stability, and to outline a seemingly stable process, which then for the most part leads to predictable state actions, the law of withdrawal calls forth an image of stability. Yet the self-referentiality of ordo-stability only works because ordo-stability is, as chapter 5 sets out, premised on a thin conception of the international rule of law, with procedural form over substantive impact or substantive protection of rights being the issue.

III. TELLING A STORY ABOUT THE INTERNATIONAL SOCIETY

The ordo-stability of the law of withdrawal is an example of international law's capacity to tell a story about how states should act in order to maintain international society. The story international law tells is conceptually different from the story of international law and its origins, which Nicholas Onuf argues is one of moves from naturalism to positivism and also interlinks with an account of

[27] W Werner, *Repetition and International Law* (Cambridge University Press, 2022) 28–29.

[28] J d'Aspremont, 'Bypassing the Authority of International Law: The Virtue of Modern Self-Referentiality' (21 September 2017) in G Hernandez and G Jokubauskaite (eds), *Constructing Authority in International Law* (2018) at https://ssrn.com/abstract=3040975 (accessed 5 October 2022).

[29] DW Kennedy, 'A New Stream of International Law Scholarship' (1988) 7 *Wisconsin International Law Journal* 1, 22.

sources.[30] The law of withdrawal is part of this story, as detailed in chapters 1–4 of this book, but it also narrates a story about how the world should operate. Anne-Marie Slaughter's interdisciplinary work on international law and international relations opens with a description of the way that both disciplines were 'intellectual constructs that lawyers, political scientists, and policymakers use to describe the world they study and seek to manipulate'.[31] The rules of identification of customary international law, for example, try to tell a story about state practice that is part of the process of deducing the emergence of rules from the behaviour of states.[32] Human rights law is often criticised for narrating, or telling a story about, a particular conception of humanity that is very Eurocentric, and individual features of the law, such as which rights are deemed fundamental or the identification of the subject of human rights, are part of constructing that story.[33] International commercial law imagines elements of what one author describes as a 'single, global market order' that implicitly reduces the 'traditional politics of nation states' to facilitate international trade.[34] Likewise, the procedural regularity and formulaic nature of state action described in the law of withdrawal is also telling a story.

The subject of this story is international society, or the wider international order. Hedley Bull's definition of international society was one focused on an ultimately, or potentially, anarchic international order that was ordered by institutions.[35] Raymond Aron, the French philosopher and sociologist, once described international order as comprising the 'minimum conditions of coexistence' between states that had the eventual aim of being able to 'live together well in one planet'.[36] Describing how both Aron and Bull's definition of international order avoided or mitigated anarchy in international society, Andrew Hurrell observed that this both reflected the 1950s and 1960s Cold War context but also spoke to a wider tradition in Western philosophy, dating back to Thomas Hobbes in the seventeenth century, of conceiving international cooperation in highly minimalist terms.[37] But through all this, the idea that there existed a

[30] N Onuf '"Tainted by Contingency": Retelling the Story of International Law' in R Falk, RBJ Walker and L Ruiz (eds), *Reframing the International: Law, Culture, Politics* (Routledge, 2002) 26–45.

[31] A-M Slaughter, 'International law in a world of liberal states' (1995) 6 *European Journal of International Law* 503, 503.

[32] J Kammerhofer, 'Uncertainty in the Formal Sources of International Law: Customary International Law and Some of Its Problems' (2004) 15 *European Journal of International Law* 523, 526–28.

[33] J Slaughter *Human Rights, Inc: The World Novel, Narrative Form, and International Law* (Fordham University Press, 2007) 18–19.

[34] P Khan, 'Speaking Law to Power: Popular Sovereignty, Human Rights, and the New International Order' (2000) 1 *Chicago Journal of International Law* 1, 6.

[35] H Bull, *The Anarchical Society: A study of Order in World Politics*, 2nd edn (Macmillan, 1995) 135–36.

[36] R Aron is quoted in Stanley Hoffman 'Report of the Conference on the Conditions of a World Order' (1966) 95 *Daedalus* 455, 456.

[37] A Hurrell, 'Order and Justice in International Relations: What is at stake' in R Foot, JL Gaddis and A Hurrell (eds), *Order and Justice in International Relations* (Oxford University Press, 2003) 24–48, 27.

framework of institutions was central; a leading synthesis of the English school of international relations describes the concept of international society as being characterised by a group of states interacting with certain common interests and within common institutions.[38] Even Bull's thiner conception of international society, premised on states' being in regular contact with one another, with interactions being 'sufficient to make a necessary element in the calculations of each other', still depends on a minimal or thin framework of law. International law contributes to international order, Bull argues, by 'setting the basic rules for coexistence among states', and helps mobilise the factors for 'compliance with rules and agreements in international society.[39] The law of withdrawal would meet Bull's definition of those basic rules.

The methodological choice of the English school in this book was almost a process of elimination. As outlined in the Introduction and throughout the book, the law of withdrawal poses conceptual challenges for many of the existing theoretical frameworks of international relations used to explain international law. Taking a narrowly positivist position, tracking the sources of law as a means of crafting a formal explanation as to why the law of withdrawal works and states are bound by it, is useful for identifying the fact of obligation but not why states should be bound by the obligations on termination, when they are leaving a legal regime behind.[40] The English school's explanation of law's institutional function captures what the law of withdrawal, and its implied ordo-stability, attempts to do. It is a story of a very functional order, but one that treats the state as a monolithic legal block with very little attention to its internal politics, even though internal politics are the driver of most modern withdrawals. This can give the impression of order and stability at the international level when in fact there can be a legitimacy crisis within an international institution, or a domestic socio-political crisis in the withdrawing state.

In this story the rules of withdrawal give a shared meaning and structure to the international system by shaping state preferences and identities, as well as their sense of obligation, broadly following constructivist theories about international law.[41] It is also one that prioritises state autonomy, albeit a bounded

[38] A Linklater and H Suganami, *The English School of International Relations: A Contemporary Reassessment* (Cambridge University Press, 2006) 52–54.

[39] Bull (n 35) 137.

[40] Arend's contention that international law is a 'set of binding rules' based upon a 'perception of legitimacy' is an example of this problem. Arend did not explore what happened at the outer end of temporal legitimacy, when, for example, a state had left or was leaving: AC Arend, 'Toward an understanding of international legal rules' in R Beck, AC Arend and R Vander Lugt (eds), *International Rules: Approaches from International Law and International Relations* (Oxford University Press, 1996) 292. See, for a general overview of international legal positivism interplay with realism, D Armstrong, T Farrell and H Lambert (eds), *International Law and International Relations*, 2nd edn (Cambridge University Press, 2018) 81–83.

[41] For an overview of the theoretical arguments in this area, see H Cohen, 'Can International Law Work? A Constructivist Expansion' (2009) 27 *Berkley Journal of International Law* 636, 639; J Brunnée and SJ Toope, 'International law and constructivism: Elements of an interactional theory of international law' (2000) 39 *Columbia Journal of Transnational Law* 19.

vision of state autonomy, confirming realist assumptions about the role of international law and power.[42] One aspect of the law of withdrawal that supports this is the idea that there are certain rights that cannot be withdrawn from, or that rights that continue after withdrawal. As chapter 4 showed, these principles, whilst founded on legal doctrine, are in practice subject to a patchwork of political negotiations and widespread non-compliance by the state party. The law of withdrawal's story of ordo-stability in international society is one that marginalises the rights of the individual, and the place of those rights is subject to a set of political dynamics where individuals are subordinated to state interests. All of this leaves a story of international society that is very thin, much like the conception of the international rule of law to which the law of withdrawal adheres most closely. A rationalist account of this story could see this as sensible, in order to encourage greater commitment of states to the treaties underpinning complex regimes.[43] Getting a state to commit to cooperation on global warming, to attract larger amounts of foreign direct investment, control nuclear weapons or commit to a human rights treaty body, can, depending on your perspective on those individual issues, be argued as a net positive for the international community and the individuals within those states. Treaty regimes are often designed to incentivise state commitment, and the conclusion of rational design theorists on this point directly links the construction of withdrawal clauses to the process of encouraging state commitment to a regime.[44] With treaty exit as sporadic as it had been until the twenty-first century, it was understandable that scholars could take the position that withdrawal was like talking about 'divorce on the wedding day'.[45] But the weaking of the authority of institutions by individual acts of withdrawal, or the threatening of rights, shows that treating withdrawal as a procedural question has consequences. Ordo-stability is a description of a fictional international order where form is more important than substance.

Therefore, a relatively thin conception of withdrawal, which focused on ordo-stability rather than substantive interests, or stability in practical terms,

[42] For an exploration of this, see RH Steinberg and JM Zasloff, 'Power and International Law' (2006) 100 *American Journal of International Law* 64, 74–76.

[43] For this argument in relation to withdrawal, see B Koremenos and A Nau, 'Exit, no exit' (2010) 21 *Duke Journal of Comparative & International Law* 81. For an overview of rationalism, see A van Aaken, 'Rationalist and Behavioralist Approaches to International Law' in JL Dunoff and MA Pollack (eds), *International Legal Theory: Foundations and Frontiers* (Cambridge University Press, 2019) 261–281.

[44] See the analysis of Koremenos in ch 2 for a concise overview of rational design; see B Koremenos "Institutionalism and International Law' in JL Dunoff and MA Pollack (eds), *Interdisciplinary Perspectives on International Law and International relations: The State of the Art* (Cambridge University Press, 2013) 59–82, 62–64.

[45] Helfer's reflection on withdrawal scholarship is illuminating in showing how attention to withdrawal grew over time; see L Helfer, 'Treaty Withdrawals in a Turbulent World: A Retrospective on Exiting Treaties' in D Lyons (ed), *Leading Works in International Law* (forthcoming) currently available at https://ssrn.com/abstract=4124308 (accessed 10 October 2022). For the wedding metaphor see J Herbst, 'Observations on the Right to Withdraw from the European Union: Who are the "Masters of the Treaties"?' (2005) 6 *German Law Journal* 1755, 1755.

was in and of itself useful. As I write this Conclusion, withdrawals are taking place around me, all procedurally stable. Responding to the climate emergency, the Dutch Government took the step of implementing domestic legislation to outlaw the use of coal by 2030. A German energy company then took action under the Energy Charter Treaty (ECT) over loses it would face, with other companies threatening similar actions.[46] In October 2022, the Dutch Minister for Energy and Climate Change announced that the Netherlands would be withdrawing from the ECT, as a means of avoiding claims against the government in the future from carbon-intensive industries as they pursued a climate change agenda that involved reducing their dependence on fossil fuels. As outlined in chapter 3, damages owed to a party arising as a result of arbitration under a treaty would still be owed to the injured party, and failure to provide compensation would be an unlawful act of the state following the Draft Articles on Responsibility of States for Internationally Wrongful Acts. So, if a fossil fuel company had a case against the state from existing losses as a result of climate change policies, it would not be terminated by ECT withdrawal. At the same time, the ECT's withdrawal clause gave a state the freedom to withdraw from the ECT in line with its political preferences, reflecting one of the core justifications of withdrawal outlined in chapter 1. Meanwhile in Strasbourg, the ECtHR is still hearing cases from the Russian Federation, even though it formally ceased to be a party to ECHR on 16 September 2022. The legal obligation to implement and enforce any finding against the state remains under the terms of Article 58 ECHR, yet as chapter 3 concluded, once 'outside the machine' there was little chance that the individuals bringing these claims would find justice. The idea of a rules-based international order in the 2020s is being treated increasingly sceptically by international relations commentators and international law scholars, but the ordo-stability of the law of withdrawal sits in the background, creating small predictable actions from states, giving systemic stability against a fragmenting international picture.[47]

[46] K Mathiesen, 'The Netherlands to leave embattled Energy Charter Treaty' *Politico* (18 October 2022) at www.politico.eu/article/netherlands-leave-embattled-energy-charter-treaty-rob-jetten/. For background, see M Khan, 'EU urged to quit energy treaty as companies sue over climate action' *Financial Times* (7 February 2021) at www.ft.com/content/b37312fb-410a-4958-a88 7-8f9bd7c5e33b.

[47] A Acharya, 'Alternative Paths of International Law and Thinking Past the Western Liberal Order' paper presented at the Change and Resilience in International Law Conference, Graduate Institute Geneva (6 October 2022).

Appendix: Sample Data on Withdrawal Clauses

I. THE CONSTRUCTION OF THE SAMPLE

A SAMPLE OF 203 treaties was looked at in the course of writing this book. The basic parameters used for constructing the sample were that, to be included, the treaty needed to be a multilateral treaty with 10 or more parties (although certain exceptions were made for more specialised treaties). These treaties were then broken down into 24 categories, in order to look at different types of treaties with different types of subject matter. The sample included optional protocols, as well as some treaties that were no longer in force but were still significant. This was done using the categorisation the United Nations Treaty System uses for different types of treaty as a guide for administering the depository, but was also refined slightly in order to capture the breadth of different issues that treaties try to control and regulate. The construction of this sample broadly reflected the research questions outlined in the Introduction to this book. Withdrawal is where a state leaves behind a legal regime created by a multilateral treaty, which can continue to function in the absence of the withdrawing state. In all of these treaties this would be legally possible.

II. BASIC RESEARCH QUESTIONS

These were the basic research questions the sample was used to answer and that are analysed in more depth in the chapters of this book

A. Treaties without Withdrawal Clauses

Out of the overall sample of 203 treaties, 24 (12 per cent) do not have a withdrawal clause, and any withdrawal from those treaties would be governed by the provisions of Article 56 VCLT:

- 1946 Protocol amending the Agreements, Conventions and Protocols on Narcotic Drugs (Lake Success Protocol).
- 1946 Constitution of the World Health Organization.
- 1946 Protocol concerning the Office international d'hygiène publique.

- 1950 Additional Protocol to the Agreement providing for the provisional application of the Draft International Customs Conventions on Touring, on Commercial Road Vehicles and on the International Transport of Goods by Road, relating to the International Transport of goods by container under the TIR Carnet Regime.
- 1952 Additional Protocol amending certain provisions of the Agreement providing for the provisional application of the Draft International Customs Conventions on Touring, on Commercial Road Vehicles and on the International Transport of Goods by Road.
- 1958 Convention on the High Seas.
- 1958 Convention on Fishing and Conservation of the Living Resources of the High Seas.
- 1958 Convention on the Continental Shelf.
- 1958 Optional Protocol of Signature concerning the Compulsory Settlement of Disputes.
- 1958 Convention on the Territorial Sea and the Contiguous Zone.
- 1959 Antarctic Treaty.
- 1965 Convention on Transit Trade of Land-Locked States.
- 1966 International Covenant on Civil and Political Rights.
- 1966 International Covenant on Economic, Social and Cultural Rights.
- 1976 Convention on the prohibition of military or any other hostile use of environmental modification techniques.
- 1979 Convention on the Elimination of All Forms of Discrimination Against Women.
- 1980 International Agreement for the Establishment of the University for Peace.
- 1980 Agreement Establishing The Common Fund for Commodities.
- 1981 African Charter on Human and Peoples' Rights.
- 1995 Additional Protocol to the Convention on Prohibitions or Restrictions on the Use of Certain Conventional Weapons which may be deemed to be Excessively Injurious or to have Indiscriminate Effects (Protocol IV, entitled Protocol on Blinding Laser Weapons).
- 1996 Protocol on Prohibitions or Restrictions on the Use of Mines, Booby-Traps and Other Devices as amended on 3 May 1996 (Protocol II, as amended on 3 May 1996) annexed to the Convention on Prohibitions or Restrictions on the Use of Certain Conventional Weapons which may be deemed to be Excessively Injurious or to have Indiscriminate Effects.
- 1997 Convention on the Law of the Non-Navigational Uses of International Watercourses.

- 2003 Protocol on Explosive Remnants of War to the Convention on Prohibitions or Restrictions on the Use of Certain Conventional Weapons which may be deemed to be Excessively Injurious or to have Indiscriminate Effects (Protocol V).
- 2006 International Convention for the Protection of All Persons from Enforced Disappearance.

In the rest of this appendix, the remaining 180 treaties will therefore be referred to as the 'relevant sample' as they are the relevant treaties in this exercise.

B. Time from Membership to Withdrawal

This describes the interval of time between a state's becoming a party to the treaty and being entitled to withdraw. The majority of the data sample falls into the 'not stated' category (approximately 52 per cent). This category was initiated by clarifying the data into a distinction between 'Not stated' (ie the treaty remains silent as to when a member state can issue notification of withdrawal) and 'Anytime' with respect to the first-time lag. As Figure 1 reflects, the majority of the sample now falls into the classification of 'after the treaty has come into force'.

Figure 1 Relevant sample on duration from becoming party to a treaty to denunciation

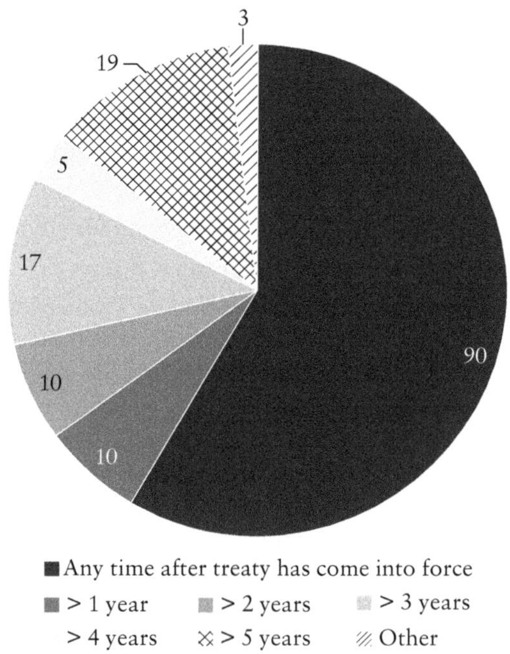

C. Time from Notification to Withdrawal

Figure 2 shows the variation in time between the notification of denunciation and denunciation's becoming effective – defined as when legal obligations cease and the withdrawing state moves from being party to a treaty to a third party.

Figure 2 Variations in time period from issuing of notification of denunciation to actual exit date

D. Notification

Where there is a withdrawal clause, withdrawal can only happen in accordance with the provisions of that treaty (Article 54(a) VCLT). If it is specified in a treaty that a notification of denunciation must be made to a specific party, that is an obligation on state parties. The overwhelming majority of treaties in the sample require notification to be made to the UN Secretary General.

Figure 3 Party to whom the notification is addressed

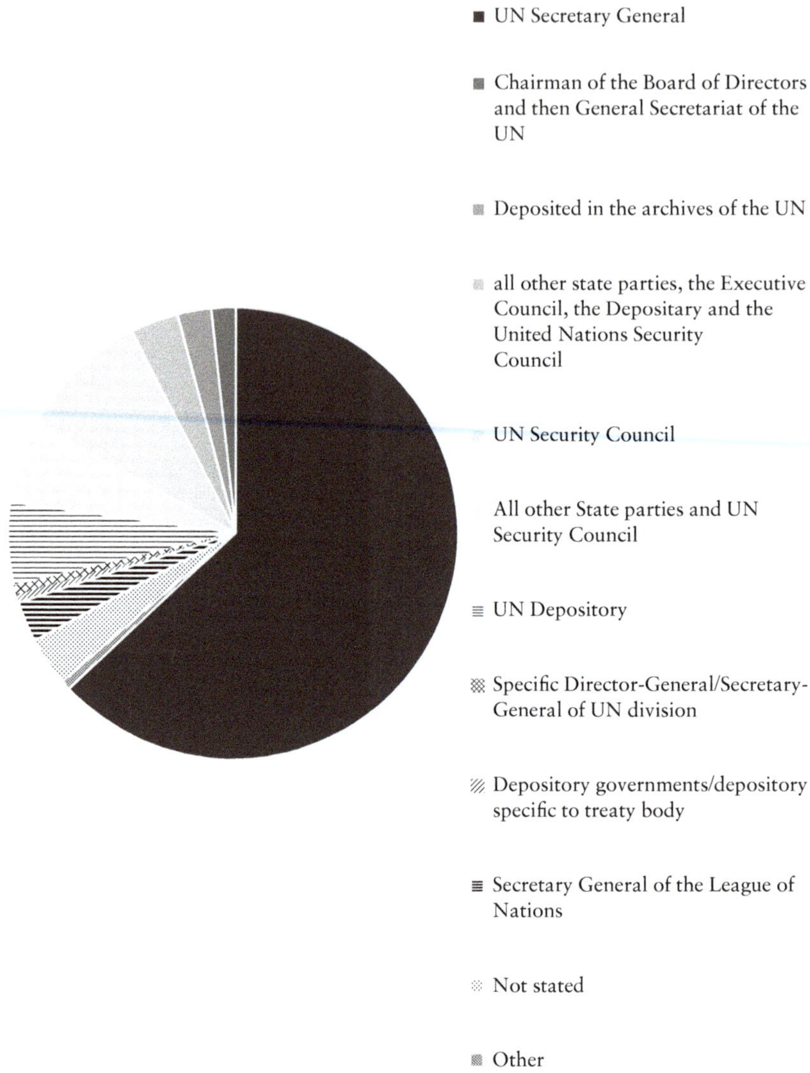

III. LIST OF ALL TREATIES INCLUDED IN THE ENTIRE SAMPLE

There follows a list of every treaty that was included in the sample. Where they were cited in the main text of the book, their full United Nations Treaty Series (UNTS) or regional/historical equivalent is used. They are grouped using the headings of the UNTS, for ease of organising this appendix, even though there are some that predate the UN or are regional treaties.

Chapter IV – Human Rights

1951 Convention on the Prevention and Punishment of the Crime of Genocide.

1966 International Convention on the Elimination of All Forms of Racial Discrimination.

1966 International Covenant on Economic, Social and Cultural Rights.

1968 Convention on the non-applicability of statutory limitations to war crimes and crimes against humanity.

1973 International Convention on the Suppression and Punishment of the Crime of Apartheid.

1979 Convention on the Elimination of All Forms of Discrimination against Women.

1984 Convention against Torture and Other Cruel, Inhuman or Degrading Treatment or Punishment.

1985 International Convention against Apartheid in Sports.

1989 Convention on the Rights of the Child.

1990 International Convention on the Protection of the Rights of All Migrant Workers and Members of their Families.

2006 Convention on the Rights of Persons with Disabilities.

2006 International Convention for the Protection of All Persons from Enforced Disappearance.

Chapter V – Refugees and Stateless Persons

1946 Constitution of the International Refugee Organization.

1951 Convention Relating to the Status of Refugees.

1954 Convention Relating to the Status of Stateless Persons.

1961 Convention on the Reduction of Statelessness.

1967 Protocol Relating to the Status of Refugees.

Chapter IV – Human Rights Optional Protocol

1989 Second Optional Protocol to the International Covenant on Civil and Political Rights, aiming at the abolition of the death penalty.

1990 International Convention on the Protection of the Rights of All Migrant Workers and Members of Their Families.

1992 Agreement establishing the Fund for the Development of the Indigenous Peoples of Latin America and the Caribbean.

2000 Optional Protocol to the Convention on the Rights of the Child on the involvement of children in armed conflict.

2000 Optional Protocol to the Convention on the Rights of the Child on the sale of children, child prostitution and child pornography.

2006 Convention on the Rights of Persons with Disabilities.

2006 Optional Protocol to the Convention on the Rights of Persons with Disabilities.

2011 Optional Protocol to the Convention on the Rights of the Child on a communications procedure.

Chapter VI: Narcotic and Psychotropic Substances

1912 International Opium Convention.

1931 Convention for Limiting the Manufacture and Regulating the Distribution of Narcotic Drugs, as amended by the Protocol signed at Lake Success, New York, on 11 December 1946.

1946 Agreement concerning the Suppression of the Manufacture of, Internal Trade in, and Use of, Prepared Opium.

1946 Agreement concerning the Suppression of Opium Smoking.

1946 Protocol amending the Agreements, Conventions and Protocols on Narcotic Drugs (Lake Success Protocol).

1948 Protocol Bringing under International Control Drugs Outside the Scope of the Convention of 13 July, 1931, for Limiting the Manufacture and Regulating the Distribution of Narcotic Drugs.

1953 Protocol for Limiting and Regulating the Cultivation of the Poppy Plant, the Production of, International and Wholesale Trade in, and use of Opium.

1961 Single Convention on Narcotic Drugs.

1971 Convention on Psychotropic Substances.

1988 United Nations Convention against Illicit Traffic in Narcotic Drugs and Psychotropic Substances.

Chapter VII: Traffic in Persons

1904 International Agreement for the Suppression of the White Slave Traffic.

1910 International Convention for the Suppression of the White Slave Traffic.

1921 Convention for the Suppression of the Traffic in Women of Full Age.

1921 International Convention for the Suppression of the Traffic in Women and Children.

1933 International Convention for the Suppression of the Traffic in Women of Full Age.

1947 Protocol signed at Lake Success, New York, on 12 November 1947, to amend the Convention for the Suppression of the Traffic in Women and Children, concluded at Geneva on 30 September.

1947 International Convention for the Suppression of the Traffic in Women and Children, concluded at Geneva on 30 September 1921, as amended by the Protocol signed at Lake Success, New York, on 12 November 1947.

1949 Protocol amending the International Agreement for the Suppression of the White Slave Traffic.

1949 International Agreement for the Suppression of the White Slave Traffic.

1950 Convention for the Suppression of the Traffic in Persons and of the Exploitation of the Prostitution of Others, Lake Success, New York, 21 March 1950.

1950 Final Protocol to the Convention for the Suppression of the Traffic in Persons and of the Exploitation of the Prostitution of Others, Lake Success, New York, 21 March 1950.

Chapter VIII: Obscene Publications

1910 Agreement for the Repression of Obscene Publications.

1923 International Convention for the Suppression of the Circulation of and Traffic in Obscene Publications.

1947 Protocol to amend the Convention for the suppression of the circulation of, and traffic in, obscene publications, concluded at Geneva on 12 September 1923, Lake Success, New York, 12 November 1947.

1947 Convention for the Suppression of the Circulation of, and Traffic in, Obscene Publications, concluded at Geneva on 12 September 1923 and amended by the Protocol signed at Lake Success, New York, on 12 November 1947.

1949 Protocol amending the Agreement for the Suppression of the Circulation of Obscene Publications.

1949 Agreement for the Suppression of the Circulation of Obscene Publications.

Chapter IX: Health

1946 Constitution of the World Health Organization.

1946 Protocol concerning the Office international d'hygiène publique.

1996 Agreement on the establishment of the International Vaccine Institute.

2003 WHO Framework Convention on Tobacco Control.

2012 Protocol to Eliminate Illicit Trade in Tobacco Products.

Chapter X: International Trade and Development

1947 General Agreement on Tariffs and Trade (GATT).

1948 Havana Charter for an International Trade Organisation.

1948 Agreement on most-favoured-nation treatment for areas of Western Germany under military occupation.

1963 Agreement establishing the African Development Bank.

1965 Convention on Transit Trade of Land-Locked States.

1965 Agreement Establishing the Asian Development Bank.

1974 Convention on the Limitation Period in the International Sale of Goods, as amended by the Protocol of 11 April 1980.

1976 Agreement establishing the International Fund for Agricultural Development.

1979 Constitution of the United Nations Industrial Development Organization.

1980 Protocol amending the Convention on the Limitation Period in the International Sale of Goods.

1980 United Nations Convention on Contracts for the International Sale of Goods.

1994 Agreement to establish the South Centre.

Chapter XI: Transport and Communications

1929 Convention for the Unification of certain rules relating to international carriage by air, (Warsaw Convention).

1944 Chicago Convention on International Civil Aviation.

1949 Agreement providing for the provisional application of the Draft International Customs Conventions on Touring, on Commercial Road Vehicles and on the International Transport of Goods by Road.

1949 Additional Protocol to the Agreement providing for the provisional application of the Draft International Customs Conventions on Touring, on Commercial Road Vehicles and on the International Transport of Goods by Road.

1950 Additional Protocol to the Agreement providing for the provisional application of the Draft International Customs Conventions on Touring, on Commercial Road Vehicles and on the International Transport of Goods by Road, relating to the International Transport of goods by container under the TIR Carnet Regime.

1952 Additional Protocol amending certain provisions of the Agreement providing for the provisional application of the Draft International Customs Conventions on Touring, on Commercial Road Vehicles and on the International Transport of Goods by Road.

1952 International Convention to Facilitate the Importation of Commercial Samples and Advertising Material.

1952 Convention on Damage Caused by Foreign Aircraft to Third Parties on the Surface (Rome Convention).

1952 Convention concerning Customs Facilities for Touring.

1954 Additional Protocol to the Convention concerning Customs Facilities for Touring, relating to the Importation of Tourist Publicity Documents and Material.

1954 Customs Convention on the Temporary Importation of Private Road Vehicles.

1954 Customs Convention on Containers.

1956 Customs Convention on the Temporary Importation of Commercial Road Vehicles.

1959 Customs Convention on the International Transport of Goods under Cover of TIR Carnets (TIR Convention).

1963 Convention on Offences and Certain Other Acts Committed on Board Aircraft (Tokyo Convention).

1970 Hague Hijacking Convention.

1971 Sabotage Convention (Convention for the Suppression of Unlawful Acts Against the Safety of Civil Aviation).

1972 Customs Convention on Containers.

1975 Customs Convention on the International Transport of Goods under Cover of TIR Carnets (TIR Convention).

1982 International Convention on the Harmonization of Frontier Controls of Goods.

1999 Convention for the Unification of Certain Rules for International Carriage by Air (Montreal Convention).

Chapter XII: Navigation

1948 Convention on the International Maritime Organization.

1974 Convention on a Code of Conduct for Liner Conferences.

Chapter XIII: Economic Statistics

1928 International Convention Relating to Economic Statistics.

1948 Protocol to International Convention Relating to Economic Statistics.

Chapter XIV: Educational and Cultural Matters

1949 Agreement for Facilitating the International Circulation of Visual and Auditory Materials of an Educational, Scientific and Cultural Character.

1950 Agreement on the Importation of Educational, Scientific and Cultural Materials.

1952 Universal Copyright Convention.

1954 Hague Convention for the Protection of Cultural Property in the Event of Armed Conflict.

1958 Convention concerning the Exchange of Official Publications and Government Documents between States.

1960 Convention against Discrimination in Education.

1961 International Convention for the Protection of Performers, Producers of Phonograms and Broadcasting Organisations.

1971 Convention for the Protection of Producers of Phonograms against Unauthorized Duplication of their Phonograms.

1972 Convention concerning the Protection of the World Cultural and Natural Heritage.

1976 Protocol to the Agreement on the Importation of Educational, Scientific and Cultural Materials of 22 November 1950.

1980 International Agreement for the Establishment of the University for Peace.

1983 Statutes of the International Centre for Genetic Engineering and Biotechnology.

2003 Convention for the Safeguarding of the Intangible Cultural Heritage.

2005 Convention on the Protection and Promotion of the Diversity of Cultural Expressions.

2005 International Convention against Doping in Sport.

2007 Protocol to the Statutes of the International Centre for Genetic Engineering and Biotechnology on the Seat of the Centre.

Chapter XVI: Status of Women

1953 Convention on the Political Rights of Women.

1957 Convention on the Nationality of Married Women.

1962 Convention on Consent to Marriage, Minimum Age for Marriage and Registration of Marriages.

Chapter XVIII: Penal Matters

1926 Slavery Convention.

1956 Supplementary Convention on the Abolition of Slavery, the Slave Trade, and Institutions and Practices Similar to Slavery.

1979 International Convention Against the Taking of Hostages.

1973 Convention on the Prevention and Punishment of Crimes against Internationally Protected Persons, including Diplomatic Agents.

1994 Convention on the Safety of United Nations and Associated Personnel.

1997 International Convention for the Suppression of Terrorist Bombings.

1999 International Convention for the Suppression of the Financing of Terrorism.

2000 United Nations Convention against Transnational Organized Crime.

2000 Protocol to Prevent, Suppress and Punish Trafficking in Persons, Especially Women and Children, supplementing the United Nations Convention against Transnational Organized Crime.

2000 Protocol against the Smuggling of Migrants by Land, Sea and Air, supplementing the United Nations Convention against Transnational Organized Crime.

2001 Protocol against the Illicit Manufacturing of and Trafficking in Firearms, Their Parts and Components and Ammunition, supplementing the United Nations Convention against Transnational Organized Crime.

2002 The Rome Statute of the International Criminal Court.

2002 Agreement on the Privileges and Immunities of the International Criminal Court.

2003 United Nations Convention against Corruption.

2005 International Convention for the Suppression of Acts of Nuclear Terrorism.

Chapter XIX: Commodities

1962 International Coffee Agreement.

1968 International Coffee Agreement.

1968 Agreement Establishing the Asian Coconut Community.

1977 Agreement Establishing the International Tea Promotion Association.

1980 Agreement Establishing The Common Fund For Commodities.

1986 Terms of Reference of the International Nickel Study Group.

1992 International Sugar Agreement.

1994 International Tropical Timber Agreement.

2001 International Coffee Agreement.

2006 International Tropical Timber Agreement.

Chapter XX: Maintenance of Obligations

1956 Convention on the Recovery Abroad of Maintenance.

Chapter XXI: Law of the Sea

1958 Convention on the Territorial Sea and the Contiguous Zone.

1958 Convention on the High Seas.

1958 Convention on Fishing and Conservation of the Living Resources of the High Seas.

1958 Convention on the Continental Shelf.

1958 Optional Protocol of Signature concerning the Compulsory Settlement of Disputes.

1982 United Nations Convention on the Law of the Sea.

1994 Agreement relating to the implementation of Part XI of the United Nations Convention on the Law of the Sea of 10 December 1982.

1995 Agreement for the Implementation of the Provisions of the United Nations Convention on the Law of the Sea of 10 December 1982 relating to the Conservation and Management of Straddling Fish Stocks and Highly Migratory Fish Stocks.

1997 Agreement on the Privileges and Immunities of the International Tribunal for the Law of the Sea.

1998 Protocol on the Privileges and Immunities of the International Seabed Authority.

Chapter XXII: Commercial Arbitration and Mediation

1958 New York Convention on the Recognition and Enforcement of Foreign Arbitral Awards.

1966 International Convention on the Settlement of Investment Disputes.

Chapter XXIV: Outer Space

1967 Treaty on Principles Governing the Activities of States in the Exploration and Use of Outer Space, including the Moon and Other Celestial Bodies (Outer Space Treaty).

1967 Agreement on the rescue of astronauts, the return of astronauts and the return of objects launched into outer space (Rescue Agreement).

1972 Convention on the international liability for damage caused by space objects (Space Liability Convention).

1974 Convention on Registration of Objects Launched into Outer Space.

1979 Agreement Governing the Activities of States on the Moon and Other Celestial Bodies (Moon Agreement).

Chapter XXV: Telecommunications

1974 Convention relating to the distribution of programme-carrying signals transmitted by satellite.

1974 Constitution of the Asia-Pacific Telecommunity.

1974 Tampere Convention on the Provision of Telecommunication Resources for Disaster Mitigation and Relief Operations.

Chapter XXVI: Disarmament

1963 Partial Nuclear Test Ban Treaty.

1968 Treaty on the Non-Proliferation of Nuclear Weapons.

1975 Biological Weapons Convention.

1976 Convention on the prohibition of military or any other hostile use of environmental modification techniques.

1980 Convention on Prohibitions or Restrictions on the Use of Certain Conventional Weapons which may be deemed to be Excessively Injurious or to have Indiscriminate Effects (with Protocols I, II and III).

1992 Convention on the Prohibition of the Development, Production, Stockpiling and Use of Chemical Weapons and on their Destruction.

1995 Additional Protocol to the Convention on Prohibitions or Restrictions on the Use of Certain Conventional Weapons which may be deemed to be Excessively Injurious or to have Indiscriminate Effects (Protocol IV, entitled Protocol on Blinding Laser Weapons).

1996 Protocol on Prohibitions or Restrictions on the Use of Mines, Booby-Traps and Other Devices as amended on 3 May 1996 (Protocol II, as amended on 3 May 1996) annexed to the Convention on Prohibitions or Restrictions on the Use of Certain Conventional Weapons which may be deemed to be Excessively Injurious or to have Indiscriminate Effects.

1996 Comprehensive Nuclear Test Ban Treaty.

1997 Chemical Weapons Convention.

1997 Convention on the Prohibition of the Use, Stockpiling, Production and Transfer of Anti-Personnel Mines and on their Destruction.

2003 Protocol on Explosive Remnants of War to the Convention on Prohibitions or Restrictions on the Use of Certain Conventional Weapons which may be deemed to be Excessively Injurious or to have Indiscriminate Effects (Protocol V).

2008 Convention on Cluster Munitions.

2013 Arms Trade Treaty.

2017 Treaty on the Prohibition of Nuclear Weapons.

Chapter XXVII: Environment

1946 International Convention for the Regulation of Whaling.

1959 Antarctic Treaty.

1973 Conservation on International Trade in Endangered Species of Wild Fauna and Flora (CITIES).

1979 Convention on the Conservation of Migratory Species of Wild Animals.

1979 Convention on long-range transboundary air pollution.

1984 Protocol to the 1979 Convention on Long-range Transboundary Air Pollution on Long-term Financing of the Co-operative Programme for Monitoring and Evaluation of the Long-range Transmission of Air Pollutants in Europe (EMEP).

1985 Protocol to the 1979 Convention on long-range transboundary air pollution concerning the control of emissions of nitrogen oxides or their transboundary fluxes.

1982 Convention on the Conservation of Salmon in the North Atlantic Ocean.

1987 Montreal Protocol on Substances that Deplete the Ozone Layer.

1989 Basel Convention on the Control of Transboundary Movements of Hazardous Wastes and their Disposal.

1991 Convention on Environmental Impact Assessment in a Transboundary Context.

1992 United Nations Framework Convention on Climate Change.

1992 Protocol on Water and Health to the 1992 Convention on the Protection and Use of Transboundary Watercourses and International Lakes.

1992 Convention on Biological Diversity.

1994 United Nations Convention to Combat Desertification in those Countries Experiencing Serious Drought and/or Desertification, Particularly in Africa.

1996 Inter American Convention for the Protection and Conservation of Sea Turtles.

1997 Convention on the Law of the Non-Navigational Uses of International Watercourses.

1997 Kyoto Protocol to the United Nations Framework Convention on Climate Change.

1998 Convention on Access to Information, Public Participation in Decision-Making and Access to Justice in Environmental Matters.

1998 Rotterdam Convention on the Prior Informed Consent Procedure for Certain Hazardous Chemicals and Pesticides in International Trade.

1999 Basel Protocol on Liability and Compensation for Damage Resulting from Transboundary Movements of Hazardous Wastes and their Disposal.

2001 Protocol on Strategic Environmental Assessment to the Convention on Environmental Impact Assessment in a Transboundary Context.

2003 Convention on the Transboundary Effects of Industrial Accidents.

2000 Cartagena Protocol on Biosafety to the Convention on Biological Diversity.

2010 Nagoya Protocol on Access to Genetic Resources and the Fair and Equitable Sharing of Benefits Arising from their Utilization to the Convention on Biological Diversity.

2001 Stockholm Convention on Persistent Organic Pollutants.

2013 Minamata Convention on Mercury.

2015 Paris Agreement on Climate Change.

Chapter XXVIII: Fiscal Matters

1979 Multilateral Convention for the Avoidance of Double Taxation of Copyright Royalties.

1979 Additional Protocol to the Multilateral Convention for the Avoidance of Double Taxation of Copyright Royalties.

1988 Convention on Mutual Administrative Assistance in Tax Matters.

Index

www.ingramcontent.com/pod-product-compliance
Ingram Content Group UK Ltd.
Pitfield, Milton Keynes, MK11 3LW, UK
UKHW020806290926
15470UKWH00003B/991

9 781509 938568